Tragedy and Melodrama

VERSIONS OF EXPERIENCE

Other Books by Robert Bechtold Heilman

AUTHOR

America in English Fiction 1760–1800 (1937)
This Great Stage: Image and Structure in King Lear (1948)
Magic in the Web: Action and Language in Othello (1956)

EDITOR

Understanding Drama: Twelve Plays [with Cleanth Brooks] (1948)
Modern Short Stories: A Critical Anthology (1950)
Jonathan Swift, *Gulliver's Travels, A Tale of a Tub, and
The Battle of the Books* (1950)
An Anthology of English Drama Before Shakespeare (1952)
Joseph Conrad, *Lord Jim* (1957)
Thomas Hardy, *The Mayor of Casterbridge* (1962)
George Eliot, *Silas Marner* (1962)
William Shakespeare, *Cymbeline* (1964)
Thomas Hardy, *Jude the Obscure* (1966)
William Shakespeare, *The Taming of the Shrew* (1966)

TRAGEDY

AND

MELODRAMA

Versions of Experience

By

ROBERT BECHTOLD HEILMAN

1968

UNIVERSITY OF WASHINGTON PRESS

Seattle and London

*The passage used as an epigraph is quoted with the kind
permission of Random House, Incorporated, and of Mary
Renault, the author of* The Bull from the Sea, *published in
1962 by Pantheon, a division of Random House.*

TO

Cleanth Brooks

AND

Robert Penn Warren

Preface

I HAD originally intended to use the word *essay* conspicuously in the title of this book, but editorial considerations resist the massing of abstractions at the outset. However, *essay* should be thought of as spiritually present in the title, for the same reason that it is actually present at more than one place in the text. *Essay* represents my own sense of what I am doing, and suggests the tone which I would like to achieve. It implies the tentative rather than the decisive, the selective rather than the inclusive; examination rather than prescription, and exploration rather than platting the ground and staking out claims. To use *treatise* or *study* would imply more rigorous formality in procedure, a more comprehensive amassing of evidence, a greater commitment to logical demonstration, and a larger hope of establishing something like proof. Ordinarily it would also mean a more extensive theoretical disquisition, and at least a steady notation of agreements and disagreements with critics whose influence has already been felt, such as Northrop Frye and Murray Krieger, Eric Bentley and Elder Olson, Francis Fergusson and George Steiner, Oscar Mandel and D. D. Raphael (not to mention their important predecessors).

That is another way of doing things, however; my own purposes appear to be better served by looking as steadily as possible at plays rather than at other ways of looking at plays. An essay is less a dialogue with specialists (who will recognize where one echoes and rejects others) than an invitation to both specialist and nonspecialist readers; though it aspires to get enough under the surface to interest the expert, it does not hesitate at the introductory note, the everyday symptom, and the looser gait if these seem likely to serve the interests of the general reader. It hopes to have its own kind of unsolemn seriousness, though its ground is hypothesis rather than thesis; it hopes to have its own identifiable order, though it traffics more in surmise than in system.

Of the words actually present in the title, *tragedy* and *melodrama* need hardly be alluded to here: the essay as a whole seeks to say what can be said about them. They take us into the tantalizing and thorny field of generic form, where agreement is rare. Though fifty years ago a practitioner of the "new criticism" of that day announced in triumph that the subject of genre was at last dead, it has never ceased acting like a live issue, evoking both popular and esoteric theorizing, virtually continuous dispute, and often the warmth of feeling that reveals, in the cool defining process, the militant underground stirring of a value-sense. Hence I approach that field, not as if presenting a solution, whether new or fashioned from the debris of earlier constructions, but as trying out a point of view. I endeavor, not to lock plays in categories, but to inspect them in a given way; not to analyze plays totally, but to describe them from a chosen vantage point. This process should reveal something significant about a play; at its best it might alter somewhat the accepted appearance of the play.

"Versions of Experience" is as laconic as title pages evidently should be. It is not, I hope, correspondingly uncommunicative. "Versions" implies the interpretative activity reflected in genre. The dramatist does not so much choose a genre as employ a point of view which gives his work a certain generic conformation. His materials are not preformed; they are open to more than one perspective; the perspective used brings into being one of the forms latent in the materials. In calling these materials *experience* I assume a relationship between drama and actuality. But I am interested much less in implying a definition of drama than in keeping present the notion that experience, in its turn, affords a perspective on drama. At least one important activity goes on both in literature and outside of it: we define catastrophe regularly in day-to-day life as well as interpret it in literature. Both dramatists and ordinary men set forth versions of experience, and there are analogies between popular attitudes and literary formulations. What is more, they interact: for better or worse, the artist may forge the conscience of his race, or the race temper the imagination of the artist. In ordinary life we frequently act, think, and feel as if we were participating in a tragedy or melodrama, or as if our experience had taken on one generic form or another. Hence I occasionally turn an eye to the life outside books and theater where the needs and strategies of our personalities have relevance for the understanding of dramatic modes.

An essay of adequate substance presumably mediates between the sketch that depends on random samples and the study that is exhaustively complete. I hope to have commented on enough plays to test my assumptions and to exhibit their utility, and to make my generalizations as persuasive as they can be made. The plays discussed are the ones that came to mind, at the moment of choice, as offering good material for the specific end in view; perhaps better choices might have been made. I come back to certain plays repeatedly because they illustrate different points; other plays appear under only one rubric when they might well appear under several; few plays are treated fully at any one point. If the ideas about tragedy and melodrama put forward here seem more widely applicable, as I hope they do, readers may be prompted to try them out on other plays that I do not consider.

I have particularly wanted the plays to come from different ages and countries, partly, of course, to secure a representative spread. Aside from that, I have chosen to consider plays from Aeschylus to the present as a timeless family of which all members are amenable to the same treatment. Though this is hardly a historical approach, it is not antihistorical; it does not deny the historical but leaves it to the students who prefer it. Plays from different areas and cultures have likenesses as well as differences; they express a common humanity as well as a social and temporal milieu; they embody constants as well as variables. Our business here, of course, is the constants of generic form that reflect certain basic attitudes to human conduct and that nourish certain kinds of aesthetic experience. It is important, indeed obligatory, that we seek out the constant as well as the changing, the common to all times as well as the unique in time. The two quests are supplementary; we are in trouble only when one tries to stamp out the other. Ordinarily the fact that men have different temperaments will guarantee the continuance of both. Yet our own time has an almost obsessive sense of historic differences, so that it may be especially fitting to reaffirm the importance, in intellectual pursuits, of integrating as well as differentiating. * We integrate, however, not by superimposing a sought unity upon real differences, but by finding, in quiet company with the differences, the likenesses in form and function that are the grounds of unity.

In the main I have wanted to have my points of view hinge on older plays, since these are at least partly free from the distractions of current events, exciting or disturbing innovations, and the passions of moot issues; on more recent work we lack distance, and we may either dismiss novelty prematurely or mistake topical and experimental sheen for inner light. But whatever the risks, representativeness means including the contemporary, and I did not wish to have a phrase such as "up to 1929" in the title. Then what had started as a discreet sampling grew into longer accounts of some individual dramatists, and in the end the bulk was excessive. Formal treatments of the moderns, as a consequence, were banished to a separate volume that is scheduled to follow this one.

I am grateful for a Guggenheim Fellowship and a Huntington Library grant which helped provide needed working time, for a University of Washington research grant that made possible the help of a research assistant, and for a Longview Foundation award which, as a response to a preliminary essay on tragedy and melodrama that appeared in the *Texas Quarterly*, served to encourage a fuller development of the subject; to Notre Dame University, Indiana University, the University of Texas, and the University of British Columbia for lecture invitations which stimulated a further working out of prelimi-

---

* For the view that literary history is a differentiating, and criticism an integrating, activity, see my article, "Historian and Critic: Notes on Attitudes," *Sewanee Review*, LXXIII (1965), 426–44.

nary notions about the genres; to the libraries of Cornell University, the University of Washington, and the University of Wisconsin for making studies available at different times; to Roy Battenhouse for an unusually thorough and perceptive criticism of the original manuscript; to Edith Baras, of the University of Washington Journals Office, for superior work, involving both editorial expertise and conscience, on the text; and to my fellow administrator Dorothee N. Bowie, whose taking on of innumerable office tasks and burdens freed additional time for reading and writing. Those ideas of Eric Voegelin that I am familiar with have always been in the back of my mind as touchstones; if I have not used them well, it is because aptitude has lagged behind aspiration. In dedicating this volume to Cleanth Brooks and Robert Penn Warren, I acknowledge how much I learned from them when we were colleagues at Louisiana State University in the late 1930's and early 1940's—for me, fortunate and exciting years which remain vivid in memory after a quarter of a century. My wife has endured, for a still longer period, regular summonses to type, to judge (tactfully, please), and, above all, to stop, look, and listen.

ROBERT B. HEILMAN

January 31, 1968

Contents

[xiii]

Tragedy and Melodrama

VERSIONS OF EXPERIENCE

(Theseus, King of Attica, recounts his meeting with newly arrived Oedipus, who declares that he will bless this land.)

"But," I whispered, "they stoned you at the altar."

"Why not?" He was calm and reasoning. "I killed my father."

. . . "Fate was your master. You did these things unknowing. Men have done worse at less cost."

He smiled. Even as I was, it awed me. "So I said always, till I became a man."

MARY RENAULT, *The Bull from the Sea*

CHAPTER ONE

Tragedy and Disaster: Assumptions

IN TIME I shall be discussing simultaneously two dramatic types which I call tragedy and melodrama. I will begin, however, by talking about tragedy. One reason for this procedure is the problems that grow out of the wide popular use of *tragedy;* another is that distinctions between tragedy and other forms derive from one's conception of tragedy. I will set forth an assumption about the nature of tragedy, trace its main consequences, and then examine a number of plays (and an occasional novel) in the light of the initial assumption and what it entails. If the light is good enough, it should be useful in placing the dramas and understanding their structure and quality. One does not so much prove or disprove an assumption as see how it works in critical practice; the test of it is less logic than use. If it affords convincing distinctions among plays generally called tragedies, it will serve some purpose.

I. TRAGEDY IN LITERATURE AND EXPERIENCE

Though we are frequently admonished to separate literature and life, we have a rather special situation here: tragedy is the name not only of a literary form but of an aspect of life. When we speak of "the tragic sense," we think of it as an attribute not only of a writer and what he writes, but of a human being who has a certain way of contemplating experience. Our spontaneous association between a kind of experience in life and a comparable experience in the imagined life of drama is not arbitrary; it is not that one restricts or determines the other but that, in both, *tragedy* implies a working of destiny, whether imposed from without or defined by inner nature. Hence a valid way of looking at literary tragedy should have some use in the placing of experience; a theory of tragic structure may have uses both in the criticism of literature and in what Arnold called the criticism of life. In time, indeed, I will propose that a sound concept of tragedy may influence social well-being. But at the moment I am only suggesting that we may find analogies between the two realms without confusing them.

I am, it should always be clear, exploring "a" way of looking at tragedy. The pages that follow should not sound final and judicial. Nor, on the other hand, should they be so lacking in conviction that the point of view becomes only a springboard for critical exercises.

II. Tragedy as a "Popular" Word

In contemporary usage *tragedy* is an important, indeed a cardinal, word. Here is a surprising fact of lexical history: an ancient term for a literary form—and a form that now has infinitely less contact with general community life than it had in Athens—has come into the most widespread daily use, written and spoken, among all classes of people. Of the small number of literary terms that have been taken over into general usage as categories of human experience, *tragedy* is the most conspicuous. *Farce* belongs to the number; *comedy* also has some use in nonliterary contexts. *Lyric, satire,* and *novel,* on the contrary, remain purely literary words. We do not say that a nonliterary event or situation "is a lyric" or "is a satire" or "is a novel" (though in a different, more specialized, way we may speak of "a romance"). We might perhaps say, of a life or a deed or an artifact, "It is a poem," but it would be artsy-booksy, if not actually precious. On the other hand, "It is a farce" is commonplace, and *comedy* appears at least in the cliché "comedy of errors." But "It is a tragedy" is universal. There may be a historical reason for this: now, when the popular imagination attaches the idea of finality to the idea of death, people crave the most resonant term for this liability.

Whatever the causes, *tragedy* is an indispensable word. It corresponds to an area of experience whose inevitability we do not question. Tragedy is an experience that we would avoid if we could; *tragedy* is a word that we like to have within reach. It is a "popular" word.

Further, *tragedy* is a "good" word; it has status; we instinctively seek it out, enjoy familiarity with it. There are always these words, less than philosophical but more than chic, that endow us with a sense of being in touch with the center of things. In the eighteenth century, *nature* was such a word. In our day *democracy* is such a word, and hence its protection is claimed not only by our demagogues and by our statesmen, but by political disciplines that are autocratic and tyrannical. *Education* has such status that no one could use it scoffingly, and it is loosely applied to a remarkably diverse set of activities. On the other hand there are "bad" words; they are "unspeakable" because they embody unthinkable concepts—for instance, *surrender*.

Words with status are popular, and popular words, like much-used clothes, are liable to distortion—a straining and stretching of the seams, with a consequent loss of shape and even identity. What was once like a tailored suit bulges into an ungainly coverall that everyone uses at will. It loses exactness; it is used for only simple or wholesale or lump meanings. It might be argued that we should ignore this gross confusion of meanings and rely on context to reveal whether *tragedy* has a trivial or a profound meaning. However, it appears to be a law of language that when one word gains several meanings, the inferior meaning will tend to force the superior meaning out of circulation; I mean that the easier, looser, lazier meaning will win out over the more exact or precise meaning, the one that demands greater care from the user. This is the Gresham's law of verbal currency. The word *acute*, long used to mean keen in mind, now survives chiefly in its crippled offspring *cute*, which means babyishly pretty or pleasing; and the word *nice* has virtually surrendered the meaning of "subtly discerning" to join the mob of hazy words signifying characterless agreeableness. *Awful* has lost all power to denote the majestically terrifying.

Terms like *lyric*, *satire*, and *novel*, because they are not popular words, are used with relative precision, without great inclusiveness or ambiguity. Not *tragedy*. It has come to mean a multitude of undifferentiated unpleasantnesses. In academic usage it does mean primarily the literary form represented, in their respective ways, by *Oedipus* and *Hamlet*. But there and elsewhere it is also used carelessly to denote a wide range of works marked by somberness of tone or unhappiness of event. The daily papers are bursting with uncomfortable, painful, or gruesome events that they, like us in our ordinary talk, regularly call "tragedies": an early death, an unexpected death by disease, a financial failure, a suicide, an epidemic, a murder, an automobile accident, a train accident, a plane accident, a successful military movement by a hostile power, a sadistic act, an error by the government, almost any act of violence, even an athletic defeat. I have seen *tragedy* applied to the death of a household pet, to the unexplained source of bloodstains, to the crash of a pilotless plane into a factory. Such loss of precision is not an idle change in fashions, like the passing of ruffs, wasp waists, men's wigs. We do not lament the loss of a meaning that has become valueless or that has been taken on by other words. We do have other words for the more scrupulous meanings eroded out of *cute*, *nice*, and *awful*. This is not the situation with *tragedy*, which has become "cheap," a bargain-basement word for which there is no "quality" alternative. *Tragedy* is cheap because it has become a gross word for every kind of misfortune, and we lack terms to distinguish these misfortunes according to human meaningfulness. This is to say that we do not have the concepts by which apparently similar experiences may be distinguished from one another. If experiences are not distinguished, some of them, at least, are not understood; if they are not understood, there is a sense in which they are not even experienced. The confusion extends beyond verbal haziness and begins to interfere with fundamental clarity of mind. If *tragedy* is capable of referring precisely to an experience that can be discriminated from all others, however similar they look, then by losing this specific image in the general warehouse of shocking unpleasantnesses we risk having a troublesome misconception of the nature of the world and of ourselves.

That is why we are engaged in something more than easy laughter at trivial journalistic errors. The errors, on the contrary, point to a defective understanding of reality. Unchecked, or at least unappreciated, they can lead to serious mistakes about literature and about the world around us.

III. TRAGIC DIVIDEDNESS

Tragedy is a specific form of experience that needs to be differentiated from all other catastrophic disturbances of life. I want now to offer an assumption about tragedy and to outline some of its consequences. My initial assumption is implied in Aristotle's definition of the tragic hero (though I am in no sense claiming Aristotelian protection). The two main terms in Aristotle's account of the hero are that he is a good man and that he gets into trouble through an error or shortcoming, for which the standard term has become "the tragic flaw." In the concept of the good man with the flaw lies the germ of what I take to be a fundamental view of tragedy. "Good man" implies a moral tenor, "flaw" the action of a force not consistent with it. Goodness and flawedness imply different incentives, different needs and desires, indeed different directions. There is a pulling apart within the personality, a disturbance, though not a pathological one, of integration. The character is not "one," but divided. This is my basic assumption about the tragic experience, whether in art or in life, and *divided*, *dividedness*, and *division* are key words that will reappear.

Tragedy connotes profound experience, then, not only because of what tragic drama has been but because the dividedness from which tragedy springs lies deep in human nature. T. E. Hulme based his social and political theories on the belief that man "encloses within him certain antinomies. There is a war of instincts inside him, and it is part of his permanent characteristics that this must always be so." [1] Literary critics repeatedly note dividedness as fundamental in characters. In a recent book on Shakespeare, Honor Matthews describes Henry V as "a man deeply divided within himself," attributes "inward healing of the divided mind" to the last act of *Winter's Tale*, alludes to Shakespeare's "vision of man's divided mind." [2] Robert Graves thinks of one whole phase of his own work thus: ". . . the poetic self has become the critic of the divided human self." [3] An author may speak of character as divided. George Eliot says of Lydgate: "He had two selves within him apparently, . . ." [4] and of Godfrey Cass's conflict: "But he had not moral courage enough to contemplate that active renunciation of Nancy as possible for him: he had only conscience and heart enough to make him forever uneasy under the weakness that forbade the renunciation."[5] Characters in plays of every age are aware of dividedness. In *Antony and Cleopatra* Maecenas says of Antony, "His taints and honours / Wag'd equal with him," and Agrippa comments, ". . . you gods will give us / Some faults to make us men" (V.i.30–33).[6] Goethe's Faust says of himself, "Alas! two souls within my breast abide, / And each from the other strives to separate." * And Meadows, the soberest voice in Christopher Fry's *A Sleep of Prisoners*, "But there's strange divisions in us, / And in every man, one side or the other."[7] These dramas are tragic or potentially tragic.

Two observers of dividedness, one a biologist and the other a literary critic, are equally interesting here. Theodosius Dobzhansky relates man's discords to the development of self-awareness:

Man became, and he still remains, a creature rent by internal contradictions. He is a paradoxical being, capable of unspeakable egotism and cruelty, but also of love, abnegation, and self-sacrifice. . . . But man is also ashamed of his defects and suffers from his depravity. He is able to construct in his imagination worlds different from the actual one, and can visualize himself in these imaginary worlds. . . . Man's biological success became a reality despite the tragic discords within him.[8]

Arnold Stein says of Shakespeare's Cleopatra that "few tragic figures can rival this full presentation of the contradictory elements out of which the tragic is made."[9] The phrases "tragic discords" and "internal contradictions," which both identify the human situation and

---

* Johann Wolfgang von Goethe, *Faust*, Part I, trans. Alice Raphael (New York: Rinehart, 1955), p. 42. The passage is near the end of Scene ii. There is a curious parody of this in Bertolt Brecht's *Saint Joan of the Stockyards*, as translated by Frank Jones: "O man, two souls have made their home / Within thy breast," in Eric Bentley (ed.), *From the Modern Repertoire* (Series 3; Bloomington: Indiana University Press, 1956), p. 372. This is in a Chorus spoken by Packers, Stockbreeders, and Black Straw Hats, all racketeers who solve a tragic situation by enthusiastically embracing doubleness:

> Seek not a choice of one alone,
> To live with both is best.
> Stay in strife and stormy weather!
> Let them battle one another!
> Keep the high and keep the lowly,
> Keep the coarse and keep the holy,
> Keep them both together!

remind us of the primary literary form that images it, suggest modes of division that include more than ideas of goodness and the flaw. We can discern three basic patterns of division, which are neither exhaustive nor always clearly distinguishable, but which will help bridge the gap between abstract theory and actual tragic experience.

Types of Division: Imperatives and Impulses

One division seems inseparable from human community; it is traceable to the existential fact that, in the ordering of life, we maintain different imperatives that correspond to different and perhaps irreconcilable needs and ideals. Eliseo Vivas has made the point that, in a certain uneven short story, the writer might have tried for "the success of the artist, who, by allowing a conflict between two sets of values, each of which has its own authentic claims, would have given us a story with genuine tragic tension." [10] Conflicting "values" with "authentic claims": here indeed is a primary source of "genuine tragic tension." Hamlet and Orestes, those heroes so distant from each other in time and place, and yet so close in the trials that they go through, cannot avenge their fathers, the victims of evil deeds, without themselves committing evil deeds. A powerfully felt bond puts such a hero afoul of an undeniable covenant. Antigone cannot be true to family duty and love, and to religious obligation, without contravening civil law; and Creon, who is tragic too and in some ways a better tragic protagonist than Antigone, cannot or at least does not maintain civil order without punitive decrees that violate human feelings and sense of justice. Yet none of these heroes could refrain from the course that leads to guilt without feeling acquiescent in a public evil.*

* Cordelia, whose tragic role is not always perceived, falls between a duty to self and a complex duty to demands outside of the self—those of filial attachment and those of political concern. She finds herself in a representative and difficult dilemma—the choice between hubris and humiliation, the extremes that one is forced into when a middle course is undiscoverable; between exerting her own will (while implicitly denying outer claims upon her) and yielding to another will (while implicitly denying the claims of her own sense of decorum). She tries to reconcile the private and public imperatives with a cryptic partial response; but flattery-hungry Lear has no head for cryptograms and reacts violently to a sense of rejection; hence Cordelia's maintenance of her own integrity contributes to the chaos that follows.

Such protagonists embody the dividedness of a humanity whose values naturally elude the confines of logic and thereby create, at the crises where choices must be made, apparently insoluble situations. The crises in drama reflect those in life. Rolf Hochhuth, author of *The Deputy* (1964), uses the term "tragic situation" for the dilemma of the Russian soldier "who was a passionate anti-Communist and who none the less had to fight with the Communist army against the [German] invaders, for the benefit of Communism just as much as for the benefit of his country" and of "many Germans, who could not possibly have wished that Hitler should triumph but who no more wished that the Russians should march all the way to the Rhine." [11] "Tragic" here means not simply "painful," as in popular usage, but requiring a choice between counterimperatives of such authority that one has to act faultily and yet cannot feel that he could act more wisely. No one can say with assurance, "It would be better if Hamlet or Antigone or Cordelia had done so and so." Nor could a fully aware person, caught between incompatible injunctions, come out of the situation untragically; his route to safety would be conventional expediency, that is, the cancellation of a part of his moral awareness. Suppose Hamlet had decided that the ghostly exhortations that he heard were simply the product of tensions within himself, that he was worrying too much, that his best move was to get adjusted to the new regime and stop brooding about conditions that he could not help anyway and which well might be only imaginary. Or that Orestes had decided that his father deserved his fate, or Cordelia that she would lose nothing by joining her sisters in apple polishing an old man in a tantrum. The resulting courses would have been safer. But what diminished persons we should have, and what a shrunken sense of reality.

To describe this fundamental human dividedness as it appears in characters like Hamlet and Orestes, we may say that they are caught in a conflict between two "imperatives." With another kind of tragic hero the split is between imperative and what I will call "impulse." I use "impulse" to denote only the emotions of self-interest, whether momentary or of some duration, since impulses that contribute to the well-being of others are not likely to conflict with imperatives.

On one side we have the moral ordinance, on the other the unruly passion. The doer is less enmeshed in the inalienable human perplexity among the modes of rectitude than he is caught between a clear mandate—the moral insight earned by the race—and personal desire or ambition, between law and lust, between what he ought to do and what he wants to do. The imperative is the voice of tradition and community, the impulse is the egotism, the appetite or fever or rage, any private urgency that runs counter to restrictions. George Eliot puts this conflict in very broad terms when she locates the tragic in the "irreparable collision between the individual and the general" and in the "terrible difficulty" of the "adjustment of our individual needs to the dire necessities of our lot." [12] In slightly different terms, tragedy shows man "confronting his own finiteness and being punished for letting his reach exceed his grasp." [13] Macbeth is mad for the throne; but what makes him tragic, unlike the ordinary run of climbers and power snatchers, is the division within him: his main strife is with his awareness of the imperatives that oppose his seizure of kingship. Likewise Faustus: in his manic snatch at godlike omnipotence he never wholly loses, try as he may, knowledge of the truth that he hopes to use and yet dissolve.

The human division in Macbeth and Faustus takes a different, but equally representative, form in Oedipus. While in using illicit means or pursuing illicit ends Macbeth and Faustus break imperatives, Oedipus wants to obey imperatives but is betrayed by the riotous impulse. One plot shows man bound to the good despite himself, the other, man unable to escape doing evil; tragedy constantly makes both assertions, the joint signs of a healthy world that escapes the incompleteness—that is, the sentimentality—of both "optimism" and despair. Oedipus strenuously seeks to escape the father-murder foretold for him, but the impulse that betrays him is an ego-serving violence that he lets fly as if it were a right. We envisage that hubris at the crossroads scene long ago; we are forced to do so by Sophocles' reinterpretation of Oedipus as crime solver in Thebes. As relentlessly dutiful detective, Oedipus so easily abuses, accuses, and threatens those who do not act in conformity with his own self-assurance that he is in danger of compounding his original crime. At the climax of his flight from incest, he marries an older woman; Jean Cocteau identifies Oedipus' impulse as a mixture of vanity and the immaturity that confuses filial and sexual. In T. S. Eliot's *Murder in the Cathedral* (1935), Archbishop Thomas' carrying out of a mandate is waylaid by personal feelings that might subvert the high enterprise: martyrdom is the imperative, and it is threatened by a profit impulse that would make a good thing of martyrdom. Cyril Tourneur's Vendice wars against palpable evils but is betrayed by a greedy lust for the sadistic mechanics of total revenge. Bertolt Brecht's Joan Dark wants to be faithful to a political mission but fails through doubt, confusion, and fear. There are many possible versions of the split between imperative and impulse.

The third representative tragic division is between impulse and impulse—the characteristic formulation in our day,* which has lost older imperatives and not found new ones, and hence often looks askance at the word *imperative*. Here *impulse* denotes any kind of desire, from gross self-seeking to noble ambition; greed may conflict with lust, one aspiration with another (generosity undermines justice in Oliver Goldsmith's *Good-Natured Man*, a comic version of an implicit theme in Shakespeare's *Timon*), or an ideal with fear or profit. The conflict of impulses often appears when Henrik Ibsen is exploring the tragic mode. In *Rosmersholm* (1886) Rosmer and Rebecca both have a lively desire to improve the common lot by enlightenment—the rationalist impulse. But they find themselves sorely troubled by older, deeper feelings—the traditionalist impulse. In *The Master Builder* (1892) Solness is caught between the satisfaction of steady success and the urgency of demonic aspiration—between a safe, conventional productivity and the Faustian impulse to make a spectacular exhibition of talent. The most nearly universal form of the division between impulse and impulse is the disparity between talents and hopes, or between possibility and aspiration. This motif, which may be comic or pathetic, comes to tragic proportions when the hero is a large enough Everyman and when his ambition images all the cravings for expansion and domination latent in the

---

* This situation is oddly anticipated by *Othello*. Not that Othello lacked a sense of imperatives; he is eager to clothe the murder of Desdemona in the garb of obligatory justice. But having satisfied the impulse to avenge an imagined wound to his pride, he is overtaken not by a sense of wronged moral order (like Oedipus, Orestes, and Dr. Faustus), but by regret. He feels less that he has incurred guilt than that he has made a bad mistake. There are, of course, different interpretations.

human personality (for instance, Bussy D'Ambois). Or tragic pride, to use a traditional term, can try to force talents into a parity with duty or mission. This may be the case of the Governess in Henry James's *Turn of the Screw*, who endeavors to contend alone against the evil she sees, without calling for aid upon the godlike uncle in the background. The story is ambiguous, we all know, but one of the themes that can be discerned in it is the tragedy of puritan total self-dependence.

Imperative and *impulse*, as used here, denote broad areas of meaning, sometimes overlapping. In general, imperative is the overriding obligation, the discipline of self that cannot be rejected without penalty, whether it is felt as divine law, moral law, civil law, or in a less codified but no less powerful way as tradition, duty, honor, "principle," or "voice of conscience." Imperative reflects communal consciousness or higher law; impulse is open to challenge, judgment, or replacement in a way that imperative is not. Impulse originates in, is rooted in, or is identified with the individual personality; though the specific feelings that impel the individual may be of the widest occurrence in human kind, they are felt as a need, a satisfaction, a fulfillment, or an aggrandizement of the individual. Imperative has authority and permanence; impulse bows to it, rebels against it, exists independent of it, or holds its power only temporarily. Imperative tends toward the self-abnegatory; impulse toward the self-assertive. The contrast is between "In His will is our peace" and willfulness, between acceptance of obligation and "I want," between acknowledging power and making power felt. On the one hand we find words like *duty* and *law;* on the other, words like *desire* and *ambition.* Impulse may take the form of "drive," which implies an enlargement of self and diminished concern with other selves. If impulse directs the individual toward the community, it is likely to create a sense of exceptionalness, so that he may wish to circumvent, surmount, control. Or on the other hand: to lead, improve, or redeem. Here we move into the other realm of impulses, those that are not self-serving, or if in some way self-serving, still not exclusively so. Love is an "impulse"; it may be heedless desire that conflicts with an imperative, or high devotion that conflicts, if with anything, only with other impulses.

We need not labor the theoretical classification of the competing forces that actuate serious conduct. I have talked about types of motives largely to make the idea of dividedness concrete. The categories are neither absolute nor rigid; they can lose clarity of outline or even coalesce intricately. The imperative may be so deeply rooted in the individual personality that it works as impulsively as hunger; on the other hand, impulses can go beyond the appetitive and have value beyond their own satisfaction; the less elementary the human being, the more "I desire" may become the equivalent of "I am required." Then there are special cases. Othello tries to camouflage savage impulse as a hard duty. John Ford's incestuous Giovanni tries to make perverse passion into an overriding law, that is, an imperative. Needless to say, it would be futile to identify every motive of dramatis personae as imperative or impulse. The important thing is the division at the center of tragedy. In tragic life, man may feel competing loyalties; aspire to a virtue or pursue a noble end, and be betrayed by a passion; seek an evil end, and be betrayed by an undismissable good; or try to fill one need, and find that another blocks his course.

We may say that he is "split." Schizophrenia, in one form the split personality as disease, may be thought of as the pathological extreme of the tragic situation. While madness is not tragic—for there are many things that are terrible but not tragic—nevertheless tragic division may push man toward madness. We see how often the Greek tragedians dramatize myths in which men and women go mad. The attacks of the Furies on Orestes and on Harry Monchensey in Eliot's *Family Reunion* (1939) are dramatic versions of mental illness. King Lear and Lady Macbeth go mad, Macbeth has hallucinations, Othello has a fit that is a temporary derangement, and Hamlet and Gloucester's son Edgar both counterfeit madness. Characters who are or become unbalanced appear continually in Jacobean drama and in Eugene O'Neill and Tennessee Williams. In all these cases there is neither coincidence nor cliché, but a true imagining, consistent over two millennia, of the direction in which human beings are pressed by the divisions in life and in themselves.

IV. CHOICES, SELF-AWARENESS, WHOLENESS

Division means choice: there are alternatives, and man must select one or the other. He must choose to murder for revenge, or remain an undutiful nonkiller; to murder for a throne, or remain bitterly uncrowned; to risk destruction in a spectacular gamble, or in safety feel faithless to a part of himself. Our reluctance to enter tragic experience must be, in the end, less an obvious fear of suffering and death than a secret dread of irreversible choices that permit few illusions or certainties about what will follow. We share with Hamlet the human tendency to indefinite postponement, to drift; we might, with Heyst in Joseph Conrad's *Victory*, choose drift. Conrad shows that even that fails. Heyst elects something that is not there to elect—security by withdrawal and passivity (Oedipus sought security by withdrawal to another place, whereas passivity might have saved him). Heyst chooses drift to avoid contaminating action, and still suffers; Orestes and Macbeth suffer intensely before they choose contaminating action that does not end suffering. Every tragic choice is both an affirmation of self and a suicide.

If division means choice, choice means strength and consciousness. Strength hardly requires discussion; inability to make choices signifies a weakness that cannot produce tragic stature. The lack of strength that often makes O'Neill's characters pathetic rather than tragic appears most fully in the refugees from life in *The Iceman Cometh*. Brick Pollitt in Tennessee Williams' *Cat on a Hot Tin Roof* may be as far gone as they. Shakespeare's Richard II hovers between the quasi-strength of willfulness and tantrums, and the recessiveness of one for whom choices are made by others. Strength is meaningless, however, if a man is not conscious of the alternatives. A drama is hardly a tragedy if the hero simply does not know, either before or after, what it is all about, if choice is automatic and effortless, or if it means only continuing in a course without knowing that there is an alternative. By its nature choice opens up the fullest range of consciousness, for here inevitably comes into play all that one knows, one's visions of ends to be sought and of what may be done, one's responsiveness to imperatives and awareness of impulses; the inspection of alternatives and, however lightning quick, of one's talents and hardiness; the perception (or pushing down) of subterranean forces that may urge one's course this way or that; the willingness (or refusal) to detect self-flattery and self-deception. The hero who falls short of such awareness, early or late, fails in the essential action of his role. Willy Loman is so consistently blind that *Death of a Salesman* becomes pathetic rather than tragic.

Further: division is not only the occasion of self-awareness or self-knowledge, but is the material of self-knowing. Division is the primary summons to understanding: it is the inconsistent and contradictory that require knowing. The unified and harmonious dissolve the world of alternatives and render the customary strivings of self-understanding irrelevant. Division is a "normal" mean between two extremes. At one extreme, division grows pathologically into schizophrenia, the negation of understanding; at the other, division shrinks, disappears, and gives way to an integration without seams. This rare unity may be one of two things—either a natural vegetable wholeness no more open to meaning than is clinical madness; or a rare spiritual perfection rendering superfluous an understanding which could be only a bland contemplation of achievement. Tragic understanding is the middle ground between two untragic extremes: at one extreme one has power to know but nothing to know; at the other, no power to know, but everything to know.

The tragic hero, then, has intelligence. If he is incapable of understanding or of coming to understanding, the effect of tragedy is not possible, and the work takes on some other generic form. The kind of consciousness (awareness, knowledge) I have been talking about is a necessary aspect of what Aristotle calls the good man. If a man faces no critical choices, that is, remains outside tragic experience, he can be "good" by rote; but the "good man" is incomplete if he encounters the divisions in the world and himself that produce moral conflict and has not the wit to recognize them. Though the good man may try to escape self-knowledge, he cannot be incapable of it; in the effort at flight lies tragedy, in incapability, at most, an ironic drama of ignorance. Intelligence, of course, does not mean wisdom. Tragedy is always about a kind of folly, perhaps even a noble folly; it is not, however, the folly of a fool, but the representative foolishness of an intelligent man, or the stupidity of a too intelligent man. Through the tragic experience man can earn wisdom; it may be an apparently profitless wisdom—like that of Eliot's Archbishop Thomas in *Murder in the Cathedral* and Celia in *The Cocktail Party*—not easily understood by the immediate world.

Finally, to portray the dividedness of life is to encompass life in its wholeness. To see the diversity of claims and urgencies that divide humanity is to approach a total view, whereas to present man as if he were a unity, undivided, is incomplete; when the artist assumes wholeness in his characters, he has a lesser vision or at least a different kind of vision. Sean O'Casey's "decline," a critic observes, "dates from the period when he ceases to have a divided mind about most of his characters," when he sees them as deserving "either unalloyed admiration or single-minded contempt." [14] Without "divided mind" he puts less into his characters. Here we can actually use a quantitative principle that is rarely appropriate in criticism: the greater tragedy is, the greater the amount of human reality—of the divisive and its consequences—that it encompasses. A writer may willingly or unknowingly settle for partialness or a pseudo wholeness. In sentimental drama a hero may be given a flaw without serious consequences, or he may be permitted to find peace without having to suffer as did Orestes—a tragic hero who found peace. Then there is the more recent sentimental fashion, in which a violent, revengeful, self-aggrandizing, malicious hero is left uncomplicated by countermotives. Saints and devils are not tragic. Sometimes a quite self-respecting drama may resolve a conflict rather handily. In both Eliot's *Elder Statesman* (1959) and O'Neill's *A Touch of the Poet* (1957), which on the surface are hardly similar, the hero gets off lightly; Lord Claverton and Cornelius Melody both undergo a fairly easy self-recognition that produces a more comfortable life.

Another kind of incompleteness, verging more subtly on the sentimental, appears in "naturalistic tragedy," that is, in the drama of the victim. There is, of course, a legitimate drama of the victim, which I shall discuss shortly. [15] But the more the victim takes over the stage—imagine, let us say, Gerhart Hauptmann's *The Weavers* (1892) as a dominant model for "serious drama"—the more the tragic division is lost sight of, and the greater the dramatists' difficulty in discovering in man the impulses which establish his complicity in his suffering. Again, man may be seen as lacking the energy or the valor to live on through the tragic experience in its entirety. In Rosmer and Rebecca, Ibsen saw the dividedness and self-recognition all right, but he rounded out their lives by the neat perfection of a double suicide; he stopped short of wholeness by not imagining in them any capacity to accept the anguish of division and to struggle for a resolution. Here we need only recall the wider human range, the sheer living with what had to be endured, in Prometheus or Oedipus or Orestes or, in a different way, Macbeth. In *Rosmersholm* Ibsen was perhaps betrayed by the theatrical lure of the double leap into the millrace; more than once he succumbed to the dark glitter of the sudden-death ending. But not always. Gregers Werle lives on, and Peer Gynt himself has to endure some painful self-inspection. In *Peer Gynt* (1867) there is an interesting minor character of a doughtiness that prevents the neurotic short cut to oblivion—the farm boy who cut off a finger to avoid military service, was publicly disgraced, but lived with his shame for a lifetime, and so earned a kind of recovery. This is only a dramatic anecdote, without amplitude, yet even in its brevity it exhibits the artist's sense of wholeness.

What Ibsen discovers here is a penitential acceptance as an alternative to despair. If a writer cannot find alternatives of this kind, the almost inevitable price is a narrowing of range. If we produce a literature of despair, it should not be mistaken for the tragic, as it may tend to be in an age which has blurred the distinctions between tragic and other experiences. True, it is possible to deal tragically with despair: Marlowe does this by presenting Dr. Faustus' despair as the last extension of his flaw, as the underside of the recklessness that had actuated his wild leap into illicit and corrupting power. But this is a thoroughly different situation from that in which the author himself despairs and therefore can see only despair for his characters. When O'Neill and Williams, and in a different way Samuel Beckett, do this, they do not achieve the authentic note of tragic completeness. For not to see what else there is, be it resignation, the wearing out of the punitive forces, the undertaking of whatever action is possible, the asking of forgiveness (as Lear does) or the forgiving of oneself (as Arthur Miller's Quentin proposes), the acceptance of retribution and suffering, the growth through suffering, the struggle for insight into self and the spiritual order which is the threshold of transformation—not to see this is to reduce the wholeness of life and hence of the literary art which interprets it and is one of our major ways of knowing it.

V. TRAGEDY: NONLITERARY USAGE

We have already found *tragedy* to be an immensely popular word—popular in the sense that it is a stand-by of daily vocabulary, called on for every kind of pain and unhappiness, giving us a pleasant sense of having entered a world of larger dignity.

But out of the wide realm of things that go wrong we have proposed one type of experience as the essentially tragic: that in which the always divided human being faces basic conflicts, perhaps rationally insoluble, between obligations, and among obligations and passions. In his strength he makes choices, electing a task with its inseparable penalties, seeking a greatness or power that he cannot have, or espousing an evil that he cannot resist; in his sentiency he hears an imperative that in prudence he might ignore; in confusion or willfulness or violence or pride he gratifies an impulse that he cannot control. He undergoes the consequences of his choice, and in suffering achieves a new or a renewed awareness of his action and himself and the order of life.

The typical situation in popular or journalistic "tragedy," however, is something like this: young man drives fast, hits truck parked on highway, and he and his fiancée are killed. Almost invariably this will be called "Tragedy on Highway 40," for it is what tragedy is to very many people—unprogrammed death. "Tragedy on Highway 40" is a great distance from the pattern of tragedy that I have sketched and that, with variations, can be discerned in Greek, Renaissance, French classical, and indeed more recent writers. Even in the most skillful journalism we would hardly be able to see inside our victims or imagine them caught in a cloudy dilemma of options or struggling between imperative and impulse; they make no choice, but are passive beings to whom something just happens; and they come into no understanding. For in that death there is little to understand, and consciousness is not sharpened but bluntly ended. It might be argued that a dramatic artist could take over the raw materials of "Tragedy on Highway 40" and so interpret them that they would symbolize human choices and responsibility. Perhaps so, but that is simply to say that nontragic events may be transmuted into tragic art; the more reason for having terms to distinguish undifferentiated raw material and a certain kind of achieved art.

Since debate about tragedy is usually a rather esoteric affair in which critics set one formal definition against another, it may be a good thing just once to set a formal definition against popular usage.

For one thing, the worlds of critical study and general practice are not so separate as they seem; the use of the same word implies a common ground which we ought to find if it is there and deny if it is not there. For another, popular usage, if I am right, contains some threats to our well-being; we have an obligation to try to make this apparent. Further, popular usage may have implications for the critical activity itself; if we can find and formulate a core conception implied by popular usage, we may be able to make more discriminating judgments in looking at the world of drama, which is our main business. We must neither snobbishly dismiss the popular nor slavishly enthrone it (the lexicographic fallacy). Rather we must mediate between a finicky discrimination and no discrimination at all by making a convincing distinction between the essentially tragic and the quasi-tragic or para-tragic—not to throw out the latter, but to understand the contrasting roles of the tragic and quasi-tragic in our emotional life and in our comprehension of reality.

"Tragedy on Highway 40" lacks the active participation by the characters, the exercise of choice, the awareness of options as equal or better or worse, the knowledge of self. When we call this "tragedy," then, we lose hold of certain ideas that we need if we are to understand and distinguish catastrophes: the idea that calamity comes from divisions within human nature and within the ordering of life; the idea that man may choose evil; the idea that potential evil within him may have power over him despite his resolution or even flight; the idea that destructive events can come out of the normal logic of character; the idea that out of terrible experiences may come the understanding of the nature of oneself and of things, and that that understanding has value. This is a serious loss. And we replace it only with the idea that tragedy is an unexpected shortening of life produced by circumstances outside ourselves; that our only relation to what happens is that of victims. Clearly, such ideas mean an irrational world; it is not to be understood; and we have nothing in ourselves to understand. As observers or victims, we can even enjoy "the misery of innocence." *

* D. D. Raphael, *The Paradox of Tragedy* (Bloomington: Indiana University Press, 1960), p. 24. Professor Raphael's view of tragedy and my own differ considerably. His full sentence, from which I have quoted one phrase, is, "Nevertheless, it seems to me, the poignancy of Tragedy

This second, diminished set of ideas is gaining on the first and inevitably encroaching on the territory proper to the first. If it gains enough strength, we may be able to think of Macbeth as only the victim of an accident in the country: he ran into malicious fortunetellers who turned him into a crazy, mixed-up throne climber. Surely this does not greatly exaggerate one of our basic habits of thought. We can hardly avoid such sentimental folly (already practiced somewhat on Lear and Othello and even on Iago) if we take the traditional word for grave disorders, cataclysmic yet referable to human character, amenable to human understanding, and conducive to intensified consciousness, and use it to mean only unhappy accidents. In saying "only unhappy accidents" I am by no means minimizing the occurrence, the extent, and the force of such events. I do not suppose that we can eliminate them, ignore them, forget them, deny their impact, or discontinue making literature of them. To call them "tragedy," however, is not a venial inaccuracy but a distortion of reality.

Tragedy and Disaster

The real need is for terms that will adequately reflect the structural differences between types of events that are only superficially alike. Sloppy as journalistic usage generally is, an occasional headline writer is admirably accurate: in place of "Tragedy on Highway 40" he may write, "Accident on Highway 40: Two Dead." There he has succeeded in putting experience into the right category, without which no thought is possible. *Accident*, however, is not quite the term we need for literary purposes, since it has been used so widely for trivial mishaps that it does not automatically connote serious trouble. For the catastrophe that is often mistaken for tragedy, the right term, I suggest, is *disaster*. *Disaster* excludes any note of triviality, and while it may refer to human disorder as an evil or a source of evils, it hardly implies choice or erring will or erring thought. *Disaster* is a sufficiently capacious term to signify fatal accidents, mortal illnesses that strike (we think) before their time, the destructive blows of a nature not yet quite tamed, and all the murderous violence that comes directly or by ricochet from the envious, the hostile, and the mad. Its

comes out chiefly in the misery of innocence." It appears to me that all theories of tragedy that turn on the ideas of innocence and victims confuse the pathetic and the tragic.

etymology and its history enlarge the usefulness of *disaster;* its service to us gains something from the astrological faith preserved in its
syllables, and from Shakespearian echoes—Horatio's "Disasters in
the sun" (*Hamlet* I.i.118), Henry's "my thwarting stars" (*3 Henry
VI* IV.vi.22), and most of all the definition of Romeo and Juliet as
"star-cross'd lovers" (Prologue, line 6). (Not so long ago Thomas
Hardy could refer casually and somewhat sentimentally to Jude's
"struggle against malignant stars"—Part IV, chap. vi. But in *The
Mayor of Casterbridge* he could also call "disastrous" a "result . . .
in no way seen or intended"—chap. xlii.) The original literal sense,
an undoing by hostile action of the stars, makes *disaster* exactly right
as a metaphor for misfortunes, bad luck, inimical blows from others—in a word, all the injuries and unhappiness that can or are
believed to come from without, that are not invited by us but imposed
upon us, that make victims of us, and that let us feel guiltless.

From now on, instead of trying to distinguish the two meanings of
tragedy—the meaning proposed in this essay and derived largely from
enduring literary practice,* and the contemporary popular meaning—I shall use *tragedy* and *disaster* to denote these areas of experi-

---

* It is probably not necessary to set up a defense against the argument
that the practice of older tragedies, and the theory implicit in the practice,
are no longer relevant because times have changed. However, the defense
would hinge on the view that older tragedies to which we still return do
not belong only to their own ages, to outmoded social and political forms.
We know them only because they belong to us too; if in one sense they are
old, in another sense they are always new, for we continue to rediscover
them as we devise new ways of formulating the constants of life. The
permanence of older tragedy appears luminously if we look at the most
fantastic of all Greek myths, the Oedipus story, and see how Sophocles has
invested it with a human veracity that no age, however different it
imagines itself to be, can gainsay: to avoid the incredible evil acts that
have been prophesied for him, Oedipus takes every precaution he can think
of but fails in that discipline of self-indulgence which alone could save
him. He leaves town—the still standard easy flight from trouble, the "new
slate," the "fresh start"—and then feels free to murder an older man who
arrogantly crosses his path, and marry an older woman. When deep
trouble overtakes his country, he is confident he can by reason get to the
root of the matter and save country and royal reputation for overcoming
crises. He suspects that others have done wrong and are plotting against
him, but he discovers the wrongdoing—in himself. It is, indeed, a universally valid pattern of human experience: man hopes by intelligence and
energy to clean up the evil in the world, but in the end his main feat is the
discovery, not of others, but of himself.

ence that, though sometimes subtly intertwined, may always be theoretically distinguished. As Albert Guerard has put it, "the tragic
attitude lays the blame not on the stars but on ourselves; . . ." [16]
   In sum: the problem occurs when we have only one word to signify
both tragedy and disaster. What then happens is that the less complex, less subtle meaning becomes dominant, for it exacts less of us.
Hence, except for what is in effect coterie usage, *tragedy* comes to
mean only disaster. Thus we lose from common life (which always
threatens creative and critical practice) such concepts as moral dilemma, the power of both good and evil over the individual, choice,
consequences, responsibility, comprehension; instead, as a way of
confronting failure and pain, we are left only with the concepts of bad
luck, hostile forces (personal or impersonal), innocence, and incom-
prehensibility: "Why did this have to happen to me?" * This shrinkage of resources will leave us confused in the presence of the facts of
life; if we misinterpret them, we are less able to face them.

VI. DISASTER AS TRAGEDY: IMPLICATIONS

   When we equate all evil with what happens to us (at the hands of
nature or of careless or malicious people), we fall into a too easy view
of life that makes life harder. We throw away intellectual tools
needed to face the complexities of actuality, where evil never moves in
one direction only, where chance and resolve, accident and will,
others and ourselves, are mingled in a trying existential disorder.
Hence we need adequate ways of "positioning" ourselves with respect
to what goes wrong, and they will hardly be easy. The 1941 attack on
Pearl Harbor, now distant enough in time to be looked at with
detachment, is a catastrophe which we can view simply or complexly.
We almost always call this a "tragedy," but at the same time we
think of it as a disaster, for we attribute it to enemy malice and
treachery. We can take a less easy stance, however, and attribute the
defeat in part to faults of our own military forces—carelessness, lack
of foresight, and, behind these, self-assurance, that is, the ancient

---

   * Doubtless many people who say "tragedy" when they mean "disaster"
would deny that they had lost one set of ideas and committed themselves to
another. True, perhaps, for some individuals. But neither an individual
nor a society can persistently use words in a certain sense without coming
unconsciously to invest that sense with a cognitive status and to acquiesce
in whatever restrictions are built into it.

flaw of pride. Thus, instead of easily blaming a distant enemy, we
have the somewhat harder task of blaming our own agents, and our
comfort is correspondingly reduced. But in this procedure we have
one luxury left: the scapegoat, by punishing whom we draw back
from the abyss of culpability. Suppose, however, we try that hard
abyss, and see the attack as attributable in part to our national policy,
attitudes, and feelings—to a pride which is not localized at a single
military base but belongs to our very way of life. Now we cannot
easily blame others, but have to look at ourselves; and by taking this
much more difficult way, we have enlarged the possibility of understanding ourselves and our history. This is the reward for moving
from the easier sense of disaster to the harder sense of tragedy.

The too easy solution is what makes the disaster principle popular.
What is too easy is axiomatically perilous. The peril appears in
characteristic intellectual, emotional, and moral errors—self-exculpation, self-pity, and the substitution of quantitative for qualitative
standards. (The intellectual, the emotional, and the moral interpene-
trate, of course, and are not wholly distinguishable; they are aspects
of one simplistic way of interpreting experience.)

In the first place the disaster principle—using the word *tragedy* but
locating the origin of the unhappiness in another person or an
impersonal force—lets us whitewash ourselves, believe ourselves, as it
has been put, "good enough," and therefore not responsible for the
calamities that overtake us. In this there is a great irony, for though
responsibility is a "good word" which only small deviant minorities
would disavow, we all have a considerable penchant for avoiding the
thing. A fringe cult may openly charge that a social order is corrupt
and therefore reject responsible participation in it. But the majority
cannot so unshrinkingly lay claim to a special integrity, and must
therefore find ways of disguising the passion for un-responsibility.
One notable disguise in our day is the oft-heard and rather reputable
theory that the modern world is too big and complex to make the idea
of individual responsibility tenable. (We can detect the subconscious
motive if we are imaginative enough to perceive that at all times the
world must have seemed equally formidable to those in it, that even in
supposedly cozier pasts men cannot have escaped feeling equally
overwhelmed by vastness, by the unknown, by the fearful pressure of
unseen forces.) But the more ingenious flight from responsibility is

the verbal habit we have been talking about—identifying all evil not with what we do but with what is done to us. When we use *tragedy* to mean not the errors of the good man but the slings and arrows of outrageous fortune, we are declaring ourselves worthy of easy redemption.

This intellectual error can even have unpleasant practical consequences, for in some ways reality does conform to our sense of it. To imply that our role is passive is subtly to invite others to cash in on our passivity; to talk as if responsibility belonged elsewhere (we can hardly, of course, disclaim responsibility for evil and claim that for good) is to establish it elsewhere, to encourage the birth of a world in which, lacking the power which shows itself only in responsibility, we may have to put up with disadvantageous terms. To let a key term in our vocabulary imply that we are always acted upon increases imperceptibly our liability to be acted upon; if we unconsciously think of ourselves as victims, we are the more likely to become victims.

By making us always victims, by presenting actuality always in terms of victims, the disaster principle encourages self-pity. No one wants to be caught in self-pity, and no well person, we may assume, wants to engage in any kind of feeling that could be diagnosed as self-pity. But the disaster principle sneaks pity in the back door. If a sufferer is really a victim, there is nothing to do but pity him; if all unhappy experience is disastrous, we must all be pitied. We begin to overvalue the literature of suffering, whether the O'Neill kind or the Beckett kind. We tend to make literary texts conform to our predispositions; happy with the cliché that Hardy pities victims of an antagonistic universe, we simply fail to see how often he attributes human suffering to naïveté, folly, wrong ideals, wrong ideas of reality, and characteristic human dividedness. Self-pity, which has to be even more devious than the flight from responsibility, may disguise itself as pity for others. When, speaking of Desdemona's supposed adultery, Othello says, and repeats, "The pity of it, Iago," he is largely feeling sorry for himself. The instinct for self-pity leads to especial enthusiasm for the man who pities, since his sympathetic wing beckons to a latent human desire to cuddle up under a warm shelter. Words like *compassion* and *compassionate* have become clichés of book reviewing; they have the air of being ultimate terms of praise. No one appears to question this, but there is an excessiveness about it that should provoke embarrassment. Compassion for actual victims, however legitimate in itself, may pre-empt attention that should go to more difficult matters; on the other hand, compassion for those who make errors may either sentimentalize them or carry the writer beyond satire into tragedy. Still, compassion is not what comes to mind when we think of Sophocles' treatment of Oedipus or Shakespeare's of Lear. It is rather completeness of understanding, insight into human division, a full sense of flaw and excellence. This getting everything into the picture is the ultimate sympathy of the author; it is his way of "loving" his characters; he must be complete rather than pitying if he is to find, for himself and us, a middle ground between indignation and tearful sorrow, between the ways of politics and those of sentimentality. Compassion belongs to omnipotent Deity, who can feed the hungry, cure the sick, and, as it is phrased in Psalms, forgive iniquity; the artist can hardly take on these functions of divinity. His business is not to forgive, but to portray human beings granting forgiveness, earning it, failing to find it, or being unable, like Dr. Faustus, to accept it.

However real and poignant the situations requiring pity, there are great areas of reality that require other responses; if we concentrate on the pitiful, we shrink into a reverie on the sadness of things in which we can hardly help feeling sorry for ourselves. We stop at what Browning uncomfortably called "droppings of warm tears," and settle for Joseph Shorthouse, the sentimental nineteenth-century novelist: "Nothing but the [sic] infinite Pity is sufficient for the infinite pathos of human life." If pitiableness leads to a tearful oneness with the character, it may on the other hand make the spectator condescend to the character or draw entirely away from him, and thus elude the recognition of himself in the tragic hero by which tragedy secures its effects. And since pity and fear are traditionally yoked in post-Aristotelian theorizing, we may note here that there is also ambiguity in fear. Is it the fear of what may happen to one? Or the fear of what one may do? The fear proper to tragic experience is sketched in the words of Perpetua in Fry's *Venus Observed* (1950):

> I'm still remembering
> I can give pain, and that in itself is loss
> Of liberty.[17]

This at least echoes, though thinly, the awareness of affinity with evil that belongs to the tragic sense. Fear of what may happen to one is a central emotion in the world of disaster.

The universalizing of disaster—i.e., the interpretation of all painful actuality as disaster—entails a third error which is essentially moral: a purely quantitative view of life. In disaster the chief unfriendly figure is death; that is, we are getting less life than we have coming to us. It is not necessary to quarrel with a universal disinclination to die, especially ahead of what looks like sound scheduling; but we should keep in mind that in our time the quest for longevity is more extensive and passionate than it has ever been before. We have taken the idea of eternity, which seems to persist fiercely in men like an instinct, and in the course of secularization have unconsciously transferred it from the spiritual to the biological realm. If we are aware of the increasing pull of the idea of immanent immortality, we can understand a growing obsession with disaster, the most acute reminder of mortality. Now disaster is the realm of quantity of life, tragedy of quality of life. If our fear of disaster, which is inevitable, so grows that it squeezes the tragic sense out of its due place, then we ignore or beg the question of quality. To say this is not to complain about the fear of death, which is a fact of life; the point is rather that the ending of life is not the sole imperfection of life, and that if we care only for amount of life and not for kind of life, we ask for trouble. The center of tragedy is not the death that may be inevitable, but what goes wrong within life, the wrong that man does, the doubleness that forbids perfect choices. Divided man faces fundamental questions of moral survival for himself and for society. To lose contact with tragedy, then, is to have a diminished sense of moral predicaments and of folly, pride, and self-deception, of all the "good man's" flaws, as the source of catastrophe; and of the kinds of resistance to the movements of egoism, and of the remedial forces in human character.

So much for the implications—the self-exoneration, the self-pity, the quantitative norm—of the set of mind that lets us habitually talk and think in terms of "Tragedy on Highway 40." Thus we confuse disaster, against which we can literally take out insurance, and tragedy, which permits no such "protection" or indemnification. We cannot insure against our committing theft, adultery, murder, or

gross injuries to body or spirit; still less against what lies behind them
—jealousy, envy, arrogance, or the illusion that we can beat the rules;
or against having, in a crisis, only a choice between the pride of
violence and the humiliation of acquiescence in the intolerable. Yet to
apply for such insurance would involve a confusion of realities no
worse than that of our everyday usage.

There is one paradoxical hope for reducing the confusion: the
peculiar hold upon us of the key word *tragedy*, which we so use as to
create the confusion. In the very sound of *tragedy* there is a note of
dignity, a scent of nobility, an aura of the heroic, that we want to
claim; in enrolling ourselves as tragic, we gain a better status in
emotional life, we become upper-class sufferers. We forget that the
dignity sought has its roots in knowing ourselves and enduring the
penalties that our choices invoke,* and that it cannot come from
sudden death or lesser blows from an unfriendly or careless world.
We do not see that, by borrowing the word *tragedy* for the bruises of
fortune or malice, we eventually erode the dignity away.

Yet however wrongheaded its course, the very quest for dignity
suggests that, if we saw what we had to do to achieve it, we would
try. If we do long for dignity, we may be the more willing to
discriminate between the terrible happening, which leads to blankness, and the terrible deed, which leads to a new consciousness of self
and the world. A rush to bargain-counter dignity may imply an
openness to the real thing.

VII. THE INTERPRETING CONSCIOUSNESS

In disaster, what happens comes from without; in tragedy, from
within. In disaster, we are victims; in tragedy, we make victims, of
others or of ourselves. In disaster, our moral quality, though it may be
revealed, is secondary; in tragedy, it is primary, the very source of all
that happens. These two contrasting structures of experience we

* Writing on an entirely different subject, Robert B. Martin makes a
statement very much in the spirit of the present section: ". . . as in all
true tragedy, knowledge and awareness are themselves an amelioration of
pain, and the consequent dignity of the individual triumphs over any
inclination to self-pity and makes the pity of others unimportant. Tragic
awareness precludes the acceptance of happiness exacted at the cost of
easy, inferior, or ignoble aims." This is in *The Accents of Persuasion:
Charlotte Brontë's Novels* (New York: Norton, 1966), p. 145.

confuse in different ways; each mode of confusion is a ploy in some way representative of our time. We call disaster tragedy, and thus we savor dignity without tasting responsibility—a sort of moral get-rich-quick scheme; or we can treat the tragic as if it were only disaster—a trick of the evasion of responsibility. In either case we elude the obligation of identifying experience accurately.

So far I have been speaking as if the two types of experience always stand clear-cut in the objective world, outside of consciousness, but ready to be received and placed by consciousness. This working assumption can now be qualified in one significant way. For the experience as immediately known or observed can be modified by a creative consciousness; there is a degree of reciprocal influence between the thing known and the knowing consciousness. Some kinds of event, of course, seem immune to transformations by consciousness. A tragic deed such as Othello's decision to execute Desdemona would seem impossible to interpret as a disaster short of insisting that Othello had a brain tumor. A disaster like an earthquake could not conceivably be made over into a tragedy originating in a choice. But some events that look like disasters are open to interpretation, and the more perceptive and mature the mind, the less inclined it will be to settle for the less rigorous way of conceiving of the event, for the concept of accident, coincidence, or even natural cause, though any of these might provide a plausible enough account. The apparently disastrous, if inspected steadfastly, may reveal deep-lying symptoms of the tragic; the tragic sense may interpret the bare fact of disaster and find, not irrationality or brute circumstance, but human meaningfulness. If we can look at the event in terms of responsibility, we gain something in intellectual security and decrease the portion of life in which we are hapless clods.

The consciousness that can gradually isolate the tragic center of the gross disaster has acted in an exemplary way on an international nightmare of more than half a century ago—the loss of the *Titanic*. On its maiden voyage the "unsinkable" triumph of modern shipbuilding collided with an iceberg and sank; many died. The world was shaken as it rarely is even by major catastrophes. Thomas Hardy wrote a poem attributing the collision to the plans of fate, which he calls Immanent Will. But the poem images the meeting of ship and iceberg as a "consummation," as an "intimate welding" of graceful

ship and "sinister mate," that is, as a bizarre intercourse in which the
lover murders his partner. These images have the effect of introducing an element of volition or of active personality into the relationship,
as if it were not entirely a casualty or a sardonic mischief of the
"Spinner of the Years." Well, in time it began to be seen that the
historical disaster which inspired Hardy's poem was what we call
"avoidable." Let us here try a restatement of the nature of tragedy:
tragedy is concerned with the inevitability of the avoidable. An "accident" takes on the coloring of tragedy when it is morally avoidable
and when we look at it in such terms. The *morally* avoidable accident
can be guarded against not by better equipment and new electronic
devices, but by a state of mind which is anterior to all technical
practices, that is, an adequate sense of reality. The accident need not
happen, for an ever alert sense of human limits and liabilities can
create an order of conduct that makes for self-preservation. But the
accident does happen because, in that division of personality in which
tragedy originates, other motives are more powerful and blot out the
course to safety. Because we know the urgency and relentlessness of
these motives, we can speak of the inevitability of the avoidable.

Everyone thought the *Titanic* could never sink; hence everyone had
the freedom of an unprecedented total security. The very name of the
ship was a boast (presumably no one recalled, however, that the
Titans were dethroned); there was unlimited pride in the final
triumph over an ages-old destructive enemy, the sea. In all the human
beings that constituted the soul of the ship, there was a contemptuous
superiority to old dangers that made the actual conduct of its life an
invitation to assault—or, to carry on with Hardy's figure, to rape. To
say this is not to moralize or to lay blame, for tragedy is a realm
beyond blame; in fact, to the kind of court of inquiry that convenes
after such catastrophes, with the intention of assigning blame, the
Titanic affair might be elusive. The heedless assurance that led to the
collision had infected everyone on land and sea; thousands of people
constituted the tragic hero of that voyage, an Everyman by sheer
numbers. There was universality, too, in the motive beneath all the
recklessness—modern pride in the conquest of nature.

So we discover the tragic reality behind the façade of disaster, and
then we understand the power to move that makes the happening
extraordinarily memorable. Whatever their magnitude or sheer incred-

ibility, mere accidents fade rather quickly toward oblivion; what gives accidents the life of memory and feeling is the immanent meaning that survives the brute shock of events. The ultimately moving experience is not the one which simply happens to us but the one which we help bring into being. Mere events take on life when they give us an image of ourselves in action.

CHAPTER TWO

This Gloomy World:
The Drama of Disaster

S O FAR I have argued that to distinguish between tragedy and disaster is a necessity of everyday life, a corrective step against the confusion created by our habitual misuse of terms, and that making this distinction is required for clarity of mind and for moral perspective and safety. In art, as in life, it is desirable to make the same distinction: to know the difference between tragedy and what I will call, for the time being, the literature of disaster. The literature of disaster comprises all those pages in which we record what has been done to us by fire, famine, the sword, and unjust men; in which our role is that of Job, plagued by our own kind, by machines, and by nature. In tragedy, as an art form, we contemplate our own errors; in the literature of disaster, we mark the errors of others and the flaws of circumstance. In tragedy we act; in the literature of disaster, we are acted upon. We court trouble if we call the literature of disaster *tragedy*, for when we do that, we implicitly equate all unhappiness with what is done to us, and in so doing we make it easy to lose awareness of what we do.

I. Generic Contrasts and Mixtures

The problem is to avoid confusing two generically different forms that look alike because both depict suffering. But in facing the problem we can commit two main errors: we can make distinctions too rigidly, and we can fall into partisanship or polemics. Individual dramas do not always fit conveniently into one category or another; the more complex they are, the more likely they are to intermingle the tragic and the disastrous. Antigone and Hamlet must both act in situations which they have not brought about; in this sense they are acted upon; something disastrous has happened to them, through the agency of others. Up to a point, then, they are "victims." But while remembering this, we see also that the plays are not constructed as accounts of what happens to the title characters, who are not treated as victims, talk though they may about the times that are out of joint; they do not choose simply to drift or to wait and hope. What happens to them is less a blow than an incitement to self-discovery, to learning their fitness for an active role. They influence more than they are influenced; it is because they can and do act that the plays exist. *Othello* also appears to have closer affiliations with the literature of disaster, for throughout the play we have a villain victimizing the hero; it is almost as though Othello were overcome by an irresistible outer force or enemy; indeed, some critics see Othello as a pathetic victim of an evil man. If we take this view, we can hardly call the play tragedy. But we do not have to use some other generic term if we perceive two facts: Othello transcends the role of victim by choosing to act evilly; and even in bending to Iago's influence he is actually failing to control a part of himself rather than giving way under outside pressure. If this is true, then he acts in the tragic style. Nevertheless a villain is there; and when there is a villain, we need to see whether he is the major source of evil visited upon others whom he victimizes, or, on the other hand, objectifies or corresponds to a prior, more fundamental source of evil in the "good man" or "hero" himself. The latter situation is tragic; the former is something else.

A caveat against the danger of pat classifications should include a reminder of the situations in *Macbeth* and *Lear* and *Oedipus*. In these plays the deeds of kings bring troubles not only upon themselves but upon their kingdoms: the tragedy of the ruler is the disaster of the realm, and the representation of this disaster is a significant part of drama. Not to be aware of it would be to underestimate the complexity of the artist's work, or the fullness of his sense of life.

So much for the danger of imposing a too pure conception of form upon existent plays that were not created to illustrate generic types—a danger for any critic who looks at form from the perspective of genre. Here he can only hope that his critical taste will not betray him. The second danger in the differentiating of tragedy and the literature of disaster is that one may fall into polemics—may overvalue the literature of disaster, which is the course more responsive to popular taste, or undervalue it, which is the likely course of the critic convinced that the tragic itself is undervalued. Perhaps the best way to exorcize the temptation to partisanship is to consider the various postures into which the critic may fall. This will mean, in effect, canvassing some of the pros and cons of the literature of disaster.

Drama of Disaster: Possible Approaches

Suppose we look at the problem in terms of the historical context. Since our age is, as we have already seen, addicted to viewing disaster as the major threat to human well-being, the strategy called for involves the risk of undervaluing the literature of disaster. The need is to recover an adequate sense of the tragic. Hence, we must emphasize that disaster is a more restricted realm, where there is always the danger of the obvious, where our sense of reality is not relentlessly tested, and where the order of feeling evoked, though it may be intense enough, is rather limited. The literature of disaster affords a lesser range of experience because it brings less of our human potential into play, and asks less of us; though it portray our doom, it is habitually easier on us than tragedy is for it leaves us free from self-inspection. As Jung has said,

The disastrous idea that everything comes to the human soul from outside and that it is born a tabula rasa is responsible for the erroneous belief that under normal circumstances the individual is in perfect order. . . . As a result of these prejudices the individual feels totally dependent on his environment and loses all capacity for introspection.[1]

Suppose, however, we ignore the historical context—the context of disordered perspectives—and look simply at the human experiences that are the raw material of the literature of disaster. The universality and the moving power of the disastrous event are facts of life. There are ways in which human beings *are* victims; it does not falsify or belittle human experience to record the sufferings of the flesh, the destructiveness of nature, the terrors of social and political disorder, the blows of evil men; these are realities, and we respond to them strongly. The artistic treatment of such matters may be overvalued. But we may not for that reason generally disparage, in itself, the artist's impulse to picture and interpret the struggle between men and the outer forces that can injure or destroy them.

Suppose we shift from the subject matter of the literature of disaster and consider the impact of that literature. Though I have suggested that it is relatively easy on us, it may still have a propaedeutic function. If less far-reaching than tragedy, it is apparently more accessible, and therefore, for a considerable number of men, it may actually be the vestibule to a more mature sense of reality. It is a rebuke to thoughtless security in the world, to dreams of invulnerability and of the conquest of enemies. It is a reminder of limits and liabilities, of the fallibility of systems, of all the quirks of circumstance that may thwart our strength and our wits. It points to the physical forces, within and around us, that forever elude our wiliest efforts to bend them permanently to our will. It comments on the irreducible remnant of irrationality in a universe that we like to see as ever more amenable to reason. It makes us look at the violence or cruelty or sadism that can break out even in what is often regarded as the apex of civilizational advance. Thus a narrower kind of literature may contribute to a broader vision of reality.

Ordinarily, however, the principal phenomena of disaster take place outside the human character; what is missing is the inner action of character, the movements of sentience and responsibility. Indeed, the literature of disaster may make the most significant actions of character impossible; it may simply portray the elimination of consciousness. Or if the sense of nonrational events is urgent and uncolored enough, it may invoke the concept of absurdity and thus impose the kind of burdens that encourage self-pity, despair, or heroics. If the disaster comes from human evil, it is the evil of others, not ourselves; we are innocent, and we can grieve, if we wish, instead of looking more steadily at ourselves. The disaster that is general rather than private destroys or injures all men alike, good and evil; thus it leads us away from qualitative differences.

Yet the literature of disaster may serve an awareness of character by choosing to distinguish among victims and by compelling the reader to be aware of different responses to different victims. If a victim is already identified as a scoundrel, his disaster will seem a blessing; we will feel differently when the disaster strikes the "good man." By responding to a difference in victims, we start to climb away from the pure menace of things upon which disaster typically focuses our attention. Or take war, which most men will classify as disaster; only the simplest literature of war will devote itself exclusively to survival; the more adult the writer, the more he moves on to the ways in which people respond to what happens to them. (War is a tantalizing subject by which a writer may be surprised into depths or tricked into shallows. When we are so disillusioned that "No one wins a war" is virtually an international cliché, our attention turns to the ambiguity of victor and victim. From this there might flow mature irony, or, on the other hand, a sense of "the pity of it all" that could easily fade into sentimentality.)

If, as I have said, disaster ordinarily evokes rather uncomplicated responses such as fear and hate, nevertheless an artist may see it in relation to a considerable range of moral options. If a making of choices enters the picture, it is likely to become the central object of attention and to push the brute event to one side. Hardship, danger, or the imminence of death may evoke complaint, resentment, fear, bravery, indifference, self-seeking, or self-absorption, or even interwoven or apparently contradictory mixtures of simple responses. In *The Private Life of the Master Race* (1934ff.), for instance, Brecht shows Germans responding to Nazi tyranny in diverse ways. He concentrates, throughout a dozen or more episodes, on the effect of constant fear on the human personality—recrimination, duplicity, hypocrisy, self-abasement, self-deception, suspicion, a dread that distorts everyday facts and actions, self-saving and indifference to others, disloyalty to and actual betrayal of others, anguished searching for reconciliation of principle and survival, despair. The dramatic plan permits only snapshots of many personalities at revealing moments: epiphanies. Some men know what they are and what they are doing; could their lives be shown more fully, the drama would turn on tragic dividedness. In general, if a writer starts with disaster but moves from the threat itself to the actions of those threatened and to the moral contrasts among them, he will be pushing the literature of disaster to its full proportions; if he can discover and explore the conflicts within those threatened, he will be approaching the realm of tragedy. But it is a hard route for him if disaster is the prime mover in his work, for in this structure it takes great qualities of imagination to force the human participants from passivity to activity, or into more than stock activity. The problem is whether the artist can move far enough beyond the simple victim to permit it to be said of his characters, "None of them are personal ciphers, as modern writers frequently have made their entrapped characters. If in a sense they are victims, it is not in a simple reflex way, not the mere products of society. In abundant measure they possess the will and passion to victimize themselves." [2]

We have been trying to see how far the literature of disaster, which in our day is very popular, can take us below the surface of moral reality, and we have noted its main possibilities and limitations. In the end we have to say that, though it may be intense and moving, and may reflect an undeniable actuality, it offers a narrower world of experience. Destructive accidents, the cataclysms of nature, the harshness of which society is capable at times, and individual acts of rapacity, whatever they bring of sorrow, and even of terror, leave out a good deal. A similar thought perhaps moved William Butler Yeats to declare that "passive suffering is not a theme for poetry." [3] Suppose all literature that dealt with mortal unhappiness were the literature of disaster. If this were true, most of the world's great tragedies would be unwritten—with some loss to our feeling for reality. For if suffering never incriminates the sufferer (whether we fail to recognize incrimination, or turn our eyes only to the cases where he is guiltless), then the world of suffering is either without meaning or obvious in meaning. The literature of this world would tempt man to thoughtless nadaism or thoughtless excelsiorism, to sinking under blows, or striking stoic poses that are the histrionic mask of despair, or laboring naïvely to do away with blows.

The business of tragedy is not only what goes wrong, but the human meaning of what goes wrong; it interprets the thing that has gone wrong in terms of the man who has done wrong. (Other catastrophes, those that are not rooted in character, may be plotted in physical or psychophysical formulas that are meaningful only in a technical sense; or else they are related to mechanics and statistics and lead to public resolutions such as "We must discover better safety devices"; in either case they are light years distant from the individual living where choices must be made.) In tragedy we find responsibility and guilt; it is there that we discover the source of evil, not in things, not in others, but in ourselves. In disaster we are without complicity in evil; in tragic life, when someone errs in heart or mind, we must look at him and say, "There, by the grace of the artist, go I."

II. Types of Victims

We want now to look at some examples of the drama of disaster. Most of these plays are conventionally called tragedies, and a few of them are complex enough to contain elements of tragedy.

In the drama of disaster we find victims of situations that range from very simple to complex. Though I do not want to get trapped in a too neat row of compartments, the actual dramas may be divided roughly according to the kinds of victimizing forces. Dramatists have been principally interested in the victims of nature, of society, of political forces, of evil individuals, and those who are victims of themselves. This last type of play sounds, of course, rather like tragedy, and the distinction must be clarified later.

III. Victims of Nature

The victim of nature is the subject of John M. Synge's *Riders to the Sea* (1904). On returning to it after some years, I was surprised to find how slight it is (it is, of course, only a one-acter), and how narrowly it clings to dignity and credibility; yet it has been anthologized and produced countless times, and for a half century it has had the status of at least a minor classic. Its very popularity, I believe, suggests the extent of our confusion about tragedy. It is the story of a fisherman's family on an island off the west coast of Ireland; Maurya, now an old woman, has lost a husband, a father-in-law, and six sons in storms or in accidents at sea; the action of the play turns on the death of the last two sons by drowning. We see the response of several survivors to a climactic series of calamities—the daughters' concern for their mother, the grief, the sense of desolation, the sense of irony, a bowing to destiny. In examining the feelings of the survivors, Synge is neither narrow nor pat; to record the variations of their grief he finds a language that, though imagistic and unusually rhythmical, is based on plainness and understatement. This style is essential to offset a hyperbole of disasters that verges on being manipulated and false. We are moved by the survivors' foreboding, fear, courage, and meditation on loss as the fate of all men; yet the play makes use of only a fraction of our total ability to be implicated. It exacts little of us. We remain fairly serene observers, sympathetic, sharing the sadness of death, but never drawn into pain such as that of incrimination.

The play is a lament; it is elegiac. When we feel an overwhelming concern for length of life, we tend to mistake elegy for tragedy; grief over the passage of things supplants contemplation of the quality of life. Death seems then not an expectable event, but a violation of order; we make it the enemy, and symbolize its hostility by pointing to its relentless, excessive attacks upon one family. In the elegiac there is a sense of the hero as victim: hence its proper relation is to disaster rather than tragedy. One of Maurya's lines is a key to all literature of disaster: "They've all gone now, and there isn't anything else the sea can do to me." Note the phrase, "can do to me." When the chief character is simply the person to whom things are done, his role as a moral agent is a small one. He is a "whole" person, without the inner divisions or the clashing loyalties that mark the meaningful human conflicts. The dominant effect is one of pathos, and its import is limited. Naturally, this is not to say that the pathos of suffering is not a legitimate subject for literary art. It is. But if we mistake it for tragic effect, we fall short in our understanding of the whole human role, and of the modes of human failure.*

* It is interesting that Synge's *Deirdre of the Sorrows*, which has tinges of the tragic, is less well-known than *Riders to the Sea*. In the basic structure of the play, the lovers Deirdre and Naisi are the "victims" of Conchubor the King, and all of them are victims of "fate," which has been voiced in prophecies. In dramatizing the legend, however, Synge makes the lovers act so as to assist a fate that technically they could avoid. When, after a seven-year idyl in flight, they return into the power of Conchubor, they are not simply tricked. There is even some complexity in their motives. Yet a new "victim motif" enters into Deirdre's decision to return: life seems a "disaster," leading to the loss of beauty and love. She cannot

David Rudkin's *Afore Night Come* [4] (first produced in 1962)
presents a victim of nature in a different key—of a human nature that
is as murderous as the sea in Synge's play, welling up rhythmically,
we infer, in a wave of destructiveness that will find someone to kill. A
group of pear pickers use a harvest scene for a death rite that ends in
a decapitation and burial. Beneficent nature ironically frames the
nature "red in tooth and claw." The small group of permanent fruit

---

bear reality (the *sic transit* of all experience), she pities herself, and the
sentimental intrudes—the danger in all literature of disaster. In Act III
there is a recovery: Deirdre quarrels with Naisi before his death, and after
his death she feels not only self-pity but guilt. Thus disaster becomes
infused with the tragic: unhappiness has not merely "happened to" them.
On the other hand, this tragic is limited: like Othello, Deirdre can
understand herself and her guilt only up to a point. In several lesser
matters there is a remarkable parallel between Deirdre's last minutes and
Othello's: Deirdre speaks of the glories of her career, reveals a hidden
knife, uses the word *pitiful* twice in her final speech, stabs herself, and
falls on the body of her lover.

Synge does not characteristically lean toward the "drama of the victim."
The Tinker's Wedding, in which a priest refuses to marry Michael Byrne
and Sarah Casey because they do not pay him enough, might easily have
been given a structure very popular in modern times: the "outsiders"
victimized by "institutions." Synge treats the situation with comic detachment; rascality appears on both sides, and a comfortable compromise is
achieved: if Michael and Sarah do not get all they have coming to them by
way of ecclesiastical blessing, they manage the priest with sufficient
agility and resourcefulness to ward off all they have coming to them by
way of punishment for misdeeds. In *The Well of the Saints* Martin and
Mary Doul might have been treated as "victims" of blindness; or of
well-meaning people who led them to a miraculous cure which would
result only in disillusionment when certain facts of life were seen for the
first time; or, in a different structure, as victims of a false cure which
would be followed by the double disaster of a return to unwanted blindness. Synge skillfully evades these sentimental traps. Given a second
chance to see, Martin and Mary choose blindness as the lesser evil, a
choice which is left ambiguous—as the love of illusion, or as the hard
adjustment to reality. Forty years later, dramatizing a similar theme in
The Iceman Cometh, O'Neill omitted the ambiguity.

It is clear, then, that Synge could take situations in which human
beings might be considered simply as victims of disaster and could see
them in the broader perspectives of comedy or tragedy. But of all his plays
(I exclude *Playboy of the Western World*) the best known is *Riders to
the Sea*, which offers little more than the plain disaster. Applying the
Aristotelian criterion of size, Joyce thought the work too short to be a
tragedy, but called it the work of a "tragic poet." See Richard Ellmann,
James Joyce (New York: Oxford University Press, 1959), p. 454.

pickers turn on an outsider (an itinerant picker) and magnify his incompetence (he is neither strong nor careful), his tricks (he tries to steal pears), his generic differentness (he is Irish and articulate), and thus find a justification for violence, but, more than that, work themselves up to, and stimulate their lust for, a killing. In part this lust may be due to the frustrations of the work and of their lives (one picker is a victim of jokes about his impotence or sterility); but principally it comes through as an autonomous fact of their being. In general, the play belongs to the large body of twentieth-century literature devoted to separating out the primitive from the uneasy fusion of the natural and the civilized that dominates post-Renaissance literature, and to thrusting it nakedly at an audience like an accusation of blindness. The program notes for the 1964 production at the Aldwych Theatre in London suggest that Rudkin's imagination was stimulated by Euripides' *Bacchae* and by a passage in which Tacitus describes a demonic outbreak of pure destructiveness, of passion to rend and tear. Such a rediscovery of the darker side of man produces a great shock, and it will doubtless take many years of familiarization with this kind of aesthetic experience before we can distinguish the facile, the meretricious, the perverse, and the more durable uses of it. However, revealing the irrational killer in Everyman so far belongs mainly to the literature of disaster and to the allegorical; these two intersect insofar as the characters, instead of maturing into full complexity, are dramatizations of concepts or single impulses. From this single-track portraiture comes a single-track emotional experience. We do not get inner conflict, but, at best, some conflict between different impulses represented in different individuals. Thus in *Afore Night Come* the murder is foreseen by Johnny "Hobnails" Carter, a worker on temporary leave from a mental hospital, who is a Cassandra character. With Cassandran difficulty, he tries to warn, and to draw away from the murder or from the sight of it, Larry Lewis, another temporary picker, a university student who represents a less primitive order of humanity. In the slight rapport achieved between them, we are offered a relationship that is a small counterweight to that of savage and victim which is at the center of the drama; it serves to afford a touch of the "relief" common in older popular dramas of disaster in which the disaster was not conceived to be total.

IV. VICTIMS OF SOCIETY

Afore Night Come is a useful transitional play. Although the murdered man is a victim of a natural force, the natural force is embodied in a group of men knit together by place, work, values, and temperament. In a sense, then, the murdered man is also a victim of society. Society as murderer, a fairly congenial theme in mid-twentieth century,* is an ultimate version of an old perspective, though one that may in time become more familiar than the indifferent or unkind society in several generations of problem plays. The relatively unqualified sense of the individual as a good man victimized by society, rather than as a deviant from the authoritative norms of society, originates in the romantic sensibility and descends to us through the plays of Ibsen's middle period (*Pillars of Society*, 1875–77, *A Doll's House*, 1878–79, *Ghosts*, 1881, and *An Enemy of the People*, 1882). These, as they recede from us in time, seem more tinged with the flamboyant air of outmoded crusades, diminishing in credibility as perspective renders clearer the artifices to which even a playwright of unusual technical skill was driven by his eagerness to make points. Presumably none of these plays would be mistaken for tragedy, but as "serious drama" concerned with social problems they are central instances of a literature of disaster that tends to crowd tragedy off the stage. To use *An Enemy of the People* as representative of the group has disadvantages, for it is the least polished of the middle-period plays; it was written rapidly, with little sense of art and with an obvious crusading intention. But if it does not represent Ibsen at his most complex, which can be very complex indeed, it illustrates the basic emotional structure of the form in which he is working.

* We come shortly to Friedrich Duerrenmatt's *The Visit* (1956); whereas Rudkin presents the murder of the individual as coming out of an instinctual need of the murderers, Duerrenmatt sees it as a quasi-judicial act that is a façade for economic profit. A third version is found in Shirley Jackson's short story *The Lottery*, in which the murder results from the formal invocation of an ancient scapegoat rite. The three works deal, respectively, with murder by society in psychological, economic, and anthropological terms (the categories overlap, of course). The scapegoat version appears also in Max Frisch's *Andorra* (1961), which presents, however, not a community ritual but concurrence in an invading enemy's anti-Semitism.

Dr. Stockmann discovers that the baths which are at the heart of the town's economy are supplied with contaminated water unfit to drink or even to bathe in; with the aid of a crusading newspaper and a public-spirited printer he expects to make the facts known, have the baths purified, and be hailed as a local benefactor. But it soon turns out that nearly everyone's economic or political interests are tied to the status quo, so that Dr. Stockmann cannot even get the story of the baths into print. Intending to publicize the facts orally, he calls a meeting in a private house, but the meeting is taken over by the entrenched interests, and the doctor is formally voted "an enemy of the people." His house is partly wrecked, he and his family are evicted, his daughter is fired from a teaching job, he is fired as director of the baths, the ship captain who lent him a room for the meeting is fired by the shipping company, a citizens' committee gets to work to boycott him professionally, and as a last blow the doctor's father-in-law spends all his money cornering depreciated bath stocks and challenges the doctor to persist in the "madness" that will wreck the investment on which his wife's and children's inheritance will depend.

In a familiar romantic pattern of thought the individual who knows the truth is the victim of the inflexibility, selfishness, and crassness of society generally. The uneven conflict has a scarcely credible simplicity. We know that, though Ibsen wrote autobiographically, he apparently got outside himself enough to entertain private reservations about Dr. Stockmann and in some aspects of the characterization even intended to laugh at himself a little. Yet the form of the play admits almost no response but sympathy for the crusader. We have to identify ourselves with right fighting wrong, and, though Dr. Stockmann's ranting style tends to interfere with this, we are asked basically to admire his integrity and courage, and to feel indignation against the corruption of the town. But even this simple fare is undercut by the contrived ironies, the incredible completeness of the alliance against the doctor, and the romantic refusal of the doctor to be downed or even downhearted (at different times Ibsen uses images which identify the doctor with Luther and with Christ). In fact, the opposition between Hovstad's "Right is always on the side of the majority" and the doctor's buoyant closing line, "the strongest man on earth is he who stands most alone," brings us close to the popular romantic theater in which total villainy is confronted by heroic fearlessness. It is always the danger when reality is understood as the battle of reckless courage against the oppressiveness of a calculating society.

The irony is that, although he seriously attenuates the emotional experience possible in the drama of disaster, Ibsen is at one point on the edge of tragedy: when the dangers to his family place Dr. Stockmann in an Antigone-like division between the claims of public and private life. But he is not permitted to face the issue seriously in either thought or feeling, for he is less a character than an allegorical figure of truth, for whom Ibsen envisages not a permanent catastrophe but only an exciting martyrdom.

Ibsen's play is the very image of the drama that offers no real choices and thrusts its audience into no new awareness. But we are forced closer to new awareness in another treatment of Ibsen's theme three-quarters of a century later—Friedrich Duerrenmatt's *The Visit* (1956). Or at least an impression of new awareness is created by the more sinister and ferocious conduct by means of which Duerrenmatt carries along, to its final shocks, his brilliant allegory of the greedy town. Like Ibsen he shows a society, driven by the profit motive, gradually but completely and inexorably turning against a man who is popular and who, like Dr. Stockmann, has visions of local preferment. But amiable Alfred Ill becomes an enemy, and a victim, of the people not because he brings a profit-cutting truth but because by merely being alive he deprives them of one million pounds: his death is the stated price the town must pay for a million-pound gift offered by a rich woman who insists that justice can be bought.

Many years before, at the age of seventeen, this woman had become a whore when Ill himself got her pregnant but disclaimed the child and attacked her character. The town begins by refusing the offer, and Claire Zachanassian, the would-be benefactress, calmly sits down to wait them out. Though they continue to protest their Western and humanitarian principles, they gradually alter under the pressure of temptation: on the one hand, in anticipation of the new wealth, they all begin buying on account, many of them at Ill's own store; on the other hand, they slowly change their attitude to the once popular Ill, whom they now begin to accuse openly of having mistreated Claire in the distant past, and who in time feels so menaced that he appeals for police protection, only to run into ambiguous replies that testify to the altering state of mind in the community. Eventually the town not only sentences Ill and executes him, doing literally what the Norwegian town does figuratively to Dr. Stockmann, but it even manages this in a climax of horrifying brazenness at a splendid community fete. The citizens equally enjoy a sense of civic virtue, praised in a number of rhetorical public statements, and a sense of great importance, attested to by the presence of visiting reporters, photographers, and radio announcers, who are finally told that Ill died of "joy" at being able to persuade his old friend Claire to make the big gift to the town. There is a closing chorus in which the citizens describe poverty as the greatest evil of all and congratulate themselves on prosperity and good fortune.

In this portrayal of the victim of the community, Duerrenmatt roughly parallels Ibsen, but he offers a less simple situation. For a while Ill has a defender, and it appears that Duerrenmatt is even complicating the community: the Schoolmaster actually tries to make the community understand what it is up to. But he cannot hold out alone, and at the final sacrifice he provides, with perhaps a touch of ambiguity, the public rationalizations; so through him the eventual monolithic unanimity of the town is the more overwhelming and the picture of human corruptibility more devastating. Again, Ill differs from most victims in that he is not innocent; in his fate there is something of nemesis, and of the understanding of nemesis, that belongs to the tragic realm. His punishment takes place through an upthrust of old evil deeds that is faintly Oedipean,* and Duerrenmatt himself believes that "in death" Ill "achieves greatness." [5] There is indeed a touch of the tragic in Ill. He is not, however, a seeker of truth; he seems to bow to the inevitable judgment of his prosecutors (like a brainwashed defendant at a treason trial), and hence the tragic drifts into the pathetic.

Perhaps it would be better to say that the focus is not on him but on the million-lusting townspeople, so that it is less what he does than

* There are several resemblances to the Oedipus story. The most marked is that an individual's wrong action in the past is the source of a blight upon the community. The individual achieves civic prominence (Oedipus became king, Ill is about to become mayor). The punishment of the individual removes the blight. The wrong action had to do with sex. The individual accepts his responsibility.

what they do that sets the tone. Thus even the pathetic is all but eliminated by the callous venality and case making of the townspeople, who, as they close in ever more tightly to kill for cash, enforce in us a response of claustrophobic dread. This is made more pressing by the knowing relentlessness of the revengeful Claire Zachanassian as she coolly waits for the townspeople to fall in line and execute Ill for her. For Ill's role to be tragic in effect, the justice meted out to him would have to be disinterested; but his own attitude to himself becomes insignificant in the face of the ruthless calculation, and behind it the scorned woman's punitive destructiveness, that usurps all attention. Hence even the standard emotional fare of the literature of disaster—pity for the victim and indignation at the evildoers—not only replaces the tragic but is in turn replaced by something else as Ill is forced into an ever narrowing cell of isolation and is finally physically surrounded by the town leaders and garroted. It is difficult to find a suitable word for the response; "revulsion" may do (if it does not suggest an unseemly shrinking from reality). The important thing here is less the term used than the fact that the symbolic extremism of the episodes pushes one out of aesthetic participation, as if through an illicit peephole one were viewing an alien depravity rather than coming into intimate knowledge of a human truth. At its extreme, the literature of disaster runs two opposite risks: it may entice us into a stereotyped situation, ready-made for easy emotional wear (*An Enemy of the People*); or it may lock us out of an eccentric or centrifugal situation which allows no balance or stability. The reader is reduced to an uncomfortable spectator of psychological machinery when the literary method is to eliminate all human complexity and take a single impulse out to an ultimate hypertrophy.

Such a drama, with its originality and ingeniousness, works like a shocking cartoon, a knockout critique in grotesque images. When it functions in this way, the literature of disaster shows its affinity with satire, which by its nature keeps us decisively outside of the reality that it presents. For it is others whose foibles satire exhibits to amuse us, and others whose vices it exhibits to gratify our vanity and our love of meting out blame. The foible or the vice is always over there outside us, in others; it is not conceivably in us. This, it need hardly be said, is a long way from tragedy. The point is made explicitly by an analyst of satire who notes that, although the tragic hero has pronounced satiric tendencies, [he also has a distinguishing] ability to ponder and to change under pressure. The satirist, however, is not so complex. He sees the world as a battlefield between a definite, clearly understood good, which he represents, and an equally clear-cut evil. No ambiguities, no doubts about himself, no sense of mystery trouble him, and he retains always his monolithic certainty.[6]

Exactly: we identify with him, as we righteously scourge the evils in which we have no part. Satire, as Swift put it, is a sort of mirror in which readers see "every body's Face but their Own; . . ."[7] Satire has no technical device for cutting through our protective *amour-propre;* if anything, it strengthens this shell by picturing foible and vice with a hyperbole that diminishes their potential relevance to ourselves. In separating us from our failings by caricaturing them, satire is allied in method with the literature of disaster that puts us to flight by its nightmarish menace: to make stark points, both pare off all richness of character and end with incomplete human beings. Instead of a fullness of life that invites a gradually deepening participation, the troubling division at the heart of tragedy, they offer an isolated virtue too easy to accept, or an isolated vice too easy to repudiate (even a vice attributed to a society leaves the reader free: to him the delinquents remain "they"). If Ibsen's Dr. Stockmann is simply an image of resurgent truth, Duerrenmatt's townspeople are images of faithless greed and Claire Zachanassian of retaliatory malice. In Alfred Ill, Duerrenmatt offers a hint of tragic range, but he mainly fills out the incomplete pattern of life with a brilliant, fantastic decor that is the expressionist garnish for cautionary tale, or what his translator, Patrick Bowles, calls a "macabre parable." We see that postrealist expressionism is often singularly like prerealist allegory.

V. Victims of the Self

If we go back to Maxim Gorki's *Lower Depths* (1902), we see the victims of society in a quite different key. The pathos of suffering appears in greater variety and is itself part of a much more varied scheme. There is not the monotone of *Riders to the Sea*, the mechanical consistency of the townspeople's alignment against reform in *An Enemy of the People*, the relentless movement of revenge and greed against the doomed figure in *The Visit*. Here we have, not the bereaved or the set upon, but the sick, the jealous, the disappointed and disillusioned, thieves, gamblers, failures and riffraff, dying by disease or violence, or subsisting on a diet of drunkenness, cheating, accusation, abuse, fights, cynicism, derisive truth telling, boasts about real or imaginary pasts or illusive distinctions in the present, and occasional bursts of false hope. Through the dialogue run a number of hints that this wretchedness originates in the inflexibility, indifference, and harshness of society. Pepel the thief says, "honor and conscience are for the rich" (Act I).[8] He is the son of a thief and so he is a thief too; he wants to break away, but in trying to save his girl he kills the landlord and, in our last view of him, is being held for the police. Kleshtch exclaims, "they won't let you live—" (Act III); both Satine and Bubnoff talk of the "they" who beat up Satine (Act I); and Satine says, "people aren't ashamed to let you live worse than a dog" (Act III). Even Luka the pilgrim, who encourages people to cling to any therapeutic faith, sums up his history, "They pounded me till I got soft" (Act I).

Yet the play is not mainly devoted to establishing the guilt of a hostile world; indeed a different situation is suggested when Satine, evidently meant to be a spokesman, insists, "Man must be respected —not degraded with pity—but respected, respected!" (Act IV). The irony of it is that these characters are so conceived that their claim is largely upon pity, though the pity is qualified by our sense of their diminished humanity. They fight and blame and accuse; self-deceptions are punctured by transient glimpses of disintegration; there is an occasional note of desire for another life, but the present is changed only by dyings and binges. Our sense of a hardly alterable slum is created by images of mire, muck, filth, rottenness; of choking, poison, and the swamp; by characters speaking to and of each other as beggars, cheats, tramps, jailbirds, ruffians, scoundrels, sluts, crooks, swindlers, devils, bastards, murderers. Though sometimes they wish and hope for escape, their enduring faith is in human beastliness; there is a Shakespearian crowding of animal imagery as the inmates call each other—and often Everyman—animal, beast, brute, bitch, mongrel, mad dog, pig, jackass, bedbug, cockroach, worm, crow, raven, wolf, and shark, and think of each other or themselves as creeping, barking, crawling, grunting, and going on all fours. In their virtual acceptance of animal status, we perceive what may be called the "disaster of personality": the going to pieces, the caving in, that means the loss of the power of recovery. There is an annihilation of soul that parallels the bodily death of physical disaster, an impotence to make or seize opportunities to get out. The prisoner's song which they sing has a heavily symbolic refrain, "I cannot break my chains."

The unbreakable chains separate the characters from the more open world of tragedy: though some of them have brief periods of insight into themselves and the world, these glimpses cannot lead toward either a reordering of self or a greater wisdom in action. What occurs is at best a static perception of loss and incapacity, not a dynamic consciousness of the full range of a self that has erred but can still understand and act. For these men and women, the glimpse of truth is hardly more than an unpleasant surprise when there is an accidental rip in the cloak of protective illusion. "I love unintelligible, obsolete words," says Satine (Act I). Whatever the pleasures offered by such words, they are hardly the language of insight. Again, the chains are unbreakable because in this world of disaster, even if the vision and strength were greater, there is too little that is recoverable; the human substance is defective; most of the organism is flaw. It is true, however, that within their enclosure some of the characters reveal, despite circumstances conducive only to enervation, a fund of energy, a gusty vigor within despair that fills out the human picture beyond an allegorical paradigm. Yet this urban underground cell, like Duerrenmatt's daylight village, keeps sinking away from the spectator instead of drawing him into it; it evokes surprise or regret or pity, but hardly the involvement or the sense of membership which would make possible the tragic experience.

O'Neill's *The Iceman Cometh* (produced, 1946) is a thematically much more complex work in which the drama of disaster hovers on the border of tragedy, sometimes crosses the line, and might enter the tragic realm entirely if it were not for the restraining power of the author's despair. Yet, despite O'Neill's enrichment of the materials, his play has extraordinary resemblances to Gorki's, and these resemblances—between a Russian play and an American play four decades apart—will suggest the extensive modern concern with disaster. Both plays deal with a large and diverse group of disreputable or broken-down characters in a squalid rooming house, living in pasts or in hopes not really trusted, failing to break out (in each play lack of

faith in human capabilities undermines a potential man-woman relationship that would involve getting away to another scene), finding
relief in quarrel, cutthroat candor, and coma, waiting for a drinking
bout such as appropriately ends each play, the crescendo of hilarity
providing the background for the suicide of one man who has found
his life intolerable. A still more striking parallel is the introduction
into each underground pseudo community of an outsider with a
remedial message, and the exploration, through him, of the doctrine
of pity for human suffering; further, each volunteer savior evokes
hostility.

But if one were making an issue of these resemblances—and there
are other parallels of detail—he would also have to note the divergen-
cies within the similar patterns. O'Neill's inmates are more decayed
and sottish, more consistently dependent on "pipe dreams" [9] (a key
image), more deficient in brute vitality; fewer of them move also in
the outer world; the disaster of personality is not attributed to social
causes at all. The salvation-offering visitors from without are quite
different in their theatrical and philosophic roles. In *The Lower
Depths* Luka works on individuals in personal talks, adjusting his
proffered help to each one's situation, whereas in *The Iceman Cometh*
Hickey not only privately urges, but publicly and formally tries to
force, everyone to accept his regimen. Luka, too mild to influence
overt action, kindly encourages any faith, illusion, or belief that
appears likely to contribute to an individual's well-being or comfort
(heaven for the dying, a cure for the alcoholic, love and escape for the
one pair that might have both); he says, "whatever you believe in,
exists . . ." (Act II). Hickey, a salesman with the "hard sell,"
relentlessly drives each man to test his illusions in action and thus to
find that they are illusions; his program is the creation of absolute
"peace" by the elimination of all pipe dreams.

Finally, the plays differ in the eventual dramatic "placing" of the
evangelists. Though Luka arouses antagonism, the gambler Satine
defends him in vigorous speeches evidently meant to have authority:
Luka "lies" out of "sheer pity" for the weak and the parasitic, who
"need lies"; truth is only for the strong and the free (Act IV). And
even in this constricted subworld there are bursts of animal vigor that
are important in the dramatization of theme: they suggest the actual
existence in the world—somewhere if not here—of the strength that

can tolerate truth. But in O'Neill's play Hickey, the destroyer of illusion, is repudiated: his prospective beneficiaries reject him, and he is so characterized that the reader must reject him. This world is not divided into those who need pipe dreams and those who do not; rather the drama declares that the flight from reality is the absolute price of life. In O'Neill's depiction of victims, knowledge of self is disaster, for it leads to malicious enmity, brutal cynicism, suicide, murder; and peace, fellowship, and life depend on dream and drink.

Hickey presents himself as a man who can bring peace because he has found peace himself—by freeing himself from pipe dreams that have led to guilt and remorse. His pipe dream was that he would break away from a lifelong career of alcoholic and sexual binges; it was given sustenance by the constant forgivingness of his wife, and he freed himself from it, we gradually learn in a skillfully maintained process of revelation, by killing his wife. But at the same time this dream-destroyer tries to hold on to another pipe dream: that he loved and pitied his wife and wanted to give her peace. Then he trips himself up and falls suddenly into the realization that he hated her. (The situation is a remarkable anticipation of an episode recounted by the judge penitent in Camus's *The Fall* [1956]: a businessman faithless to a faithful wife "was literally enraged to be in the wrong, to be cut off from receiving, or granting himself, a certificate of virtue. . . . Eventually, living in the wrong became unbearable to him. . . . He killed her." [10]) When Hickey finds out what he was really up to, he cries out that he hasn't "got a single damned lying hope or pipe dream left" and declares himself ready for "the Chair" (Act IV). Our last view of Hickey is all irony: the anti-illusionist seeking to recover an illusion, and the madman desperately trying to think of himself, at his one moment of insight, as insane (he uses the word, or synonyms for it, seven times in the speeches before his final exit).

But the irony of Hickey's inconsistency, though it reinforces the theme and might in another play be of major consequence, is almost insignificant in contrast with the demonic, calculated irony on which the play turns: O'Neill's brilliant polemic stratagem of having the traditional castigation of the vice of self-deception, as well as the constructive counsels that might be given in psychotherapy, come from the mouth of a gross fornicator and a cunning salesman who has become a homicidal maniac. This old hand in vice—a meaner Iago, with a "magnetic personality," insight into human weakness, and skill in profiting from it—is given the coloring of a reformer and a do-gooder, even of the zealot who will force his medicines down the throats of those who he thinks need them. There could hardly be a more intensely hostile assault upon the doctrine that human salvation lies in discovering the truth and undergoing the pain that it may bring. In this drama of ideas O'Neill does not, however, betray his hand from the start: he does not get our backs up by immediately labeling the truth-bringer a phony and then simply playing for the cynical grimace at his falsity. Hickey is made initially plausible and draws us partly into his camp. Though a firm look at reality may seem a rather unpromising prescription for this barful of sodden wrecks, our beliefs are at least passively on Hickey's side, for it is possible that he may offer a key to betterment. Having been prepared to grant him "authority"—he has strength of personality, he makes some devastatingly sharp analyses of Larry Slade, the "philosopher" of the place, and he is able to act in the world—we then discover that he is a murderer and madman who, having wrecked his own life, must drive others into a similar destruction ("So you've got to kill them [dreams] like I did mine" [Act III]). O'Neill gets a maximum shock out of this—not to mention the delayed shock of our realization that he is defining the therapy of self-understanding as a cruel and vindictive fraud. And he seems clearly to desire the shock as a means of opening our eyes to his vision.

Yet this shock is not the same thing as the bald surprise of the slick popular play. In his dramaturgy O'Neill shows both competence and self-respect: the horror that is revealed in Hickey, though it has the force of a blow, is prepared for through two and a half acts before he confesses that he has shot his wife. The inmates abuse him in a variety of ways—as a liar, as a bringer of "bad luck," as being "not human," and, dozens of times, as being crazy and driving them crazy. Though these attacks are partly suspect because they originate in self-defensiveness, still they work cumulatively to make us ready for a truth not yet apparent. Our semiconscious doubt of his explicit objectives, and our readiness for the interpretation of him that O'Neill is finally to make, are most strongly influenced by the imagery of death that Hickey evokes in Acts III and IV. That Hickey has "the touch of death" or "brings death" is said repeatedly by Larry Slade, the one derelict who still has a mind; then under Hickey's influence the men almost "murder" each other, Harry the proprietor feels and looks "like a corpse," and Hickey himself is worried because his patients "play dead." And in a brilliant grotesque modulation of the theme of death, the drinkers bitterly complain that the liquor itself "has no life in it": only after Hickey is dragged off to jail does it again make them forgetful and merry.

In his desire to universalize the action, O'Neill uses an infusion of allegory. One of the bums is known as "Jimmy Tomorrow," a metaphor for illusion that could be applied to most of the company. The proprietor is named Harry Hope; his sponging lodgers only too obviously "live on hope." Another device of universalization O'Neill might have got from Conrad—the wide distribution of the group by nationality, status, and former way of life. But one of O'Neill's problems is to convert his small barroom society into a microcosm, to make it seem something more than an enclave of ruin on all sides of which, however much out of sight, is a realm of normalcy. He does not, I believe, find a way of convincing us that he is picturing a representative humanity. Despite the powerful dramatization of theme, we are spectators a long way from the arena of disasters, held momentarily by shock and by a nightmarish distortion, but not drawn in by a sense of identity which art can make inescapable. Our separateness is, as always, a mark of an effect other than the tragic. We might be more drawn in if it were possible to feel in the play a larger theme: the theme that might be present is the defense of the life of myth, imagination, and faith against a dogmatic rationalism, the latter presented with diabolic cleverness as the revenge against society of the man who has lost his faith. But the range of the characters is too narrow for them to symbolize myth or reason successfully; it is difficult to think of Harry Hope's dependents as more than sick men or weaklings, and difficult—though perhaps less so—to think of Hickey as more than a quasi-rational scoundrel in a final vast project of the salesmanship that has always meant for him a slick psychological exercise of the power impulse.*

* Ibsen's *The Wild Duck* (1883–84), to which *The Iceman Cometh* has extraordinary resemblances, tries more convincingly for representativeness by centering the life of illusion in a relatively "normal" family

Certain reminiscences of Conrad shed light on O'Neill's move away from the tragic toward the disastrous. O'Neill defends pipe dreams, and Conrad the dream; however, for O'Neill the pipe dream is simply an insulation against unbearable reality, while for Conrad

---

with identifiable common routines of life and by making the illusion breaker not an ostensibly genial Yahoo but a misguided idealist.

The number of ways in which Ibsen anticipated (by sixty years) O'Neill's debunking of the illusion breaker is remarkable. Like many of the O'Neill characters, Old Ekdal lives in a past that he has brought into the present in illusionary form: once a great hunter, he now happily shoots birds and rabbits in a pseudo forest rigged up in an attic; his son Hjalmar, also strongly attracted to this play life, lives on dreams of being the support of his father, the father of his daughter, an unusually gifted fellow, a potential inventor. His uneducated but sensible wife has created a workable domestic life by refraining from an officious correction of her husband's misconceptions. But Gregers Werle virtually ruins their life by carrying out his "mission." He forces upon Hjalmar the "claim of the ideal," which starts with a massive dose of disagreeable facts. (My quotations are from the translation by Mrs. F. E. Archer.) O'Neill's Hickey found his mission to the Hope inmates through hatred of his wife, Gregers through hatred of his father; each has to bear down hard on unwilling subjects for reform, and each is presented by his creator as subtly influenced by the power motive; each is confident that he knows just how his subject will respond to his coaching, but each is surprised by the low spirits that he produces ("dulness, gloom, oppression," Gregers calls it). In each play the new possessor of truth becomes unbearably quarrelsome and is inclined to put off until "tomorrow" the full implementation of the new life. And just as Hickey is opposed by Larry Slade, who charges that in breaking up pipe dreams Hickey brings "death," so Gregers is strongly attacked by Dr. Relling, who not only defends "life-illusions" as essential but also, we find, has been helping others to create sustaining illusions. And if Ibsen's characters exist in a less alcoholic atmosphere than that of Harry Hope's bar, nevertheless Ibsen perhaps anticipates O'Neill in this matter too, for Relling and his roommate are said to go in for riotous evenings, and Hjalmar, after he has been plunged into truth, joins them in a drinking orgy.

But if Ibsen's victims of a crusader for truth are more nearly related to general humanity than are O'Neill's, nevertheless Ibsen too has selected characters of considerable weakness—a choice likely to be made both by the dramatist of disaster and by the dramatist whose sense of character is influenced by his desire to exhibit the harmfulness of a code of values. Thus, even as early as the 1880's, there is a movement toward the Mr. Zero who would not be formally discovered until the 1920's. And in exhibiting the need of the weak to be protected against the terrors of self-knowledge, the dramatists have a common impulse to blacken the apostle of enlightenment: Gregers is a prig, and Hickey a rascal, and both are merciless.

the dream redeems the act, pulls man above the lowest level of conduct toward whatever virtues he can achieve. So Conrad believes that Lord Jim can endure the shame of his act of betrayal and can undergo a moral self-recovery and meet honorable death, whereas O'Neill clearly believes that for Don Parritt the only way out after his act of betrayal is a quick leap from the fire escape. Like Lord Jim, Parritt approaches a new knowledge in that he gradually surrenders the folds of deception with which for a time he has tried to hide the nature of his deed, but O'Neill's despair cuts off the wide range of experience that might follow when man stops lying.

Larry Slade, the ex-anarchist, and Axel Heyst in Conrad's *Victory* both cherish the illusion that they live in passive disillusionment on the shores of life, and both, in an interesting parallel, are ironically drawn into the stream by pity. Heyst learns that involvement means being overtaken by good as well as by evil, by love as well as by hate, and he acknowledges the guilt of retreat into inaction. Through pity, Larry defends the alcoholic dreamers against Hickey and in effect condemns Parritt to death as the only route from the sufferings of guilt to "peace." (Though with major differences, he parallels Gorki's Luka, who says, "Truth may spell death to you!" [Act II], "Truth doesn't always heal a wounded soul" [Act III], and who tells of a man who committed suicide when he lost faith in the actual existence of a "land of righteousness" [Act III].) Although in these ways and others Larry learns that actually he is not detached, he does not act (even too late); there is no galvanic shock of self-perception but only a gloomy acknowledgment of defeat in which it is difficult not to descry self-indulgence. "Be God, there's no hope! I'll never be a success in the grandstand—or anywhere else! Life is too much for me! I'll be a weak fool looking with pity at two sides of everything till the day I die!" (Act IV). Larry's key phrases—"no hope" and "too much for me" and "weak fool"—reveal the artist looking at life in terms of victims, acted on rather than acting. This view of character is a clue to the sense of constrictedness that is frequently present, not only in O'Neill, but in the literature of disaster generally.

The Self: Disaster vs. Tragedy

When the forces that men cannot cope with are identified less with society than with "life" itself, the failure that is presented is what I have already called the "disaster of personality" or the "disaster of self." But it is also true that the origin of the tragic situation is within the self. At the risk of too epigrammatic a contrast, we may say that the disaster of the self (as distinguished from natural or political or social disaster) has its origin in weakness, the tragedy of self in strength. In disaster, individuals are not up to traditional requirements; in tragedy they are not held down by traditional requirements and eventually find themselves not up to the special rules that they propose for themselves. One aesthetic leads to Mr. Zero, the other to Dr. Faustus; one character says, "Pity me," and the other, "I have sinned." In the former, there is little for the hero to know—not more than a negation ("I am weak"); in the latter, what can be known is the vast range of self-magnifications that are the inner form of the world's evil. Yet little as there is to know in the disaster of the self, O'Neill sees even that knowledge as intolerable, and defines the role of pity * as the defense of self-ignorance against its enemies. The ultimate shock of the play is that "Know thyself" is interpreted as the counsel of madness or malice that leads neither to peace nor to wisdom but produces only savage cynicism, murderous fighting, suicide, or living death. The sense of disaster simply eliminates the tragic situation. But the sense of disaster is powerfully dramatized.

VI. Victims of Political Forces

An enlightening contrast to *The Iceman Cometh* is provided by another play of the same year,[11] Robert Sherwood's *There Shall Be No Night*, which is also a drama of disaster. Here we have another category of disaster, the politico-military, a familiar stage theme through at least four decades of the twentieth century. Though the work of Max Frisch is an exception, the theme generally appears to evoke a journalistic treatment, that is, to call for the voicing of pride

---

* Hickey distinguishes between two kinds of pity—the wrong kind that encourages "some poor guy to go on kidding himself with a lie" and the kind that by revealing the truth "will make him contented with what he is." What the play says is that the latter program is impossible, indeed mad (though in one sentence of his final speech even Larry tacitly accepts Hickey's distinction). O'Neill's play as a whole might be based on the position of Gorki's Luka, a position which, if I do not misread it, Gorki's play as a whole modifies by distinguishing between those who can stand the truth and those who cannot.

and alarm, warning and exhortation. The constant threats of disaster since 1914, we may assume, inhibit author and audience alike. When contemporary events are frightening and dangerous, it is not easy to examine them with the full sense of character evident in the better nontopical dramas of such playwrights as O'Neill, Williams, Eliot, and Brecht.

At any rate, dealing with the Russian attack on Finland in 1939, *There Shall Be No Night* does not surmount the problems of the topical drama. It recounts the disaster to Finland and the heroism with which it was met and maintains a tone of hopefulness by stressing the endurance of the "human spirit," but in character it discovers only the expectable virtues, a mild thoughtfulness, and, in a German scholar-diplomat, intellectual offensiveness. The human picture is neither intense nor deep enough to make a strong drama of disaster, not to mention a tragic interpretation of the event. Yet the irony of it is that in all his key speeches, which contain the intellectual core of the play, the male lead (Dr. Kaarlo Valkonen, a Finnish neurologist) speaks with a tragic sense of reality. Instead of simply inveighing against enemies, as might be expected in a drama of political crisis, he speaks of the war as one of the symptoms of human failure. What will happen after the war? "How long will . . . men possess the spiritual strength that enables them to be free?" We try to get rid of the "tribulation" that in Paul's words leads to "patience," "experience," and "hope"; we ignore Jung's dictum, "There is no coming to consciousness without pain." We count on "pills and serums to protect us from our enemies." Nevertheless Dr. Valkonen believes (perhaps prematurely) that the world is experiencing a serious "coming to consciousness" and that for the first time "individual men are fighting to know themselves." The "revelation" which he sees prophesied in the "there shall be no night" of Revelations 21:25 is "the revealing to us of ourselves—of what we are—and of what we may be." In that is the source of strength for the survival of a mankind that has not yet adequately heeded the injunction—Dr. Valkonen quotes it in a radio address from Helsinki to America—"Know thyself" (Scene i).

One playwright asserts that knowing the self is unbearable, another that it is a necessity for the continuance of humanity. The contrast is between the point of view that leads away from tragedy and the point of view that is essential to it. Yet the pressing of the values of self-knowledge does not make *There Shall Be No Night* a tragedy, for these values are only expressed editorially, not rendered in the movement of character. Sherwood simply creates a conventional drama of disaster, with a counterpoint of physical defeat and moral victory, acted by essentially flat characters. We do not see anyone struggling from a ruinous blindness toward a saving self-awareness. Sherwood's drama is markedly inferior to O'Neill's, for if O'Neill works in terms of a much narrower concept, nevertheless his concept is relentlessly and bitterly dramatized in the action of characters who in the main are not stereotypes.

The topical drama of disaster—the presentation of victims of actual political tyrannies—achieves a greater range and depth in Frances Goodrich and Albert Hackett's stage version of *The Diary of Anne Frank* (1955), if at so little distance in time we are capable of detached judgment. While we are shown discipline, forbearance, generosity, the persistence of faith, and even a limited happiness among Jews in a long hiding from Nazis in Amsterdam, the tensions latent in the situation are better explored than in Sherwood's play: the Jewish victims show not only their virtues but, within limits, selfishness, jealousy, fear, meanness, and near violence. What I am getting at is that the emotional experience afforded by the drama of disaster, which is always in danger of being limited to pity for suffering or admiration for courage, is here made more mature because our "sympathy"—our "feeling with" the sufferers—has also to include some less gratifying self-centered impulses. Animosities break out when Mr. Van Daan steals food from his fellow victims and Mrs. Frank wants to throw him out of their sanctuary, though this will surely mean his death. When Mr. Frank protests, "We don't need the Nazis to destroy us. We're destroying ourselves" (II.iii), and when shortly afterward Mr. Van Daan and Mrs. Frank are overcome by shame—he at his thefts, and she at her furious will to punish him—the play enters momentarily into the realm of tragedy. It samples dramatically what is only talked about in the Sherwood play. The episode is brief; the self-serving acts that could injure others end before real harm is done; thus the theme of guilt is no more than glimpsed.

Yet even this quick excursion beyond innocence into the divisions of personality is remarkable in a play which, by its very choice of subject, is in characteristic danger of offering audience and reader a "too easy" experience. There is the appeal of adventure, with a series of dangers apparently surmounted, with the enemy held off until the last minute, and with the Nazi evil almost brushed out of sight by the final serenity of Mr. Frank. There is the charm of the young girl who is both bright and sweet, combined with the pathos of innocent hopefulness during a prolonged crisis. We are freed from the guilt of anti-Semitism because we absolutely separate ourselves from the Nazis (nothing in the play forces us into a sense of even momentary identification with them); and if we are not Jewish, we have an especial distance even from the suffering of the victims. We do enter, of course, into the human experiences of the sufferers, but since the Jewish situation—that of the designated victim—is not universalized, we really stay outside the disastrous event that creates the experience; hence we have an unusual freedom from the kind of pain that accompanies the artistic interpretation of disaster—not to mention the pain of tragedy. This is what I mean by a "too easy" experience. The live topic begets an air of immediacy, but on this stage we are still fenced off from harsh reality. We thrill, cry, smile, and hate, from a safe distance. Except for the brief moments when some of the admirable victims act ignobly, we pay no price. Emotionally we are home free.

VII. Victims of Evil Men

We have looked at dramas of disaster dealing with victims of nature, of society, of the self, of malignant political forces. We find one other major kind of victim—the victim of the evil individual—a favorite topic of Elizabethans and Jacobeans, whose picture of revenges and of motiveless malignity fairly well exhausted the possibilities. Except for occasional revivals of old Italian evildoers, as in Shelley's *Cenci* (1819), the sense of the monstrous for a considerable time found its outlet in fantastic beings of the Frankenstein-Dracula stamp. However, Heathcliff, Mr. Hyde, Raskolnikov, and Stavrogin were reminders of the dark side of human personality, which in time was to become a major theme of twentieth-century fiction. Meanwhile, nineteenth- and twentieth-century dramas of disaster were characteristically devoting themselves to the victims of self and victims of social or political groups (the disaster of personality and the disaster of history). But more recently, as we have already seen, drama has been coming into a new awareness of victims destroyed by the murderousness or the malice—or perhaps simply the symbolic gestures—of other individuals.

Duerrenmatt's *The Visit*, which we have already looked at as a drama of the victim of society, is in part a revival of the revenge play, and Claire Zachanassian is a Renaissance revenger in avant-garde modern costume. She revenges herself on a betrayer of half a century before by offering her home town a million pounds for his death; she has already softened up the townspeople by buying all the local businesses and closing them, so that the town is stagnant and shabby. Her demonic calculation, thoroughness, and determination bring to mind the diabolic character often attributed to older revengers (Iago was repeatedly called a "devil"), and the identification is carefully spelled out in Claire's own words: ". . . I've grown into hell itself"; "I'm unkillable" (Act I); "[My husband was] a real devil. I've copied him completely" (Act II). In all of her actions, as we shall see in a moment, she illustrates a theological definition of Satan, whose "rule . . . is possible only through the ruin of other creatures. That is the ultimate meaning of demonic possession." [12] Her traditional role is defined in other terms when the Schoolmaster, every inch a humanist, says to her, "You make me think of a heroine from antiquity: of Medea . . . cast away those evil thoughts of revenge, don't try us till we break." Claire, however, goes Medea one better by giving more scope to her revenge; she replies to the Schoolmaster: "The world turned me into a whore. I shall turn the world into a brothel" (Act III). Her retaliatory passion is like that animating a feud, one of the severe forms of external conflict between wholly undivided personalities. Undivided personalities tend to become generalized clutters of details that illustrate, but do not qualify, the determining idea. Claire's need for "the ruin of other creatures" is expressed with ironic playfulness in her Gilbert-and-Sullivanish husband-hopping; in the course of the play we see the rather rapid passage of husbands seven, eight, and nine. As her financial power turns them all, including a Nobel-Prize-winning physicist, into errand boys, she becomes something of the bitch goddess success, and this, we see, is a subtle version of the revenger: she bends everyone to her will in such a way that his capacity for independent choices is destroyed. One form of revenge upon people is to make them incapable of tragic perception and experience: Claire has made the town that once rejected her a murderer by giving it wealth and the corollary of wealth, "culture," and at the end we see the town rejoicing in its material salvation and evincing no sign that it will ever know itself or what it has done. Its riches are its "ruin." Duerrenmatt's satirical rigor has made the town a special kind of victim—rather than evoking pity for its suffering, it evokes horror by taking its degradation for a heavenly blessing.

The departure from tragedy is less marked in the treatment of Claire's primary victim, her betrayer Alfred Ill. Though he is destroyed by the townspeople, his rejection of his own innocence provides a tragic note that gives some point to Duerrenmatt's subtitle, "eine tragische Komödie." His is the only experience of inner division and of enlightenment. The townspeople have conquered their original tentative division and see only by neon lights. Claire remains the undifferentiated revenger, though she can indulge in sentimental retrospection and, near the end, in a moment of introspection: "But my love could not die. Neither could it live. It grew into an evil thing, like me . . ." (Act III). She is capable only of the passionless, detached notation of an emotional mechanism, of causes and effects as if in a psychological laboratory. She records; she does not judge. She knows what happens, not its quality. Her use of wealth to murder Ill is as unfelt as the town's murder of Ill to get wealth. The play is dominantly about undivided characters working their will on others.

Webster's The Duchess of Malfi

The undividedness, of course, is imposed by an artist who is essentially satirical. There is less contrivance, and a much more spontaneous—and indeed explosive—feeling in a great drama of disaster, John Webster's *The Duchess of Malfi* (produced about 1614). Here the innocent heroine is hounded, tortured, and finally murdered by a pair of sadistic brothers whom she has displeased. As a drama of the victim, it differs in one way from *The Visit*, in quite another way from *The Diary of Anne Frank*. The difference from *Anne Frank* is underlined by a single marked resemblance between the two plays. In each, the title character is a person of unusual charm and imagination who is destroyed by a relentless depravity that, the more it is actively present in the drama, the more completely it must carry spectators from the pity characteristic of the disaster situation into a horror that accompanies savage outbreaks of human evil. When such depravity is institutionalized, as in the Frank play, rather than concentrated in an individual, we might expect the drama to gain in complexity. But the opposite is ironically true here. For Webster's drama of the cruel brothers is much more complex than the drama of the corrupt political order. In fact, it is the most complex of the plays that we consider in this section. Since in the differentiation of tragedy and disaster it raises more critical problems than do the others, a fuller inspection of it is in order.

At the beginning of the action, the Duchess of Malfi, a widow, is ordered by her brothers, a Duke and a Cardinal, not to remarry. But she marries her steward Antonio, a decent man who returns her love. She makes love to him in a style that combines gay playfulness, strong feeling, and dignity; weds him in a private ceremony and bears him three children; out of innocent trustingness betrays his identity to Bosola, an agent of her brother; counterplots as well as she can in a futile effort to save her family and herself; is driven by persecution and torture, which she bears with fortitude, to a despair in which she welcomes the death inflicted by her brothers' hired assassins. Webster has endowed the Duchess with gifts of character and personality that have charmed many generations, but he has not treated her as a tragic heroine: her marriage to her steward is not an act of pride or lust, or a violation of any imperatives which are given authority by terms of the drama: in a love match that is presented as its own justification, she has simply run afoul of the irrational purposes of her brothers, who from the start appear as willful and unscrupulous wielders of power and whose victim she becomes. She does not "earn" her fate. That this organization of materials is something other than tragic (though the play is traditionally called a tragedy) is in part explained by Aristotle's argument, when he is naming the kinds of plots to be avoided in tragedy, that "it is not advisable to show good men falling from good fortune to bad fortune, for this is not fearful nor pitiable but abominable." [13] Nor, it may be added, are her actions such that she must assay, or judge, or newly understand her motives and her courses. Like Desdemona, of whom she is reminiscent in some details, she can only suffer and yield to her executioner; though her tactics, like Desdemona's, may misfire, they are not moral errors.

When there is a community of victims, as in the Anne Frank play, the interplay and tensions among them can provide all the stage material. When there is a single victim, or only one major victim, the dramatic structure is naturally different: here we need to have the evil men in full view. We get just that. Webster offers a comprehensive picture of human evil concentrated in several virtually symbolic characters; Duke Ferdinand of Calabria and the Cardinal are permitted an almost novelistic quantity of words to express their commands to the Duchess, their chagrin and fury at her conduct, and their abuse of her. Their revenge on her is protracted like an exercise in sadism; instead of tragic perception, we find the psychological exploration of maniacal power lust. As Peter Alexander has said, "Villainy is not a tragic theme even when raised to the level of genius." [14] The danger in the brothers' villainy, which is not without mad genius, is of a grotesque extremism that can defeat this kind of literature of disaster in its essential function—the dramatizing of gross evil in terms that catch its reality and its general relevance.

In other ways *The Duchess of Malfi* helps mark the dividing line between tragedy and disaster. The agents of evil do not correspond to elements within the tragic heroine (or her consort Antonio); she is not morally responsible for their efficacy in the world; the play does not present a complex, unified reality but two discrete worlds, one of which is bent on destroying the other. Goneril and Regan, on the contrary, come into destructive power as projections of a part of Lear's divided nature; in a paradoxical combination of whim and perverse calculation he gives them the world; and that world becomes the creature of their whim and perverse calculation. Lear has made his world in a way that the Duchess has not. As Webster presents evil in the two brothers, it is autonomous—a human analogue of the force of nature, the flood or holocaust, that destroys blindly. This is not to deny the existence of autonomous evil; there are phenomena that apparently have to be treated as spontaneous exceptions to the ordinary courses of personality. But eccentric cases do not make the world of tragedy. The President of the United States is empowered to designate as "disaster areas" parts of the country that have undergone heavy accidental damage; fortunately the term is, as it should be, "disaster area," and not "tragedy area." Similarly in the moral realm we find disaster areas, areas in which evil forces overwhelm and destroy.

The world in which the Duchess of Malfi lives is such a disaster area. But if natural disasters and human disasters are alike in that they destroy "innocent" victims, they differ in that human agents of disaster may have or profess certain motives. The quality of the literature of disaster depends in part on how convincingly it presents motives (or lack of motives). In popular literature, as we know, villains easily become laughable stereotypes of rapacity or other vices, though we do not question the vices as a fact of human character. In Webster's play, the brothers have a relentlessness so hyperbolic that it is on the edge of seeming a tour de force. Webster tries to naturalize their rather surrealistic passion by having them voice certain motives: "honor" in the sense that remarriage would evidence an inadmissible passion; "honor" in the sense that Antonio is socially ineligible; the obligation of "revenge," whether for the Duchess' flouting their commands or breaching the family pride. But later Ferdinand bluntly denies that "the meanness of her match" meant anything to him and says it was an "infinite mass of treasure" he was hoping for (IV.ii.301–4).

In one respect the treatment of motives, which are stated casually and are inconsistent, is very unsatisfactory; with the brothers as with that other enunciator of implausible motives, Iago, we appear to be forced into a symbolic reading of character. But in another sense there is an advantage, for the unconvincingness of the stated motives alerts us, as with Iago, to the possible presence of an unrecognized and unacknowledged motive. With Ferdinand, though not with the Cardinal, we do find pieces of evidence fitting together to give us a picture of him that makes him credible in characterological terms. From the start, Ferdinand's language about the Duchess is charged with sexual images. After he knows that she has a lover, he is hysterical and fears lest "my imagination will carry me / To see her in the shameful act of sin" (II.v.54–55); he does imagine a "strong-thigh'd bargeman" as her lover (line 57); in his fury he would "dip the sheets they lie in, in pitch or sulphur, / Wrap them in't, and then light them like a match" (lines 90–91); he chooses a nocturnal intimacy for giving her a poniard and subjecting her to lingering abuse. Hence we see the real meaning of his words when, after her death, he says of her marriage that it "drew a stream of gall quite through my heart" (IV.ii.306), and we see why he goes mad. For his pangs, and his style of speech and action, are those of a frustrated lover, though he may not know, or be able to let himself know, that he is a lover. Consciously or not,[15] Webster has drawn a telling picture of incestuous passion that is psychologically the most meaningful element in the disastrous events that destroy the Duchess.

The justification of this sorting out of the erotic impulse in Ferdinand is that it reveals something about the drama of disaster. Though the presence of motives distinguishes the disaster brought about by human agents from that brought about by natural forces, yet here, ironically, the motive itself permits us to see an affinity between the types of disaster: just as incest is a rare breaking of taboos, so is disaster generally a violation of an apparently dependable order. In disaster, we find special, insensate outbreaks against established patterns and inherited expectations. Tragedy encompasses the troubles that arise from the norms of character; the literature of disaster, the troubles that arise from special flings of event and character. These special flings may be recurrent—storms, wars, accidents, exotic lusts —but they are felt as violations of the expected, shocks, contraventions of the rules and probabilities we ordinarily live by. But tragic deeds are profoundly expectable. Tragic pride is deep in human character, so that we naturally move toward a sense of identity with the hero in whom it has gained the upper hand. It might be argued, perhaps, that Oedipus' actually marrying his mother is, simply as an event, more unlikely to happen than Ferdinand's being erotically attracted to his sister. But out of the incredible Oedipus story Sophocles has made a tragedy in which, in a highly representative way, a man is betrayed at once by his intemperateness and by his pride in rational control of destiny; while the Ferdinand story, for all of its intensity of feeling, remains a specialized, eccentric tale of disastrous perversity.

Yet Webster wrote in an age of great tragedy, and he tends to superimpose something of tragic form upon his plot. As the play goes on, he imputes to Ferdinand and the Cardinal a tinge of the moral consciousness which leads to tragic self-understanding. But again Webster is excessive, theatrical rather than dramatic; he moves either too slowly or too fast; there is a protracted exacerbation of feelings as the brothers drag toward death, but many sudden twists of action that are more surprising than inevitable. As soon as the Duchess is dead, Ferdinand turns violently on his hired executioner, Bosola, blaming his agent rather than himself; then with equal rapidity he goes mad. This madness, a familiar outcome for dramatic protagonists, hardly establishes moral revulsion in Ferdinand, for we have had no prior evidence of capacity for remorse in him. But what we can do is see the madness as an ultimate stage of the inner tensions rooted in his sexual passion. This tells us something about Webster: that he presents less the tragic movement of personality than the clinical progress of an unstable personality, one that has always been hysterical in manner. Hence we could anticipate Webster's use of madness—as a clinical spectacle rather than as a symbol of moral condition. Though he shows talent in elaborating the verbal style of the madman, indeed in using variations on the madness speeches in *Lear*, Webster does not make Ferdinand's madness, as Shakespeare does Lear's, a paradoxical instrument of revelation.

For most of Act V the Cardinal is still indefatigably plotting, with only his sudden wearying of his mistress as a possible symptom of diminishing worldliness. Then without warning, three-quarters of the way through Act V, he announces in a soliloquy:

> O, my conscience!
> I would pray now: but the devil takes away my heart
> For having any confidence in prayer.
> [V.iv.30–32]

Again he complains, "How tedious is a guilty conscience!" and when he is wounded, he concludes,

> O justice!
> I suffer now for what hath former bin:
> Sorrow is held the eldest child of sin.
> [V.v.72–74]

These conventional motions of conscience,* presented only in the

---

* The Jacobean convention of repentance in the villain is an interesting phenomenon. In its persistence we can see the extension of tragic practice into works in which the underlying sensibility is not tragic, that is, in which the sense of evil in the world is not balanced by a sense of the counterpowers of resistance and recovery. But in the afterglow of the high tragic achievement there is still a formalized reminiscence of the tragic rhythm: a quick coda of remorse is tagged on to long movements of evil. Compare the fleeting moments of moral awareness attributed to Ferdinand and the Cardinal with the longer-lasting sentience of Lear, Macbeth, Othello, and for that matter even Claudius.

lines quoted, do not achieve dramatic vitality; Webster is much more interested, for example, in the elaborate contrived irony of the Cardinal's having forestalled, by his own devious designs, the very rescue for which he calls loudly and which is within reach when he is attacked by Bosola. From the multiple ramifications of disaster there is no more than a bare inclining toward tragedy. The brothers remain in the category of "wicked men" whose "falling from good fortune to bad fortune," Aristotle points out with especial care, is not a suitable tragic plot.

But if Ferdinand and the Cardinal are not made convincingly remorseful, the fact is less significant than the fact that the play is not theirs; though in the clumsy construction they survive the Duchess for an overlong stay on the stage, the focus is on her. At best the treatment of the brothers could permit tragic accents in the portrayal of secondary characters. Now Webster's situation as the potential tragic dramatist who is deflected into another form—whether he will not see his material tragically and therefore does not organize it for tragic effects, or simply cannot find the ordering of the material which will be conducive to the maximum tragic effect—is best represented by his treatment of Bosola. Bosola is the most likely tragic figure in the cast. He is more truly divided than the others, for as the play goes on, he is increasingly moved by contradictory impulses; though initially he appears as a cynically disillusioned and opportunistic hanger-on venting frustrations in railing at vice, he has in him something of the "good man" repeatedly driven, by a medley of influences, to choose evil. Yet two aspects of Webster's characterization are obstacles to Bosola's actually achieving tragic stature. For one thing, Bosola's sardonic disgust (his "nausée") and rationalized self-seeking are so deep that they are not perceptibly challenged by other motives until the play is three-quarters over. Not until Ferdinand has tortured the Duchess does Bosola first begin to show sympathy for her; at this point he urges the Duke to relent and declares that he will not again see the Duchess unless "The business shall be comfort" (IV.i.164). Then in the next scene he superintends the murder of the Duchess and with a cruel witticism orders that of her woman Cariola (IV.ii.268–69).

The point is that Webster has difficulty in portraying a direct conflict of motives; he shows the divided character acting first under one rather clear-cut impulse, and then under another. Again, the revulsion which Bosola attributes to himself is not clearly distinguishable from a stereotyped repentance; he does not experience a real reversal of feeling until Ferdinand not only refuses to reward him, but actually blames him, for the death of the Duchess. His mood is penalties for others rather than penitence for himself. The second, and more important, limiting of the tragic potential in Bosola is that he does not initiate major actions, but stays in a subordinate role as the brothers' operative against the Duchess and Antonio; he does not determine what happens until, in pursuit of "just revenge" after the Duchess' death, he brings about the concluding round robin of killings. Webster is unable to imagine him at the center of things where his actions would be the cardinal ones, although Bosola is sufficiently complex to be the most interesting person in the play. He is capable of virtually all treacheries for hire, and his rant against falseness is in part simply an index of his offended egotism; yet this rant is ambiguous, for it also helps evoke in us a tentative belief in his moral sense and thus partly prepares for his fierce turning against the brothers after he has betrayed the Duchess to them. For him alone is Webster able to imagine a partial self-confrontation, mixed though it is with both self-defense and blame of others. But Webster does not take a step that would move the play as a whole out of the realm of disaster —that is, giving the central dramatic place and full development to Bosola's critical self-recognition.

With the main focus on the innocence of the Duchess and the almost unrelieved villainy of the brothers, and with the stage given over to a stream of plottings, sufferings, unexpected turns, irrelevant emotional stimuli, wonders, and tortures, *The Duchess of Malfi* contains all the theatricalities of crude popular entertainment. Indeed it goes far beyond the "horror shows" of our day in its uninhibited exhibition of perversities.* But what differentiates it from these, what

* This seems true not only for the *Dracula* genre of entertainment but for the more aspiring drama that reflects the underside of human nature rediscovered in the twentieth century. There is a marked tendency for the drama of darkness to slide into philosophical murkiness; dramatists tend to use irrationality and destructiveness, not as evidence of character, but as breath-taking accidents in a drama whose essence is argument or polemic about value and meaning. Stage action becomes, not the overt form of human drama, but a visible ballet of the author's meditations.

gives it strength and dignity, is a poetic power akin to Shakespeare's. Besides, it is the only play in our present group in which the poetic language has a major influence on the dramatic whole. It is this language—the language of great tragedy—that qualifies the drama of disaster and, if it does not carry that drama beyond itself, pushes it toward all the greatness of which it is capable. Hence we need to examine Webster's language more fully than that of the other dramatists of disaster.

Webster's Language

Webster's verbal medium has great range and flexibility: its adjustability to different uses is barely suggested by two early passages that are not far apart. The first of these is Bosola's blunt and cynical comment on himself:

> What's my place?
> The provisorship o' th' horse? say then my corruption
> Grew out of horse-dung: I am your creature.
> [I.i.311–13]

The second is the Duchess' gay and tender quip in love making:

> Go, go brag
> You have left me heartless; mine is in your bosom:
> I hope 'twill multiply love there. You do tremble:
> Make not your heart so dead a piece of flesh
> To fear more than to love me.
> [I.i.514–18]

But the individual passages are not often autarchic or self-contained in their poetic resources; many of Webster's most striking lines import some of their strength from large imagistic groups that extend throughout the play. The world of disaster that Webster pictures is created in part by the prevalence of animal imagery and the imagery

---

These may be more or less profound or novel. Peter Weiss's *The Persecution and Assassination of Marat as Performed by the Inmates of the Asylum of Charenton under the Direction of the Marquis de Sade* promises horrors galore but turns out to be a protracted debate, rendered less dramatic by Brechtian distancing, between familiar social idealism and familiar cynicism. (This comment is based on the London, 1964, stage presentation of the English version by Geoffrey Skelton, in a verse adaptation by Adrian Mitchell.)

of disease (the two are joined in Ferdinand's lycanthropy); the general and specific terms of illness are supported by the continual appearance of such words as *melancholy*, *corruption*, and *rotten*.

What is worse, the world eaten into by sickness and dehumanization suffers from a corrupt and malevolent will: we sense this in a small but persistent poison theme that comprises both literal and metaphorical poisoning (disease happens, but poison may be administered); and our sense of falseness is rendered overwhelming by a massive pattern of what I will call the "façade," that is, of the visible surface which conceals or belies what is within. The façade dominates actions and poetry: at some time every major character pretends to a feeling or role which is not his. To survive, even the good are forced into this, though "simple virtue," as the Duchess puts it, "was never made / To seem the thing it is not" (I.i.513–14). Ferdinand sends false messages of friendship; Bosola once enters "visarded," another time "like an Old Man"; the Duchess uses a "feigned crime" to "shield our honours"; the Cardinal proposes to "feign myself in danger"; the Duchess is "plagu'd in art" when Ferdinand lets her see wax images that she takes to be the bodies of her dead children. Characters constantly talk of the difference between inner and outer, or covering up, falsifying: ". . . is merely outside"—"the devil / Candies all sins o'er"—"Keep your old garb of melancholy"—"faces do belie their hearts"—"A visor and a mask . . . / . . . are never built for goodness"—"I'll conceal this secret"—"this outward form of man"—"feign a pilgrimage"—"that counterfeit face"—"wrap thy poison'd pills / In gold and sugar"—"never in mine own shape"— "Off, painted honour"—"nets to entrap you"—"lay fair marble colours / Upon your rotten purposes"—"Fie upon / His counterfeiting" —"thy greatness was only outward." When the Duchess asks the masked Bosola, "What devil art thou, that counterfeits heaven's thunder?" (III.v.116), her words record thematically the state of this desperate world.

The language itself builds up an extraordinary sense of disaster. Though events themselves may have an enormity that challenges imaginative acceptance, the language subtly does its work to incline us toward suspension of disbelief. It is especially effective in developing the theme of darkness. The first characterization of the Duchess, spoken by Antonio, ends, "She stains the time past, lights the time to come" (I.i.214)—that is, by not being in the past, deprives it of brightness, makes it dark. From the start the Duchess is identified with light, and then light is destroyed. When Ferdinand, upon discovering that she has a lover, rages like a maniac, his climactic threat—in the concluding lines of Act II—takes this form: "I'll find scorpions to string my whips, / And fix her in a general eclipse" (II.v.101–2). Ferdinand's obsession with that light may take the form of wanting to extinguish it, or of symbolically extinguishing it by treating it as nonlight. When he makes his first theatrical night entry into the Duchess' apartment (with a "false key"), he opens his abuse of his sister with the stagey apostrophe, "Virtue, where art thou hid? what hideous thing / Is it that doth eclipse thee?" (III.ii.81–82).[16] Here the Duchess is made the dark body that cuts off light. The same conception of her appears in another line of his a little later: "You have shook hands with Reputation, / And made him invisible" (lines 157–58). And in the next line the Duke's strange need to associate the Duchess with darkness (in terms of his latent passion for her, it is ambiguous) appears in a "vow" which he takes several times and which makes possible one of the theatrical effects of Act IV: "I will never see you more" (III.ii.159, 165). So when he comes to torture her, again at night, the lights must be put out: despite the immediate shock of the mere spectacle, and despite our awareness of his conscious purpose and his unconscious motives, we do not miss the symbolic implications of the scene.

But if Ferdinand, as a compulsive darkener of the world, is quite successful, nevertheless the light that he has destroyed recoils upon him ironically. This is brilliantly revealed in Webster's poetry. The first climax of the light imagery is the most famous line in the play, spoken by Ferdinand after the Duchess' death: "Cover her face: mine eyes dazzle: she died young" (IV.ii.281). What looks like a tardy realization of her beauty is rich in other meaning that has been created during the play: the light that he sought to eclipse, and then tried to bury in darkness, is still there even after her death, and he is overcome by it. It would be wrong, I think, to emphasize exclusively, or to rule out entirely, the presence of an erotic history in these lines. Whatever the precise terms required, it is clear that the shock of the destruction of what he had to destroy, destroys him. An experience that had in it something of the passional and something of the aesthetic, and that we cannot avoid seeing in symbolic terms as an attack of evil upon good, presents itself finally to him in such moral terms as his nature permits. Webster manages it all deftly with the light imagery. "Let me see her face again," Ferdinand says a little later (line 291); as her light continues to impinge on him, he loses what he earlier called the "most imperfect light of human reason" (III.ii.90). His last words on the border line of insanity appropriately continue the theme: "I'll go hunt the badger by owl-light: / 'Tis a deed of darkness" (IV.ii.360–61). The symbolic overtones of these lines during Ferdinand's transformation palliate the theatrical speed of his decline into allegorical lycanthropy.

The second climax of the light imagery comes in several of Bosola's valedictory lines:

> Oh this gloomy world!
> In what a shadow, or deep pit of darkness,
> Doth, womanish and fearful, mankind live!
> [V.v.124–26]

He speaks in character. Yet his words do more than state his mood: they give us the dominant tone of the play. The lines are strong in themselves,[17] but their strength is greatly increased because they belong to a pattern built into the poetry and action of the play. The "darkness" is not simply a conventional figure for bad times; it is the state of the world that has lost all that is symbolized by the radiant light of the Duchess. The world has not only lost that light: it has perversely destroyed it. This is Webster's version of disaster.

VIII. THE REALM OF DISASTER

"This gloomy world": it is an apt phrase for the reality that Webster sees. But "this gloomy world" is also an apt phrase for the reality discovered by all our dramatists of disaster. In other plays at which we have looked we have found characters speaking like Bosola. In *Riders to the Sea* Maurya says, "there isn't anything else the sea can do to me." In *The Iceman Cometh* Larry sums up, "Be God, there's no hope! . . . Life is too much for me." What is done to me, what is too much for me—that is the heart of the gloomy world. The plays of the gloomy world deal largely with shadows and darkness imposed rather than chosen. This is the realm of disaster—the desolation of life when the sea or other forces of nature find their victims; the death and suffering of those who are the victims of societal power, political ruthlessness, or war; the disintegration of those who cannot cope with the exigencies of the life in which they find themselves, the sad maneuvers of victims of disillusionment, the beating down of those who get in the way of evil men.

The realm of actual disaster that is the raw material of literary art is a large one. We do not underestimate the immediacy or anguish of that realm, or fail in sympathy with those injured or betrayed by such events, nor do we uncritically disparage the literature that draws its life from the life and death of victims, if we say, once again, that such fates are something other than tragic, and that the drama portraying such fates is not of the tragic order. It can be repeated: many things that are terrible are not tragic.

CHAPTER THREE

The Structure of Melodrama

I N PRESSING the distinction between the tragic and the disastrous, I have said repeatedly that many kinds of misfortune and injury, of catastrophes leading to suffering and death, of evil from without, of defeat and unhappiness, are not tragic. The literature that is based on such materials I have called the "literature of disaster." Though this term is cumbersome, I have so far excluded alternatives, partly for the sake of emphasis, partly to avoid terminological interruptions and detours. But "literature of disaster" is a limiting term; the specific materials that it names are a part of a much more inclusive class. To this broader class belongs all nontragic conflict that invokes ideas of good and evil. Dramas of disaster are the most important part of the nontragic, and are most in need of critical attention, for they are most likely to be taken for tragedy; but still they are only a part of the nontragic whole, and they need to be seen in their relationship to it.

I. DRAMA OF DISASTER: AN ASPECT OF MELODRAMA

For the general realm of the nontragic, of which the literature of disaster is a substantial part, I shall henceforward use the term *melodrama;* and the next business will be an examination of the structure of melodrama, and of the structural relations between dramas of disaster and other forms of melodrama. But first there is the problem of the name. To take *melodrama*, which is usually a derogatory term that means popular, machine-made entertainments, and to apply it to a wide range of literature that includes much serious work and that may achieve excellence of its own kind, may seem capricious to the point of scandal. I hope that the term will not be distracting now, and will not seem scandalous after I have made an effort to explain the choice of it.

Three points can be made by way of justification and clarification. The first is a proposition: that, if an existent term is potentially capacious enough, as I believe *melodrama* is, it is better to use it than to coin a new term which may be no more satisfactory.* In sticking to an old term, one gives up a certain novelty that may in itself seem enlightening and thus encourage assent; but one ought to refrain from multiplying terms, lest in the end they seem only to clutter the critical landscape and betray the ploy of conspicuous innovation. The second is a definition of point of view: I will use *melodrama* as a neutral descriptive term, not as a pejorative; my interest is in classification, not in repeating old denigrations. Within the category, plays may range from contemptible to distinguished; if a considerable number drift toward the lower level of achievement, it is not that this is inevitable but that certain structural characteristics of the type tend to make it rather accessible to inferior writers. This leads to the third and most important point, which concerns the logical implications of the form: the very qualities usually connoted by the word *melodrama* lead us, I am convinced, toward the serious meanings which I shall attach to it. That is, what we call "popular melodrama" has reduced

---

* The kinds of plays that I have included under "dramas of disaster" have been variously called naturalistic tragedy, romantic tragedy, problem play, social drama, serious drama, psychological drama, and so forth. The terms are too numerous to be helpful. Those that include the word *tragedy* seem to me to be inaccurate; the others are too diffuse. They are loosely descriptive, and they give up on the problem of structure. One cannot conceive of "serious drama" as having an identifiable structure that will be found, whatever its variations, in all the instances of the genre. On the other hand *melodrama* implies, I believe, not only a definite structure but one that is found in many plays different in tone and texture. It has also the advantage that to most people *melodrama* and *tragedy* will seem mutually exclusive.

to stereotypes and thus has trivialized the basic structural characteristics of a literary form that can be managed soberly and reputably. If this is true, then perhaps this loose general term can be transformed into a precise instrument for making critical distinctions.

Melodrama: Conventional Meanings

Nevertheless, the strain must be acknowledged. *Melodrama* certainly connotes a rather frivolous art form that makes the most obvious kind of appeal to an uncritical populace. Its character and style are suggested by such phrases as the following: pursuit and capture, imprisonment and escape, false accusation, cold-blooded villain, innocence beleaguered, virtue triumphant, eternal fidelity, mysterious identity, lovers reconciled, fraudulence revealed, threats survived, enemies foiled; the whole realm of adventure from dangerous exploits to foreign-legion doings to struggles in exotic scenes to intrigue, spying, and secret missions; the whole realm of mystery from the supernatural to esoteric science to the whodunit; the whole realm of vice and crime from the terror or horror of the evil deed to the detection of the evildoer to the reform of corrupt persons or situations.[1] It is the world of shock and thrill and sensationalism, of what is regularly called "gripping" and "poignant." It also traffics in ideas; it may make use of fundamental concepts and values, perhaps challengingly, but more often in a hackneyed or easily acceptable way. In a century and a half its color has variously been revolutionary, democratic, antitotalitarian, reformist (against gambling, slavery, drinking, dope addiction, and so forth). The form is represented with unusual amplitude in an early example, Thomas Morton's *Speed the Plough* (1798), which, along with various popular comic effects, contains upper-class injustice, *nouveau riche* snobbery, poor-man's integrity, a lover who almost gives up the poor girl for the rich one, bigamy, economic threats and a mysterious *deus ex machina*, secret grief, irrational enmity, mysterious identity, old villainy disclosed in a blood-curdling confessional and healed by remarkable accidents and counterplotting, a castle fire and a rescue, and an appeal to patriotic sentiments.

When we turn from Morton's luxuriant theatrical mélange to Lillian Hellman's anti-Nazi play, *Watch on the Rhine* (1941), we may at first seem to be in a different world. The later play is more somber and sophisticated; it cannot help having vitality when the kind of political danger it dramatizes is still present (though all such plays may in time come to seem to us no more essentially interesting than *Uncle Tom's Cabin* is now). But in the main it has a simple villain-hero structure: the evil Nazis, represented on the stage by a cynical and corrupt fellow-traveling Roumanian count, are opposed by a high-minded but practical underground worker (much the same figure as Dr. Valkonen in Sherwood's *There Shall Be No Night*), who has the sympathy of his American wife, their children, and his wife's rather charming family. Here is the easy emotional appeal that tends to be found in melodrama; we have no choice but to hate the Nazis and to love everybody else. What is more, we are offered familiar pleasures by devices of entertainment not entirely unlike those in *Speed the Plough* but less easy to isolate because they belong to our own conventions: two amusing quippish servants, a comically pedantic child, the pathos of suffering but uncomplaining children; a feather-brained, willful, but basically dependable matriarch; a clean-cut young American lawyer; the charming American girl who throws over her husband (the loathsome fellow-traveler) for the young lawyer; daring underground work, spying, threats, bribes, and murder. Only in detail are these different from their counterparts that invite the stock responses of the regular television audiences.

Yet in several respects Miss Hellman moves toward less obvious melodrama by altering the stereotype and thus forcing the audience into responses less easy than the conventional ones. The forthright American mother and her lawyer son vent indignation and angry disgust on the Roumanian collaborator with the Nazis: this is a popular exercise that we all love to leap into, but the author undercuts it by making it appear pointless, of no help to serious anti-Nazi work. Much more important: Kurt Müller, the anti-Nazi, is shown as selfless and high-minded; suddenly, without warning, he skillfully knocks down and kills the Roumanian who may betray him and his cause. Thus our easy enjoyment of gratifying political emotions is complicated by the shock of murder before our eyes: a less palatable reality intrudes into our comfortable pleasure of siding with simple unmixed good against simple evil. We are still "with" the hero, of course, for it is a Nazi he is killing; but we have to pay a higher price for being on his side. Now notice how the author goes on to deal with the problem of the hero as murderer. She is unwilling to stop, as does the entertainer playing to stock responses, with an elementary assertion of self-defense as justification. Rather she has Kurt say, of such a killing, "But for whatever reason it is done, and whoever does it—you understand me—it is all bad. I want you to remember that. Whoever does it, it is bad" (Act III). At least the questionable element is understood and made explicit. But the moral problem of means is present only in the form of detached, rational comment. If Kurt's ethical observation took the form of a profound personal feeling, that is, if the action were to include Kurt's conflict with his own guilt, his split between political and moral imperatives, the play would be moving toward tragedy. But tragic terms are not those to which the author is committed; it is not part of her plan to carry the moral cruxes beyond verbal formulation and into full dramatic life.

To sum up: in standard usage, *melodrama* implies the simple pleasures of conventional or straightforward conflict, decked out in the various excitement of threats, surprises, risks, rival lovers, disguises, and physical combat, all this against a background of ideas and emotions widely accepted at the time. If we look at this theatrical mélange in an example (*Speed the Plough*) which is distant in time, in which the details are long out of fashion, and in which the conflict —unjust lord versus honorable farmer—is no longer relevant to actual life, we find it tedious or laughable. But if we look at a more recent example (*Watch on the Rhine*) in which the decor is familiar and the conflict—aggressive totalitarianism versus our own political order—is quite relevant to life, a comparable theatrical mélange seems more convincing and moving. With what justice, then, do we call them both melodrama? We have already noted the similarity of many devices by which they are made popularly "appealing": these depend on the utterly clear, untaxing arrangement of human laughableness, human loathsomeness, and human admirableness, as these are commonly identified in the author's day. But beneath the surface of immediate theatrical winsomeness, the intimate core of the form is the conflict of villains and heroes—the standard brands of villains and heroes. This conflict is so familiar and in its most popular forms is presented with such supersimplicity (the work of cynical artificers) that we dismiss it as the unreal battle of antagonists whom we contemptuously call "good guys" and "bad guys."

In general usage the term *melodrama* certainly implies the combat of "good guys" and "bad guys." But if we use such terms derisively, nevertheless the terms themselves suggest an interpretation of experience which is not limited to the simple-minded. For however dull or trite or grotesque the actions of these good and bad antagonists may be, the plots are simply a debased popular form of a stable central structure that appears in all times and in trivial and sober plays alike: [2] in this structure, man is pitted against a force outside of himself—a specific enemy, a hostile group, a social force, a natural event, an accident or coincidence. This is one of the persistent fundamental structures of literature, whether it appears in a silly or meretricious form in a cinema or television thriller, or is elaborated with dignity and power in *The Trojan Women* or *Romeo and Juliet*. It draws upon permanent human attitudes, some perilous and some preserving, whether we disavow these when they become ludicrous in a western, or scarcely recognize them in an extraordinary struggle into which we have been drawn by artistic skill—the story of Annapurna, *Nigger of the Narcissus*, *War and Peace*, *Richard III*, or *The Duchess of Malfi*.[3]

II. MELODRAMA: CHARACTERIZATION AND PATTERNS

In the structure of melodrama, man is essentially "whole"; this key word implies neither greatness nor moral perfection, but rather an absence of the basic inner conflict that, if it is present, must inevitably claim our primary attention. Melodrama accepts wholeness without question; for its purposes, man's loyalties and his directions are neither uncertain nor conflicting. He is not troubled by motives that would distract him from the outer struggle in which he is engaged. He may indeed be humanly incomplete; but his incompleteness is not the issue. It is in tragedy that man is divided; in melodrama, his troubles, though they may reflect some weakness or inadequacy, do not arise from the urgency of unreconciled impulses. In tragedy the conflict is within man; in melodrama, it is between men, or between men and things. Tragedy is concerned with the nature of man, melodrama with the habits of men (and things). A habit normally reflects part of a nature, and that part functions as if it were the whole. In melodrama we accept the part for the whole; this is a convention of the form.

We have seen virtually "whole" or undivided characters in Dr. Stockmann, contending against community stupidity and greed, and in Dr. Valkonen and Kurt Müller, fighting against Communists and Nazis. They are created, though it seem disparaging to say it, by the same conception of character that appears in popular heroes pitted against cattle rustlers, hold-up men, smugglers, and dope rings. If our attention is focused initially on dangers to be fought, the fighting pre-empts the scene, and we do not often go into the characters of the heroes or others who are doing the fighting. However dissimilar the external conflicts dramatized, there is a strong conventional pull in the generic form itself once the writer is committed to it. Certain formulations of reality lead automatically to the conventional agreement not to inspect characters, or at least not to go on and discover inner contradictions that would usurp attention. If our sense of reality leads us to see experience as an opposition of good and evil, or of power and weakness, we are not likely to look questioningly at the individuals that embody these elements. If a dramatist puts victims on the stage, he rarely examines their characters. Hence we find an almost entirely unified nature in Synge's Maurya, in the Franks, in the Duchess of Malfi. On the other hand, we have whole or undivided characters of evil in Duerrenmatt's citizens who murder for money and in the brothers who torture and destroy the Duchess of Malfi. In general, these are of the same basic substance as the gallery of villains fought against by popular heroes, though in all treatment of "pure" villains, the kind of detail used may lead to stereotypes or to high individualization. Finally, in the wretched inmates of the grim sanctuaries depicted by Gorki and O'Neill there is another kind of wholeness: that of half beings almost totally cut off from any counterimpulses that would leave them split between retreat and participation. Wholeness, in other words, is a technical structure of character and personality; in itself it is morally neutral; it means simply that in goodness or in badness, in strength or in weakness, the protagonist is, at the level of significant action, not a composition of divergent inner forces that would push him into the arena of choice and self-knowledge. When a writer adopts this structure of character and personality, he also necessarily adopts a certain structure of relationships between characters, and what he writes is melodrama. He may, of course, write melodrama for a variety of motives—from the profitable delighting of the multitude to the most intense conviction about the nature of reality; and he may produce the trivial or the serious, the meretricious or the honorable. We will come later to the qualitative distinctions possible within the generic structure.

We need now to take a further look at our original problem—the problem of how a term which connotes stock plots for uncritical audiences can also be used to denote serious interpretations of experience, of how popular adventure tales and thrillers can be said to be of the same essence, the same form, as sober dramas of failure and defeat. The first part of this is not too hard: in both "popular melodrama" and such political problem plays as *Watch on the Rhine* we can see, despite all differences in detail, the same structure, the same opposition of good and evil elements as the source of tension. What may seem less obvious is the kinship between popular melodrama and the "drama of disaster" which, in its various manifestations, we examined in the two preceding chapters. We may tend to resist the identification because at first glance we are struck by a discrepancy in tone. For in popular melodrama we normally find what we may call "drama of triumph"; this may seem like an unmodifiable opposite of "drama of disaster." In one respect it is. But the antithesis is on the surface. Inwardly, "dramas of triumph" and "dramas of disaster" have the same form.

Dynamic Form: Victors and Victims

So far we have characterized the genre of melodrama in two ways: the characters are whole rather than divided, and the conflict is not within them but between them and various forces outside themselves (persons, groups, events, nature). This analysis is still incomplete in that it treats the form as if it were static. Like all other literary forms, melodrama is not static. It has not only its own pattern but also its own dynamics. Structure has to do with both. It implies not only a basic arrangement of antagonists but certain kinds of movement between them; to phrase the matter a little differently, melodrama has certain definable structures of action. This is what enables us to deal with the apparent contradiction pointed out above: that two different versions of the same basic form may have quite different tones (and therefore may seem formally distinct). In all versions of the melodramatic genre—from popular theatrical synthesis to serious problem plays to dramas of disaster—the "static" form is the same: there is some variation of the conflict between man and elements outside himself (hero versus villain, man versus nature). But the dynamic form, or the structure of the action, varies. When the "undivided" protagonist is facing an outer "enemy," the conflict can be resolved in several ways (though these ways are limited in number). It may end in impasse or compromise. Or it may end in defeat for the "hero," or in his victory. One kind of movement or structure of action will result in one tone, another in a quite different tone. But whatever the varieties of tone, the fundamental form—the way of formulating experience—is unchanged.

This is the key point: the disastrous ending and the "happy ending" are not marks of different formal entities. The "drama of disaster" and the "drama of triumph" are not different genres at all, but are simply alternative forms of melodrama. They are at opposite ends of the spectrum of melodrama. At one end man is beaten down by his antagonist; at the other end he comes out on top (or occasionally both survive, in exhaustion, or in the restless truce when both rest for the next round of melodramatic conflict, or perhaps in compromise, which is the related idiom of comedy). At one end, man is victim; at the other end, victor. The nature of the conflict is the same: the dramatist gives us one structure of action or the other by his choice of point of view.

If man's antagonist is nature, the artist may believe in, and may therefore dramatize, either man's vulnerability or his conquering power. From the artist's sense of man's vulnerability will come visions of defeat—by the sea, as in Synge's *Riders to the Sea*, or by the combined action of man and natural forces in nuclear destruction, as in Arch Oboler's *Night of the Auk* (1956).⁴ The contrasting sense of man's power will produce visions of triumph—in tales of discovery and invention, and in dramas of medical break-through such as Sidney Howard's *Yellow Jack* (1934). Thornton Wilder's *The Skin of Our Teeth* (1942) does it in both ways: it presents a series of cosmic disasters (ice age, flood, world war) as inherent in man's fate and yet also shows man as victor, not by eradicating misfortune, but by durably surviving it. If man's antagonist is the socio-political world, the individual may be a victim, as often in the long line of dramas extending from the Romantics (*Sturm und Drang*, the early Schiller,[5] Coleridge, Shelley) through later nineteenth-century problem plays (such as those of H. A. Jones and A. W. Pinero) and Ibsen in his social studies to later drama of "protest" such as that of Clifford Odets; a special modern variant, as we have seen, is the drama of disaster growing out of the rise of Nazism and Communism (given a new sophistication by Max Frisch and Eugène Ionesco). In the melodrama of society the sense of man as victor appears most reputably in the view that such virtues as integrity and faith survive despite the blows suffered by men and the apparent hopelessness of the immediate task; it appears most uncritically in the hundreds of popular subliterary plays that depict the triumph of the "good guys" against the group, the punishment of corruption, and the reform of unjust conditions. Finally, if the antagonist is the vicious individual, we may see man betrayed and destroyed, as he is by the long line of Elizabethan and Jacobean villains, or we may see him subduing "bad guys," as he often does in later periods: defeating seducers and other schemers in the eighteenth century, foiling rapacious mortgage holders in the nineteenth, and hunting down a multitude of criminals and subversives in the twentieth.

There is, I suspect, a traceable continuity in the underlying polar attitudes that create one type or another of the basic melodramatic structure, and the history of man's self-interpretation could surely be illuminated by plotting the constant attitudes against the variable antagonists: if the sense of human hopelessness is the constant, the destructive force as it appears to the Elizabethans is the villainous individual (the tyrant or machiavel), whereas the destructive force that appears to modern eyes is society generally, or the vicious group or force, or most conspicuously man's own weakness, his inherent capacity for going to pieces. The modern who inherits Webster's sense of the gloom of the world is surely O'Neill, with his pictures of collapse and wretched failure, from *The Emperor Jones* (1921) to *The Iceman Cometh* (1946) and *Long Day's Journey into Night* (1955). History and synoptic completeness, however, are not my intention. In this section I want only to name enough examples to present concretely the types of melodramatic structure, and to have the examples sufficiently spread in time to suggest that the types persist in various historical contexts.

III. Psychological Structure

So far I have been talking about literary structures: the arrangement of the constituent elements of a work and the general patterns of interaction among these elements. I want now to speculate about the psychological structure of melodrama. By this I mean the kinds of need that give rise to, and the kinds of experience and satisfactions afforded by, these literary structures.* Why do they exist at all? In most general terms, what they afford is the pleasure of experiencing wholeness—not the troublesome, uneasy wholeness that exists when all of one's divergent motives remain within the field of consciousness, nor the rare integration of powers that may be earned by long discipline; but rather the sensation of wholeness that is created when one responds with a single impulse or potential which functions as if it were his whole personality. In this quasi-wholeness† man is freed from the anguish of choice, and from the pain of struggling with

---

* We might speak of the "melodramatic catharsis," but that term would complicate the discussion by introducing the divergent hypotheses of the nature of "catharsis" itself. Were I to use the term, I would give it the sense of "working off" or "working out" or simply "working." "Working out" is a useful term because it suggests both "working out of the system" and "workout" in the sense of "exercise." My own emphasis would be more on the "workout," the "exercising" of certain impulses, and less on the "elimination" that it may be argued is a by-product of the "exercise." In fact, a "working" may involve a "working in" as well as a "working out"—i.e., the creation of a habit that makes its own demands. At this point one slides from Aristotle back to Plato and realizes that the Aristotelian term is a liability unless it is used simply as a general metaphor for the not easily definable psychic aspect of aesthetic experience. However, cf. Eric Bentley, who introduces Freudian tools in evaluating the experience of melodrama (*Life of the Drama*, note 1 of this chapter).

† For literal consistency I should use *quasi-wholeness* throughout to denote the emotional or moral singleness characteristic of, and induced by, melodrama. But the term is cumbersome; with steady repetition it may sound pedantic; and it may seem disparaging when, for an experience that has its own legitimacy, the term should be neutrally descriptive. Ordinarily, then, I shall simply use *wholeness*. Though I also use *wholeness* to denote the inclusive activity of being that belongs to tragedy, there should be little risk of confusion. Modifiers within a statement, or the context within which the statement occurs, should always make clear whether the reference is to the tragic state (all impulses active: courage *and* cowardice) or to the melodramatic state (singleness of feeling: courage *or* cowardice).

counterimpulses that inhibit or distort his single direct "action." If there is danger, he is courageous,* and he is not distracted by fear, or the itch to save his skin, or the calculation of his chances, or the profit motive. Or he is noble and dedicated, unhampered by self-seeking, by disgust at the venality of his compatriots, or by dubiety about the formally proclaimed ends of the struggle. Or he can be serene in adversity, untroubled by the thoughtlessness of others, unmoved by the temptation to rebuke the selfish and the complaining, to look out for himself, and to rail against fate. Thus Dr. Valkonen, Kurt Müller, and the stage version of Anne Frank's father: through them, melodrama affords audience and reader an experience of remarkable, satisfying oneness of feeling. Through Kurt Müller, as well as through a large host of much more stereotyped heroes contending against wrong or crime, one enjoys the wholeness of a practical competence that leads to swift and sure action; one is untroubled by psychic or physical fumbling, by indecisiveness, by awareness of alternate courses, by weak muscles or strong counterimperatives. One comes under the agreeable yoke of what I will call a *monopathy;* by monopathy I mean the singleness of feeling that gives one the sense of wholeness. The unifying feeling may be found almost anywhere in the spectrum of emotional possibilities. A sense of oneness may come from a monopathy of hope, but also from a monopathy of hopelessness; from a monopathy of contempt for the petty, discontent with destiny, indignation at evildoing or apparent evildoing, or castigation of the guilt of others.

Let us examine a little further the notion that a monopathy may represent any one of a wide range of affective states. The monopathic pleasure of melodrama is of course immediately apparent at the end of the spectrum where the mood is triumphal, and where the delights of mastery are proffered. Yet the monopathic satisfaction is also provided, however paradoxical this may seem at first glance, by dramas of disaster. While the very word *disaster* names the unwanted, the dreaded, or the unthinkable, nevertheless the event itself is capable of

* The modern reaction against the facile heroic is in danger of falling into a contrasting simplicity, the facile unheroic: stories of World War II so universally report the dominance of fear in the protagonist that a generation of readers is largely spared the puzzling temptations of heroism. More recently, of course, we have gone further and trafficked widely in the facile "antiheroic."

providing an aesthetic experience in which there are gratifying sensa-
tions of wholeness. This is most obviously true when the literature of
disaster exploits the "going down fighting" theme or works to induce
a "good cry": the normal chaos of emotions yields to a monopathy of
shared bravery or of grief or pity. However much our human nature,
or a part of it, creates a desire to stay on top, there are actually
emotional compensations (even rewards or enticements) in going
under, in being defeated or overwhelmed or victimized. One is saved
the troublesome pains of responsibility for evil, of choice among
unclear options, or actions that may turn out to be misconceived; one
can hate evil without the need of making countermoves that may be
futile; one can take a kind of comfort in the very insuperability of
obstacles or the irresistibility of opposing forces; one can find an
affirmative pleasure in the relief from tormenting uncertainty, or can
yield to the lure of passivity, or can even welcome death.

In such ways may disaster—that which we would pray out of life if
we could—penetrate to centers of human responsiveness, none the less
active because less acknowledged than others; in all of these ways of
responding, dividedness is replaced by a quasi-wholeness, and we find
the security of an ordering monopathy. Among all these gratifications
perhaps the greatest, to which we shall return later, is the unity of
innocence. Through the Duchess of Malfi, for instance, we have an
unusually complete experience of monopathic innocence.

IV. THE WORLD OF MELODRAMA

Melodrama, in sum, includes the whole realm of conflicts undergone by characters who are presented as undivided or at least without
divisions of such magnitude that they must be at the dramatic center;
hence melodrama includes a range of actions that extends from disaster to success, from defeat to victory, and a range of effects from the
strongest conviction of frustration and failure that serious art can
dramatize, to the most frivolous assurance of triumph that a mass-cir-
culation writer can confect. The issue here is not the reordering of the
self, but the reordering of one's relations with others, with the world
of people or things; not the knowledge of self but the maintenance of
self, in its assumption of wholeness, until conflicts are won or lost.
There is a continuous spectrum of possibilities, from the popular play
in which the hostile force can be beaten to the drama of disaster in

which the hostile force is unbeatable; at one extreme we view man in his strength, at the other in his weakness. These variations of the melodramatic structure have their emotional concomitants. In one direction we are lured toward high confidence, in the other, toward despair; in one direction toward self-glorification, in the other, toward feeling sorry for ourselves. Since the experience is monopathic, it gravitates naturally, if not necessarily, toward the extreme formulation that encourages overly simple feelings. In this we recognize a vice, and a vice to which, we know, few hearts are immune. Here we have to keep in mind two contradictory aspects of melodramatic structures. On the one hand they reflect aspects of reality, and we require them; on the other, they cater to longings that can easily get out of control. The less responsible the catering instinct, the greater the risk of the emotional bargain counter. In the monopathic structure, based as it is on the victor-victim polarity, there is no counter-feeling to offset the dominant emotion: the approval of victory easily expands into the delights of self-congratulation, and sadness for the defeated glides gently into the melancholy pleasures of self-pity. In melodrama, victory is not tempered with the rigors of cost accounting, nor defeat with the reckoning of spiritual growth.

But if such complications are introduced, we have dividedness of vision; when we see reality dividedly, we can no longer enjoy a monopathic identification with characters that are simply winning or being overwhelmed; and when this singleness of sentiment is gone, the melodramatic form presses toward the outer limits of possibility. Marlowe's Barabas, in *The Jew of Malta*, is defined as a machiavel, that is, a villain; but when all of his victims turn out to be as bad as he is, the feeling evoked is no longer so simple a matter. Cyril Tourneur gives Vendice, in *The Revenger's Tragedy*, every justification for carrying out vengeance against his enemies, but then attributes to Vendice such fiendish glee in his retaliation that he cannot retain the sympathy likely to be given to the worm who turns on evil foes. If the pursuit of justice and the sadistic pleasure in torturing others became conflicting elements in Vendice, and if the conflict were a determinant of action, then this high-level melodrama would be transformed into the tragic.

CHAPTER FOUR

Tragic and Melodramatic Realms: Explorations I

WE BEGAN by distinguishing tragedy and disaster, and by looking at a number of plays which are often thought of as tragedies but which really have the structure of dramas of disaster. We continued the theoretical examination of disaster by observing the relationship between dramas of disaster and the immense world of popular plays that may be called dramas of triumph; dramas of disaster and those of triumph we found to be polar developments of a common form, and to this common form we have applied the generic term *melodrama*. We have tried to isolate the genre of melodrama and to identify the unity which underlies its diverse outer forms. We move now to a more inclusive theme—the relation between melodrama as a whole, and tragedy. Our problem is the geography and politics of two contiguous and complementary realms which fluctuate between an impulse to partial fusion and an impulse to total independence.

I. BASIC CONTRASTS

In characterizing these realms we shall do overtly what up until now we have often done implicitly, that is, consider the tragic and the melodramatic both as artistic structures and as general categories of human experience. It is worth repeating that the analogy of the literary and the existential lies deep in our habits of definition: we use the literary term *tragedy*, whether accurately or not, to define numerous nonliterary happenings; and many an observer of the tenser human moments has ruefully concluded, "Life is always taking the form of a melodrama." Men not only write tragedy and melodrama but also, in quite nonliterary contexts, view human experience tragically or melodramatically.

I have proposed that the identifying mark of the tragic character is dividedness: that he is caught between different imperatives each of which has its own validity, or that he is split between different forces or motives or values. In other words, his nature is dual or multifold, and the different or competing elements are present at the same time, are operative in the dramatic situation, and are known to us as realities that have to be reckoned with. In melodrama, on the other hand, character is viewed as essentially undivided; whether intentionally or unknowingly, a part is taken for the whole, and it does duty for the whole; the complicating elements are eliminated or made ineffectual; there is an impression of unity of being and singleness of direction. In structure of feeling, the form is what I have called "monopathic"; tragedy, by the same nomenclature, is "polypathic." Though melodrama would generally seem a less inclusive form than tragedy, monopathic concentration may even make melodrama in some ways more overwhelming: the uninhibited violence of passions —lust, revenge, sadism—often gives Jacobean drama, or the plays of Duerrenmatt and Frisch, an almost unbearable force. In *The Duchess of Malfi*, everything contributes to a sense of ruin that is staggering. In tragedy, on the other hand, the sense of ruin coexists with other elements; impulses and options are dual or multifold, we are drawn now this way and now that, and the awareness that is exacted is much more complex and troubling. Not that the spectacle of the aged Lear as a victim of madness and the storm is not overwhelming too. It is. But it cannot inspire simply a monopathic pity, which is at the center of our response to the torment of the Duchess of Malfi. For we do not forget that Lear, under the dominion of the dark side of his being, has created the storm himself. Profound pity for Lear as victim, yes, but also acknowledgment of the paradoxical presence of justice, and sense of irony—all are present in a disturbing polypathic experience.

In melodrama, man is seen in his strength or in his weakness; in tragedy, in his strength and his weakness at once. In melodrama, he is victorious or he is defeated; in tragedy, he experiences defeat in victory, or victory in defeat. In melodrama, man is guilty or innocent; in tragedy, his guilt and his innocence coexist. In melodrama, man is bad—that is, a villain—or good, whether as victor over evil or as a victim who does not deserve his fate; in tragedy, his goodness is intermingled with the power and inclination to do evil. In melodrama, man's will is broken, or it conquers; in tragedy, it is tempered in the suffering that comes with, or brings about, new knowledge. As these comparisons suggest, it is possible to think of tragedy, in more than one respect, as resembling the mean between two extremes, drawing something from both, while melodrama tends to develop each extreme in its pure state. Tragedy, with its inclusive vision of good and evil, never sees man's excellence divorced from his proneness to love the wrong, nor, on the other hand, does it see the evil that he does divorced from his capacity for spiritual recovery: for achieving new insights, accepting guilt, reordering the will, preserving or re-establishing the moral order by which the quality of action may be known. But melodrama, in separating good and evil and treating them as independent wholes, has a natural inclination toward the extreme monopathic attitudes: toward a triumphal spirit, an unqualified hopefulness, a belief that good is chosen without anguish, and integrity maintained despite danger; or, at the other extreme, toward all the black despairs that have entered the dramatic vision—despair of man's surviving against the villainy of others or of himself, as in Elizabethan and Jacobean playwrights; despair of the general state of the world, as in *Sturm und Drang* poets; despair of man's ability to endure himself, as in O'Neill; despair of man in his infinite corruptibility, as in some of Duerrenmatt and Beckett (and in such fiction as George Orwell's *1984*).

One way to amplify understanding of a character type, I suggested earlier, is to discover its pathological form. The pathological extreme of the tragic condition is schizophrenia, where normal dividedness is magnified into a split that is sheer illness. The pathological extreme of the melodramatic condition is paranoia[1]—in one phase, the sense of one's own grandeur and, implicitly, of the downfall of others; in another phase, the sense of a hostile "they" who are conspiring to make one their victim (a state dramatized with bold symbolism, in Christopher Fry's *Sleep of Prisoners*, by a verbless speech of David King's: "They, they, they, they"). Or, to continue the contrast by means of a quite different analogy: melodrama has affinities with politics, tragedy with religion.

In the competition for public power that is pragmatic politics,* one conquers or is conquered; the public stance of every party, the operating "platform" of every contestant, is that what is going on is a conflict between right and wrong; the wholeness of all antagonists is a working assumption that need not even be articulated, and the participating public is apparently as indifferent to the antagonists' inner state as they themselves are and generally have to be as long as their life is gladiatorial. "Our side" is the "good man," and "they" are the "flaw"; the Aristotelian tragic hero is broken up into two separate competitors, whose combat is the public form of political activity as we know it. Unlike the tragic hero, the political hero is a part of the human whole doing duty for the whole, that is, representing this or that crystallization of feeling or desire that is identified with "the good," and striving to put opposing forces out of business. The political leader is the hero of melodrama, and his opponent the villain; if he does not consciously seek this formulation, we tend unconsciously to impose it on him and his antagonist.

But religion (to omit here the metaphysical dimension) is concerned precisely with the whole man, and at the center of its view of man is a sense of his dividedness, of the copresence of counterimpulses always striving for dominance, of the fact that throughout life he is a dual creature with equal possibilities of coming to salvation or to damnation. And, if I do not misinterpret the religious view, another of its premises is the importance of man's understanding his own

* Eric Voegelin reminds me, in a personal letter, that this is only one view of politics, that of Hobbes and of others, such as Carl Schmitt, who derive from him, and that it is "in radical opposition to the classic conception of Aristotle: that the essence of politics is the *philia politike*, the friendship which institutes a cooperative community among men, and that this friendship is possible among men insofar as they participate in the common *nous*, in the spirit or mind." Here I do not go into the subject of the ultimate nature of political reality, but apply the theory of melodrama only to the public phenomena of political activity in those countries where competition between parties is the mechanism for securing control of governmental forms.

divided nature. Within the realm of literature, it is tragedy that interprets that nature always suspended between damnation and salvation and that places primary value upon, and indeed serves to heighten, man's knowledge of his own being.

Timeless vs. Topical

To make one final statement of the contrast between these basic forms and attitudes: tragedy is drawn toward the permanent and the transcendent, whereas melodrama gravitates toward the topical. Both, obviously, have roots in emotional patterns that belong to the nature of man rather than to periods or civilizations, but they tend respectively to find formulations that are timeless or time-bound. "Contemplation is something that exists outside of time, and so is the tragic sense," says Tennessee Williams. "Snatching the eternal out of the desperately fleeting," he adds, "is the great magic trick of human existence." [2] For us, the fleeting is virtually all-absorbing: it occupies most of our consciousness, most of our processes of communicating with each other. The immense machinery of journalism, all of political life, the concern with social problems, even science itself insofar as it is committed to "target research"—these are focused on the immediate, the contemporary, on what will not be the same tomorrow. Much of melodrama is akin to these modes of examining the present that pre-empt all of the awareness of most men and most of the awareness of those who sometimes escape from the "fleeting." Hence it is possible to say that, if we are to have an adequate view of man, our age needs tragedy, with its sense of constants.

If it is natural for melodrama to be an ally of history, it is equally true that tragedy, "snatching the eternal," has affinities with myth. Tragedy habitually selects themes of more than historical relevance; hence the well-known persistence of mythological subjects,[3] not only in Greek tragedy, of course, but in that of later centuries from the Renaissance on. Recently, as if in reply to our characteristic historicism, to our insistent definition of discrete particularities in time, playwrights have shown an extraordinary interest in ancient mythical subjects (in the hastiest sampling one recalls O'Neill's and Sartre's use of Aeschylus, Eliot's use of Aeschylus and Sophocles and twice of Euripides, the Oedipus plays by Cocteau and Gide, the Antigone of Brecht and Anouilh, the Hercules of Duerrenmatt, the Orpheus of

Tennessee Williams) and in such a modern mythical figure as Don Juan.[4] It is stating the obvious to say that Shakespeare's use of historical or semihistorical characters is grounded not in his sense of the ages to which they belonged, or of the problems of those ages or even of his own,[5] but in his imaginative perception of the constants which they embody—the constants which he re-created so well that all subsequent ages have found his characters intelligible in their own terms. The "imperatives" to which, as I have argued, tragic heroes characteristically respond with part of their beings represent a moral reality that does not change when "times change." If a twentieth-century man does not literally feel the duty of a punitive matricide as Orestes did, what still is entirely valid for him is the drama that Aeschylus found in this revenge—the conflict of imperatives, and imperatives for which analogous modern formulations may generally be found. In the region of constants lies the drama of self, of man's relations with himself; the realm of melodrama comprises his relations with others. It is this realm that drifts toward the topical. I say "drifts" because I do not want to overstate the point: when the drama of disaster represents evil as an absolute, not attached to particular social or political forms, but simply as a possibility of human nature, obviously it is a long way from topicality. Here it approaches the tragic search into the depths, and that is of course why it is most likely to be mistaken for tragedy. Shakespeare's Iago and Webster's Duke of Calabria come out of similar visions, and hence the dramatic forms in which they act their roles may seem to be identical; but Iago is subordinated to a tragic design, and the Duke has a glaring prominence in a less subtle melodramatic pattern.

But these embodiments of unconditioned evil belong in the main to an older melodrama; for several centuries the melodramatic sense of evil has discovered not so much timeless monsters as evildoers representative of their own times and interpretable by the historical context. Indeed, this begins as early as the Renaissance; along with machiavellian villains and Jacobean figures of pure evil, made possible by a sense of man's corrupt nature, were evildoers of a particular historical cast. These might be monarchs (as in *Edward II* and *Richard III*), and tragedy itself was widely thought to be a warning to them. Or the wrongdoers might be ambitious rebels who could not accept royal justice (as in *1 Henry IV*), or the various local or national tyrants that populate drama through the seventeenth century. By the eighteenth century, evil is beginning to be found in different quarters, though in no less topical forms; in Lillo's *London Merchant* (1731), the robbery and murder committed by George Barnwell are blamed on Millwood the prostitute, and Millwood's vicious life is in turn blamed on society. Edward Moore's *The Gamester* (1753) shows gamblers ruining a weak hero. Moore's chief rascal is a seducer as well as a money grabber: we can trace lust and avarice in shifting manifestations as social and economic changes open up new points of view. The upper-class rake or seducer popularized by Richardson went on to a long life in popular plays that exploited the democratic sentiment. Lords who threw the innocent into dungeons were eventually supplanted on the stage by landlords who threw the innocent out of cottages; this general theme was extended in many stage varieties of what has been called the "Marxist melodrama." [6] More recently we have grim pictures of Snopeses surging out of shacks and becoming lords of the land, and still the old lords reappear, newly decked out, in Beckett's Pozzo. The fear of tyranny once directed against kings is now turned on Fascists, Communists, "Establishments," and majorities generally. Whether in "shows" that simply play for the current stock responses, or in the large body of "problem plays" that strive to evoke questions or influence attitudes, the melodramatic form seizes upon the topics that spring up with the turns of history and consciousness—slavery, "big business," slums, totalitarianism, the mechanization of life, war, the varieties of segregationism—and, from whatever point of view it may adopt, finds the chosen issue to be the local habitation of evil. Few playwrights are able to universalize topical issues, that is, to discover in them patterns of reality that give the plays life after their own day.*

* Ibsen could do this, though he did not always do it. Nothing is deader than a problem play after the problem has died and been interred in history; it then becomes primary material for social historians. But certain problems generate popular art forms that survive the problem—usually in stereotypes that seem to be required by imaginations enclosed within a rigid concept of reality. At the same time, the practical disappearance of the problem is almost always a prerequisite for the artist's treating it as more than a historical topic. The problems of "the West" have produced, on the one hand, "westerns," on the other such an adult piece of fiction as Walter Clark's *The Oxbow Incident*. To sum up: when the sentiments and attitudes that are appropriate to a historical situation at the moment of

So much for the efforts to pile up distinctions between two basic sets of habits and attitudes. I have meant to suggest rather than to insist. It would not be helpful to propose absolute, unvarying boundary lines; in both literature and life there are few instances of pure types. The literary work or the human personality leans in one direction or the other; it rarely plunges to an extreme. But one cannot judge the individual work, or the person's way of confronting reality —one cannot say that here is a melodramatic style with an infusion of the tragic, or here is a tragic cast of mind that includes something of the melodramatic—without discriminating the theoretical poles of attraction. The test of these theoretical constructions is their helpfulness in identifying the literary structures of individual works or in understanding the strategies of spirit that men devise to face an imperfect world.

II. The Role of Melodrama

I proceed from the preliminary distinctions between types to a delineation of the tragic and the melodramatic as independent and complementary activities, each with its own nature and function. I will approach this indirectly, through a further note on the psychological structure of melodrama.

If the preceding comparisons are valid, they indicate that the emotional experience of melodrama is a less inclusive one than that of tragedy. What melodrama typically offers is the exaltation of victory, indignation at wrongdoing, the pitiableness of victims, the frustration of the indeterminate outcome, the warming participation in courage, the despair of defeat, the shock of disaster, the sadness of death. These may indeed be much complicated, as O'Neill sometimes complicates his dramas of despair, but once they have begun to take hold, they tend to inhibit exploration of more ambiguous emotional possibilities. We cannot help taking pleasure in limited emotions; in monopathy we are spared all contradictions and contingencies. With

---

crisis persist in art after the situation has vanished, an aesthetic cliché is created; when the historical situation, having passed, is seen anew at a later time in the light of fresh sentiments and attitudes, we have the conditions for creative art. Some of these matters are treated more fully in my article, "The Western Theme: Exploiters and Explorers," *Partisan Review*, XXVIII (1961), 286ff.

a part of ourselves we unknowingly try to pressure artists, and even events, to yield these limited emotions. If we can, we keep the joy of conquest incomplete by shutting off the complementary—that is, the completing—feelings: sense of exhaustion, fear of injustice to others, shock at our own ruthlessness, disillusionment with the ends achieved. In indignation, we eliminate complicity and guilt; in despair, the heavy strain of finding ways of not simply giving up and going under.

An incomplete emotion is one which mirrors only part of the actual or possible human engagement in the given circumstances. For this reason it is likely to be very intense, gaining concentration from diminished amplitude: the full emotional potential runs off in a single channel, with a stimulating rush. The art, or the experience, that offers us this makes a powerful appeal. Though *Long Day's Journey into Night* endeavors to work from the inner contradictions of the Tyrones, what comes through, in the end, is a simple but devastating sense of frustration and defeat. It is this monopathic pressure, this forcing of emotion into one narrow course, that doubtless accounts for one critic's accepting *Long Day's Journey* as "perhaps the finest play (and tragedy) ever written on this continent." [7] "On this continent" is the safety valve in the hyperbole. But even so, we see how O'Neill's insistent sense of defeat blinds the critic to the essentially untragic note of the static, nagging, and trivial lives depicted. The critic is characteristically modern in being moved by the disaster of personality, that form of melodrama in which atrophy of the will replaces a tragic hypertrophy of will. How much more perceptive is Nicola Chiaromonte's appraisal: "For three hours O'Neill compels us to take part in this monotonous and obstinate round of suffering; it would, we feel, be stupid, were it not for his sincerity." [8]

To make these notes on the partialness of melodramatic experience may seem like a call to arms against melodrama. I intend no such thing. On the contrary, I want to point out the legitimate role of melodrama, and the ways in which the form may be considered a necessity. Take, for instance, the long line of problem plays which so rarely live beyond their own time: in them the melodramatic spirit performs a historical task of taking sides and stirring up debate on moot issues of behavior. In literature, melodrama is the principal vehicle of protest and dissent; or, more accurately, it is the vehicle of protestants and dissenters when they are in a polemic rather than a soul-searching mood. As a polemic form, it may also be used by the order that is attacked, but it is less used in reaction because the existent order tends simply to hang on, to maintain itself by political means. If the existent order uses artistic means, they are likely to be in the comic form, as with Aristophanes. One cannot imagine an anti-angry-young-man or anti-beatnik drama, but there is a fair supply of angry-youth drama and beatnik verse. Dissent uses words to create a position; it has no institutional being, and it relies on art forms as a way of giving quasi-institutional status to individual efforts. Hence the melodrama of problems assumes most frequently the style of protest. It is the addiction to melodramatic postures which leads to an overvaluing of "protest" and "dissent" and "rebellion" as aesthetic materials and to the untenable view that they are always at the center of great art. From these may come, given enough talent, great melodramatic art (homily, satire, invective, the "black comedy" rather popular in the 1960's, and so on), but one would hardly think of such terms in endeavoring to account for the quality of the world's great drama and fiction.

In a more general sense, melodrama is the realm of social action, public action, action within the world; tragedy is the realm of private action, action within the soul. Melodrama is concerned with making right prevail in the world and between persons, or with observing that it does not prevail; tragedy, with the problem of right in the self. The tragic figure may act vigorously in the world, as Oedipus and Macbeth do, but his public action is important mainly for its revelation of the private reality. We are hardly concerned at all about the plague in Thebes, and we are only secondarily concerned about the political illness of Scotland. Tragedy, much as it may and does take note of social and political effects, is less concerned with them than with the truth for and of the individual. Each realm—the public and the private—has its own moral impulse, though, as we shall see, the morality may be stereotyped, rigid, imperceptive, or false. Both types of action have their claims—the realization that marks T. S. Eliot's progress from the priggish antiworldliness of *Family Reunion* to the double vision, in *The Cocktail Party*, of life in the world and spiritual life.

We can now see why the wholeness or oneness of being that is postulated in melodrama is inevitable: man has to assume wholeness to act in the world. He cannot act if he is beset by guilt or by conflicting impulses that make choice exhausting or impossible. "Existentially speaking, the acting man can be efficient and self-assured only insofar as his consciousness is non-reflective." [9] He must take his own wholeness for granted if he is to carry out a policing function, attack the police, make a theory of social justice effective, defeat a bigot or a cheat, survive against enemies, defend the institutions that he is identified with, or attack other institutions. He may be born with, or seize for himself, or have forced upon him the relatively simple organization of sensibility required to work for a party or to meet a crisis. He may be naturally "single-minded" or "single-hearted" (the terms of praise for a unity that only rarely precedes or survives the hour of stress); he may force himself to be so by ignoring or putting aside all the elements of personality which make him normally more complex than a combatant, whether attacking or attacked, can be. He may be trained for "singleness": the discipline of the nation's service academies has to be aimed at a monopathic reconstruction of the individual psyche, at the creation of a "nonreflective consciousness" essential to armed-forces action. The price is, of course, the limitation of sensibility which not many officers escape and which evokes two opposite responses in the civilian community: a distrust of military men for other roles where a wider human consciousness is desirable, and a seeking out of military men as administrators by bodies that hope to impose a unitary order upon diverse actuality. To return to the private man: a threat or a challenge may "make him whole" for the time by subordinating his entire personality to courage, if he is capable of it, or to tenacity, obedience, or fearful flight. Stress makes the unified hero or coward, the samaritan or the savage. One part takes over, as we have said, and does duty for the whole. Opportunity may bring forth a great virtue, a whole-souled acquisitiveness, or a monopathic vindictiveness; occasion may confer on divided man the oneness for a selfless act, for a killing in the market, or for a murder in the bedroom.

Aspects of Wholeness

Wholeness in this sense is morally neutral; it is an artificial unity —the simple condition of action with or against others. It may appear in competition, in struggle toward a generally approved end, in nobility or barbarism, in triumph or surrender. In the more constant competitions as well as in the violent crises of life, it may be seized by, or thrust upon, whole classes as a special possession: all the members of the class become "whole" in goodness or in evil, depending on the point of view. Participants in a struggle of employer versus employee, party versus party, capitalist versus socialist, dare not open their consciousness to their own defects or their opponents' virtues. Voluble defenders of the freedom of the press must ignore the fallibility and self-seeking of some journalists whose style of freedom may actually be injurious to individuals or to society. Ideally no one relishes the concept of morally privileged classes, but it is the implicit working assumption of every group driven by the need of wholeness in public conflict.

Snobbery is an instance of the melodramatic habit of mind: by it a man confers on himself a wholeness needed for competitive purposes, and he secures this wholeness by absolutizing a single value, real or imagined, such as class, school, or intellect, some historical condition, or some talent. Thus the practicing snob is able to "defeat" contestants for honor by simply ignoring all other kinds of merit that they may possess, and by exempting himself from measurement by any other norms. This personal Napoleonism is not generally lovable; one can think of it as at a great moral distance from the singleness of the heroic explorer or mountain climber. Yet both are monopathic phenomena that are structurally akin; in both, the individual is finding an inner "combat stance," a unity of feeling that will give him competitive strength against things or persons. The single-standard melodrama which is exemplified in snobbery appears also in such cultish movements as, say, prohibitionism: in the quest of public action there is a forced unifying of life by a single value—a concentration of good on one side and of evil on the other. Though snobbery is localized in the individual, and panaceas are the work of groups, they are interestingly alike in essential melodramatic spirit: since they cannot be practiced in private, they eliminate privacy; their stage must be all the world.

The wholeness required in melodrama, to repeat, is a quasi-wholeness created when an individual or group gives complete jurisdiction to one of the parts. The wholeness with which tragedy is concerned is the sum total of inconsistent parts, all of which are active: in this sense the tragic personality is divided. Paradoxically, it is whole because it is divided. In tragic life the implied end is not simply survival, or successful competition, or triumph, not simply saving one's life or reforming the lives of others, but insight into oneself and understanding of moral reality. Here man is to know not what is wrong with others but what is wrong with himself; his attention is focused not on evil in the world but on his own capacity for doing evil; he does not have an enemy to do battle against or a villain to unmask, but an inner being and a general truth to become acquainted with. If he is adult, he cannot say, as Anne Frank did, that all men are really good at heart * and thus declare a sort of moral amnesty for himself. Nor can he fall into the self-soothing tactic by which society can acknowledge that evil exists but still escape its burdens—the tactic of making evil a foreign monopoly: Renaissance England was inclined to localize evil in Italy, and in the 1960's we often tend to treat it as a Russian or Chinese export. Rather, if he is to achieve tragic wholeness, man must be able to say, with Goethe, that he has heard of no crime that he cannot imagine himself committing, or with Flaubert, "Madame Bovary, c'est moi," or with R. L. Stevenson that there is "nothing so monstrous but we can believe it of ourselves." [10] This is the realm not of innocence but of guilt, not of campaigning but of contemplation. Just as man cannot act in the world if he is divided within, so he cannot act in the privacy of the self if he is controlled by the artificially limited consciousness of melodrama. By nature and habit he may be so addicted to outer problems that he is incapable of self-knowledge. Or objective crises—war, for instance—may interfere with the tragic life.

Once the two modes of life are delineated, one conclusion seems obvious: that here are complementary forms of reality. They exist, and we must know how to live in both. We cannot really imagine a life that is all melodrama and no tragedy, for this would make the public absolute, and ignore the inner conflict. It would be still more

---

* When the playwrights who dramatized the *Diary* had Anne's statement, which is appropriate to her, repeated by Mr. Frank with apparent acceptance at the end, they were implying a philosophical summation not justified by the world presented in the play. In effect, then, they were offering a placebo to all of the public who respond warmly to assurances that all men are innocent.

difficult—in our day, virtually impossible—to imagine a life that is all tragedy and no melodrama, for this would break down the community into innumerable private cells. We cannot have a life that is all public or all private, all historical or all timeless. We can postulate an ideal coexistence or intermingling or reciprocal modification, or even a public life so adult that community itself is the province of morally self-aware action. We can also remain aware that one realm of life may encroach on the other, be mistaken for the other, or make its demand at the wrong time. Amid these counterclaims, the abiding problem is to avoid being melodramatic when the tragic is called for, or tragic when the melodramatic is called for, and, still more, to avoid being one while having the illusion of being the other.

III. The Attractions of Melodrama

At the theoretical level we define the two counterclaims upon us and state the validity that each has. When we move on to a glance at the historical moment, we must consider whether the two claims are being held in proper tension. Perhaps in different ages the tragic or the melodramatic impulse tends to be dominant. In view of the conspicuous habits of Western man, we would hardly expect the tragic mood ever to be excessive. On the whole it is the melodramatic which can be generally counted upon to take care of itself and not to be crowded out of an adequate role. It has gained great strength in the twentieth century. We appear strongly addicted to the melodramatic —to a public competitive life, to finding and putting down evils, to promoting causes, to an unexamined busyness, and, at the other extreme, to equally unmixed moods of disengagement, defeat, and despair; and, in either case, to an assumption of our own wholeness. Our free use of the word *tragedy*—the starting point of this essay—is an easy substitute for genuine tragic experience.

We call many things tragedy, but we do not characteristically write tragedy; this is a literary truism that critics regularly speculate about; often they tend unconsciously to justify the age by saying that that which we do not write cannot, for whatever reason, be written. Yet it is possible that we simply are not comfortable with the kind of self-knowledge imposed by tragic life. The trouble is not our obsession with longevity, for death is not the essence of tragedy (despite our dislike of death as a fact of life, we relish it as an aesthetic experience: inflicting it, or having it with glory, or sadly suffering it as an undeserved disaster). It is rather that tragedy inhibits the easiest kind of responses; it excludes a comfortable blindness; it is hard on the easier kinds of self-esteem. To be aware of divided-ness is not the most serene form of consciousness. We long to escape into action or, conversely, into inactivity. Contemplation may become painful by betraying us at any moment into a sense of our own liabilities, but expending energy in a cause can be a kind of restora-tive or therapy. The cause may actually be evil: Sartre has argued that anti-Semitism is a mode of response to inner troubles. The cause that most men are likely to choose is the accepted one—charities, educational revisions, civic reforms, social reordering, and so on—so that public attachment to it wins approval from without, and this strengthens approval from within. Or the cause may be a minority one —rescuing some recipient of popular disesteem, opposing national policy, challenging middle-class attitudes, or taking simpler exercises *pour épater le bourgeois* (the forms of combat most attractive to intellectuals and artists in melodramatic mood): here one runs coun-ter to some accepted belief or prejudice, and such conflict confers a reassuring sense of individuality, courage, and integrity. Our most recent device of *épatage* is contemptuous withdrawal or total condem-nation: the now familiar charge that "everyone over thirty is corrupt" is so extraordinarily complete an example of the complacent and unreflective melodramatic spirit that it is in effect a parody of that spirit.

Still, activism is the dominant social mode. Our penchant for this melodrama in the world is reflected in certain student attitudes to drama. Of the serious dramatists who may be called "popular," it is Eliot who, in my own experience, makes students most uncomforta-ble and inclined to be resentful. His principal characters are con-cerned with a state of being, not with external problems to solve, and this seems puzzling, even perverse. If Thomas is willing to be a martyr, it must be that he suffers from a pathological enlargement of the death wish. Certain of Arthur Miller's heroes, however, are easier to live with. In part, they come out of more familiar backgrounds; they belong to common life; they have more animal vitality. But quite aside from all these obvious matters is the fact that they suit our preferences in other ways. Willy Loman and Eddie Carbone, for

instance, have limited understanding, they rarely know what they
have done or are doing, they live and die as activists, unhappy but
uncomprehending. They do not force the reader into self-knowledge,
into the pain of an experienced dividedness; instead he can rest in the
simpler response of enjoying the energy and pitying the misfortunes.
There is a similar response to *Waiting for Godot* (1952): it is easy
to bypass the ambiguities and see in Beckett the portrayer of innocent
man afflicted, without desert, by *tedium vitae* and deluded by indifferent divinity. Nor does O'Neill push one toward self-knowledge; at
least in *The Iceman Cometh* he asserts that self-knowledge cannot be
borne. In that, and even more markedly in his almost unqualified
sense of disaster, he arouses the melodramatic sentiment. That sentiment characteristically relates troubles to outer forces; it is what led a
student of mine to declare that at the end of Marlowe's *Dr. Faustus*
God has become the villain. The student not only did not see that
Faustus has determined the ending by making a choice which even at
the last minute, in effect, he reaffirms, but also failed to understand
that moral life involves penalties as well as rewards and that the
mythic dramatization of values is equally aware of both. Hence the
romantic dualism of innocent man and hostile deity: God is only an
arbitrary punitive force, and man's sufferings are inflicted on him
from without. In the melodramatic formulation of life, we either
demand that God be a sort of super Santa Claus or declare him
unworthy of belief.

The hankering for melodrama infuses some of our socio-political
attitudes and ideals. Most oratory on the subject of liberty implies
that freedom means only being *against* something—dissenting, resisting, finding some group or force or concept to reject; and I have heard
a distinguished American historian [11] wildly cheered for encouraging
this stance on historical grounds. If we are strongly attracted to the
spirit of opposition, our past helps explain the attitude: so many of us
or our forebears came to America because we were against something
—some institution, or measure, or point of view—that we almost instinctively cling to the habit of challenge or denial. The habit gains
support when new leaders of life and thought, emerging from under-
privileged backgrounds with ideas molded by a sense of oppressors
and victims, instinctively use this dualism as the natural formulation
of all human data. We have an almost paranoid suspicion that some-

one is trying to put something over on us. We naturally keep looking for bad men to blame and campaign against.

As at the theater, we are ready for villains. In tragic life, on the contrary, no villain need be—to quote one of Meredith's best-known lines. In our national melodrama, royalty and nobility were the first villains; aristocracy always was and still is the name for a hostile force to be guarded against; other popular villains have been bosses, capitalists or socialists (the "Marxist melodrama"), labor, the bourgeoisie, even intellectuals; and the turning upon, or away from, society as a whole by the hippies, whose self-approval apparently exceeds that of most challengers, can be seen as an ultimate logical extension of one of that society's own favorite habits. A study of stage villains would lead to a fairly inclusive history of the American theater, and, through it, of a host of American antipathies. The point is that blaming classes of people has such quick psychological rewards that we unconsciously try to make reality conform to the melodramatic pattern; it is the old business of making the part truth do duty for the whole. In fighting villains we become heroes. The most eccentric fringe groups are not immune to the traditional charms of this posture.

The assumed accrual of moral capital from a regular practice of objecting, resisting, and denying lies behind a very interesting segment of dialogue in a recent Arthur Miller play, *After the Fall* (1964). Quentin, a lawyer who has "authority" in the play, says to a client of his, Harley Barnes: "I am not sure what we are upholding any more—are we good by merely saying no to evil? Even in a righteous 'no' there's some disguise. Isn't it necessary—to say—. . . to finally say yes—to *something?*" (Act II). Miller gives great dramatic weight to the question by having Quentin ask it of Barnes when Barnes is about to testify before a congressional investigating committee and is, indeed, going to "take the 5th Amendment." That is, Barnes will say "no" and feel sure that he is doing right. This is not a time when anyone could give an easy assent to the idea of affirmation (Harley looks at Quentin "indignantly, suspiciously"). That Miller could make his character ask the question under the most difficult circumstances shows how much importance he attached to the issue. He is taking the rare step of saying "no" to the absolute value of saying "no."

The "some disguise" in even a "righteous no" is, of course, drawing a veil over personal guiltiness. Warring against apparent injustice is invariably more attractive than either probing for one's own lapses from justice or making unclear decisions between options neither of which permits one to be an unflawed hero. It is the latter difficulty that Avrahm Yarmolinsky has in mind when he makes, though in other terms, a contrast of the melodramatic and tragic situations. Yarmolinsky argues that Dostoevski, in his "exaltation of suffering," "failed to recognize the distinction that Kierkegaard drew between 'tribulations' and 'temptations': on the one hand, suffering which is due to external causes and which can and should be eliminated, and on the other, unavoidable suffering which results from a situation involving a moral choice." [12] The suffering that accompanies moral choice has its roots in the tragic dividedness that we will ignore or force into limbo if we can; we are content if we can identify all suffering with that "which is due to external causes" and if we can act on the hopeful theory that it "can and should be eliminated."

A moral choice may be painful because one can respond with only part of himself while other parts protest, or because one responds with the wrong part and tensely hopes to get by with it. Meredith not only said that tragedy needed no villains but went on to state the dynamics of tragic life: "We are betrayed by what is false within." This is so lucid and compact that it is very accessible, and what is accessible may soon sound glib. But there is no glibness of thought in this definition that is almost classical in its centrality. In life and art we often prefer finding villains (men, classes, machines, cosmos) to discovering inner falsities. It is the melodramatic comfort against the tragic discomfort. Partisanship is invigorating, defining, even life giving; it is the easiest distraction from, and quasi therapy for, inner turmoil. It permits us, as a writer on the American-Russian confrontation puts it, to "have too high an opinion of ourselves, and too low an opinion of our enemies, . . ." [13] In a "cold war" all resources are directed against the enemy; hence a society can "turn its energies of mind and passion away from examining itself." [14]

The Melodrama of War

In *Sleep of Prisoners* (1951) Christopher Fry dramatizes the human longing for an uncritical, self-strengthening combative stance in David King, the quarrelsome, almost paranoid, fighter and activist (in one of his manifestations, a Cain figure). "I've got to know which side I'm on," David insists in the final episode; "I've got to be on a side." Here speaks a representative human urgency. It is this melodramatic impulse that gives us a rather strong, if unacknowledged, inclination to war, hot as well as cold. The prescription of "moral equivalents" to war shows a sound estimate of our longing for the melodramatic way, but it apparently overestimates the power of the equivalents to channel energy and create a sense of unity (whether in the individual or the corporate personality). The evidence of our conduct suggests more than a lingering desire for the real thing. No professed public goal evokes less passion, or even interest, than disarmament. Openly we make the motions of warring against war, for we apparently have to believe that we believe in peace, but we would be let down if we won and were stuck with only the moral equivalents. As it is put in Anouilh's *The Fighting Cock* (1959), "Wars are easy. Peacetime is when the trouble starts." [15] Openly we shrink from the hardships of war, its shocks, its terrors, and its griefs; but quietly, inwardly, and perhaps unconsciously we find in it the joy of wholeness, the exhilarating freedom from doubt and self-awareness, the gratifying order in which evil is without and we can ride unified and inspirited on a wave of blame and indignation. James W. Hall notes that the bohemian-beatnik social "rebellion arises not because a war begins, or continues, but because it ends . . . war gives civilians a sense of an over-riding common purpose, a kind of enforced, synthetic sense of community. . . . The war ends, but the taste for intensity and community has been inculcated. . . ." [16] Hall's terms differ from mine, but he does use "rebellion," which exactly implies "blame and indignation." It is noteworthy that antiwar demonstrations are predominantly against a war, not against war; that they provide the psychological satisfactions of fighting an outer enemy; and that they often make outright use of military tactics.

Novelists and dramatists regularly testify to the singular appeals of war; though they name different motives for the love of war, their pictures do not vary much. In *Electra* (1963) Henry Treece says, "Men . . . make great show of despising war, . . . Yet, deep down in them is a love of war; not of the fighting itself, perhaps, but of the freedom war gives. . . ." [17] This is quite like a passage in Simone de Beauvoir's *The Mandarins* (1954), in which Henri Perron says to resistance workers who kill collaborators after the war: "It's breaking your heart to think that all the adventure is over; you're just trying to prolong it." In the same novel Anne Dubreuilh gives a grimmer picture of the peacetime malaise: "People don't have their daily ration of horror any more, so they're beginning to torture themselves again." [18] This in turn might almost come from the scene in *Coriolanus* in which several servants of Aufidius, anticipating the resumption of war, are filled with joy, and for fifteen lines itemize the delights of war and the defects of peace. The key line is, "Ay, and [peace] makes men hate one another" (IV.v.245–46)—in our terms, it makes them find a domestic melodrama to substitute for the international one. The Sergeant in Brecht's *Mother Courage* (1938–39) does not praise war; he simply notes its hold on man. "Of course, a war's like any good deal: hard to get going. But when it does, it's a pisser, and they're all scared of peace. . . ." [19]

This whole psychic situation is anatomized with great shrewdness in a number of passages in Act III of Thornton Wilder's *The Skin of Our Teeth* (1942), a play which, to the extent that it is a commentary on American life, ranges from the fairly obvious to the subtle insight of the speeches about the war's end. The maid Sabina, who has been a camp follower, exclaims, "God forgive me but I enjoyed the war. Everybody's at their best in wartime. . . ." The play as a whole does not repudiate Sabina by presenting her view as eccentric or shameful. Indeed, she has already quoted her master—Mr. Antrobus, the Everyman of the play—as saying "that now that the war's over we'll all have to settle down and be perfect." Sabina, we suspect, is not quoting quite accurately, but behind her words we see an idea that is consistent with the tenor of the play and of Mr. Antrobus' mind. These words delineate exactly the problem of peace: the resumption of tragic consciousness, or the return to all the imperfections and disorders that could be sidetracked or unfelt for the duration. Wilder emphasizes this point unmistakably when he has Mr. Antrobus turn furiously on his son Henry, who is the Cain figure in the Everyman family. At this point Henry is not only the rather nasty problem child of the earlier acts, but has been literally identified as "a representation of strong unreconciled evil." It is Henry at home that Mr. Antrobus finds almost unendurable. He cries out, "I wish I were back at war still, because it's easier to fight you than to live with you.

War's a pleasure—do you hear me?—War's a pleasure compared to what faces us now: trying to build up a peacetime with you in the middle of it." [20] This speech is written out of a fine perception of human nature: the longing to fight the outside enemy rather than deal with the trouble close to home. It is important that Henry, the figure of evil, is the son of Mr. Antrobus, just as Goneril and Regan, the chief embodiments of evil in *Lear*, are the daughters of the tragic hero: kinship is an excellent symbol of evil that is not a plague from without, but an intimate reality, in effect within the good man himself, a part of him in the same sense that his child is part of him, separate but inseparable. It is from this home front that one takes flight, beckoned to freedom by war. The scenes that I have quoted from Wilder's play, which is in the form of an episodic comic epic, put brilliantly the charms of war to hearts that believe themselves committed to peace. In literary terms, Wilder conveys not only the pull of the melodramatic but the essence of melodrama and tragedy: melodrama presents the joys of war, with its occasional sorrows; and tragedy, the sorrows of peace, with its occasional joys.

IV. TRAGIC EXCESS

It is the nature of human life, as I said in Section II of this chapter, to require a cooperation of these two modes, and it is healthful not to be practicing one when we ought to be, or think that we are, practicing the other. In our moment of history, we strongly tend to think and feel in melodramatic terms. The antithetical kind of unbalance, the untimely invocation of the tragic, is theoretically possible, but it will probably seem not a strong enough likelihood to demand elaborate discussion. Pure cases of "tragic excess" are rare, but related to them are various kinds of withdrawal and disability that have always attracted some interest among writers. The weakness and general incapacity that have caught the eye of more than one modern dramatist may not be cases in point, but some of the plays will help illustrate the problems.

There are interesting borderline cases in English novels of the eighteenth and nineteenth centuries. The novels are comic, and this in itself is significant: to hold the tragic view when all about you are content with melodrama is likely, provided you do not attempt to impose your view on others, to seem no more than an innocuous and laughable eccentricity. When the title character of Tobias Smollett's *The Expedition of Humphry Clinker* is falsely accused of highway robbery and is arraigned before Mr. Justice Buzzard, he makes equivocal replies, with the result that his irascible employer, Matthew Bramble, exclaims, "In the name of God, if you are innocent, say so." At which Humphry cries out, "No . . . God forbid, that I should call myself innocent, while my conscience is burthened with sin." [21] In this episode Humphry does have the innocence that is always assumed of or sought by the hero of melodrama, so that there is comic incongruity in his introducing a sense of guilt that may be expected in tragedy. It is interesting that in this tale of the world the only character who could be thought capable of such self-consciousness is a servant who is "an original."

In Anthony Trollope's *The Warden* we again have a title character who, in the eyes of his more worldly family and colleagues, creates gratuitous and annoying problems by defecting from melodramatic standards. Here, however, the key episode is crucial; the individual is not without power to act; and the story as a whole turns on the ironic discrepancy of the two modes of action. The legal attack on the conduct of the wardenship has been repulsed, and Mr. Harding is in the clear. At that moment he calls on the great lawyer, Sir Abraham Haphazard, simply to know what is "right." Now, from the legal point of view it is "madness" to raise such an issue, and Sir Abraham is afflicted with "utter astonishment" when Mr. Harding proposes to resign because he feels that, though the legal case is won, his position is questionable.[22] Mr. Harding is virtually alone in wanting to look at himself, know whether he is guilty, and find a morally satisfactory solution; with one exception, all the other churchmen simply want to win the melodrama of the legal conflict. They represent the church militant, and they are in worldly despair over his troublesome perversity.

In both these novels the unexpected emergence of the tragic view serves comic ends; the "guilty" person is not artistically placed in a position in which his hypersensitive self-evaluation could be construed as simple failure to cope with an obvious claim of the world upon him. Other characters do regard Humphry and Mr. Harding as failing in a public situation, but these critics represent, not authority, but a conflicting point of view. In Shakespeare, however, there are two clear-

cut cases in which men with responsibilities—Richard II and Henry
VI—turn from a demanding outer world to an inquest upon or a
pursuit of an inner world. In Acts I and II we see Richard turning
from the business of being a king, as it were, by off-the-cuff and
irresolute actions; since this style is quite marked, his unyielding
persistence in seizing Gaunt's property and going off on the Irish
campaign seems hardly consistent (unless we interpret stubbornness
as the only steadfastness possible to the impulsive man). However,
for two acts the dramatic characterization of Richard is sketchy; only
in retrospect do we understand that his malfeasance is obscurely
related to his instinctive looking within. Then in Act III, Scene ii
begins that flowering of the self-contemplative man, of the peculiar
self-consciousness of the histrionic personality, that dominates the rest
of the play. It is of course a truism that Richard is a self-dramatizing,
self-imaging man, often embarrassing in the pictures of himself
which he lingeringly designs and all but caresses. He serves our
purposes here, however, insofar as his self-concern becomes an obsessive mode of activity that inhibits other modes. He might flash one
quick, reckless stroke, such as he fleetingly envisages: "Shall we . . .
send / Defiance to the traitor, and so die?" (III.iii.129–30); he might
attempt a vigorous Macbeth-like or Richard III-like last-ditch struggle, however desperate the odds may be; he might with candor and
dignity acknowledge failure and win esteem in the crisis.* We mention alternatives only to throw into relief Richard's hyperbolic exploitation of the pathos that he detects in the circumstances; besides, he
speaks of these circumstances as if they had come upon him without
any collaboration on his part. His excess is the thing: the elaboration
of detail in each moment of self-painting, and the piling of moment
upon moment while those possessing and using power are transfixed as
audience. They watch Richard watching his own performance; they
are a dim play outside a play, only intruding now and then with the
solid force of the world's will, as if groundlings, about to hold a
political meeting, were clearing the stage of players.

---

* Granted that Shakespeare was under some pressure from historic
facts, but these would have permitted a more energetic and vehement
Richard; besides, as he shows by transforming Richard's child bride into a
mature woman, Shakespeare could flout history when it served his purposes to do so.

Richard's is not a tragic excess, but something so like it as to illustrate its functioning. Take the mirror scene (IV.i.265ff.); here we have to do with a symbol of self-placement such as Swift would use brilliantly in portraying Gulliver after his return from the land of the Houyhnhnms. But Richard uses it, not in the privacy of true contemplation, but before an audience; it is analogous to praying on the street corners. He uses it, not to see into his soul, but to note the irony of the facial lineaments that, though apparently unchanged to the eye, have undergone an incredible loss of power. Richard views himself not morally but aesthetically; he labors under a self-immobilizing exaggeration, not of guilt, but of spectacle. He infuses "the pity of it all" with "the irony of it all"; he has a share of the sick ironist bound to a narrow bed of itemizing discrepancies while others act— the type later given comic fullness in Jane Austen's Mr. Bennet. In sum, the enlarged sense of oneself as a good actor, like an enlarged sense of oneself as an evildoer, may become a disabling illness.

Though in modern eyes a more interesting person than Henry VI, Richard is, for our purposes, more specialized; Henry comes closer to exemplifying that kind of nagging conscience which drives the potential tragic hero into or close to an incapacitating morbidity less tragic than pitiable or even exasperating. The trilogy defines Henry in effect as the "good man," and it would not be difficult to see one or another of his royal ineptitudes as the expression of a "flaw" with which he would have to come to terms. The trouble is that he is better endowed for coming to terms with misdeeds than for committing them, that is, for acknowledgment and remorse than for the willful violence in which the tragic catastrophe characteristically originates. He represents a disproportioning of the elements of the hero, a distortion of the kind we are observing in this section. Habitually we think of the tragic hero as strong, as capable of and even given to violence; Henry is given to passivity, and it is customary to define him as a weak man. This will do up to a point; Shakespeare provides more than enough justification for it by rather frequent scenes such as he would still be employing in *Richard II*—court debates and quarrels in which the King, far from controlling them, can hardly gain anyone's ear. Henry, also, constantly bows to the will of others, says "Do what you will," formally cedes his prerogatives, or simply throws up his hands. But there are weaknesses and weaknesses, and what appears in Henry is less a failure of energy than an employment of energy irrelevant to the demands upon him. When bitter quarrels threaten the realm, he uses the power of the throne only to enunciate ethical sentiments (*1 Henry VI* III.i.127–28; IV.i.161). He prefers "my study and my books" to a political marriage, which he calls "wanton dalliance with a paramour" (V.i.22–23), and Margaret of Anjou soon complains about "holiness," "Ave-Maries on his beads," and so on (*2 Henry VI* I.iii.58ff.). We see the basic outlines of his mode of energizing: when he is urgently pressed by the state of the world, he turns the more eagerly to the state of his soul, and the country suffers (I.i.259). He is taken in by a manufactured miracle (II.i.66); when faithful Gloucester is murdered, Henry's chief concern is to avoid unjust suspicions (III.ii.139); he objects to Warwick's phrase "monstrous life" applied to the late Cardinal Beaufort, an unscrupulous politician, "for we are sinners all" (III.iii.31). He hopes that God will "succour" them when Jack Cade rebels (IV.iv.55); he hardly does more than exclaim about infidelity when York rebels (V.i.166; ii.73). He acknowledges, "my title's weak" (*3 Henry VI* I.i.134) and gives away his throne, for future delivery; his only justification is that the rebels "enforc'd me" (line 229), and he observes that "things ill-got had ever bad success" (II.ii.46). While the crucial battle is going on, Henry wanders off alone, says, "To whom God will, there be the victory!" (II.v.15); wishes he were a shepherd, grieves for the bereaved, asserts that he is worse off than they (lines 22ff., 94ff., 123–24). Re-established on the throne by Warwick, Henry promptly "resigns" the "government" to Warwick and vows to "lead a private life / And in devotion spend my latter days" (IV.vi.42–43). Yet even after this he inconsistently cherishes the belief that the people love him and will be faithful to him because he has been responsive to them, prompt to act, full of pity and mercy, neither grasping nor revengeful (IV.viii.38–50)—virtually the only passage in which an ironic effect is derived from his thinking well of himself rather than from his expecting the best of the human race.

The point of these samplings of Henry's speeches is not his lame conduct of the throne, which does not need demonstrating, but the cast of mind that makes him a poor king. In contrast with the much more frequent human inclination to exercise power, engage in combat, and set up simplistic confrontations that make possible a continual flight from self, Henry is the rare person so concerned with the spiritual self, with achieving goodness and being the agent of goodness, that he is incapable of the pragmatic assessment of situations and the resolute action that are his primary obligations. His is the ironic case of the person who fails to become a tragic hero through a hypertrophy of the tragic capacity and a penchant for the untimely exercise of it. That is to say that he is overendowed with that need for rectitude without which the great exemplars of hubris would be, not tragic heroes, but violent barbarians and single-natured villains, in a word, melodramatic characters. If a tragedy is the story of a man who must move from a melodramatic to a tragic sense of reality, Henry's story is that of a man who needs to move from a quasi-tragic to a melodramatic sense, i.e., an awareness of his obligatory role in the unreflective, power-oriented world in which he finds himself. As is inevitable in an individual who can be used to illustrate one extreme in a scheme of types, Henry is an attenuated figure lacking the girth of personality that distinguishes the great characters of Shakespeare's high tragic period.

V. Guilt Neurosis and Innocence Neurosis

In glancing at instances of the flight from the tragic into activity in the world, and of the surprising appearance of the tragic or the quasi-tragic in the arena of worldly action, we have not considered situations that are unmistakably of pathological intensity. For these, we would have to go to such Tennessee Williams characters as Blanche DuBois and Brick Pollitt. Granted, the border lines of the pathological are not always clear-cut, and placing given instances of state of mind on one side or the other of the line often evokes considerable difference of opinion. It is possible to argue that Richard II and Henry VI go so far in confronting public situations with private, recessive styles that they actually exemplify serious disorder. But whatever ambiguity may be present in the individual play or person, we can think of theoretical lines extending outward, from a center of recognizable balance, to extremes of divergent eccentricities. It should be illuminating to explore this theoretical possibility and to note the contents of either kind of consciousness as it develops abnormal proportions.

The extreme of the tragic sense that has got out of control is what we commonly call the "guilt neurosis." On the other hand, then, the melodramatic sense that has got away from all the restrictions of reality produces what we may call the "innocence neurosis." It is not an altogether rare indisposition. The narrator in Camus's *The Fall* remarks, "The idea that comes most naturally to man, as if from his very nature, is the idea of his innocence." [23] In defeat the innocence neurosis makes one always a victim who does not deserve his fate, and who finds it irrational and untimely; in victory it makes one guiltless; and in all the actions of life, in the conflicts as yet unresolved, it makes one the voice of justice and honor. All around him is guilt of some kind. "We are all exceptional cases," continues the Camus narrator. "We all want to appeal against something! Each of us insists on being innocent at all costs, even if he has to accuse the whole human race and heaven itself." Under difficulty, innocence tempts a certain personality to despair—to melodramatic despair of the world (as distinguished from the tragic despair of oneself); to a sense of the hopelessness of things; to imputing to others an infidelity to right ends, and to oneself a special quality which is likely to be irreparably injured by the abrasion of thoughtless or hostile circumstance. This state of mind may appear as self-pity or as the more vigorous cousin of self-pity, self-righteousness, or, if it is more concerned with things than with self, as either existentialist dismay or "defeatism." "Defeatism" is likely to be used, disparagingly, by the possessor of innocence at the other end of the melodramatic spectrum, where the sentiment of conquest dances blithely, in reveries of achievement (the Mitty mode) or in tireless assaults upon the imperfections of the world. Or again, innocence may be simply a gratifying possession in itself: Henri Perron, in Simone de Beauvoir's *The Mandarins*, "was floating in a bath of innocence, and innocence can be every bit as exhilarating as voluptuousness." [24]

Unbridled innocence may express itself in ignorance and immaturity. "The mark of the immature man," it has been said, "is that he wants to die nobly for a cause, while the mark of the mature man is that he wants to live humbly for one." [25] One's relationship to a cause is a measure of one's whole relationship to the world. Maturity is the maintenance of an equilibrium between the extremes of acceptance and rejection; in the immaturity of excessive innocence, one either gives up before the world as it is or decides to "change all that."

Toward the discrepancy between the ideal and the actual in mundane affairs, several attitudes are possible. The "comic" attitude accepts incongruity as a fact of life but also perceives that incongruity may be in part modified by the spirit of compromise (in Congreve, fops, with an excess of urbanity, and rustics, with a deficiency of urbanity, move toward a norm whose best representatives are tolerant and generous). The comic is closely related to, indeed is one of the aesthetic versions of, the "normal" melodramatic, that is, a steady watchfulness, somewhere between indifference and reformist fanaticism, against people who do wrong and things that go wrong. But in its abnormal or morbid states the melodramatic spirit cannot tolerate the discrepancy between the ideal and the actual. In one strategy it becomes millennial: it tries to obliterate the actual by tugging it relentlessly toward the ideal, and thus it leads to the severe tensions of reformism and coercion, and to the eventual shocks of disillusionment.

Gregers Werle in *The Wild Duck* is an archetypal representative of this method—the promotion of the "ideal" by frontal attack, by wrecking an unideal but satisfying life. Gregers survives into the twentieth century, in which his type has attracted the eye of at least three writers—Dorothy Sayers, Robert Penn Warren, and Friedrich Duerrenmatt. In *The Devil to Pay* (1939) Miss Sayers acutely defines a twentieth-century version of Dr. Faustus: she interprets him as "the type of the impulsive reformer" who seeks, as various lines of the play put it, to "change / Sorrow to happiness in a twinkling," "abolish pain and suffering from the world," and "with a sudden lightning smite the world perfect." * As long as he sticks to this

---

* Dorothy L. Sayers, *Four Sacred Plays* (London: Gollancz, 1948), pp. 113, 140, 149, 156. Apropos of the reformer who, snubbed by stubborn history, rebounds into "primal innocence," Miss Sayers makes her Mephistopheles say, "Since first man fell into sophistication I have found no way to ruin him so effective as his restoration to a state of nature" (p. 173). Her interpretation of Faustus finds a parallel in Graham Greene's presentation of Alden Pyle in *The Quiet American*. This view of a man who would "with a sudden lightning smite the world perfect" apparently aroused some resentment among American readers. Greene, I think, complicated the work more than was generally realized; Pyle is seen entirely through the eyes of an English journalist, Thomas Fowler, who is surely not meant to have final authority. He comes very close to being too "patient of the facts," and it is difficult to suppose that Greene lacked the aesthetic sophistication to see him in perspective.

course, he is in flight from tragic experience. What this course does to his personality is noted in William Havard's comment on Warren's work:

In the act of rebellion against the evils of the world, the moral type obsessed with the ideal of total human justice or perfection loses the possibility of a true sense of self-identification . . . and he contributes to his personal corruption and eventual destruction through the identification of himself with the idea to an extent which permits him to act entirely outside any moral restraints. He identifies his individual will with the absolute; in his angry virtue he excuses and justifies all.

Miss Sayers and Mr. Warren come remarkably close together in their estimates of the aftermath to which the perfectionist is doomed: Miss Sayers' statement that he retreats into "primal innocence" and "nostalgia of . . . the primitive" could be the literal prescription for the course pursued by Jerry Beaumont in Warren's *World Enough and Time*. But Warren's "morally mature" man, as Havard says, elects neither "a turning to the 'blank cup of nature' in search of innocence nor an act of wilful rebellion against the evil of the world." [26] Friedrich Duerrenmatt has a comparable understanding of the personality of the impatient ideological remolder of the world. In *An Angel Comes to Babylon* (1954) Nebuchadnezzar is busy forcing a sociopolitical "New Order" upon Babylon; when he is frustrated he becomes outraged and wants to revenge himself upon all the uncooperative. On the other hand, two forcible reformers in *The Marriage of Mr. Mississippi* (1952)—enforcers respectively of the Mosaic law and the Marxist law—are activated by revengefulness against a world that had once treated them badly. They will now make the world be good according to their own wills.

All such characters are aptly described by phrases in Miss Sayers' portrait of melodramatic man. He is, she says, "impatient of the facts" and heedless of "the ineluctable nature of things." It is indeed a tolerance of the actual that is lost in this compulsory spiritual security (the theomorphizing of man), and tolerance of the actual is essential to survival. But this has its own danger: at the opposite melodramatic extreme this tolerance, instead of being obliterated in the effort to establish the ideal by law or fiat, may itself obliterate the ideal by surrendering unconditionally to the prevalent modes of worldly "realism." This "fallacy of realism" is always a threat. For the purposes of our present analysis what is especially interesting is the ironic resemblance between the man who would change the world and the man who would sell out to it. Like many pairs of extremes, the crusader and the opportunist have much in common. One is immature, too young to know that evil has deep roots; the other is hypermature, too soon too old to know that many deep roots do not feed evil. But both stay innocent, the one as he imposes his own righteousness on the world, the other as the world imposes its un-righteousness on him. This is the innocence neurosis: that illusion of guiltlessness which, for clarity's sake, is to be distinguished from the tactical assumption of guiltlessness to meet an emergency.

We have been trying to see what happens when the melodramatic impulse gets out of hand. Now let us see what happens when the tragic sense gets out of hand, a subject which we approached by considering Richard II and Henry VI. If the uninhibited melodra-matic means a predominance of action in the world and a neglect of the problem of the self, then an excess of the tragic—if that hypotheti-cal condition be imaginable for us now—leads toward withdrawal from action, toward a monopolizing contemplation of an introspective cast. One can postulate, at least in theory, a state of affairs in which the business of the world does not get done because the potential doers are morally self-absorbed—pondering, while Rome burns, the dis-cords of their own heartstrings. Perhaps an unarticulated desire to counter the separation from the world that is latent in the tragic consciousness gave rise and currency to the Renaissance theory that tragedy was a warning to kings: this view would bring the form itself into the realm of public action. If the tragic sense can get out of hand by monopolizing the energy which should be shared by other activi-ties, it can also get out of order. This it may do, like the melodramatic sense, in two ways: the way of conquest, and the way of surrender. Zestful conquest in the world is paralleled by zestful conquest in the self: "I am the captain of my soul"—a triumphant voluntarism as illusive as the chiliastic premise in the world. The opposite excess is the helplessness before a sense of guilt that, because one exagger-ates its proportions or one's own weakness, leads to paralysis in the world.

Perhaps the best exemplar of the guilt neurosis in drama is Rosmer in Ibsen's *Rosmersholm*. In him we do not formally see "paralysis in

the world," for the worldly arena disappears from the play; but we do
see the strains of guilt creating a general incapacity for action amid
difficulties. Rosmer has wanted to "ennoble" men, to make "all that is
good in human nature" triumph, to end "malignant wrangling" and
bring about "Happiness for all—through all" (Act III).[27] In this
quest Rosmer might be the very model for Miss Sayers' portrait of the
"impulsive reformer" who wants to "abolish pain and suffering from
the world." But when he begins to suspect that his wife understood
better than he did the emotional urgency in his relationship with
Rebecca West, Rosmer develops "gnawing doubts," and he concludes, "I can never again know . . . Peaceful, happy innocence"
(Act II). Hence, as for social improvement, "Not through me."
There can be no happiness "for me," for happiness "is above all
things the calm, glad certainty of innocence." He knows "what guilt
means." He falls into "gloomy thoughts" that he can "never shake
. . . off." He "loved" Rebecca without knowing it: "That is why
there is guilt on my soul." His cause must fail "because no cause ever
triumphs that has its origin in sin" (Act III). Once an exemplar of
the innocence neurosis, Rosmer now cannot act because of the guilt
neurosis. His sense of the wrong he did his wife, though he acted
unknowingly, becomes obsessive, and the contemplation of it takes up
all his energy and removes him from the campaign to better human
life. He has an overbalance of the tragic sensitivity. It is as if, in
Shakespearian terms, he has retreated within a soliloquy that has
pushed the world into sideline oblivion.

Yet at the same time he serves our purposes doubly, for he exemplifies the human tendency to leap from one extreme position to another.
First he is a total reformer; then he is in total retreat. He leaps from
one melodramatic extreme, where man cannot tolerate the discrepancy between the ideal and the actual in the world, to the tragic
extreme where one cannot endure the discrepancy in the self; from the
radical's dream to total despair: "My faith in myself is utterly dead
. . . —And I know of nothing in the world worth living for" (Act
IV). He is an early example of the personality with which Tennessee
Williams would deal many times—the one that goes to pieces when
an image of the self cannot be maintained. Rosmer underlines his
sickness of being by a question which is really a statement: "—have I
not fled from the battle before it was well begun?" So, with a sophisti-

cal interpretation of it as an affirmative act, he draws Rebecca into a double suicide.*

In both of the extremes into which Rosmer falls, there is a sensitiveness which makes actuality seem unendurable. Yet in both, paradoxically, there is a kind of callousness: a protective hardening of the skin against the complex adult sensitivity that is constantly exacted by the "ineluctable nature of things," and a substitution for it of an easier—that is, a monopathic—discomfort. The inability to live with conflicting demands within the self may lead to either of two simpler extremes of feeling: either a tense, troubled aspiration, an ever-anxious stretching away from the actual, a painful state usually called "perfectionism," and self-punishment; or, in the opposite direction, to a cynical acceptance of the self as unredeemable. One state will be on the border of self-loathing, the other may move from self-forgiveness to self-indulgence. The man who suffers from congenital innocence puts all the blame on others; the man who suffers from incurable guiltiness puts all the blame on himself. The melodramatic cynic falls in with the world; the tragic cynic falls in with himself. The one has to dress his innocence in the style of a scoundrel because the world assures him that that is what he is; the other has to be a scoundrel because his heart assures him that he cannot be anything else.

Withdrawal and Self-Punishment

But of the spiritual disorders that represent an intensification of a normal attitude, the varieties of cynicism are less interesting than the anxiety states produced by a habitual awareness of evil without or within. In an excess of tragic awareness, self-understanding can become oppressive, self-consciousness punitive. Johannes Rosmer goes to pieces when a sudden revelation about an event in the past brings on a new, acute sense of guilt. But there is also the chronic sufferer; the poet William Cowper is a case in point from real life. Somewhere between is Hamlet, who is almost immobilized by his anguished reflectiveness, by his wrestling with a plurality of motives, and by a gnawing sense of moral incompetence. Yet he has still the capacity to break through into action that, however it may indiscriminately min-

* Cf. the double suicide at the end of Ionesco's *The Chairs:* the natural exhaustion of two aged people rather than the premature going under of two people evidently in the "prime of life."

gle justice and injustice, defensible end and faulty impulse, is relevant
to the situation in which he feels responsible for action.

The clinical extreme of incapacitation in affairs, the visible evidence of severe inner illness, is exemplified by Harry Monchensey in
Eliot's *The Family Reunion*. Like Rosmer, he feels guilt in the death
of his wife, and he magnifies it; the occasion releases an all-encom-
passing sense of spiritual maladjustment, which, if it were the ultimate fact in his history, would be only permanent illness. Like his
forebear Orestes, he finds his way out of the morbid excess of tragic
awareness. He does this by a literal struggle of personality (in contrast with the complex symbolic escape from the toils of retributive
malaise that Aeschylus devises for Orestes). The residual strength
for recovering from the clinical state is what, in the end, distinguishes
the tragic hero from the sick man; in the hero are all the facets of the
divided personality, so that the result is not permanent imbalance or
collapse. Lear comes out of the darkness; Lady Macbeth does not.
Lady Macbeth is interesting because, simply by going mad, she
resembles the character who has gone to pieces from an overbalance
of tragic awareness. As always, illness is not tragic; the disaster of
personality is not unlike a natural disaster. Yet there is a difference:
Lady Macbeth is not a static victim but has contributed, by a choice
rooted in her own impulses, to her disaster. The problem is to identify
the precise source of the illness that takes her out of the arena of
worldly competition. One might infer the latent presence in her of a
great moral sensitivity choked down much more successfully than is
her husband's and therefore of less daily trouble; what hits her,
however, appears less a rebound of an insulted area of consciousness
than the psychic exhaustion of driving her husband to a series of
desperate steps and then maintaining an unbearably difficult public
situation. Her "withdrawal" is in contrast with that compelled by the
relentless inward-probing eye.

Tennessee Williams is helpful here because of his recurrent interest in women who withdraw from the world. Laura Wingfield in *The
Glass Menagerie* (1945) is partly crippled, is agonizingly shy, vom-
its when she must take a typing test, is made almost physically ill by
the arrival of a dinner guest; she takes refuge in playing records and
collecting glass figures of animals. Here, certainly, is an inadequacy
that can be called illness, but it is a *donnée*, a primary psychological

fact; though Laura withdraws into herself, her withdrawal is not the product of the moral hypersensitivity that we have called tragic excess. Nor are the grounds of *The Glass Menagerie* tragic: there is little disruption of the single-mindedness of the mother, Amanda Wingfield, and of her son Tom, as they move on their separate campaigns in the world—she to supervise family life, and he to escape it through travel and verse.*

In *A Streetcar Named Desire* (1947) Williams again takes up the theme of the woman who cannot "cope": in the final scene Blanche DuBois is taken off to a mental hospital. Here again the situation is pathetic rather than tragic. Yet Williams has now achieved a more complex treatment of human personality: Blanche combines the qualities of the two women of *The Glass Menagerie*—the daughter's weakness and need for private refuges which here become outright fantasies, and the mother's tendency to use her self-conscious genteel delicacy as an instrument of policy, and her persistence toward her own ends. In addition, whether from a vigorous sexuality that is a primary quality, or in response to psychic needs originating elsewhere, Blanche has become promiscuous, while maintaining a façade of sexual squeamishness. With this mingling of elements Blanche is more than a one-dimensional character: she can be fragile, false, gentle, pretentious, ladylike, insensitively demanding, and trouble-making by turns. Though she has a vestigial hold on true excellences, they drift into the artifices of self-seeking or simply self-preservation. Yet the diverse folds of her nature are being smoothed out into merely pitiable illness—alcoholism and madness. We do not know how she

* Though in one of his prefaces Williams speaks rather disparagingly of the older "realistic play," *The Glass Menagerie* has strong affiliations with a familiar form of realistic drama, the problem play, and with its patterns of emotional appeal: sympathy for the girl who cannot break out, admiration for the young man who does break out, and painful laughter at the mother whose style, if it does not create the prison, makes it a more dismal enclosure. Williams does attempt to complicate the mother—not, however, by a conflict of motives, but by a situation in which she becomes an object of both satire and pity. He does not quite pull it off: his strength lies in a satirical portrayal of vanity, rigid and obsolete ideas, and nagging, and at the end he has to rely on a stage direction to assert her "dignity and tragic beauty." The quotations from *Streetcar* which follow in the text are from the 1953 American edition (New York: Dramatists Play Service). Some editions have only scene divisions.

has contributed actively, if at all, to her fate; the present does not so much dramatically embody her past as admit brief reports on it; and these generally present her as a victim. She talks much of difficult times, many deaths to be lived through. She tells Mitch of first ecstatic love, of early marriage to a boy who turned out to be a homosexual and who, after she told him of her disgust, committed suicide (II.ii). Blanche's sister Stella also cites that story (III.i) and later offers Stanley this general interpretation of Blanche: "Nobody, nobody was tender and trusting as she was. But people like you abused her, and forced her to change" (III.ii). Stella may merely be putting the situation in its best light, but the text provides us with no evidence that substantially alters the picture of Blanche as a pathetic victim of destructive forces.*

In a disaster of personality such as Blanche DuBois's, the incapacity for survival in the ordinary world illuminates by contrast that failure to go on in which an unbearable weight of scruple is the source of illness. The self-scrutiny that becomes flagellation, the nagging guilt that eats inward destructively rather than initiates spiritual action, is brilliantly presented in Hardy's *Jude the Obscure*. Sue Bridehead is the character who cannot be cured of guilt-sickness but falls ever deeper into it; thus she affords one of the most clear-cut examples of tragic possibility that does not mature because excess leads, instead, to what we have called the "disaster of personality." Sue has always suffered from an inner division—a conflict that Hardy never discusses directly but dramatizes with extraordinary effective-

* Williams, however, is interested in "character," and that is what tends to disappear when the case of the individual who opts out is translated into an idiom of the 1960's. In James Saunders' *Next Time I'll Sing to You* (produced, 1962), the career of a hermit simply serves as a point of departure for a dialogue in which the nadaistic predominates. The subject of the dialogue is a historical hermit who had spent forty years alone in a cave. The participants—including a straight man who is philosophic, a cynic, a joker, a naïve girl, and the hermit himself—talk about his role like actors rehearsing a play. The drama consists rather in the conflict of points of view than in the development of character; it is like a witty "panel discussion" on television. The wag and the cynic conclude that the hermit, who has illusions of sainthood, has "dislocated his soul" and jestingly apply psychiatric "manipulation." As we note elsewhere, the stage becomes less an arena for actors than a discussion table where different voices may be heard, but where the chief note appears to be that nothingness is all.

ness in a long series of sudden shifts of demeanor, inconsistencies, changes of direction, and reversals that finally drive even patient Jude into angry expostulation. Sue is formally a rationalist rebel against conventions of various kinds, especially those that surround sexual attitudes and practices; but only profound jealousy of Jude's former wife, Arabella, can drive Sue, who has run away from her husband and is already in effect living with Jude, into becoming his mistress. This does not really solve her problem; the basic discords remain, pushed below the surface but bound to erupt when special blows or pressures disturb her precarious working equilibrium. The shock that destroys her factitious order is the violent death of the children: the eldest murders the two younger ones and commits suicide. Here, as often in modern formulations, a crisis is produced less by what the protagonist himself has done than by the impact upon him of events in which his own will has little or no part. True, Sue's will has been active in that she has imposed upon herself a pattern of life for which she does not have the resources, but it is not really this hubris that she discovers (though once she does say, of her rationalist opinions, "I was wrong—proud in my own conceit!" [Part VI, chap. iii]). The death of the children she takes as a judgment for living with Jude, and she then develops so profound a sense of guilt that it becomes an unalterable way of life: illness as a solution. Her self-castigation is fierce and unrelenting: ". . . we have been selfish, careless, even impious, . . . my monstrous errors, and all my sinful ways! . . . I am such a vile creature—too worthless to mix with ordinary human beings! . . . —you don't know my badness. . . ." (Part VI, chap. iii); "a poor wicked woman who is trying to mend!" (Part VI, chap. iv); [28] "We should mortify the flesh—the terrible flesh—the curse of Adam! . . . Self-renunciation—that's everything! I cannot humiliate myself too much. I should like to prick myself all over with pins and bleed out the badness that's in me!" (chap. iii). So, though she acknowledges that she loves Jude, she forces herself to go back to her legal husband Richard, whom she loathes—first to a nominal marriage, and then, as "penance," to "the ultimate thing. . . . I must do it—I must! I must drink to the dregs!" (chap. ix).[29] She has fulfilled her need by finding a scarcely endurable punishment that will continue until she dies. (In the concept of marriage as punishment Sue anticipates the title character of Duerrenmatt's *Marriage of Mr.*

Mississippi.) Scruple has become a whip and a wheel: the self-aware-ness needed for tragedy has become hypertrophic and monstrous, a factitious order is secured in a monopathy of anguish, and disaster stretches ahead interminably.*

When the tragic sentiment exists without the action that is proper to it, we have what might be called, by current fashion, the "tragedy complex." This may be a form of emotional self-indulgence; while the most familiar form of sentimentality is to be unable to believe any evil of oneself, it is equally sentimental to be able to believe only evil or failure of oneself. This may mean to retire into the egotism of pain, to give up, to find comfort only in discomfort, to devise roles of suffering that may be inwardly nourishing or outwardly remunerative, or even to wield the power of weakness. On the other hand, the tragic senti-ment may mean an assumption of primacy in a felt community of guilt, a keen ear for the call of public obligation. Rolf Hochhuth insists that the "individual . . . must always bear the responsibility not only for his family but for the entire community." [30] Obviously such an enlargement of private responsibility is a different thing from the pathological. It may conform to public truth, as with Oedipus; it

---

* The alternative is of course suicide; this is the way out for the girl simply named Zoe in James Saunders' *A Scent of Flowers* (produced, 1964). Zoe is, in effect, another version of Sue: she has inner contradic-tions finally summed up, on the one hand, in an affair with a married man and, on the other, in a strong attraction to the Catholic Church (with a lighted cigarette she burns a cross on her arm). However, Saunders is more interested in the clinical origins of Zoe's state (parents' broken marriage, very sensible but unloving stepmother) and in the ineffective-ness of all those who would help her or to whom she turns for help. One of these is a gay and imaginative uncle who amuses her with fairy stories, and on a crucial occasion, as he later puts it, with a "dirty fairy story" that leads to a sexual approach to her; this horrifies her and contributes directly to her suicide. The uncle's self-knowledge and remorse, occasionally breaking through his façade of ironic commentary, are a brief touch of the tragic in a play otherwise essentially pathetic. It makes much of the old tradition of the dead person who converses or seems to converse with the living (*Blithe Spirit, Outward Bound, Passing of the Third Floor Back*), and finally does a clever take-off on the Ophelia burial scene in *Hamlet*. A remark by John A. Meixner applies to all these cases of madness and death, whether literal or figurative, that we have noted: ". . . the resolu-tion of withdrawal, by suicide and insanity, from a world which is too horrible" is "not the resolution finally of great tragedy, . . ." This is in "The Saddest Story," *Kenyon Review*, XXII (1960), 264.

may mean the acceptance of a sacrificial role, as in *Murder in the Cathedral*. But it may also be, to return to the theme of morbidity, the self-glorification of a sick man, with the sad contentment of a secular Christ on a dream cross.* The ambiguity of self-sacrifice has been noted by Gide in a passage criticizing "Moralists and novelists" under the influence of La Rochefoucauld: "They have radically mis-prized the . . . human need for self-immolation—a need that on occasion can lead to the most fantastic vice or to the most sublime virtue." [31] Whether the manifestations are neurotic or healthy, the drawing of general responsibility to oneself is in sharp contrast with the melodramatic strategy: in that way of life one deals with general guilt by finding a public victim, that is, a scapegoat. At one ailing extreme, consciousness takes on excessive burdens; at the other, no burdens at all.

VI. THE CLAIMS OF MELODRAMA

In examining the abnormalities which I have called "guilt neu-rosis" and "innocence neurosis," I have perhaps been describing exceptional cases. We need not debate the fact or the degree of their exceptionalness. If they are exceptional, they are still representative in their own way, that is, they have the meaning which sickness always has for health. If they have this, they will provide additional means of distinguishing the tragic and melodramatic perspectives, which exist normally in life as well as in literary art. Tragedy is the world of self-awareness and contemplation, but if on the one hand we have to keep pointing out that our age neglects it, we have also to acknowl-edge that it is impossible to be tragic all the time; insofar as one has

---

* The martyr complex is at least suggested by certain romantic self-conceptions held by artists. See the chapter, "Poeta Dolorosus," in Walter H. Sokel's *The Writer in Extremis: Expressionism in Twentieth-Century German Literature* (Stanford, Calif.: Stanford University Press, 1959). Sokel remarks, "If the artist is compared to Christ it is, to be sure, a Christ seen through the lenses of the Storm and Stress and its worship of genius . . ." (p. 64). Again we may observe in pathological conditions a distinction between tragedy and melodrama: the tragic disorder is the "Christ complex," in which the person is overwhelmed by universal guilt and doomed, he believes, to suffering of the redemptive sort; the melo-dramatic disorder is the "Messiah complex," in which the person becomes a conqueror by carrying "the word" (it is doubtless not an accident that modern slang embodies the concept of the logos).

choices, one must know when to discover himself and when to act a part in the world of nature and of men. The most determined partisan of tragedy could not deny that melodrama is inevitable, at least as we conceive of reality now. For us, the two great centers of reality are public policy and the management of nature; we metaphysicalize the socio-political and the scientific, and so we are committed to these melodramas outside of self-knowledge. This is our world, and we are not freed from action in it. As liberals or conservatives, nationalists or internationalists, risk capitalists or social planners, glorying in our strength or fearing our weakness, we act our roles in the melodrama of history, expediently taking on the wholeness, the innocence, that frees us for public contention.

But the claim of melodrama is rooted not only in the nature of the world as we have constituted it, but in our own nature, in our own needs. Tragedy has powerful legitimate claims, but at times we must get away from it. We might paraphrase Anatole France's epigram on the sublime [32] and say, "Même le tragique ennuye." There is a sense in which *ennuyer* is the right word. It would not of course apply to the tensions of tragic crises, but it would become suitable as the tragic experience of detached understanding palled. The plain looking at self, the never complete assessment of the personal reality, has its limits, and we crave the reassuring excitement of action: when all dispassion is spent, the commitments of melodrama reinvigorate us. In another sense, *ennuyer* is not a strong enough word, for the tragic consciousness may become not merely dull or unproductive, but actually unendurable, or at least painfully troubling and perhaps injurious. As George Eliot put it in *Silas Marner*, apropos of Nancy Cass's self-castigation: "This excessive rumination and self-questioning is perhaps a morbid habit inevitable to a mind of much moral sensibility when shut out from its due share of outward activity and of practical claims on its affections . . . [and when] there are . . . no peremptory demands to divert energy from vain regret or superfluous scruple" (chap. xvii). Suffering can get out of hand and inhibit the "due share of outward activity." It may manifest itself in impotence in the very realm of responsibility, as in Henry VI; it may lead to disintegration, as in Blanche DuBois; it may end in a rejection of "practical claims on [the] affections" and a turning toward a self-inflicted incarceration in punitive misery, as in Sue Bridehead. These kinds of malady, including the "guilt neurosis," threaten all sentient people.

The problem fascinated Ibsen, and he returned to it several times as he explored different operations of the "sickly conscience." [33] In *The Wild Duck* Gregers Werle exhibits one version of the malady when, with the intention of righting the wrongs done by his father, he applies a doctrinaire idealism in managing his own life and in trying to remodel the life of a friend. In *The Master Builder* Solness tries to escape the disease, or to deny its hold upon himself, by a self-assertive, venturesome act—the symbolic climb to the tower of his newest edifice. The fullest treatment of the sickly conscience, however, is the analysis of Rosmer in *Rosmersholm*, whose growth of knowledge and hence of guilt incapacitates him for living. Obviously, suicide is not a "normal" flight from tragic pain. The fact that Rosmer dies emphasizes the strain of dividedness from which most men need to fly at times; they must escape from the anguish of a real wholeness into a therapeutic quasi-wholeness, and if their state is not pathological, they find it within life. Twice Ibsen portrays spirited women—Hilda Wangel in *The Master Builder* and Rebecca West in *Rosmersholm* —who in effect offer a reckless or ruthless pursuit of ends as a healthy alternative to the "sickly conscience." Their version of the melodramatic salvation is to autonomize "drive." It is one of the possible routes to pragmatic unity in worldly action: it may serve in the ordinary competitions of life, in the promotion of causes,* the pursuit of personal or community ends, or of private or group ends (whether or not these are generally sanctioned). Claudius plunges from anguish into plans for murder, Hamlet from his own painful divisions into forthright action; Celia, in Eliot's *Cocktail Party*, wants to find her way from a sense of "sin" into a unifying mode of action; we see Orestes making every effort to escape from the domination of Furies

---

* It is possible that the world owes a considerable amount of crusading to people who are unconsciously in vigorous flight from division and need almost constantly the therapy of "pragmatic unity." The sort of repellent rigidity that we sometimes find in the year-in-and-year-out workers in public causes—even when we approve the causes—reflects, perhaps, a laborious willing of wholeness; what appears as self-righteousness may be the effect of a half-felt "self-wrongness" under forced submission to "right" ends. "How lean men grow who try to save the world," remarks Mephistopheles in Dorothy Sayers' *The Devil to Pay*, with a glance at Cassius.

and go back into ordinary life; Bosola can leap from bitterness and self-confrontation into further destructive moves against the Duchess of Malfi.

A man can escape not only from suffering to energizing, from passion to action, but from one kind of feeling to another. There is the illuminating experience of an American who had occasion to visit, after the 1939 war, and before there was time for reconstruction, the bombed areas in England and in Germany. He reported that he felt much more uneasy in devastated Frankfort than in devastated London. In Germany he found it difficult to free himself from the guilt that seemed inevitably entailed in that vast destruction. But in London he was free to feel indignation at another's wantonness, and this emotion was immeasurably more agreeable than guilt. Precisely: his trip from Germany to England is an excellent symbol of the saving flight from the realm of tragedy to the realm of melodrama—not a final forgetting and rejection of burdens, but a temporary relief from them. Hickey, in *The Iceman Cometh*, puts the need thus: "There's a limit to the guilt you can feel and the forgiveness and pity you can take! You have to begin blaming someone else, too" (Act IV). However little we may relish Hickey as truthteller, his words do put the case for one melodramatic sentiment: blame is one of the psychic aids to survival.* It is at least so for some people. Yet three nineteenth-century novelists, in noting the same situation, gave it a different emphasis. In *Silas Marner* George Eliot let Hickey's sentiment be expressed by Priscilla Lammeter, who, as a rather comic chatterbox, simply does not speak with authority: ". . . there's nothing kills a man so soon as having nobody to find fault with but himself. It's a deal the best way o' being master, to let somebody else do the ordering, and keep the blaming in your own hands" (chap. xvii). Gogol directly criticizes a General Betrishchev, who retired from the

---

* While I was working on this section, I remarked to a colleague, without explanation or definitions, that I was writing about the "melodrama of blame." My colleague, evidently feeling that the use of the word *melodrama* was too flippant for the context, retorted, quickly and almost challengingly, "But you have to blame in order to survive." An intellectual with an intelligent grownup's self-consciousness, he furnished evidence not only of the ordinary need of the melodramatic posture, but of the tendency to justify it without reservation—a contemporary tendency, I have suggested.

service because of troubles, "putting the blame on some hostile party and lacking the magnanimity to blame himself for anything." [34] Dostoevski remarks ironically that "generally speaking, every public scandal cheers a Russian up no end." [35] Not only Russians, but everyone wants to feel "right," and one of the ways of doing this is to put the finger on those who are wrong.* We move happily into what E. M. Forster brilliantly called "the outer world of telegrams and anger" (*Howards End*), into the exhilarating life of *J'accuse* and *écrasez l'infame*. We can enjoy being "too angry with the world to see it clearly." [36] Our innocence rings out cheeringly, because we are not implicated in a given evil, such as anti-Dreyfusism, or do not know we are, or forget we are, or because by attacking it we are scourged or purged. Blame is a moral sedative, of course, and for modern man a life without some sedatives is unimaginable; but we have only to mention sedatives to be reminded that there is such a thing as an overdose.

Indignation and Genre

Indignation is stirring, exalting. It has a public function: it concentrates energies for the rigors of combat, whether for war or for its moral equivalents. It has a private function: as a unifier of emotions, it cures the painful divergency of feelings present in states of high self-awareness, and it is a preventive of the melancholic states that

* This stance leads to the kind of rhetoric which, to a reader of any experience, seems laughable. The rhetoric is exactly adapted to the melodramatic situation: it is total defense or attack, with all qualifications out, and hence moves inevitably toward the "high sounding" or the "noble." The "sentiments" exemplified in the speeches of Joseph Surface are another rhetorical reflection of the melodramatic perspective: they embody a program of "good" conduct in implicit opposition to bad conduct. Incidentally, the burlesquing of such rhetoric may involve, in addition to the overt fun making, an oblique indulgence in the pleasures of the melodramatic style. It is possible, also, that the entertainment in such older stage fare as *The Drunkard* is ambiguous: behind the self-conscious laughter at obsolete styles may lurk a secret engagement in a kind of conflict that, whatever the playful absurdities of the detail, has deep roots in our emotional habits.

The rhetoric of self-justification has interesting forms. One of these is to state a private preference as a general law, to transpose "I prefer to live in New York" into "New York is the only place to live." In this way, as in melodrama, one is not a willful person but identifies oneself with a principle of right conduct.

occur at the other end of the melodramatic spectrum.[37] It is the ultimate unquestioning, unquestionable assertion of our own rectitude. Through it we soar into simple, untragic excitement. "Perhaps the ultimate statement made by tragedy," suggests David Daiches, "is that the moral universe is more complicated and more self-contradictory than we can allow ourselves to think in our daily lives." [38] The opposite of the "complicated" and the "self-contradictory," as we have seen, is war, and, as James Cox has observed, "the moral indignation required to prosecute [wars] is a simplification of life into a morality play." [39] If war is lacking, one can war against a minority. The anti-Semite, according to Sartre, "chooses to live permanently in the state of anger and indignation which normal people undergo only rarely. He also chooses to run away from his own deep inconsistency by assuming the rock-like solidity of a person governed by an irresistible passion." [40] Indignation is easily come by or administered; we become indignant readily, for in a culture heavy with melodrama there are many popular, easily recognizable symbols of evil that pop into view or can be brought into play with little effort, and make us respond quickly. Hence indignation has a danger in public life: it is only too available, as an instrument of manipulation, to anyone who wants to use groups or nations to his own ends, and to secure blind actions instead of a scrutiny of options.

Novelists of two centuries and four countries have noted the way in which indignation may be used toward an end, discovered by a needy ego, or enjoyed simply as a form of emotional high life. In *The Warden* Trollope writes astringently of "Eager pushing politicians" who in the House of Commons attacked grasping priests "with very telling indignation" (chap. ii). In *Dead Souls* (1842) Gogol describes " 'frustrated' men . . . strange and uncomfortable characters who cannot endure not only injustices, but what they believe to be injustices [cf. Sayers' Faustus] . . . demanding indulgences for themselves but full of intolerance for others, they made a very great impression . . . by . . . their noble indignation against society." [41] Their "noble indignation" so misleads one man that he loses both his sense of reality and his job. The narrator of Camus's *The Fall*, a lawyer who has managed at least a sardonic self-assessment, says of his self-conscious appearances in court, "I am sure you would have admired . . . the restrained indignation of my speeches. . . ." [42]

Simone de Beauvoir presents Nadine, in *The Mandarins*, as a character who loses no "opportunities to become indignant," who, indeed, "would refuse to understand in order not to spoil the pleasure of venting her indignation." [43] Saul Bellow's Moses Herzog observes, "While in the parlors of indignation the right-thinking citizen brings his heart to a boil." [44] Indignation has also a danger for the practitioner: an emotion at once so easy and so satisfying may easily become a habit. What is admirable as a tonic may be harmful as a diet. Hence the severe disparagement by the narrator in Walter Allen's *All in a Lifetime* (1959) who, by now a relatively wise old man, declares, "ever since I have been on guard against feelings of moral indignation in myself. I almost think now that moral indignation is the most suspect and most worthless of all emotions." [45]

To return from the emotion to the problem of genre: ". . . to be ruled by indignation, however righteous," Edward Rosenberry observes, "is to subvert tragedy to melodrama." [46] Exactly. One may agree to this, however, and still acknowledge that, as a temporary alleviation for troubles of mind and heart, the indignant-melodramatic posture may not be entirely worthless. Well persons in need of relief do not become drug addicts or followers of medicine men. Rather, living as much of a melodrama as the conditions of life require and experiencing as much of its emotional content as is necessary to well-being, they are thus freed for the other realm of activities that are centered in the problems of dividedness and of self-knowledge. So we come full circle: if man must at times escape from tragedy to melodrama, melodramatic activity may restore him for the more exacting life of tragedy.*

---

* Obviously the issue turns on the old problem of whether a certain kind of emotional exercise creates a deleterious habit or effects a salutary purge (the Platonic and Aristotelian views on the effect of tragic poetry). It is not altogether settled by the distinction between the well and the ill, since this is an old borderline dispute, doubtless never to be wholly resolved.

We cannot speak of indignation without noting the problem of satire and how it works. We have previously pointed out the affinity between the melodramatic and the satirical: both pit an essentially "whole" individual against an outside entity. (Hence I find untenable Wyndham Lewis' idea of the coalescence of satire and tragedy in a "*grinning* tragedy," for the conception ignores the structural differences and depends upon a loose popular use of the word *tragedy*. Cf. Elliott, *The Power of Satire*, p. 226.

Cf. also the present volume, Chapter 2, note 6, and the Kernan passage cited there.) It follows that it is the nature of satire, not to offer enlightenment, but to gratify a pre-existent antagonism. At most, perhaps, it might have the effect of enlightenment by crystallizing a vague hostility that has not yet found its precise intellectual and moral structure. Cf. Edward W. Rosenheim, Jr., *Swift and the Satirist's Art* (Chicago: University of Chicago Press, 1963), pp. 12–13.

Beyond this lies the problem of the psychological working of the satirical experience. Like melodrama, satire separates people into victims and victors, and we can consider the probable response of each. It seems safe to assume that satire rarely has a beneficial impact on the "victims," that is, the imperfect human beings who (in their types, attitudes, conduct, styles) are its object; it is highly unlikely that it leads them to a new perspective on themselves. It may create a related but different effect, a kind of undefined uneasiness, and this may express itself in plums or poison for the satirist (cf. Elliott, *The Power of Satire*, p. 266); in either case we can see the target leaping for protection against darts and knowledge. As in melodrama of triumph, virtually all readers will identify themselves with the "victors," i.e., the implicit possessors of right thought and action in whose name the shafts are aimed at the delinquents. For these, satire is a source of great pleasure; it is a fine channel for what we denote by the cliché term "aggressiveness," for the impulse to show contempt and inflict injury. Obviously, this experience is a source, not of self-knowledge, but of self-esteem. Does it lead, then, simply to complacency? Or, alternatively, does it permit the working off (the "catharsis") of a disturbing antipathy, and thus free the person for other pursuits? Perhaps we can distinguish between those for whom it has this effect, and those who become addicted to satire as a necessity of habitual malice.

A still more complicated subject is that of the nature of the satirist's experience. Is he a man living out a melodrama in his work, the voice of righteousness against evil? Apropos of our context, the role of indignation, Martin Price makes a sharp summary antithesis: "A man may write satire because he is indignant, but he may also cultivate his indignation in order to write satire." This is in *To the Palace of Wisdom* (Garden City, N.Y.: Doubleday, 1964), p. 16.

CHAPTER FIVE

Tragic and Melodramatic Realms:
Explorations II

WE HAVE noted the legitimate claims of the melodramatic: the necessity for action in the world, and our own need to escape a sense of guilt and dividedness which may become destructive and to take refuge in the pragmatic innocence and unity of relationships in the world. In pragmatic innocence we discover the guilt of others, whether we skirmish successfully against it, or only become innocent victims of it. Thomas Mann has put the psychic and even moral case for the melodramatic activity: "Hitler had the great merit of producing a simplification of the emotions, of calling forth a wholly unequivocal No, a clear and deadly hatred. The years of struggle against him had been morally a good era." [1]

I. FLIGHTS IN OPPOSITE DIRECTIONS

We do not often have such clear menaces to call forth a total No. Since a real menace does paradoxically afford us a sanctuary from the stresses of personality, with its confused clamor of No and Yes, we can understand the semiconscious search for menaces that can become sanctuaries. On the other hand, well people do not stay in the sanctuary of melodrama indefinitely; they sense it as a limited enclosure and seek wider, even if more troubling, horizons. We have contradictory impulses: if we flee tragedy, some saving impulse generally leads us back to it.* The return flight to the tragic awareness is put with fine concision by Jeremiah Beaumont in Robert Penn Warren's *World Enough and Time:* "For I had sought innocence, and had fled into the brute wilderness where all is innocence, for all is the same in that darkness, and even the shameful canker is innocence. But that innocence is what man cannot endure and be man, and now I flee from innocence and toward my guilt. . . ." [2] The direct, conscious flight from innocence is not a frequent way of growing into tragic consciousness, since it is an ultimate form of that acknowledgment of guilt which always comes hard. Yet Jeremiah's flight provides us with a useful pattern of understanding. In fact, there is a scale of possible attitudes toward the defects of life which we tend to perceive first as social or political ills. The simplest attitude is one of "protest"; there is an evil for which an individual or group is to be declared responsible and punished. The ritual of blame and penalty is familiar in history and in polemic literature. Who was guilty—the captain of the *Stockholm*, or the captain of the *Andrea Doria?* † Get

---

* The frequent discovery of fear and even cowardice by the novelists of two world wars may be a reaction against melodramatic quasi-wholeness. It is possible, of course, that the wide notation of fear may be a subtle form of self-pity: "I am a victim of the war; it has no claim on me, but is making demands; I am innocent, and in no way need I pretend to accept the values that it tries to impose; if I admit that I am afraid, this is really a way of pointing to a tyranny that I should be free of." Thus the very admission of the unheroic may be a way, not of complicating character by displaying the flaw in the good man, but of converting the experience from the heroic melodrama into its cousin, the melodrama of defeat. I rather doubt that this is what happens, but it should be offered as a possibility. For there is a sour note in the contemporary fashion of the unheroic: the notation of weakness, though it may take something from the style of tragedy, may be a strategy of self-exculpation amid disaster or of surrender, as if to a catastrophe of nature.

† The collision of the *Stockholm* and the *Andrea Doria* (1956) not far from New York seemed so incredible that it evoked, I believe, considerable detached speculation. Even though this may never have been formulated in such a question as, "What happened here that mirrors us to ourselves?" still the general curiosity was different from the insurance melodrama in which all participants wanted to affix blame on someone else. For once it appeared difficult to invoke the greatest metaphor of nonresponsibility,

the evidence and penalize the culprit. For many people of honesty and intelligence, this is the whole duty of man. We do not decry this quest for justice if we point to another level of approach: the kind of examination in which the vigor of inquiry survives the certainty of sure black-and-white results. Ibsen remarked at one time that he was less intent upon finding answers than upon asking questions, and something of this attitude appears even in such a topical play as *A Doll's House*. In this attitude one asks, not "Who killed cock robin, and what shall we do to him?" but "What kind of man is the killer?" and "What is his relation to me?"

If we have asked this last question, we have gone on toward the final stage of a progressive understanding which began with the simplicities of detection and punishment: in this stage we look at the misdeed from the inside, that is, through the consciousness of a doer who is capable of coming to knowledge of himself. He is an Everyman, and we all share in the possibilities of evil—as well as of good—concentrated in him. Now the evil is no longer isolated, a local infection to be dealt with by a board of health acting for us; we no longer postulate a utopia cleaned up by right-minded and technically proficient community action. We may move from easy castigation of others in a manner like that of the American abolitionist Theodore Weld, who "withdrew from active propagandizing because . . . he found that 'he himself needed reforming' and that he 'had been laboring to destroy evil in the same spirit as his antagonists.' " [3] Thus we come to know more about the nature of man, and to give up illusions about him and about ourselves. In one respect this means recognizing his, and our, instinct and capacity for evil, and retreating from dreams of innocence. At the same time it means reasserting the human capacity for insight, for man's seeing himself in a new perspective.

The pleasures of finger pointing—a danger of the picket-and-protest way of life—are so strong that it is not easy to give them up and move on to a self-knowledge and perhaps self-incrimination. Iago's stiff upper lip, criminal's though it is, is in favor with us: "From this

---

"act of God," that summation of cosmic melodrama which may mean objectively a natural cataclysm or subjectively a participant's quest of his own innocence.

time forth I will never speak word." * The reluctance to make admissions slides into self-concealment from the self. This makes Hermann Hesse insist that men should "flee from innocence." The issue is put with great immediacy in some autobiographical words spoken by the hero of *Steppenwolf*:

> Now and again I have expressed the opinion that every nation, and even every person, would do better, instead of rocking himself to sleep with political catchwords about war-guilt, to ask himself how far his own faults and negligences and evil tendencies are guilty of the war and all the other wrongs of the world, and that there lies the only possible means of avoiding the next war. They don't forgive me that, for, of course, they are themselves all guiltless, the Kaiser, the generals, the trade magnates, the politicians, the papers. Not one of them has the least thing to blame himself for. Not one has any guilt. . . . To reflect for one moment, to examine himself for a while and ask what share he has in the world's confusion and wickedness—look you, nobody wants to do that.

Hesse puts his finger on the universal passion to see life as a melodrama instead of a tragedy. From 1922 on he pointed more than once to man's weakness for blaming others and thus escaping a sense of his own guilt.[4] So he helped maintain the tragic consciousness in the artist's characteristic way: forging the conscience of the race by subtly communicating to it his sense of reality.

II. POINT OF VIEW AND GENRE

The sense of reality determines the point of view and hence the central form of the work. In the conversion of raw material into drama, the writer will produce melodrama if he adopts one point of view, tragedy if he adopts another. The artist's choice of point of

---

* Iago's speech is oddly echoed in the final speech of Franceschina, the title character of John Marston's almost contemporary *The Dutch Courtesan* (1605); in her, however, the note of melodramatic toughness is hardly consistent with the medley of farce and homily that have gone before. To shift from literature to life: the confession and self-accusation that used to be an aspect of Russian political trials, and even of Russian political life generally, were abhorrent in the West because they seemed false, a parody of the tragic achievement of self-knowledge. Yet to some extent, perhaps, we resist the whole idea of self-accusation, even while admiring the assumption of responsibility which is implicit in it. The coexistence of contradictory attitudes is expectable: the fluctuating conflict of the melodramatic and tragic instincts.

view, in turn, is a consequence (and therefore an index) of his way of perceiving the materials. His philosophic understanding is the basic influence upon the form of the work, the structuring of materials. It may compel his very selection of materials: one kind of pessimism may draw him to physical or natural or circumstantial catastrophes that cannot allow him much interpretative freedom. He may find himself limited to the pathetic, as in *Riders to the Sea*, or the irony of events, as in *The Bridge of San Luis Rey*. Such materials would hardly permit tragic effects unless the writer, by a truly heroic transformation, could present catastrophes as in some way "chosen" by those who experience them.

But if what he has before him is a story, not of catastrophes outside the realm of choice, but of human misdoing, he does have various options; and what kind of work he writes depends on his sense of meaning. What does he see in the misdeeds that have caught his eye? A story about a victim? Or a story about a doer of wrong? Most important: can he conceive of a wrongdoer who is still a sentient person, endowed with a moral awareness with which he must reckon? Or to ask the same question in terms of artistic form: does the dramatist have the reader adopt the point of view of the victim of evil, or the point of view of the doer? Can he make the doer an Everyman in whom the reader is forced to see himself? Here is the fundamental inner decision that will take the drama toward one genre or another. If for the artist the center of reality is the victim of evil, and it is the victim's perspective of events that determines the form, the result will be a melodrama of disaster or a problem play; but if the artist finds reality centering in the consciousness of the doer, and communicates with us primarily through that consciousness, he will write in the tragic form. He could of course write from the point of view of a morally unsentient doer of evil; he would then have a special kind of melodrama, with strong overtones of the tour de force—as in Alain Robbe-Grillet's *The Voyeur* (1955), in which, because there is nowhere else to go, the reader is forced to share the identity of a homicidal pervert.* This is a special development of modern experimentation; its possibilities are not yet clear. As far as the great mass

* This way of positioning the reader is not altogether a rarity in mid-twentieth century, when innovation often takes the form of adopting a specialized, extramural, or "sick" point of view and apparently giving this

of literary evidence goes, the work "belongs" to the wrongdoer (e.g., Macbeth) only when the wrongdoing is understood as a deviation and we are aware that the wrongdoer is suppressing, or moving toward a resumption of, full consciousness.

Suppose a playwright has his imagination stirred by a plot in which a woman is cruelly treated by relatives who do not like her marriage. What does he see at the center of it—the problem of the cruel relatives, or the problem of the sufferer? Is she in any way responsible for her suffering, or is she simply a victim? Are the cruel relatives simply monsters, or is their cruelty meaningful as an illness or a flaw that, though terrible, is somehow understandable? Is their cruelty total, as in allegory, or is it an evil possibility in characters that have the main lineaments of humanity? The materials have to be understood or "felt" by the artist in one way or another; it is his sensibility, the quality of his insight, that is responsible for the form of the work, and his answers to the preceding questions will push him toward a melodramatic or a tragic form. Now suppose that our hypothetical playwright, as he works out his plot, finds it necessary that the cruel relatives have an undercover agent to carry out their evil designs. This agent begins to develop his own character, indeed, turns out to be an only partly willing agent, led by his own distortions of personality into deeds that he will later repent of and will try to expiate by inflicting revenge on those whose own acts of vengeance he has aided. Here, unmistakably, is a complex character, who has got into his creator's imagination and grown to such proportions that he is worthy of primary attention. But the dramatist is unable to let this character take over; instead he is charmed by the pure suffering of the woman, and fascinated by the pure villainy of her relatives. So to the

---

authority; there are familiar instances in Samuel Beckett, Edward Albee, John Osborne, and Harold Pinter. Here the melodrama of the outsider against the establishment, using these words in the most inclusive possible sense, carries a romantic attitude on toward an attenuated extreme and at the same time, despite the original decor, drifts back toward an older allegory or morality play. For the maimed personality—as in *The Zoo Story*, *Endgame*, and *Look Back in Anger*—speaks less for the human personality, in either of the major postures that we are considering here, than it does for fragments of the psyche and for concepts; in its unconscious adaptation of pre-Renaissance forms, it is a sort of theatrical pre-Raphaelitism. Despite the philosophic divergence, such works are akin to Hugo von Hofmannsthal's *Everyman*.

victim he gives first place, and to the villains second place, and allots only a lesser role to the villains' agent, whose conflicting passions make him more interesting than any of them.

Here are, of course, the outlines of Webster's *The Duchess of Malfi*, which we discussed in Chapter 2. By looking at the material in this abstract and nameless form, I have hoped to escape the impact of the actual, completed play, to look at the raw materials of the plot as though they were unformed, and hence to see them as open to several kinds of treatment, nontragic and tragic. This procedure is a way of emphasizing the fact that Webster chose, or was compelled, to organize the materials in a particular way. He could not take the Duchess beyond innocence, or give her brothers a share of innocence, or subordinate all of them to the richer character of Bosola, who craves innocence while choosing guilt. He has simply put us on the side of the suffering Duchess and against her evil brothers. His choice of this point of view reveals his way of intuiting the story.

On the other hand it is easy to imagine how certain familiar tragedies might, under the hand of artists with a different orientation, have turned out to be melodramas. Sophocles might have dramatized the Oedipus story from the point of view of Creon: there would have been plenty of conflict in this arrangement of sides, what with Oedipus' suspicions of and hostility to Creon. Creon might have been the district attorney, ferreting out the origins of illness in the state, pressing home the case against the miscreant King, and eventually cleaning up Thebes. We would have the easy experience of being identified with decency, order, and justice; the only pangs to be shared would be those of the temporary distress caused by royal misconduct; and we could salve our limited suffering by blaming the King. If we think of the story in terms of this familiar simplicity, we are the more able to recognize what a vast feat of the imagination Sophocles has performed in making us participate in a life which, though it is a web of fantastic episodes, yet makes an extraordinarily inclusive sweep through human feelings: the delusion of security, readiness for responsibility, paranoid suspiciousness, persistence under difficulty, explosive intemperateness, resistance to easy ways out of present trouble, willfulness, determination, indulgence in accusation, courage, boastfulness, acceptance of guilt, pride in intellect, self-understanding. In sum, Sophocles has overcome enormous odds to force us into tragic experience. He has taken a wildly incredible story of parricide and incest and so placed us at the center of it that we have to undergo a world of human reality.*

His achievement through point of view stands out more sharply if we note the choices made by some modern dramatists when they look at such materials. Though not always, they are likely to be driven toward the pathological, as was O'Neill with the *Oresteia* and Cocteau with the *Oedipus Rex*. We are fascinated by the schemata of pathology, especially when these wield power through novelty and appear to revise the physical and psychological landscape. The sole point here is that pathological phenomena have to overcome great handicaps to contribute to tragic effect. The characters are likely to be partial people instead of whole people; the clinic is an exotic realm, not a mirror of our own; it may shock or hypnotize or even delight (compare the madhouse which no one leaves in Weiss's Marat-Sade play [1964], the sanitarium in Duerrenmatt's *The Physicists* [1962], and the asylum scenes in *Peer Gynt* [1867]), but it does not invite; we stay outside, clinging to our wellness. We are not in the density and sweep of tragic experience, but are separated from the sick, looking in at them as we might at specimens in an exhibit case. Despite a great deal of ingenious and even absorbing detail, Cocteau in *The Infernal Machine* (1934) trivializes the Oedipus story: he gives us the Oedipus complex instead of a complex Oedipus. At Cocteau's obtuse honor-roll juvenile and his neurotic mamma we simply gaze in astonishment, often captivated by the inventive machinery, but hardly convinced by the trappings of allegory by which a modish side-show avers that it encloses a significant myth.

---

* Shakespeare might have written *Macbeth* from the point of view of Macduff and Malcolm. We would then be allied with the "good government" people; the action of the play would turn entirely on the deposition of a bloody tyrant. What we would not have, except perhaps in glimpses, is the intimate experience of Macbeth's ambition, surely representative ambition, in conflict with the rest of his personality; we would not have the "feeling knowledge" of it that is now the rich center of the play. We would not live through his strenuous efforts to translate desire into destiny and to choke off consciousness of all moral obstacles. Instead we would see Macbeth as a kind of Hitler, and the human origins of evil in the state would be away from us, lodged in a deviate; we would remain good citizens, frightened but not torn, innocent opponents of ruthless power snatchers.

It takes a great dramatist to envisage the malfunctionings of human life, not as stemming from the eccentricities and barbarisms of "others" but as rooted in the characteristic longings and temptations of Everyman, and to organize his visions of reality in ways that force us into identity with that Everyman. To repeat: this is a technical problem of point of view, but the point of view is determined or made possible by the sense of where the potential for evil lies. Melodrama is separatist: in it, guilt belongs to nations, classes, parties to which we do not belong, or to monstrous individuals, with whom we are not identified; trouble springs from causes in nature and in some natures, but not really in human nature generally, or at least not in *my* nature. I am innocent—the paranoid isolation that lies at the logical end of the melodramatic line. But if this separatism has played a rather heavy role in modern theater, the melodramatic view is never wholly satisfying, and we find constant signs of movement toward the tragic consciousness. It has always been important to Eliot, even where he was deliberately using the comedy-of-manners mode. O'Neill was fascinated by it, though in his most intense and passionate play he had to deny the human power to endure it. Tennessee Williams, as we shall see, is strongly attracted to it more than once, most notably in *Streetcar Named Desire* and *Cat on a Hot Tin Roof*. Arthur Miller has developed steadily toward the tragic perspective; though *After the Fall* has a melodramatic structure based on Quentin's dominant habit of judging others, a key point in the play is the formal dismissal of the belief in one's own innocence that Quentin implicitly exemplifies. Some of the best expressionists are drawn to inner ills that are characteristically human rather than eccentric or clinical.

III. Crisis, Survival, and Genre

In certain periods the tragic consciousness may not be possible. When war or other crises raise problems of physical survival, it may not be expedient to examine one's own guilt. These conditions may demand only vigorous unreflective action, and the tragic vision is perhaps a flower of times when troubles are not immediate and pressing. We may have to think of "disaster areas" in time that are comparable to those in physical place. There are historical "moments" of disaster—the moments when what is cherished ends. Some of these moments are long, some brief. Ironically, however, shorter moments of disaster can lengthen into hours, and hours into "periods," because in a dim way we are willing to have them do so. The atmosphere of disaster, if not the blunt fact of disaster, has a mysterious attractiveness, and it is the apparently unanswerable justification for the prolonged stoppage or postponement of troubling introspection. A crisis in society, or even in personal relations, is an extension of the charms of war into nonmilitary scenes. Exciting conflict subdues reflection. As the title character of Anouilh's *Becket* (1959) says to King Henry, "In a week we will face the King of France's army and there will be simple answers to everything at last." [5] Simple polemics—literal war or figurative fighting—are exhilarating; we are able to take the polemic in liberal doses. With us, this is the favorite form of eternal vigilance. Melodrama, as we have seen, is the aesthetic version of polemics, and for that reason we take to it readily, on the whole more readily than to the contemplative that appears in both the true comic and the tragic.

Polemic zeal may present itself to us as the love of survival. The right to survive seems so fundamental that in a crisis we automatically lay aside all questions of deserts and guilt; hence we are gratified if we can convert all troubling inner states into the sentiment of survival. Since the primacy of survival strikes us as axiomatic, it may seem almost outrageous to inquire whether physical survival is actually an obligation that supersedes all others. But it is one thing to survive against a natural danger; it is another to survive in a war that one has provoked; it is still another to survive by not hearing imperatives that might lead to death. Again the problem is what I have defined as the distinction between quantity of life and quality of life, which may be seen in hyperbolically pure form in the credos of Falstaff and Hotspur. If the survivalist temper had been stronger in Hamlet, he might have lived more easily. Yet mere survival fails to satisfy us, and we have to dignify the polemic exploit by insisting, not on personal or group survival, but on the survival of the idea which is greater than we as individuals or groups—the idea of "democracy" or "Western civilization" or "Christian civilization." Fortunately we are also able to make jokes about our survivalism, as in the sergeant's sarcasm to the private: "What do you want to do? Live forever?"

When we see present life as a fight for survival, we are least inclined to yield to the tragic sense. In view of the crisis atmosphere of modern life, it is perhaps surprising that we have as many manifestations of the tragic awareness as we have, surprising that a major novelist can have a character stop in mid-melodrama of survival, reverse his course, and resolve that his need is to "flee from innocence." Granted, Warren's *World Enough and Time* is about a nineteenth-century character. Tragic drama tends to be written long after the supposed occurrence of the events that provide the plot—after the myth has lost its urgency and immediacy as a confrontation of reality, as in the high period of Greek tragedy, or after the Britons, Scots, Danes, Italians, and Romans had done the deeds that were transformed into Shakespeare's plots. Tragedy is less an analysis of current life than it is a post-mortem. My point here is that the longer we can keep on viewing our own history as a battle, the longer we can live polemically in the present, the more likely we are to be able to eliminate all post-mortems and what they tell us about current reality.

We may assume that the seductive power of melodrama is not permanent and that at some time a tragic artist will offer us an understanding of the modern world quite different from that which is available to us who live in it polemically, and who variously hurl shafts against materialism and ecclesiasticism, rationalism and mysticism, totalitarianism and anarchism, and whatever antagonisms we believe threaten us in an unending crisis. Primarily he will have to discover the nature of our own complicity, to find the roots of this in human impulses, and so present this that no reader could deny his own involvement. European writers have made some interesting approaches to the problem. Arthur Koestler's *Darkness at Noon* (1951), as dramatized by Sidney Kingsley, looks at communism, not as an evil that good men should put down, but as a way of life that a good man can be drawn into. Sartre's *Altona* (1959) examines Nazism and its ability to thrive by drawing on human characteristics that are not found only among sick people. Max Frisch repeatedly treats political enormities of the Nazi type as traceable to universal human characteristics.

One would like to see an artist deal comparably with situations closer to home. One possibility for the native tragic hero is the man who, starting as a political idealist, becomes so entangled in devious means that he brings about his own ruin and the near ruin of his political community. Yet his motives are those of his age: impatience of limits, immanent material utopianism, the "intemperate and willful assault upon reality which so characterizes the modern world. . . ."[6] A still more profound tragic hero would be the "good man" embodying all the impulses that go into racism. The dramatist's problem would be to make him undeniably the Everyman in whom we see ourselves, not the partial man, the simply evil man, the person other than ourselves whom we can blame, as we easily do in melodramatic mood. Fight evils in the world we must; that melodrama is not to be avoided. But the wisest of leaders against racism have been saying that public ameliorative acts, essential as they are, will not go far without a change of heart. That is to say, in my terms, that the ultimate action has to go beyond the melodramatic and become tragic. The tragedy of Everyman as racist would have extraordinary resonance: inner life and public catastrophe, and the evil of the past rising to doom the present. But perhaps that tragedy can be written only in retrospect.

IV. POLEMICS AND GENRE

Man has contradictory impulses, as we have seen: now he seeks the tragic, now he flees from it. The very flight from the tragic may be an important constituent of tragic action: in one tragic structure, indeed, the hero tries to live in a melodrama and comes to learn that he must live in a tragedy.[7] He tries, in other terms we have used, to take a part for the whole, but he cannot long escape the whole.

Gloucester tries to take the actual political world for the whole of life, to live as it does and get along in it, to survive "by not hearing imperatives that might lead to death." But the imperatives become louder, and eventually he acknowledges the tragic wholeness. At the opposite extreme, Gregers Werle tries to take his own ideal construction for the whole of life and to make actuality conform to it, for both himself and the Hjalmar Ekdal family. The recalcitrance of the actual wakens him to the partialness of the ideal. An analogous situation is that of Dorothy Sayers' reformist Faustus. O'Neill's Emperor Jones subjects his realm to the yoke of a rationalist materialism whose profits, he believes, are the truth of life; but he is destroyed when the other part of the whole—the forgotten irrational—asserts itself. Lear tries to take his own will as the whole determinant of history, and learns that many wills, and more than one renunciation, enter into the whole. Macbeth strives to make his "vaulting ambition" alone mold a world for him, doing duty for the whole scale of human values— values that he struggles to suppress as they rebelliously surge up to raise disorder in his mind.

The endeavor to live the partial life of melodrama may mean that one chooses the polemic mode when it is not suitable. Though many men, as we have seen, appear to need the spirit of blame at times or even all the time, a character may invoke it simply as a means, perhaps unconscious, of evading tragic awareness. This human tactic, in recent times a commonplace of psychological knowledge, has always had an obvious utility on the stage, and the finger of blame has been a staple of popular melodramatic theater since the eighteenth century. What kind of art comes out of the polemic style depends on how well the dramatist understands both its meaning and the range of other options that lie before his character. Three plays, two of the eighteenth century, and one of the twentieth—George Lillo's *London Merchant* (1731), Richard Sheridan's *School for Scandal* (1777), and John Osborne's *Look Back in Anger* (1956)—provide examples of different attitudes in dramatists. Lillo aspires to tragedy, but is led astray by an irresistible impulse to assume the shrill tones of condemnation. With one hand Lillo makes Barnwell tragically responsible for his own downfall; with the other he undermines tragic effect by rhetorically blaming Barnwell's downfall on the prostitute Millwood, and Millwood's, in turn, on society. Not only does this finger pointing muddle the focus, but it helps reduce Barnwell's self-accusation, already sentimental, to hysterical self-abasement.

The other two plays are, of course, in a different mode—Sheridan's is partly comedy of manners, and Osborne's is what might be called "bleak comedy" *—but what they do is relevant to our discussion.

---

* By "bleak comedy" I mean that form of adjustment to the world (the archetypal action of comedy) in which too much of adult sentience and wisdom has to be left out. Cf. "black comedy," the term that has been applied to Joe Orton's *Entertaining Mr. Sloane* (1963): the adjustment is accomplished with so much loss of adult moral sentience that the mood is cynical. This is the tradition of Machiavelli's *Mandragola*. "Light comedy" is the form in which the obstacles to adjustment are not severe enough to inhibit a solution in terms of dominant current values (e.g., Lessing's *Minna von Barnhelm* or, in opera, the story of Mozart's *Così fan tutte*). "Full comedy" is that in which adjustment rests on a tension between sense

Formally antisentimental, Sheridan suffers from the sentimental temper of his times; he seems to be taken in by Lady Teazle's self-righteous attacks on Joseph Surface. These are evidently meant to show
that she is repentant, but because her denunciatory finger pointing is
a gross evasion of her own complicity, we remain unconvinced. Osborne, if I read him aright, is more clearheaded about what his maker
of indictments is up to. The very title, *Look Back in Anger*, furnishes
a clue to the character whose métier is blame; Jimmy Porter, however, looks not only "back" but around in a 360 degree circle and
delivers tirades in all directions, with a Gulliverian indiscriminateness
that embraces every kind of target, from familiar middle-class hypoc-
risies, assorted affectations, and modes of thought uncongenial to
himself, on to apparently innocuous individuals whose collapse and
surrender, if he can get it, will be a boon to his needy ego. The
wide-ranging inclusiveness of his verbal machine-gunning, his centrality in the play, his sheer energy, and the charismatic quality that
we are supposed to believe he has for three people give him a certain
ambiguity; perhaps the man screaming indictments, who makes some
shrewd hits, is the truth-bearing hero after all. Yet whatever sympathy the author may have had for his protagonist, he nevertheless so
constructs the drama as to make it finally a detached and ironic study
of the prosecutor of everybody. The other characters—Alison, Jimmy's wife; Helena, his temporary mistress; and even Colonel Redfern,
Alison's father, the old India army man who is the born butt of the
obsessive critic of mores—all are able to look at themselves and to
acknowledge error and wrongdoing; but Osborne keeps Jimmy in a
fixed posture of unflawed rectitude hurling abuse at the flawed
remainder of the world. Colonel Redfern credits Jimmy with "honesty," but what comes across is the tireless fury of a Timon, undis-

---

of the world and value judgments (e.g., Congreve's *Way of the World*).
Or say "full comedy" works from norms of good sense and right feeling:
"light" makes it easy for the norms by setting up only token opposition;
"black" substitutes opportunist calculation for the norms, as the only
way out of disaster; "bleak" reduces the norms to self-centered sentiment.
"Bleak" is old-style romantic modified by the author's loss of the characters' illusions (e.g., *Madame Bovary*). One can apply these standards even
when the adjustment is only to the domestic and not to the social world:
Coward's *Hay Fever* and Osborne's *Look Back in Anger* both deal with
outsiders; Osborne translates Coward's "light" into "bleak."

guised, to be sure, but with a quite unprobed self-coddling, a monstrous self-adulation.

When Alison says that "perhaps" Jimmy married her for "revenge" (II.ii),[8] she puts into words what one has already sensed: that as a man of blame Jimmy not only has affiliations with the old malcontent but is a version of the ancient revenger. Timon-like as he is in his rants, the true vocation of misanthropy demands generalized repudiation of mankind; not that Jimmy's aversions are restricted, but that his punitive style is animated by an especial need to humiliate and wound individuals, and by a real warming up to work when he senses a mangled victim going to pieces in front of him. Osborne shows him as magnifying slights, and even forcing them, as if to justify his frenzy, and permits the inference that his chief grievance is a world that will not take him at his own estimate. In search of grounds for revenge on everybody, Jimmy proposes a trauma: his father's long dying when he was ten. Not only does he use conventional sentimental phrases about himself, but he also insists without embarrassment, "I was the only one who cared," and claims exceptional suffering. "Doesn't it matter to you—what people do to me?" (II.i). Again he theatricalizes the death of a friend's mother as a unique trial for him; on each occasion of a death his own feeling is the only thing that counts for him, and he has contempt for the emotions of others, which he regards as an intrusion into his higher reality.

With a good deal of originality Osborne has exactly dramatized a truth sharply phrased by Mrs. G. B. Shaw: ". . . sentimental people are always unkind. They think of their own sentiments, and not of the feelings of the other person."[9] As Jimmy's wife puts it, "Oh, don't try and take his suffering away from him—he'd be lost without it" (II.i). Several times he relaxes his killer role to insist to Alison that he "needs" her (e.g., II.i), an apparently complicating and possibly endearing weakness that raises the problem: what need? Osborne does not shirk it: Jimmy "wants," as Alison puts it, "a kind of cross between a mother and a Greek courtesan, a henchwoman, a mixture of Cleopatra and Boswell" (III.ii). The other side of such vulgar dreams is a familiar paranoid attitude; as Jimmy puts it, "Either you're with me or against me" (III.i). And Alison states his need finally when she comes back to him: "I was . . . so stupid, and ugly and ridiculous. This is what he's been longing for me to feel. . . .

I'm in the fire, and I'm burning, and all I want is to die! . . . this is what he wanted from me! . . . I'm in the mud at last! I'm grovelling! I'm crawling!" (III.ii). It is the ultimate revenge: not murder, but triumph by humiliation of the single symbolic victim (achieved, ironically, just after he has been talking grandly about a "burning virility of mind and spirit that looks for something as powerful as itself"). Then he can turn warmly to her and resume their affectionate game of bear and squirrel in a snug animals' refuge, or, as Alison has put it earlier, "Playful, careless creatures in their own cosy zoo for two" (II.i).

This regression into a miniature sanctuary is a skillful ending that picks up earlier dramatic elements: there are constant hints of Jimmy as carnivorous beast. He has, among other things, "freebooting cruelty" (first stage direction). ". . . He's got to draw blood somehow" (stage direction). Alison says, "—he got savage, like tonight." Jimmy says, in his characteristic spirit of blame, that it is "living . . . with another human being" that has made him "predatory and suspicious" (Act I). Helena: "It's as if he wanted to kill some one. . . . I've never seen such hatred in someone's eyes before." Alison: ". . . I felt as though I'd been dropped in a jungle. I couldn't believe two people . . . could be so savage. . . ." Helena: "This menagerie." Stage direction: "He can smell blood again. . . ." "He's drawn blood at last" (II.i). But for all his own talk about "strength" and "life," the killer is soft about himself: Osborne traces his logical course from predator to pet. The master of blame, who does not grow beyond the flail and the whip, is bound in the end to find refuge in fantasy, and adjustment in a cage-playpen: romantic retreat, modern version.*

---

* In some details of physical appearance, attitudes, and style, Jimmy manages to sound like a D. H. Lawrence without creative talent. His marriage "above" his class, his sexual potency, and his "need" of his wife are also reminiscent of Stanley Kowalski in Tennessee Williams' somewhat Laurentian *Streetcar Named Desire*. But Stanley and Stella are living in an actual world, and there are some striking differences in sex doctrine: whereas Stella can tell her sister Blanche, "But there are things that happen between a man and a woman in the dark—that sort of makes everything else seem—unimportant" (I.iv), Helena (granted, a mistress, not a wife) tells Alison, "He wants one world, and I want another, and lying in that bed won't ever change it" (IV.ii). In *Inadmissible Evidence* (1964), longer and duller, Osborne traces the public and private breakup of the Jimmy Porter character.

In tragedies and dramas of disaster, the quality is partly determined by the artistic placing of blame. The villainous Ferdinand in Webster's *Duchess of Malfi* has his sister killed and then furiously abuses his murderous agent Bosola. In this scene Webster certainly manages to suggest that Ferdinand is suffering from self-knowledge, though we never see Ferdinand really move from melodramatic to tragic consciousness, from blaming his tool to blaming himself. Antony flies into bursts of blame against Cleopatra and Caesar, but here the dramatist knows very well that these are stratagems. Antony is presented as never able to break away satisfactorily from consciousness of his divided life; his resort to melodrama is less a foolish snatching at moral security than an outpouring of frustration and desperation. In O'Neill's *Long Day's Journey into Night* the Tyrones all but live on recrimination. This is interrupted by moments of self-accusation, but these are more like sporadic and unwanted flashes of light in a deep fog—there is an actual fog in the play, and Edmund praises it as conducive to forgetfulness—than a growing, reliable sense of truth.

Blame and Self-Blame: Shakespeare

Characters who surmount the passion to blame belong largely to Shakespeare's high tragic period; it takes him time to work into this more complex characterization, and then his practice is marked by some recession from it. *Titus Andronicus* (1594) needs no additional disparagement, but the play is relevant here in that the spirit of blame is almost the sole motivation of the principal characters: unqualified blame expands into massive resentfulness, revengefulness, and malignity, and this is explored with hyperbolic thoroughness. Ironically, the play is so written that Titus, like Lear, could be held responsible for all the subsequent disasters to himself and others, and might have been made to move from retaliation to an understanding of his own role; but Shakespeare is not yet ready to base drama on this movement of character. Analogous to Titus' unmixed determination to get even is Aaron's single-minded rigidity in evil: "If one good deed in all my life I did, / I do repent it from my very soul" (V.iii.189–90).

Five years later, in *Julius Caesar* (1599), Shakespeare managed a much more sophisticated play; yet it is still one in which the drama derives mainly from a partisan vehemence hardly modified by self-questioning. Initially, of course, blame is lavished upon Caesar; we have the melodrama of "purgers" (II.i.180) against the "ambitious" man, the "tyrant." Brutus has some mixture of feelings, but they do not essentially disturb the mood of the public-spirited censor. Antony blames "these butchers" (III.i.255), prophesies "Domestic fury and fierce civil strife" (line 263), and sets it in motion. Brutus and Cassius blame each other, though at first they move slightly in the opposite direction by making acknowledgments and offering apologies (IV.iii.115ff.). Yet the final note is that of Brutus' almost monolithic self-assurance as he overrules Cassius' battle proposals (lines 203ff.), faces Caesar's ghost (lines 275ff.), ignores Cassius' I-told-you-so reminder that he had wanted Antony killed with Caesar, and trades taunts and cries of "traitor" with Octavius and Antony.

In *Timon of Athens* (1607?) Shakespeare returns to the angry man; not only is the characterization of Timon one-dimensional, but Timon is made to maintain an unvarying stance of accusation throughout Acts IV and V. It is the nature of the misanthrope to engage in intellectual melodrama, hurling multiple indictments in justification of his vindictiveness. Timon has contributed to his own wretchedness by founding an illusion of security on the unspoken premise that hearts can be bought, but he cannot grasp the truth when he is frantically firing barrages of abuse at others. The title hero of *Coriolanus* (1608–9?) also has something of Timon in him; he has earned of his community a regard that Timon has not, but whereas Timon suffers from a familiar ignorance of human nature, Coriolanus wants to override familiar "custom" (II.ii.140) that his "proud heart" (II.iii.161) cannot abide. When his sheer lack of discipline makes him vulnerable to scheming politicians and he is banished, he breaks out furiously, "You common cry of curs! . . . I banish you!" (III.iii.120–23). He carries the spirit of blame into the ultimate form of action, joining with an enemy against his country, and then the massive conviction of rightness that underlies blame leads him naïvely to negotiate a settlement without consulting his new partner Aufidius. Arrested, he bursts again into denunciation; now it is Aufidius who is "this cur" and "False hound!" (V.vi.107, 113), and Coriolanus' unbreakable self-ignorance appears almost humorously in his thoroughly nonironic, " 'tis the first time that ever / I was forc'd to scold" (lines 105–6). He retains his rigid sense of grievance until he dies.

To a considerable extent Othello seems of a piece with these earlier and later heroes, for an important element in his make-up is his fondness for blaming others and justifying himself. Once the nature of his murderous deed has become clear to him, he spends virtually as much time blaming Iago as blaming himself. Indeed, an almost habitual tendency to find guilt elsewhere and to view himself in a roseate light hinders, I believe, his coming into the fullest possible tragic realization. But whether or not this is true—and in this matter there is difference of opinion—he is in the general pattern that we have described: the dramatic movement from the partial polemic life into, or at least toward, the wholeness of tragic awareness. Compared with Titus, Timon, and Coriolanus, Othello has made a palpable move toward the self-comprehension which markedly alters the melodramatic structure.

This alteration is more palpable in *Lear*, in which the hero carries out his misdeeds early in the play and therefore has a longer time for moral reorientation. In *Othello*, also, the central evil deed has its essence in Othello's consent to it and execution of it, whereas in *Lear* there are acts of malignity that, though Lear made them possible, are done not only without his participation but in direct opposition to his own will. Hence Lear is not simply deceiving himself when he castigates his daughters for their gross self-seeking. Nevertheless, he wants to live a melodrama, a life of dealing out blame, as long as he can; he clings to the wholeness of the victim and the plaintiff and resists acknowledging his own intemperateness and injustice. So there is a long, wonderfully imagined process of his exhausting the polemic emotions and, through an understanding of self, coming into a larger sense of life. At first his acknowledgment of his fault comes through only in isolated phrases—"too late repents," "O most small fault, / . . . in Cordelia . . . ," "this gate, that let thy folly in," "I did her wrong" (I.iv.279, 288–89, 293; I.v.25); then comes the longer "Poor naked wretches" speech, including the admission, "O, I have ta'en / Too little care of this" (III.iv.32–33); and finally his humility before Cordelia—"You have some cause . . . ," "Pray you now, forget and forgive," and "I'll kneel down / And ask of thee forgiveness" (IV.vii.75, 85; V.iii.10–11). At this point, defeated and broken, Lear is a more complete man than he was as an all-powerful and imperious ruler.

Blame and Self-Blame: Euripides and Sophocles

The theme of characters who turn from blame of others to self-blame appears not only in Shakespeare but in classical dramatists—and interestingly enough, in Euripides. Much as he is given to that form of melodrama which may best be named "romantic comedy" (*Alcestis, Helen, Iphigenia in Tauris*), and to the melodrama of the victim (*The Trojan Women*) and the victim as revenger (*Medea*), Euripides can look with great detachment at characters endeavoring to erect a melodramatic attitude into a way of life, and, like writers with a more consistent tragic awareness, can uncover the inadequacy of their efforts. In *Electra* both Electra and Orestes blame Clytemnestra and Aegisthus for the murder of their father Agamemnon, and plot revenge; and Clytemnestra, in turn, seeks justification for her life by a constantly reiterated, indeed naggingly insistent, blame of Agamemnon for having offered their daughter Iphigenia as a religious sacrifice. But Euripides has Electra declare, with apparent authority and without challenge from Clytemnestra, that Clytemnestra's basic motive was not grief for Iphigenia ("your pretext") but her illicit passion for Aegisthus. Then Euripides sees Clytemnestra as tired of, and willing to relinquish, the role of district attorney and judge in the case of Agamemnon; when she says, "With what insensate fury I drove myself to take / My grand revenge! How bitterly I regret it now!" she has reached a point at which she could become the tragic heroine. Meanwhile Euripides is taking a fresh and independent look at the posture of revenge, the ultimate crystallization of the instinct to blame, as it appears in Clytemnestra's children. Electra lives for revenge, but Euripides shows, in effect, that the kind of wholeness she achieves by becoming the professional prosecutor of Clytemnestra leaves much out; in her monomania she has become self-pitying, tense, even neurotic. Orestes, on the other hand, is hardly the monopathic revenger; his doubts about both tactics and outcome reveal a more complete awareness that finally emerges in a forthright statement of his dilemma vis-à-vis murdered father and living mother: "Avenging him I am pure; but killing her, condemned." [10] It is a concise statement of the whole realm of conflicting imperatives. Electra, not unlike Lady Macbeth, drives him on to committing the act on which her heart is set. But once the deed is done, Electra shares in Orestes' guilt and remorse; she gives up blame and makes no effort at justification; Euripides has fully imagined the course of the human being trying to live in a melodrama of blame and eventually moving into a less self-protective realm.

In *Oedipus the King* we have the same structure, but with the salient parts more sharply accented. Oedipus is a great star in the melodrama of blame because, though he has none of Lear's reasons for fury at injustice, he blames frequently and violently—Creon, Tiresias, Jocasta, and the Herdsman. But despite his flair for detecting untruth which does not exist, he never loses the ability to get through to truth and to acknowledge it; nor does he shirk self-blame; more fully than many tragic heroes he becomes aware of the tragic wholeness. Oedipus knows all of the self from which he has attempted to escape into a lesser domain that attracts many heroes.

Tragic Action: Escape and Return

I have been trying to illustrate that basic form of tragic action which can be described as the flight from tragedy followed by the inexorable return to tragedy. We can restate this idea thus: tragedy has its roots in man's efforts to escape his destiny, and its conclusion in his reunion with destiny. His destiny is the total of the liabilities that are his as an individual and as a generic human being: the inability to live or possess or enjoy without limits, to know only his own will; to avoid imperfect, painful, and perhaps ruinous choices; to be sure that he will not do wrong, or to escape penalties. He cannot force life into a unity under a single passion or idea, a dream of power, a love of freedom, or a longing for security. Yet it is also his destiny, as existent tragedies interpret it, that when his liabilities overtake him, even ruinously, he is not simply weak, cynical, corrupt, or stupid and ignorant. In the tragic view, he tries to seize but learns to lose or renounce; he acts punitively, revengefully, or maliciously, but does not finally deceive himself about his actions; he does what he thinks he must do, but comes to know the doubleness of what he has done, and to accept penalty or undertake reparation; he instinctively sees the ailments of the world as disasters and as the misdeeds of others, but he comes to discover his own complicity; in a word, he reasons badly, but he comes to understand; he errs terribly, but he finds a mode of recovery. In this sense we may say it is man's good fortune that tragedy catches up with him; this is what saves him from irreparable disaster. "Tragedy is *not* 'the truth realized too late.' It is man's way of coming to his senses in time." [11]

V. The Tragic Continuity

Tragedy, then, implies a kind of recovery. Tragedy is the idiom of an imperfect humanity that remains capable of moral recuperation; tragedy implies a durable order of life, in which failure is always possible, but in which it is understood, not mistaken for a final blow, the road to nothing. In tragedy there is spiritual survival. It is possible to say, without sentimentality, that "great tragedy . . . confirms the optimistic view of a man's ability to transcend himself spiritually." [12] Melodrama is the idiom of either a victorious world, successfully disposing of concentrations of evil, or a declining world, undone by evil or fatally weakened by its sense of the unconquerable hosts arrayed against it. Melodrama is concerned with the struggle for physical, social, or political survival. Its end is victory or defeat, whereas tragedy defines life as the paradoxical union of the two. Another critic has spelled this out in more detail: "The greatness and the paradox of tragedy is that it discovers in human madness, in human senility, and even in humanity's bestial wickedness the glimmer of a transformed humanity that is dignified and noble and perhaps just barely possible." [13]

Man may meet disaster with nobility, and the literature of disaster —war plays, for instance—may reflect this in a pleasurably reassuring way that does not falsify humanity. Tragedy acts differently: it is not concerned with the given virtues of those who are overwhelmed, but with the achievement, reinforcement, or recovery of certain virtues in men who are suffering in consequence of their own choices. What it implies, then, is continuity—an ongoing of man's saving qualities, rooted in but transcending the individual life. In disaster, life and consciousness are simply cut off, or cut down to futile remnants; in tragedy, life may or may not be cut off, but death, if it comes, is a lesser event than the new growth of the hero. The action testifies that self-knowledge and moral clarity persist. These depend on values that it once seemed impossible to serve or that had been willfully forgotten, pushed aside, or rejected, but that are now seen to survive contradictions, forgetting, and rejection, and to endure. I use "continuity" to refer to this persistence of the moral basis of life, as distinguished from the survival of physical and societal bodies that is the concern of melodrama. Hart Crane was saying something of this kind when he spoke of the "acceptance of tragedy" as implying a belief in an "eternal life" that followed "in spite of all annihilation." [14]

The Sentient Hero

The tragic continuity depends upon the possibility of imagining representative heroes with a certain kind of sensitivity. Here sensitivity means a keen and full normal perceptiveness, not any one of the forms of hypersensitivity that serve other artistic purposes: the hyperaesthesia of Poe's Roderick Usher, suitable for a study of the disaster of personality; the special vulnerability with which Hardy endows such heroes as Clym Yeobright and Jude Fawley in elaborating his doctrine of the more sentient man as inevitable victim; the hyperalgesia which for O'Neill is so central a human attribute that he can only paint men's anguish, as in *Long Day's Journey into Night*, or dramatize the need of narcotic illusions in *The Iceman Cometh;* or the neurotic tendency which leads some Tennessee Williams characters to go to pieces or court destruction. To secure the tragic effect, the artist must be able not only to look at wrongdoing from the point of view of the doer, but also to conceive of that doer as endowed with the intelligence that will enable him to look at himself with understanding. Otherwise man only exists or ceases to exist. Often in O'Neill's later plays the characters simply drag on until they can be saved by the end of things. This is something other than the tragic continuity.

So far we have spoken of the hero's sensitivity as a potential which is made actual in the course of the drama. In one kind of drama the flaw may be viewed as a temporary failure of intelligence. We see this pattern in both Macbeth and Dr. Faustus, who may be said to know enough from the start but who for their own reasons must deny what they know, and who find that knowledge in one way or another forced back upon them. There is a still subtler denial of the known in Arthur Koestler's Rubashov, whose sense of truth almost totally surrenders to a cold rational ideal, but who comes to see his own complicity in postrevolutionary inhumanity and can say, "That's the horror." [15] The concept of the tragic process as either an actualizing or a recovery of a needed perceptivity makes it possible to think of tragedy as implying, among other things, a "self-healing" human order. The difficulty of this metaphor is that it may seem to mean an easy, automatic process. I disavow any such meaning. "Self-healing order" should call attention to two aspects of tragedy: to the fact that what goes wrong is a wound or an injury rather than a destruction; and to the fact that the injured organism is capable of being restored.

The self-healing process is exhibited in its most fascinating way in the kind of tragic structure in which the hero, instead of recovering or developing sentiency in the latter part of the tragic rhythm, acts from the beginning because he is an especially sentient person. He responds to a state of affairs which he did not bring about but which compels him to act. A hazardous situation forces itself upon him, not like a destructive natural force of which he is a passive victim, but because he is a sentient man whose awareness requires him to respond in a certain way. A number of great tragedies would not exist if playwrights could not have imagined the responsiveness of heroes to situations that, though dangerous and equivocal, seem in their wrongness to obligate the hero to a perilous entry. Antigone, Orestes, and Hamlet are at the opposite pole from the unfeeling cloddishness that would save them from jeopardy. But though they act in response to troubles that arise outside themselves, they do not find themselves in either of the characteristic melodramatic situations. They are not simply losers in social conflict, beaten down by superior forces; nor are they simply victors, triumphing over evil. They never have the less exacting monopathic consciousness of participants in melodrama. Before he moves, Orestes strives for an assurance of rectitude in his course; the tone of the *Choephoroi* is always somber; the parricide is barely finished before Orestes is overwhelmed by retribution. In Euripides' version, Orestes has even less certainty of rightness in a course where he is agonizingly aware of conflicting imperatives. Antigone is never at ease; in the forbidden act of burial there is, as her stridency shows, willfulness as well as religious dutifulness; nor does she meet death without bitterness. The strain of role has contorted the personality of Euripides' Electra, so that she takes on a frantic and obsessed style; once Clytemnestra is murdered, Electra is quickly plunged into a new sense of guilt.

The unmelodramatic complications in Antigone and Electra are multiplied in Hamlet: his sensitivity is uniquely troubling, for while it makes him responsive to supernatural admonitions, it also hinders him in the execution of his resolves. He names the "cursed spite" and suspects the "craven scruple"; he is split between what he accepts as duty and a not easily defined incapacity for that duty. The hero in the Hamlet situation always finds it difficult to have clarity, to be free of doubt, to act and yet maintain the illusion of innocence. The sensitivity which brings him to act against the civil authority leads him into a role that strains his powers; unlike Dr. Faustus, the man who would be God, he is the man who must try to be God. Even in his dutifulness there is a measure of hubris. In this subtle union of virtue and pride, he becomes a sacrificial figure; yet he is a victor in that his sacrifice is not futile. He has been the instrument for what I have called the self-healing moral order. The tragic "continuity" means less the readjustment of a public situation, though this does take place, than the persistence in pragmatic history of a saving kind of consciousness, which is transmitted by being experienced in representative figures. The total loss popularly connoted by the word *tragedy* does not occur; rather something vital is saved—the kind of moral awareness which is distinguishable from the cynicism of a narrower world view, and from the despair that belongs to disaster. It is not simply that life goes on, but that the quality of life is maintained.

The interrelationship of the sensitivity of the hero and of moral continuity appears in a special way in both the Aeschylus and the Eliot versions of the Orestes myth: here we see, as it were, a rectification of spirit through the exhaustion of a curse upon the house. The curse is played out when an individual, though he continues the pattern of reciprocal aggressions that constitute the family history, is sentient enough also to feel his guilt and thus to take on an expiatory role. The barbaric potential breaks out—a regular form of tragic action—but is seen to be capable of replacement or transformation. What occurs might be called the tragic conversion: a fund of psychic energy is turned from a destroying to a preserving function. Rather than simply inaugurating a new series of revenges, Orestes suffers and is "made whole"; his own metamorphosis is repeated in universal symbolic terms when Athena persuades the Erinyes to take on a new character as the Eumenides.[16]

In *The Family Reunion* the curse is lovelessness—a life of ignorance, formalities in place of feeling, and maternal power-seeking that drives Harry, the eldest son, into severe nervous disorders. But the fact that he can become ill means that, in contrast with the callousness of many of the family, he has a special nature: when he discovers knowledge and love, he can undertake a new life of spirit. Salvation is made possible when, in the barren life of the family, there appears one human being with an adequate sensitivity to their state. As Agatha says to Harry:

> It is possible that sin may strain and struggle
> In its dark instinctive birth, to come to consciousness
> And so find expurgation. It is possible
> You are the consciousness of your unhappy family,
> Its bird sent flying through the purgatorial flame.
>
> .   .   .   .
>
> The burden's yours now, yours
> The burden of all the family.
> [II.ii]

Though Harry is a minor version of the tragic hero and is not a successful character,* nevertheless the treatment of him carries out

---

* The sharpest criticisms of *The Family Reunion* have been made by Eliot himself in *Poetry and Drama* (Cambridge, Mass.: Harvard University Press, 1951), pp. 32–37. Among other faults he notes that Harry is "an insufferable prig." This is true, but it may be worth noting that Hamlet and Antigone are also not entirely without priggishness—the hazard, perhaps, of a person who assumes the sacrificial role. Self-righteousness becomes a palliative of inevitable suffering; at the opposite extreme is the popular melodramatic hero who undertakes public burdens: he is likely to be all self-righteousness, without a palliative of suffering.

Eliot's plots are sometimes reminiscent of other plots than those which are his "sources," and comparisons may be useful. The treatment of Harry's mother can be compared with that of the mother in Sidney Howard's *The Silver Cord* (1926). There are close resemblances between a central situation in *The Family Reunion* and a central situation in Ibsen's *John Gabriel Borkman* (1897): in each there is an unmarried woman (Agatha, Ella Rentheim) who has been in love with her sister's husband and who is or has been close to her sister's son; in each case the wife (Lady Monchensey, Mrs. Borkman) accuses the sister of trying to take away both her husband and her son. In each case the mother plans that the son shall restore or carry on the family fortunes, and in each case the valuable function of stressing the qualitative recovery that is always a phase of, or is latent in, the tragic experience.

VI. Past, Present, and Future

The ancient and modern treatments of Orestes both end with a sense of spiritual achievement, and this carries with it, though it may be unspoken, a sense of futurity. Hence, as this essay has termed it, the tragic continuity. It is to be distinguished on the one hand from other kinds of continuity and on the other from the sheer hopeless stoppages that are the suitable endings of melodramas of despair. Tennessee Williams illustrates both of these—the continuity of fertility and physical vitality in *Streetcar Named Desire*, and the sheer black-out of *Suddenly Last Summer*. But in the former, to do Williams justice, he does not fall into mere "life" worship.* Nor does his

---

the son, with the help or approval of the aunt, escapes to an extramural destiny. These similarities are useful because they assist in clarifying the differences in the treatment of the son; these are so marked that one could read Eliot's play as an answer to Ibsen's, a rather subtle restatement of his general attack on Ibsen (cf. F. O. Matthiessen, *The Achievement of T. S. Eliot* [3rd ed.; New York and London: Oxford University Press, 1958], pp. 156ff.). For while Harry goes off on a redemptive mission, Erhart Borkman specifically repudiates all missions: he runs off to "happiness" and "life" as symbolized in an older woman who takes along a younger girl to solace Erhart when he will have tired of his senior mistress. Ibsen's central character, however, is the father, John Gabriel Borkman—a megalomaniac who has great tragic potential but whom Ibsen presents, finally, as shunning self-knowledge for self-defensiveness (the melodramatic mode) and a nostalgic savoring of old dreams of empire.

* Biolatry is another of the secular Calvinisms on which the lesser melodrama thrives, and the popularity of its simplifications is perhaps to be expected. It divides all men into the elect, who are "on the side of life," and the damned, who are for death. Hence it eliminates all of the complexities—the ways of living, the ways of dying, the different meanings of both, the conflicting claims—that belong to a tragic view, or for that matter to the style of mature melodrama; it almost eliminates an adult sense of character and values. "Reverence for life" is the sentimental formulation; it shifts to an indiscriminating universalism. Its terms will not bear analysis, since "reverence for life" means either respect for the right of men to continue living, which is not new (though the Decalogue is not exactly chic at present) and which no one denies, or worship of all living people, which no one can or should practice. In the former case there is an error of style, an inappropriate hyperbole ("reverence" for "pay due regard to"); in the latter, an error of thought, a failure to make elementary qualitative distinctions.

sense of disaster lead him to end in a dismal static present, dragging on toward death, such as we find in Gorki's *Lower Depths* and O'Neill's *Mourning Becomes Electra*, *The Iceman Cometh*, and *Long Day's Journey*.

A present may end a past or fulfill it. Dramas that are in or near the tragic mode turn frequently on the unfolding of a past that is continuous in the present: we see this in *Oedipus* and *Hamlet* and repeatedly in Ibsen and O'Neill, and more than once, though with a different tone, in Eliot and Williams. This introduction of a past that is revealed in and lives in the present offers a real source of richness. But it does not distinguish the tragic vision as does the portrayal of a present that extends into the future; in this view of reality, man salvages, from the ruins of the present, the essential human powers on which continuity depends (a quite different thing from a melodramatic victory over an enemy). This may take place whether spiritual regeneration coexists with a new well-being in life, as in Orestes; or man lives on in a paradoxical union of suffering and new wisdom, as does Oedipus; or comes to a new insight before dying, as does Lear.

In the O'Neill and Gorki plays mentioned above nothing is salvaged; all is collapse and decay. In contrast with this is the Shakespearian tragic ending in which the pieces are picked up and there is a partial resumption of order after explosive disorder; the elegiac is qualified by distant notes of rebirth. This ending, of course, is a convention, a formalized management of proprieties that had authority in their day. Yet the convention itself is significant: it could not exist, we may conjecture, without faith in a transmittable order of values, and belief in continuity; the ending is a symbol of something earned in the tragic action, in contrast with the total sense of loss in dramas of de-

---

If life worship simply means that fertility and vitality are desirable, it has a legitimate role in the comedy of nature, that form of literature which notes the passing of a decadent order and hails the reviving forces. *Streetcar Named Desire* and *The Cherry Orchard*—which by the way have many similarities—are cases in point. They are concerned with that final phase of a recurrent social history in which refinement has exceeded vitality, and a new rough vigor must come in to begin a new cycle. Most biolaters, however, fail to recognize the need for a tension between refinement and vigor, and tend to regard all refinement (form, discipline) as "on the side of death." In the end, biolatry most often fails to define "life" inclusively enough or with sufficient discrimination; hence its wide appeal.

spair and disaster. The dramatist's own sense of continuity may be more or less profound, and he may build the convention firmly into the plot or employ it casually, like a verbal tag. The essential ongoingness, it should be apparent, lies in the potentiality for understanding and renewal that the dramatist can imagine in his protagonists. But he can also show the effective continuance in life of characters whose substantialness, in themselves and in affairs, has been well established. In *Macbeth*, for instance, Shakespeare treats Malcolm and Macduff in this way. In *Hamlet*, Horatio and Fortinbras attest to the objective persistence of order that is conceivable partly because all the participants in the debacle have experienced, whether tardily or inconsistently, at least moments of moral alertness. In *Lear* the voices of Edgar and Albany, by no means latecomers to the action, are the symbols of continuity. The treatment of Albany is especially effective because his gradual coming into understanding parallels Lear's and, for that matter, Gloucester's: the course of salvation is shown overtly in both private and public life. The insight gained by the dying protagonist is carried on by those who can grasp it and who live on.

In concluding *The Duchess of Malfi* (1611), Webster, whose bent is all melodramatic, bows to the tragic convention by having Delio speak for Antonio's son as inheritor. But this is an afterthought, unprepared; Webster's conviction is all of "this gloomy world," and there is no real carry-over of supposed new-found strength into the future. At the end of *The Maid's Tragedy* Beaumont and Fletcher are so busy displaying a collection of broken hearts that the new king's resolve for the future is as pat as the curtain moral of sentimental drama. In Heywood's *A Woman Killed with Kindness* (1603) there are many healthy survivors, but in this sentimental piece there is no real earning of continuity; moral insight is not achieved through struggle, but virtually swamps all the too eager recipients of it. Yet these chroniclers of domestic wretchedness do have some sense of wider context: all is not lost.

We can have an intimation of the future and a sense of continuity when the dramatist maintains a vision of the constants of life. In *Dr. Faustus* Marlowe presents the constant values both as spiritual possessions, always intimately felt, and as supernatural beings with objective existence. At the end we see only the demonic beings, with the scholar in their possession. This ending runs so counter to post-romantic sensibility that we can hear Marlowe's Dr. Faustus pitied, not because he has mistaken the nature of reality and of his relationship to it, but as if he were the victim of a kind of ruthless interruption of a noble exploit, of a tyranny which in an outdated world view smashes a merited bliss. Readers forget that "demonic action is powerless to achieve human damnation without the willing cooperation of man." [17] So for relief they turn to Goethe, who with his glorification of energy and discontent offers a more comforting, and therefore less probing, treatment of the myth. But there is much misreading of Marlowe's play. If at the end the diabolic forces live on in such power as they have, so do the divine ones. The symbols of order persist; order endures; man may fail, but he can understand his course. Life does not end in a blur or a blot, in simple confusion or destruction, in incomprehension or cynicism; what remains is a clear vision of spiritual realities—of man recognizing himself in his constant struggle between damnation and salvation. In a real sense, then, "Tragedy is a hymn to life; it is at the opposite pole from elegy." [18]

CHAPTER SIX

Movements Between the Poles: The Renaissance

WE CAN gain another perspective on tragic and melodramatic forms by seeing how they complement each other, mingle, or compete in the works of individual dramatists and in the drama of a historical period. So far we have been looking at the forms in largely theoretical terms, noting their psychological genesis and functioning, their relationship to social and political attitudes and to the postures that men assume toward themselves and others. We have treated tragedy and melodrama as literary and theatrical crystallizations of basic modes of feeling and consciousness, modes that are essential in defining experience but that can become attenuated, distorted, or excessive and hence push drama in a number of different directions. Since the modes of feeling and consciousness evidently persist from age to age, our exploration of forms and their human bases has been thematic rather than historical. We can now usefully introduce a historical perspective into the consideration of forms. Renaissance drama provides admirable materials.

I. HISTORICAL APPLICATION

To introduce a sense of chronology and temporal boundaries should have a double advantage. On the one hand, in looking at the structural types as they have been employed by a single dramatist or by a group of dramatists in one period, we should fill out our picture of the types themselves—refining, modifying, adding concreteness, and above all understanding the variations that can occur in a relatively short compass of time. On the other hand, the concepts of tragedy and melodrama, even when we observe them in this partly fluid state, should be useful in charting kinds of historical movement. We test them by using them as poles for the placement of a given collection of dramas. The concepts provide a way into history, while the historical body of materials sheds additional light on the concepts.

The "placement" of dramas by the use of theoretical notions means not the affixing of labels, but the identifying of structural tendencies which lead to different dramatic colorations. A play can be a composition of actions in different modes. The tragedy of Macbeth, to repeat an earlier remark, is the disaster of Scotland; the tragedy of Lear, the disaster of Britain; the tragedy of Oedipus, the disaster of Thebes. The different kinds of action may alternate, as in *Macbeth*, or be to all effects fused, as in *Lear*. Still, both plays are consistently dual, just as *The Spanish Tragedy* is consistently a revenge melodrama and *Othello* is consistently a drama of a divided personality, without echoes in the public realm. There are some plays, however, that seem committed to a single-faceted personality (as in the revenger) or to a conflict between such personalities (Brutus against Caesar or against the triumvirate; Montagues against Capulets) and then endow the protagonist with other motives or a disturbing consciousness that leads the structure from one polarity toward the other. Hence a "movement" in the play itself, the result of a change in the dramatist's attitude to the character, or a revised imagining of the character in more expansive or constricted terms than those used initially. When that happens, we can say that a play "moves" from melodrama to tragedy, or the reverse. In *Richard II*, for instance, there is a singular shifting of generic ground.

Likewise we may say that the works of a single dramatist move from melodrama toward tragedy, or the reverse. It took Shakespeare some years, in the histories and tragedies, to move from a one-dimensional to a multi-dimensional range of character, from conflicts between to conflicts within characters. Though it has all kinds of variations, his earlier dramatic organization is largely melodramatic;

dividedness in characters is infrequent or unusual, and the self-knowledge which is an expectable consequence of dividedness is trifling or
nonexistent (e.g., in Richard III, Romeo, Brutus). Again, after the
middle period in which the sense of character is most emphatically
tragic, Shakespeare moves, slightly in Antony and more markedly in
Coriolanus, toward a concept of personality in which the most powerful element is less challenged by other motives and is hence less
likely to become the subject of critical awareness by its possessor.
That is, there is a movement toward the melodramatic ordering of
experience.

Finally, plays by different dramatists may be compared in these
terms. It is a truism that revenge plays reach a fruition in *Hamlet*.
Something has happened to the form: the protagonist has taken on a
degree of sentience that makes his relations with himself no less
important than his relations with others. Within the family of revenge
plays the melodramatic sense of reality, without disappearing, has
yielded ground to the tragic sense of reality. On the other hand, when
we follow the revenge convention on through Jacobean drama, we see
—amid divergent formal changes that make it risky to generalize—a
traceable tendency to cut back character to a single motive, to attenuate and exacerbate. In the brothers who harry to death the Duchess of
Malfi, the melodramatic shaping of personality pushes univalence so
far that it becomes disorder.

Within a body of works (a canon, a type, or a period), "movements" are variable; opposite movements may occur side by side. By
isolating one group of dramas we can discern a maturing of form, an
achieving of the fullest conception of the materials natural to it (for
our purposes, the nature of the persons whose wills and passions
create the visible action). Another group illustrates decadence, that
is, the breakdown of the fullest conception and the enlargement or
hypertrophy of abstracted parts, often with a strange gleaming that
accompanies an unwonted or distorted focus. These countermove-
ments, with more than one modification, occur representatively in
English Renaissance drama, in which the large number of plays
produced in a relatively short time make a rich ground for observing
the historical utility of formal concepts. Marlowe's plays are few
enough to permit a complete tracing of one man's work. Though
Shakespeare can only be sampled, it happens that three early histories

provide excellent illustrations of interplay between tragic and melo-dramatic perspectives. In Shakespeare's contemporaries and succes-sors there is a perennially interesting body of work that, despite the conventional label of "Jacobean tragedy," reveals more than one complication of generic form. We can see, then, variations within the work of one writer, from one writer's work to another's, and within the over-all production of a period. Always, of course, we shall be looking at individual plays. Whatever its generic configuration, each play, in itself and in its relation with others, should contribute to our understanding of generic norms.

II. Generic Variations in Marlowe

Marlowe's career is so short—all his writing for the theater was done in six or seven years—and the dates of his plays are so uncertain that we cannot satisfactorily describe his work in terms of a generic "movement." It would be convenient if Marlowe's most brilliant work came at the end, and sometimes *Dr. Faustus* is considered late; but more often it is put close to the beginning, right next to *Tambur-laine*. If this dating is sound, it provides us with a singular juxtaposi-tion of two contrasting plays of remarkable generic purity—one an almost classical melodrama of a certain kind, and the other, for all the corruptions of the text, a tragedy with an exemplary absence of modal variation.

The formal consistency in both of these plays is in contrast with the tonal insecurity of *The Jew of Malta*, where we can observe a rather interesting movement from one kind of structural pattern to another. *The Jew* starts off as a melodrama of a machiavellian villain, Barabas the Jew, whose malice and faithlessness are to make him into a loathsome monster. Marlowe, however, lets the play veer away from the initial pattern into something else. Since the Jew is regarded by the other characters as a legitimate victim, they all turn into victimiz-ers; in so doing they betray a rascality that cuts them off from any sympathy as Barabas revengefully works out ingenious machinations against them. Among all those whom Barabas is in conflict with or tries to cheat or injure—the Maltese leaders, the Turkish leaders, the heads of the Christian monastic orders, his own slave Ithamore, and Ithamore's blackmailing accomplices—there is not one who elicits our partisanship against Barabas. The situation is exactly that of the picaresque mode, in which we are on the side of the man who lives by his wits at the expense of others. We are kept there by the basic rule of picaresque art, which is either that we do not see the con man's gulls or that they deserve what they get. Barabas, a solitary competitor, meets all plots and catastrophes with such energy, cleverness, and resourcefulness, and so skillfully turns the schemes of others to his own advantage, that we relish his gamesmanship, which is both dashing and cunning. The melodramatic has turned into the picaresque, with that elimination or mechanization of feeling that deprives even grossness, injury, and death of their power to affect us as they do when they are experienced by ordinarily sentient human beings. Like all picaresque heroes, Barabas is brought down in the end: he overreaches himself by a dazzling scheme whose failure, on the whole, we regret. The one character who does not conform to the picaresque is Barabas' daughter Abigail; she has an authenticity of feeling that makes her suffering real and Barabas' murder of her shocking. As if aware of the problem of tone, Marlowe removes Abigail from the picture quickly at the end of Act III and sets Barabas off immediately on his cleverest operation—hoodwinking a pair of crooked friars—but the inconsistency is there, and it cannot be interpreted away. Still, aside from the murder episode and the other episodes in which Abigail is involved, the play achieves a higher degree of unity if it is regarded as a picaresque drama rather than as a revenge melodrama or as what "Machiavel" calls it in his prologue—"the tragedy of a Jew."

Against this background we can see more clearly Marlowe's achievement, evidently an earlier one, in maintaining a melodramatic consistency in *Tamburlaine*. Here is the ultimate pageant of the victor, of the triumphant conqueror who goes on insatiably from one slaughter of enemies to another; he becomes authentic by the very press of his victims, of all nationalities and ages, and of both sexes, impaled, decapitated, burned, and drowned; with Tamburlaine we soar over the world, or with the victims go down in suffering and grief; with him we are arrogant to the weak, or with them reprove the barbarous use of power. We can probably have it several ways at once, or quickly shift from one unambiguous emotional posture to another; for neither in the relationships nor in the scope of individual personalities is there the subtlety or depth that would force us into an exacting, troubling experience where incompatible claims are both urgently present. Not that there is an entire simplicity in Tamburlaine, for he is half the maniacal sadist and half the captain of a championship football team; half the cruel despoiler of the world and half the national conquistador who in past ages fashioned one empire after another; half bloody gangster and half self-made entrepreneur. But behind both these personalities there is a totally untragic unity— the unity of energy, drive, the violent pressure from within that is at once competitive, acquisitive, aggressive, revengeful; the exuberance of physical strength and psychic zest, and the talent for ordering these against giant targets.

It is not clear that Tamburlaine has a real grievance. As the "baseborn" Scythian, the shepherd, the upstart, he may be taking revenge on the world of kings, and insofar as there is something of this in the background, he has milder cousins in the resentful modern "outsiders," in John Osborne's small men who with big invectives attempt a verbal slaughter of near innocents. Revenge is a ritually channeled destructiveness; with Tamburlaine the urge to destroy hardly needs rite or occasion; it is autonomous, the spontaneous, unsanctioned revenge on those who offend, not by doing an injury or by being better than one is, but by being in the way, by blocking the universal passage of one's own solar rays. It is a revolt, not against authority, but against all other authorities. The play is a pure melodrama of total egotism, an egotism that can crudely murder millions or fiendishly humiliate monarchs kept alive in order that their grotesque abasement may fantastically mirror the champion's glory.

Tamburlaine is free from division. He has no doubts of any kind. His will is his imperative, and he has no problem of competing impulses. He magically draws rival persons and possibly rival feelings into his own central orbit. His prisoner Zenocrate falls in love with him, and when he spares her father he practices, in a new key, the magnanimity which he often talks about but by which he normally means only virile ruthlessness. His virility is all military. So he is a Puritan and middle-class family man. He does not let the little death distract his energy from the big killing. He does not *épater le bourgeois;* he wipes out establishment after establishment, and substitutes his own. He is all the uninhibited human dreams of triumph realized. Like the true melodramatic hero, he has a great fund of indignation. It is a purer, less morally congratulatory indignation than most. His greatest indignation is against his fatal illness. "Shall sickness prove me now to be a man . . .?" (Part 2, V.iii.44).[1] He blames the gods and would attack them: "Come, let us march against the powers of heaven . . ." (line 48). Tamburlaine feels the first onset of his illness just after he has been burning holy books, challenging Mahomet ("Whom I have thought a god"), and declaring his allegiance to some "God, full of revenging wrath"—"if any god [there is]," he adds—who is hardly more than a copy of himself (Part 2, V.i, iii). Marlowe might have treated this as a tragic nemesis, but he does not do so. The dying Emperor's grief and anguish are modified by no awareness of hubris. There is no move toward Faustus.

Tamburlaine the Great is dramatized hyperbole; nothing counterbalances or inhibits this outpouring of holocaustic power that defines the man. Hyperbole is the melodrama of rhetoric; here, rhetoric and drama are scarcely distinguishable. Being rushes into words, which are charged with the sentiments of conquest, the triumph of one over all. At best there is the tension of the straining ego, the struggle by style to magnify a glory felt to be pressing beyond human limits. One frenzied giant, declaring himself heaven's scourge, does not render others timid and puny, but stirs them also to giantism in words; demonic fury calls forth resounding magniloquence, aspiring to diabolic certitude and venom. Tamburlaine and other leaders are like intoxicated actors trying, with total voice and wild mouth, to leap to the heights of roles they imagine to be soaring above them. They are the creatures of a poet who can build mighty lines into crescendo after crescendo without quite swelling into bombast; but in such melodrama there is always a pressure for escalation, and bigger and stronger doses of words cannot always be found. We keep crossing back and forth over the same rhetorical plateaus and peaks. There is a succession of flitings, epic boasts, serried catalogues, tumultuous sonorities, rolling exotic onomasticons, mouth-filling names, and numbers massed like troops. At every crisis the rhetorical outburst becomes an end in itself, or at least the exercise ground for technical skills in verbal dueling. A speech is an aria; the atmosphere is operatic; every king is a vocal virtuoso. Melodrama passes over, if not altogether into rousing musical theater, at least into romantic epic, where, as in Boiardo, Ariosto, and Tasso, any scene may crash from soaring thoughts into burlesque. That Marlowe never quite sinks testifies to his genius; we can see the ancestral line running downhill from him into the rodomontade of Restoration heroic drama. In the end, however, the purity of the melodramatic characterization means a thinness of substance for stylistic commutation; we know where the flights are going and we do not soar any more; the onomatomania seems mannered, and even the mighty line drapes power with monotony.

Since we have often alluded to *Doctor Faustus* elsewhere, an elaborate comment here would be repetitive. Only one thing need be said: it is extraordinary that within a year or two, or at most within four or five years, a young dramatist should have done two distinguished dramas with such contrasting premises of characterization as *Tamburlaine* and *Doctor Faustus*. We hear often of what they have in common—a solitary titanism in imagining worlds to conquer and in striving to subdue; both gamble everything in securing and expending power. It is plain, too, that the realm of one is physical battles and empire, of the other, arcane magic and the mysterious reaches of the cosmos where heaven may be challenged with a subtler power. But Tamburlaine is sheer demonic drive, single in being, with no trace of counterimpulse to impede endless assaults upon kings and kingdoms. Take away half the animal passion, the torrential rage, replace it by machiavellian scheming, and the result is the Jew of Malta. Let the egoistic energy and the heaven-conquering spirit stand, but add to them a knowledge of consequences, of nemesis, of moral order, of the price the "I" pays to ascend the throne of the universe, and the result is Dr. Faustus. The warrior is one of the most remarkably undivided characters in literature; the scholar an exemplary embodiment of Everyman's divisions that are the genesis of tragedy. Both have a kind of completeness that makes them almost schematic. In few melodramatic victors is there so total a concentration of means upon ends; in few tragic heroes is there so strenuous and unending a clash between the lust to possess and the biting awareness of immitigable sanctions, the scorning of these and the sensitivity to them, the anguished snatch at salvation and the crippling despair. It would not seem possible that a single creative mind, not yet practiced enough to be disciplined, could so quickly have leaped from one polar method of

characterization to the other; we would expect a more gradual shifting of generic modes. The double accomplishment may have been
exhausting; or it may be that Marlowe's death came before he could
recover from this twofold outpouring of creative energy and again
approach the same heights.

Marlowe's Lesser Work

For, if the usual dating is correct, the rest of his career represented, if not a downhill movement, at least a lower level of performance. He did not again write tragedy, and the other melodramatic
works—with a partial exception for *Edward II*—did not approach the
heights of *Tamburlaine*. *Tamburlaine* looks monumental beside *The
Massacre at Paris*, in which the dominant impression of episodicity
and lack of focus is mitigated only by the continuing reappearances of
the Duke of Guise throughout five-sixths of the play. Though Tamburlaine is often histrionic and hysterical, he achieves grandeur beside the miscellaneous company of kings, dukes, and churchmen,
who, even when playing at *coups d'état* for thrones, seem like pettily
malicious schemers and back-alley cutthroats. This is simply to say
that in *The Massacre* Marlowe retrenched the melodramatic scope of
character so sharply that he achieved little of the intensity possible
within it. If the melodramatic personality is to be explored successfully, it needs centering and time and continuity; Marlowe has so
crammed a short play with years and events and political rivals that
no individuality can mature. In contrast, even the *Henry VI* plays
seem massive and disciplined. *Dido*, however, continues—or anticipates, as some scholars think—the operatic vein in *Tamburlaine;* but
the key is different and the variety is greater. The divine interventions
look backward toward the romantic comedies of Euripides and ahead
toward the mode of Offenbach; the playfully ironic and the pathetic
overtake the epic, which was evidently meant to lead the procession.
Three lovers die because love has gone unrequited; we can almost
hear the triad of death-agony solos before the final curtain. Meanwhile Aeneas has got himself off to Italy at last, after uncertainties
that might have been enlarged into a tragic conflict but that hardly go
beyond the superficial irresolution of an underdeveloped character.
His departure is simply the occasion for the long final grief of Dido,
which is not made tragic by the title *The Tragedy of Dido*.

Like *The Massacre, Edward II* forces so many years of history into the space of a play that the rush of events inhibits characterization; even at that, however, it makes a partial return toward the melodramatic achievement of *Tamburlaine.* Different as they are—*Tamburlaine,* the operatic chronicle, and *Edward II,* the dramatic chronicle —each deals with an obsessed character; and if Edward has nothing of Tamburlaine's cyclonic powers of devastation, still he manages to stand out amidst a large cast and to achieve a lesser vein of memorability. While Tamburlaine is a talented destroyer of others, Edward has a genius for being destroyed by others; Marlowe shifts from a union of will and power to a combination of willfulness and weakness. Edward is a genuine personality in whom we can detect human habits, especially the flair for wanting one's own way in defiance of the ways of the world. He is the victim of the world who, like most such victims, refuses to conciliate it—not out of stubborn uprightness against oppression or corruption, but out of that perverse quasi integrity which interprets the legitimate claims of others as an indignity. He is the man who goes under because he will never go around but must always go over, who is finally on his knees to all because he will never curtsey to any. He is the man of bad habits who, instead of practicing secret vices, flaunts his addiction in public and believes that others will cede their own habits out of deference. In his special form he has the Marlovian hero's dream of immunity: England will have to take the disreputable Gaveston (and later Spencer) and like it. Whereas Faustus will make the cosmos bow, Edward will make the nation bow; Faustus will control through a new, antitraditional grasp of truth, Edward through a traditional exercise of role. Neither has adequate power or sense of reality. Faustus senses this from the start, and through his effort to deny it becomes tragic; Edward lacks the mind to grasp that he has erred and to see himself in moral perspective. He faces not nemesis but enemies.

When the enemies are too strong, that man who has tried to impose his will suffers from the will of others and becomes a victim; so we get a double melodramatic exposure of Edward. The king who could promise "lakes of gore" (III.ii.135) in revenge for the death of Gaveston, who can quickly order "off with both their heads" (III.iii.62) when he captures the barons who killed Gaveston, who rails at "villains" and "traitors" (IV.iii.38, 47), and who indeed fights vigorously, now asks "compassion of my state," declares "this life contemplative is heaven" (IV.vi.11, 20), and sadly wishes

> O might I never open these eyes again,
> Never again lift up this drooping head,
> O never more lift up this dying heart!
> [IV.vi.41–43]

We have that transformation of the foolish king into the pitiable man that is better known in Shakespeare's Richard II.

This kind of pitiable man is neither the innocent victim nor the uncomplaining sufferer, but the man who, both sinned against and sinning, feels more sinned against than sinning, and whose blaming of others' misdeeds excludes all awareness of his own. Since we will examine in detail the strategic movements of the personality when we come to *Richard II*, we need not here do more than note them. Marlowe lavishes a good deal of care upon the details of thought and feeling by which Edward contemplates his own suffering and instinctively employs all devices for the evocation of sympathy. Marlowe endows Edward with such skill in stirring pity for the dethroned king that it seems almost unfair to recall the incompetent and irresponsible king who held the throne. In fact, the playwright fascinated elsewhere by pitiless triumph is here almost obsessed by pitiful defeat: in presenting the mistreatment, torture, and murder of Edward, Marlowe discloses an appetite for prolonged suffering that might appear in a Jacobean sensationalist or in a provisioner for the modern theater of cruelty. In sum, he so manages *Edward II* as to secure several quite different melodramatic effects. Marlowe plainly does not wish to make use of the tragic potential in his plot; and the combination of Edward's self-pity and the victors' pitiless mistreatment of him which dominates the last third of the play does not permit the full and robustious melodramatic grandeur that *Tamburlaine* reaches more than once.

III. THREE SHAKESPEARE CHRONICLE PLAYS

Whereas Marlowe burst through suddenly to his heights, Shakespeare approached his gradually; whereas Marlowe shifted, almost without taking a breath, from achievement in melodrama to achievement in tragedy, Shakespeare moved deliberately from one to the other. In Shakespeare there is elaborate experimentation, and an almost evolutionary development; this may help account for the greater richness in his employment of the two structures. He did not surpass Marlowe in the intensity that comes from presenting exhaustively a single strong personality; but to this he added the intensities of other personalities and of complex relationships; hence the widening out into his characteristic massiveness of effect. The movement from Marlowe to Shakespeare—to consider the two canons simply as stages in English drama—is from a slenderer to a greater achievement in both melodrama and tragedy, and from a single brilliant work in tragedy to a series of magnificent works. That large historical development need not be elaborated here. In Shakespeare's own development, however, there are several aspects of movement that are worth examining.

Within the traditional category of "tragedies," there is a visible widening out of sense of character—from *Titus* to *Romeo and Juliet* and *Julius Caesar*, and then from these to *Hamlet* and its successors. But in the dramas of the 1590's the protagonists still have markedly less dividedness than do those of the major tragedies. In *Titus* we have largely humors, or one humor in different manifestations; Romeo is a lover whose troubles are almost exclusively outer ones; the perturbations that afflict Brutus are those of the political arena (this is less true of Cassius). However, if to these plays we add the chronicle plays of the mid-nineties, we get a broader view of the experimentations preceding the high period of the tragedies, and perhaps of a more inclusive movement toward that period.

King John

King John (*ca.* 1594), though much less commanding than *Richard III* and *Richard II* of about the same period, nevertheless is interesting for the considerable variety of effects that Shakespeare either seeks out, or unwittingly secures, within a melodramatic structure. The direct confrontations of political conflict are diverse, at least some of them have an ironic element, and they do not always evoke clearly patterned responses. There is an opening touch of hostilities where the appeal is purely patriotic; then comes the extended Faulconbridge family quarrel, where the advantage is all with bastardy and imaginative freedom. In Act II, the clash between England and

France is interwoven with a dynastic squabble which does not make an unequivocal call upon loyalties, and is punctuated by an exchange of sneering incivilities between royal-family mothers that has a strongly distancing effect. The sheer melodrama of war is undermined by the obstinate self-protective neutrality of the city of Angiers, prepared to yield only to a proved winner; by the almost comically ironic decision of the competing armies to join in sacking Angiers and to fight it out for the ruins later; by the sudden makeshift pacification through the marriage of Lewis and Blanch; and finally by the Bastard's jeering speech at "Commodity" as the corrupt world's sole principle. Then there is an entirely new direction of feeling as the French King is caught between his agreement with England and heavy papal pressure to break it; this leads into an England-against-the-world melodrama, but it is quickly modified by King John's plotting for the death of Prince Arthur. The appeal to patriotic sentiment is consistently ambiguous; Faulconbridge's energy and zeal carry the appeal directly, while the King's defects of character interfere with it. The main actions are so full of ironic reversals that the reader, following an apparent clue to expected feeling, is repeatedly rebuffed. John wants Arthur dead; then the Barons want him alive; then John blames the murderer whom he had incited to do the job; then he finds that the murderer had failed in his assignment; then Arthur in effect commits suicide; then the murderer who failed is blamed for the murder he did not carry out. Throughout Act V, where the action is nearly all military, there is a comparable series of ironic reversals that make the affair quite different from a triumph by Henry V or a defeat for Richard III.

It is possible to argue that Shakespeare simply did not hold his materials together very well. But if, as critics have maintained, he was put off by the difficulties inherent in King John as a subject, it may also be argued that these led him into extremely interesting, and by no means unsuccessful, departures from the more straightforward effects that would be served by a larger, better integrated royal character. Aside from the variations we have already noted, Shakespeare repeatedly gives prominence, for a dozen lines or as many as a hundred, to a private feeling or a kind of conduct that alters the nation-at-war pattern of feeling and actions. With a throne at stake, and his mother Constance fiercely defending his rights, Arthur "weeps" and wishes he were dead: "I am not worth this coil that's made for me" (II.i.165). In the fifty closing lines of the long scene in which King Philip of France, threatened by Rome, resolves to war upon England, the key figure is Blanch, tied by blood to the English and by marriage to the French. The appeal to partisanship is all but wiped out by the desperation of her divided loyalties: "I having hold of both, / They whirl asunder and dismember me. . . . Whoever wins, on that side shall I lose" (III.i.329–30, 335). After Arthur has been captured in the battle, his mother is grief-stricken; but she is so indefatigable in the clamorous rhetoric of bereavement that the Cardinal says, "You hold too heinous a respect of grief," and King Philip adds, "You are as fond of grief as of your child" (III.iv.90, 92). Good sense interposes against a legitimate emotion which has over-played its own legitimacy. And then, after a 75-line intervening dialogue, Shakespeare writes a 130-line scene in which Arthur, a typically attractive "little prince," instead of going pathetically to his death, charms Hubert de Burgh, the executioner appointed by King John, into going back on his promise to the King (IV.i). It is after this that Arthur appears on the castle wall, half terrified, half desperate; willing to escape if possible, but also suicidal; he leaps and is killed. Among the ironies that surround this action is that three English lords so loathe it that they defect to the French even when the French invasion is threatening the English throne (IV.iii). The throne cannot command the responses of patriotic melodrama; the Bastard does make this appeal, but he uniquely combines the national hero with the sardonic ironist and severe moralist.

Richard III

The point is that even in a chronicle play which is intrinsically melodramatic, Shakespeare is constantly experimenting, modifying, complicating, widening out, not only with actional surprises and a series of ironies, but with touches of character that partly turn on inner discords. The process is also apparent in *Richard III* (*ca.* 1593) and *Richard II* (*ca.* 1595), notably in the treatment of the title characters, who are central and unifying in a way that King John is not. Both are of the melodramatic order, but in each we can see, if not actually a movement toward tragedy, at least formal modifications that imaginably represent a growing sense of tragedy. We could put it the other way and say that in each we see a different departure from an ideal tragic balance: Richard III embodies a defect, Richard II an excess, of what we have called tragic consciousness. But *Richard II* is not susceptible of easy classification, and later we shall need to examine fully the diverse formal pressures within it.

Both plays, of course, can be looked at as variations on Marlowe themes. The resemblances between Richard II and Edward II are commonplace knowledge; what interests us is that in these plays Marlowe was, evidently, past his peak, while Shakespeare was still approaching his. If we look at Richard III as a version of Tamburlaine,* we can see contrasts that may have defining value. Both protagonists have a gift for conquest, for taking by storm and for humiliating others, whether out of spontaneous power lust or out of a vengefulness of nature which makes the mere existence of other throne holders a slight. But whereas Tamburlaine is a naïve, volcanic brute, Richard is a calculating machiavel. Both are violent and ruthless, but one is a barbarian questing for glory, the other a modern schemer, decisive in act but undecided about ends. Tamburlaine has the bloody innocence of a killer without soul, Richard the sinister duplicity of an entrepreneur whose perverted soul enables him to charm, lie, and murder at will. Tamburlaine apotheosizes the military conquerors whom most nations have admired; Richard is a melodramatic villain. But he is a complex villain, and it is in the exploration of his complexities that Shakespeare writes an unusual melodrama, with more order and power than *King John*, and, in one scene at least, with a hint of tragedy.

In some ways *Richard III* seems to play to a simpler organization of feelings than *King John*, for here there is a series of victims to be

---

* Tamburlaine and three Shakespeare characters can be arranged in a line of relationship that suggests an interesting set of modifications in a type. Tamburlaine and Richard III are related in that they are both political entrepreneurs without scruple, but one has the continuing success of naïve, spirited might, while the other has too tortuous a personality to command power and loyalty indefinitely. Take from Richard III the political orientation of energy, and leave the instinctive revengefulness against a world that slights one's own ego simply by being independent, and you have Iago, the agile and persuasive man of malice who has a private instead of a public arena. Take away the destructive malice, but leave the egotism, agility, and defect of scruple, and you have Iachimo in *Cymbeline*.

pitied, and a monstrous villain to be loathed. It is not quite so simple as that, however, for Richard is not the only user of "policy" in the play, and strong, legitimate feeling and "practice" are intertwined in a way that creates an equivocal impact. Several characters feel the remorse that, when it is integral to the hero's experience, helps give a drama tragic tone. Of the murderers of Clarence, one feels the pangs of conscience strongly enough to give up his fee (I.iv.284); to both murderers of the sons of Edward IV are imputed "conscience and remorse" (IV.iii.20). Hastings, en route to death, laments the folly and overconfidence which contributed to his own disaster and to the misery of England (III.iv.82ff.). Buckingham even more emphatically recounts the moral errors that become clear to him as he is on the way to execution (V.i.3ff.). Though these are minor and tentative approaches to the drama of self-knowledge, they show early preparation for the great tragedies.

What Shakespeare does to Richard himself serves not to make him any less a villain but to modify, in more ways than one, the straightforward response to him. On the one hand, of course, the combination of Tartuffe and trigger man makes him the more to be dreaded. On the other hand, the combination of deviousness and daring, of boldness and gamesmanship, gives him a certain fascination. His brilliant tour de force of seeming to be pulled against his will from religious to political life would give him a picaresque flair if his victims were not everywhere present. The precocious wooing, against hopeless odds, perhaps attracts to him a faint touch of the admiration elicited by the utterly cool gambler. Though in these devices Shakespeare might instinctively be trying to diminish the distance between reader and Richard, elsewhere he seems to be intuiting in Richard a discordant element of a sort we call "modern"—the periodic *nausée*. At certain times Richard has an almost Puritan disgust at the human responses brought about by his own pressure upon others: we see it unmistakably in the sneers at Anne after she yields to his protracted love-making (I.ii.228ff.) and at Queen Elizabeth after he thinks she has accepted his proposal for her daughter's (his niece's) hand (IV.iv.431). Likewise it is obscurely present, I believe, in his sharp reversal of attitude to his chief tool Buckingham almost as soon as he mounts the throne (IV.ii.1ff.). Such matters are the evidence, even in an early play, of a fresh and variegated characterization that makes *Richard III* more than a trite melodrama.

At one point, as we have said, *Richard III* pushes toward tragedy —toward division and self-knowledge in Richard; this is in the long nighttime scene before the battle of Bosworth Field, when the ghosts of Richard's victims come parading before the sleeping commanders, each spirit or group of spirits first condemning Richard and then encouraging Richmond. This intervention of transcendental forces, which serves to underline the simple conflict of good and evil in the coming battle, is rather mechanical and undramatic, technically backward looking rather than experimental. As if aware that these balanced testimonials to evil done and to true reparation are not vitalizing the action, Shakespeare follows it up immediately with a thirty-line soliloquy by Richard that for the first and only time breaks the dominant symmetry of the long scene (V.iii). This soliloquy, since it is the only extended statement by Richard not matched in Richmond's lines,[2] catches the eye. Waking up suddenly after the dream of the hostile spirits, Richard is terrified, and in his terror talks of his "coward conscience" (line 179) and his "trembling flesh" (line 181), and, more than that, discovers that he "hates" himself (line 189), names his crimes (lines 195–98), and feels "despair" and finds that no one "loves" or "pities" him (lines 200–201).

Such a self-survey is not plausible in Richard, since there has been no preparation at all for even a small inrush of moral sensitivity. But if under shock Richard falls momentarily into conventional views that ordinarily he would despise, he plausibly tends, at this moment, to feel fright rather than remorse, to catalogue painful facts rather than to wish them different. He can apply harsh words to himself but still by battle time recover sufficiently to call "conscience" a word for "cowards" and to cheer his comrades thus: "Our strong arms be our conscience" (lines 309, 311). I am making two suggestions here— first, that Shakespeare is working to keep his character consistent despite an exceptional intrusion of conscience, and second, and more significant for a study of genre, that these motions of conscience—all problems of plausibility aside—show an early tendency in Shakespeare to interpose a tragic perspective even for a character at the center of a brilliant melodrama. If Richard III is defective, as we put it earlier, in tragic consciousness, the remarkable thing is that he has something like it even for a moment.

Richard II

In the examination of "movements toward" tragedy, *Richard II* (*ca.* 1595) is still more interesting. Here Shakespeare virtually jumps from Richard III to an opposite extreme—from a pressingly aggressive man to an increasingly recessive one, from one who has no feelings for the victims he keeps on making to one with floods of feeling for the victim he keeps on becoming. Richard III is too tough in his wholeness to be a tragic hero; Richard II, as we noted in Chapter 4, is a man whose stamina is too much undercut by hypersensitivity to be the tragic hero. He has a fatal excess of a potentially tragic quality, and it is misdirected. Yet Shakespeare dramatizes his career with a generic complexity that forbids quick labeling.

One could legitimately describe *Richard II* as a melodrama that "moves toward" a tragic orientation, or as a possible tragedy that eventually takes melodramatic form. Though the latter appears to be more accurate, let us look briefly at the former: *Richard II* as initially a melodrama—a conflict of sides for power, or in part a conflict between good and evil rulers—that veers toward tragedy as the stage is taken over by a highly introspective character. Indeed, the inaugural note is almost archetypally melodramatic: the furious assertion of rival rectitudes by Bolingbroke and Mowbray which occupies almost two hundred lines of Act I, Scene i, and almost another one hundred in Act I, Scene iii, creates an atmosphere of combat between "whole" men bent only on surviving or triumphing in the world. This is far removed from tragedy, as is indeed the main line of subsequent action in which we see "good" statesmen gradually joining against "bad" Richard. But then the focus shifts from the overt conflict to the sensibility of defeated Richard, and the meditative-philosophic inevitably suggests something closer to the tragic than are duels, civil broils, and coups. The something closer, of course, has difficulty in materializing because of Richard's overwhelming grief for himself. Yet at one or two moments Richard fleetingly views himself in the light of the moral realism that is at the center of tragedy, and slips for a second from self-pity to self-placement. In just one line, speaking to the Queen, he attributes their troubles to "our profane hours"

(V.i.25); but then he is promptly off into fifteen lines on "tales / Of woeful ages" and "the lamentable tale of me" (lines 41, 44). Later, in solitary captivity in Pomfret Castle he hears music and is led into reflecting that if one does not "keep time" the "sweet music" becomes "sour" (V.v.42); then he develops a simile between life and music. Now, he says, he can "check time broke" (line 46), that is, censure bad time. He continues:

> But for the concord of my state and time
> Had not an ear to hear my true time broke.
> I wasted time, and now doth Time waste me.
> [V.v.47–49]

Here the exploration of the metaphor leads naturally to the partial note of self-judgment; although brief, it is managed with a technical grace in contrast with the rather crude, though much lengthier, interjection of the conscience issue in *Richard III* two years earlier. Still the appearance of the tragic sensibility is hardly more than a flicker; from there on, Richard develops his time trope principally as a description of his lamentable circumstances. The music which was his starting point becomes, at the end of the speech, "a sign of love; and love to Richard / Is a strange brooch in this all-hating world" (lines 65–66). This sense of enmity everywhere has a tinge of the paranoid which, as we noted earlier, is the clinical form of the melodramatic posture. This is in Richard's more characteristic vein: the pathos of solitude and deprivation.

We can proceed more surely by following the alternative movement, that from tragedy to melodrama. There are various ways of revealing, early in a play, a tragic commitment: the dramatist can begin with an apparently evil man but indicate the presence of contradictory elements in his make-up and hence introduce the tragic dividedness (in this sense Claudius could be a tragic hero). The traditional procedure, of course, is to present the "good" man with the "flaw," and its emergence in the error whose consequences are the body of the play. It is this kind of structure to which, however consciously or unconsciously, Shakespeare seems drawn. Throughout Act I Richard's lines and conduct are those of a well-intentioned ruler who needs only a little more clarity, consistency, and decisiveness to be impressive or at least adequate. Not until his harshness to dying

Gaunt and his confiscation of Gaunt's property (II.i) does he make an error of commission before our eyes. Yet we are hurried over these actions (in which Richard speaks only about thirty lines), and we note Richard's readiness for the arduous Irish campaign; hence we do not have an overpowering sense of his administrative misconduct, which seems a small affair in comparison, say, with such political evildoing as that of Lear and Macbeth.

It is not that Shakespeare totally forgets the historical Richard or ignores his sources, for an ample calendar of Richard's misdeeds is made available, but the record is introduced in a way that is technically interesting: the case against Richard is made almost entirely in the statements of others. We see very little of his corrupt favorites ruining the state. We hardly see Richard himself do wrong; rather we hear others report wrongs (Gaunt, York, and other lords in Act II, Scene i; Bolingbroke and the rebels in II.iii and III.i). Though these reports are the prologue to and accompaniment of rebellion, they do not acquire full dramatic substance; and we rather tend to slide over them and regard Richard with the sympathy that normally accrues to an Everyman whose defects do not outnumber his virtues.* It is possible that in this management of Acts I and II there is simply dramaturgic confusion, and that Shakespeare was turning Holinshed into dialogue without being certain where he was going. But it is also possible to suppose that he was instinctively shying away from that easy blackness of character that would have left him with slender dramatic alternatives once Bolingbroke returned and confronted Richard. If that is true, he was, in our terms, sensing the situation tragically rather than melodramatically, imagining a divided rather than a whole character.

The problem, then, is what happens when Richard commands the stage in Act III, Scenes ii and iii, the second half of the short Act IV, and Act V, Scenes i and v. We have already commented on his intense preoccupation with himself and his fate, in what is less a moral hypersensitivity than a histrionic narcissism (Chapter 4). Critics have spoken of him as having a "character" that constitutes a "theme . . . essentially lyrical," and as "a great minor poet," "a touching

---

* Richard was given an almost completely favorable interpretation in the 1964 production at Stratford-on-Avon.

person," "a sympathetic figure." [3] In endeavoring to place him more precisely, and in seeing how the portrayal of him affects the generic structure of the play, we may profitably observe the themes that his verses develop and the kind of appeal that he makes for sympathy, that is, the human congeniality of the posture he assumes. Richard might, for instance, see himself at least in part through the eyes of others, or he might understand the import of such mistaken deeds as Shakespeare has actually let him do in the drama; one who is so fond of sun images might lyrically experience a dawning light whose painful brightness would demand of auditors the uneasy sympathy that embraces a shared sense of incrimination. Macbeth does this. He imposes on an adequate reader the close knowledge of divided motives: the desire to act by obligation, challenged by the ambition that can become murderous. Though Richard might represent, and become aware of, a comparable division, the remarkable fact of his conduct from Wales to Pomfret Castle is his assiduity in maintaining an almost unbroken oneness which appeals not to pity but, with a subtler seductiveness, to a love of singleness not disrupted by competing impulses.

We are simply trying to see what the personality is, and what responses of our own it actuates, what it draws us toward or into. Richard finds a protective over-all oneness that is the sum of several constituent onenesses. He has, notably, the oneness of the victim; only a concessive phrase or two disturbs slightly the hedge of guiltlessness about the deposed king. He is not facing people who have a cause but simply "foes," "enemies," "thieves and robbers" (III.ii.12, 18, 22, 39); he imagines his friends are deserters and calls them "villains, vipers" (line 129). Bolingbroke has taken all; there is "nothing can we call our own but death" (line 152); yet death victimizes him too —an "antic" "Scoffing his state and grinning at his pomp" (lines 162–63). So Richard is "subjected thus" (line 176). He "Must . . . submit," "Must . . . be depos'd" (III.iii.143–44) and "be buried"

> . . . where subjects' feet
> May hourly trample on their sovereign's head;
> For on my heart they tread now whilst I live,
> And buried once, why not upon my head?
> [III.iii.155–59]

He acknowledges only force as an issue: "For do we must what force will have us do" (line 207). He finds no "truth" in "twelve thousand" men (IV.i.171). Bolingbroke "may my glories and my state depose," "for I must nothing be" (lines 192, 201). But "Conveyers are you all, / That rise thus nimbly by a true king's fall" (lines 317–18); "Bad men . . . violate / A twofold marriage" and make him "Doubly divorc'd" (V.i.71–72).

The point is that Richard's presentation of himself as a victim of force and injustice invites assent by appealing to a strong human inclination that is normally exploited in melodramatic form. Richard's view is not entirely without factual justification, and since the play does not as a whole challenge the view or subject it to ironic comment, the appeal becomes the stronger and hence contributes to removing the play from the tragic realm. When Richard identifies himself with Christ by repeatedly terming his opponents Judases and Pilates (III.ii.132; IV.i.170, 239–40) and by referring to his "sour cross" (IV.i.241), he pushes as far as it will go the strategy of substituting a polarity of his good and others' evil for the medley of good and evil in the soul. It is an accent rather than a theme, and Shakespeare does not run the danger of letting it be picked up by hostile observers; hence, it seems likely to aid rather than interfere with Richard's subtle appeal to the love of being on the right side.

If Richard's role as Christ will not bear much examining, his position as king is strong, and so he makes the most of divine right; of accusations of treason, violations of oaths to God's anointed, and seizure of God's power; and of predictions of heavenly wrath against the deposers (cf. III.ii.50–62; III.iii.72–100; IV.i.229–42; V.i.55–68). This exclusive reliance upon legal position, as if the deposition were a spontaneous uncaused evil, is dramatically interesting. A tragic treatment of the theme might present various inner conflicts; of these, the most likely would be that between a sense of technical inviolability and a sense of human, and royal, fallibility ("the conscience of the King" is a recurrent motif in Shakespeare). The point is that Richard rules out such complications, probable as they are, and limits his consciousness to a single one of the facets of truth open to his view. We know how much authority this facet had: Shakespeare shows Henry IV's distress over his insecure claim to the crown. Our problem, however, is not the touchy one of divine right and royal failure in itself, but of Richard's chosen innocence, of his finding, in our terms, oneness by clinging to the single value that theoretically renders him unassailable. In that sense his role exemplifies another functioning of melodramatic feeling. It excites, we may suppose, a ready responsiveness even in ages that have lost not only the monarchic sentiment but also the sense of its metaphysical roots. For Richard appeals not to an obsolete feeling but to one historic form of a constant impulse: the longing for protection by prerogative, justification by office, the security in enduring forms outside the wavering and inconsistent self—in a word, an Everyman's divine right that the mind rarely ceases to quest for. Such wholeness is a refuge from tragic dividedness, and it invites a sympathy that may have more weight than our own sense of the intellectual dubiety of his theoretical claims.

The third form of wholeness that Richard instinctively adopts may seem even more difficult to relate to representative habits of feeling. This we can approach through what is usually called Richard's sentimentality, a word whose very mention runs the risk of placing us at a critical distance from him. But we may find that he is up to something by no means distant from the more obscure underside of human personality. Sentimentality normally implies a clinging to an emotional experience which has become a pleasurable end in itself. We can go a step further and say that this experience is made possible by the elimination of emotional counterclaims; we can linger in one emotion by giving over to it the energy saved by the exclusion of other emotions, however relevant. Hence we can see the relation between the sentimental and the melodramatic: what is central to each is a singleness of feeling made possible by the paring away of whatever does not contribute to it. Aside from claiming the singleness of the victim and that of the possessor of divine right, Richard holds himself in one affective mood, the elegiac: he embraces tears, sorrow, "grim Necessity," his own nullity, death, even despair. This is the only wholeness that Shakespeare lets be challenged by the dramatic structure: the Queen, in a momentary reminiscence of Henry VI's Margaret and anticipation of Lady Macbeth, suggests that Richard is "Transform'd and weak'ned" and that he could be more like the lion

(V.i.27–34). Richard refuses to reject "base humility" and play at "king of beasts"; he picks up immediately the melancholy subject of their parting, and the Queen is drawn quickly into the anguish of separation. She has failed to spur the King into a style that would modify his ruling passion.

"Let's talk of graves, of worms, and epitaphs" (III.ii.145) marks Richard's entry into a mood that remains almost totally unbroken. Note some characteristic phrases: "rainy eyes," "nothing can we call our own but death," "sad stories of the death of kings," "feel want, / Taste grief, need friends," "pine away," "woe's slave," "I have none [of hope]" (III.ii.146, 152, 156, 175–76, 209, 210, 213); "a little grave, / A little, little grave, an obscure grave," "make foul weather with despised tears," "make some pretty match with shedding tears," "Two kinsmen digg'd their graves with weeping eyes" (III.iii.153–54, 161, 165, 169); "full of tears am I, / Drinking my griefs whilst you mount up on high," "still am I king of [griefs]," "Your cares set up do not pluck my cares down," "soon lie Richard in an earthy pit," "Mine eyes are full of tears, I cannot see," "I have no name, no title," "How soon my sorrow hath destroy'd my face," "the tortur'd soul" (IV.i.188–89, 193, 195, 219, 244, 255, 291, 298); "the senseless brands will sympathize / . . . And in compassion weep the fire out," "So two, together weeping, make one woe" (V.i.46–48, 86); "eas'd / With being nothing" (V.v.40–41). One of the most striking of these speeches is his ironic rebuke to Aumerle for words of encouragement which, Richard says after another setback, "didst lead me forth / Of that sweet way I was in to despair" (III.ii.204–5). He quickly gets back into the "sweet way . . . to despair."

No serious note of responsibility enters to disturb an experience which is, in our terms, monopathic; the grief is never for the deed done, but always for the deed suffered. Even the occasional flash of indignation dies away in lingering lament. Shakespeare has brilliantly portrayed a personality adept in pushing away the sources of division and in exhaustively utilizing every device of wholeness—even that mode of surrender which clings to sorrow and death, and all but says, "You'll be sorry when I die." That brilliance does not mean greatness, for the exclusions essential to Richard's form of wholeness seriously limit the human range. Yet Shakespeare doubtless did not consider the portrait as altogether unfavorable; * many readers have found Richard "sympathetic," and his way of handling his disaster can be ingratiating; one who simply scorned him would be felt to be making an inadequate response.

The irony of it is that whatever sympathy accrues to Richard is not elicited by virtues that can be publicly acclaimed; not only does he have few, if any, of these, but the modes of his wholeness are likely to evoke formal disapproval—the sense of being victimized, the claim to special immunity, and, above all, the long-drawn-out tasting of pathos and doom. Shakespeare has pulled off a tour de force: making the style of his protagonist run head on into a public sense of adult manly conduct, penetrate through a heavy layer of open dissent, win an un-articulated sympathy from unacknowledged inclinations, and find an assent in private impulses that, if all counterclaims are ignored, can become addictions. Aside from some philosophical circles, despair is not normally in good odor; yet Richard's "sweet way . . . to despair" surely reduces to a casual phrase a kind of monopathic simplifying that we have already observed in the spectrum of melodramatic re-sponses (Chapter 4)—the strange comfort of going under, with per-haps a dressing of soft pity and sharp irony. Further, giving up has its own perverse triumph, which we accept as a characteristic impulse in suicides. But while Richard is instinctively exploiting the pathos of going down, he is intermittently attacking or needling Bolingbroke: the polemic mode enjoying the technical or theoretical triumph of divine right. This reaches a climax when, in his death speech, he exclaims, "Mount, mount, my soul! thy seat is up on high" (V.v.112), and thus asserts an ultimate victory of spirit. The depths and the heights at once: the monopathy of the victor piled upon that of the victim. Two extremes of melodramatic consciousness and experience: in this mode of appeal there is much latent power.

Richard II is not a simple play. Its use of the melodramatic struc-ture of personality is subtle and sophisticated; it has a complexness not wholly unlike that of tragedy. Hence its oscillations between the tragic and melodramatic poles, and its eventually stronger attraction

---

* As indicated by the devotion of a few followers, that of a groom in Act V, Scene v, and especially that of the Queen, who was evidently given adult years by Shakespeare for this purpose.

to the latter of these, constitute an unusual revelation of generic interplay.

IV. GENERIC TYPES: REVENGE DRAMA

If we look at noncomic drama as it approaches Shakespeare's period of greatest achievement, we see an irregular development with just enough complexities to forbid an easy charting. The record from Shakespeare's high period to the closing of the theaters is a still more complicated interweaving of diverse aesthetic strands. We customarily think of the main course of events as a decline. This will do, at least as a mnemonic device. But like most mnemonic devices, this one simplifies a pattern that in its fullness is rather taxing. At best the pattern resembles the *trompe l'oeil*, for how one reads it depends on one's perspective. If we think of Shakespeare's four main tragedies as an absolute high in tragedy and move ahead almost a decade to *The Duchess of Malfi* (*ca.* 1614), we have to see Webster as a disintegrator: he takes the complex character of tragedy, breaks it up into its constituent elements, and embodies these in different dramatis personae. Duke Ferdinand and the Cardinal are the malicious and destructive side of human nature; the madness that comes to the one, and the brief remorse attributed to the other, are much less symptoms of tragic awareness than late additional twists in the theatricalization of evil character. On the other side, the Duchess and Antonio are versions of human goodness; the "flaws" which some readers have labored to find in them, on the assumption that the play is a tragedy and must conform to the rules, are at most of a highly technical sort and can convince no reader that this pair are essentially tragic actors rather than victims. In a history of tragedy, then, *The Duchess of Malfi* would be an important representative of the generic shift that follows a breakdown of that full character without which tragedy cannot exist.

That is the point of view that we tend to use. Yet it is not obligatory. Alongside developments in tragedy, melodrama continued to be very popular, and writers in it, though they did a great deal of repeating, also did some experimenting. If we look at Webster from the vantage point of procedures in melodrama, what do we see? In this context, surely, he is a talented innovator. In *The Duchess of Malfi* he invests the victims with a strength and dignity that make

them permanent exemplars of what humanity can achieve while losing everything. Likewise he pursues his ostensible revengers so far
into their psyches that we begin to understand revenge as the ritual
front for sick personalities whose natural outlet is sadism; Webster is
especially subtle in revealing an incestuous passion as the center of
Ferdinand's perversities. Such analyses were the new turn in revenge
melodrama. There are other brilliant innovations worth glancing at.
In *The Revenger's Tragedy* (1607), for instance, Tourneur embodied the voice of outraged virtue in a man who had a case for revenge
but even more conspicuously a flair for trapping, torturing, and
taunting victims. In *The White Devil* (1611) Webster innovated in
a quite different way: he found charm in evildoers.

In looking at serious drama in the first four decades of the seventeenth century, we can see it as a transforming of tragedy or an
exploiting of melodrama. Once the option is stated, however, it is
plain that we cannot choose between points of view but have to use
both. Some men write melodrama, for better or worse; some write
tragedy for better or worse. What is more, some waver between two
modes, and a few successfully use both. To inspect the formal variations and modulations within one period may reveal something about
both the period and the forms. Such an inspection obviously has to be
selective. Since the dozen or so non-Shakespearian dramas that most
consistently attract attention show not only resemblances but very
marked differences, they should perhaps yield an adequate preliminary view of the dramatic tendencies of their age; since they belong to
an age that, despite its own inner diversities, has an integral quality,
they demonstrate especially well the multiple possibilities in two basic
structures.

To begin with the simplest forms: pure melodrama not only did not
yield to tragedy, but it continued an independent existence in the
hands of writers who could not or did not think of character in terms
of tragic dividedness. They may have altered the details, but they
adhered to a basic pattern of external conflicts in which moral issues
are taken for granted and the action turns on physical survival.
Revenge melodrama had great longevity; not only were revenge plays
numerous, but the treatment of the revenge theme in unsophisticated
characterological terms went on as though actual improvements in the
form had not been noticed and had hence failed to alter anyone's

expectations of what might be done. We find an example at the beginning of the period—John Marston's *Antonio's Revenge* (1599) —and another at the end—James Shirley's *The Cardinal* (1641).

Marston and Shirley

John Marston is worth mentioning here because we see him going on with a simple form when Shakespeare had already improved on it several times and would shortly do *Hamlet*. After writing an essentially romantic drama of triumph in *Antonio and Mellida* (the virtuous survive evil machinations), Marston reversed the script in *Antonio's Revenge: The Second Part of Antonio and Mellida* and gave all the evil victories to a machiavellian villain, until at the very end he is done in. Piero, the Duke of Venice, is a frantically murderous plotter who seems designed only to provide a monstrous object of revenge; revenge on him becomes a holy crusade that justifies all killings and tortures that the revengers, with whom we are supposed to be allied, can rush into or coolly devise. Such a play imposes the maximum of irrational suffering on some characters and thus releases, in approved retaliatory activity, all the homicidally aggressive impulses that the human being is capable of. Antonio and his fellow revengers act out the savage fantasies of getting even that could possess a child half maddened by a sense of grievance. Not that they lack a grievance, but that their characters have the same singleness of motivation that appears in the monstrous Duke Piero. Such employments of the melodramatic structure of character need not be traced in detail. In *Antonio's Revenge*, however, there are signs of a tendency that later would develop more fully—the tendency to protract scenes of strong emotional impact; the characters begin to savor their own emotions and thus to play for a response of the same kind from the audience. At the beginning of Act I, and repeatedly in later scenes, Piero clings to an extended lunatic rejoicing in his murders and allied plots; Antonio mourns and contemplates revenge at notable length, as do other victims of Piero (III.i; IV.ii); the preliminaries of the final revenge scene and the actual execution of revenge, with the relish in torturing Piero, are unmistakably held (V.i, ii). We can see the emergence of that unstable relationship between action and feeling that is characteristic of decadence.

James Shirley's *The Cardinal*, one of the latest of the prewar dramas, has been said to show the influence of Webster's *The Duchess of Malfi*, but the resemblance is limited to a few details of the plot —the murderous hostility of a Cardinal and his nephew to a countess who happens to love the wrong man. While *The Duchess of Malfi* is a great drama of disaster that has some resemblances to tragedy, *The Cardinal* is a straight melodrama of revenge which has some ingenuity in the plotting but no complication of character. Shirley's Duchess prefers D'Alvarez to Columbo, the Cardinal's nephew; Columbo kills D'Alvarez (Columbo is disguised as a masker, like Vendice in Tourneur's *Revenger's Tragedy*); and Hernando, a colonel whom Columbo has called a coward, kills him. The Cardinal, seething with retaliatory passion, plans to avoid the unsubtle revenge of simply killing the Duchess (who by now has joined the long roll of pseudo-mad people in this family of dramas), but first to rape and then poison her. Before he accomplishes the first, he is superficially wounded by Hernando, who then kills himself; eventually the Duchess and the Cardinal both die by poison, although only after a laboriously ingenious series of "twists."

One would scarcely think that fifty years had elapsed since *The Jew of Malta* and forty since *Antonio's Revenge*. Yet Shirley is still exploiting an early style of popular drama; the characters, the motives, and the main patterns of interaction are taken for granted, and the only novelty is in some of the specific machinations of revenge and in the introduction of passages of sardonic comedy. These partly conceal the mechanical employment of an old style which becomes an end in itself rather than an instrument of human revelation. The Duchess and Hernando are entirely good people, different only in that the Duchess principally suffers while Hernando manages to get in a blow or two against antagonists before coming to an unhappy end; Columbo and the Cardinal are malicious revengers committed to inflicting as much pain as possible on their victims. No character has even superficial divisions of being. *The Cardinal*, then, sums up that form of decadence in which a formula is used idly, that is, without taking characters beyond psychological routines; in the opposite form of decadence, as we shall see later, the conscious struggle for novelty leads to special psychological cases and strained emotional solicitations. These extremes of melodrama, in which it becomes either stereotypical or centrifugal, contrast with its high achievements: revenge melodrama could produce a Iago, the archetypal man who wants to destroy a better order of being; an Othello, the jealous man who puts a façade of justice upon revenge but learns what he has done, or most of what he has done; and a Hamlet, one of the few revengers who can achieve a tragic anguish over his own motives.

Jonson's Sejanus

Ben Jonson's *Sejanus, His Fall* (1603), written in the middle of Shakespeare's high tragic period, is commonly called a tragedy. However, it is a political melodrama without a touch of the tragic; its portrayal of reality perhaps is widened, though its dramatic quality is correspondingly thinned out, by Jonson's giving rein to his strong satiric bent. It is melodrama insofar as it is concerned with undivided characters; there is no drama within character, for none of the dramatis personae is conceived in depth. The stage is occupied largely by political figures whose sole concern is to seize power, to get rid of possible rivals, to stay on the right side of those who have power, and to flee those brought down by the revolving wheel of fortune. The emperor Tiberius is an interesting supervisory machiavel, whose continuing political shrewdness and control scarcely seem consistent with the lavish practice of multiple vices continually imputed to him; he disappears in mid-play to function thereafter as an unseen, apparently inconsistent, and in the end beneficently wily *deus*, not *ex machina*, but in a distant haven pulling the wires to spring the trap on Sejanus and thus bring down a tool aspiring to be a rival.

Sejanus himself is a kind of Richard III, lusting after power, and as a procurer of it cunning and unscrupulous enough almost to satisfy his lust: Sejanus' excess of ambition finally leads Tiberius to remove and execute him. Sejanus is not only a ruthless viceroy but a scornful rationalist; * rather like Edmund in *Lear* he jeers at the superstitions of those who report unfavorable omens, and sneers, "What excellent fools / Religion makes of men!" (V.i.69–70).[4] In a more complex character this might be a symbol of tragic hubris; Sejanus, however, is not so much Faustian as he is a worshiper of Fortuna, who brings

---

* In this age there is an interesting series of self-conscious unbelievers: Marlowe's Tamburlaine and, with major qualifications, Faustus; Sejanus and Massinger's Domitian; Tourneur's D'Amville. Faustus is the only one treated tragically.

ups and downs without relation to moral desert. The downfall of an evil man, as we know from Aristotle, is not tragic; and when Sejanus starts to tumble, Jonson sensibly gets rid of him in a hurry, since, however much time he had, he would be incapable of self-inspection. It appears that Macro, Tiberius' agent in disposing of Sejanus, will be little different.

The lesser characters are of two classes: the sycophants and agents of Sejanus, and the victims of Sejanus who are eliminated. The latter are either rivals for power or good citizens and senators who dislike the way things are going; they are voices of truth and justice, that is to say, one-dimensional characters on the right side of the fence. They seem without power; instead of getting into political conflict, they act as sharp commentators on the lamentable ways of the world (two survive to the end and have the final word). It is through them that Jonson the political satirist tends constantly to replace the writer of political melodrama (though satire, opposing the man of right vision to the man of wrong deed, has affinities with melodrama). These right-minded observers who hardly participate in the plot have so many lines that the reader is, as it were, put into the pit and made to listen to other members of the audience carry on discerning and often pungent discussion of doings on the political stage. Often we do see the political stage itself—indeed, the long Act V, working up with a good deal of ambiguity to the disgrace of Sejanus, is like a skillful mystery story approaching its climax—but we are constantly drawn back to the shrewd, disillusioned, and often sardonic observers. This appears most clearly at the end. After Macro has formally denounced Sejanus in the name of Tiberius, and it is clear that Sejanus has not even a chance to fight, Jonson continues the scene for over two hundred lines—for what? To have the authoritative commentators report and condemn the mob violence against the dead body of Sejanus and against his children. The melodrama proper would end with the deposition of evil Sejanus; but he almost becomes an object of sympathy as Jonson prolongs an already long play to satirize the cruel and fickle mob. And the satirical spirit needs, not to bring an integral plot to a conclusion, but to keep uncovering new objects for chastisement.

Sejanus is long-winded, ungainly, and at times too insistent; but occasionally it offers the kind of excitement that comes when the general line of action is clear-cut but the working out of the details is not. It presents a familiar world of *agents provocateurs*, informers, guilt by association, trumped-up charges, "enemies of the state," and even book burning. The language is often brisk, colloquial, clipped— the right medium for satiric observation of chicanery in government, and crassness, credulity, and unreason in the people. Above all, it puts the reader steadily in the comfortable, undemanding position of the right-minded observer detecting complementary vices in ruler and mob.*

V. Innovations in Melodrama

If melodrama continued to be written, even long after Shake-speare's time, in various relatively conventional ways, it also under-went other developments, original and at times brilliant. During Shakespeare's professional lifetime three dramatists had, within a

---

* *Sejanus* may logically be compared with Philip Massinger's *The Roman Actor*, which, appearing in 1626, shows the chronological spread of the form. Also a political melodrama, *The Roman Actor* differs from *Sejanus* in several ways. Massinger's language is less brisk; the dialogue is more rhetorical. Yet *The Roman Actor* has a greater tragic potential than *Sejanus*, even though Massinger does not bring it off. Massinger lacks Jonson's satirical bent, which works against tragic effect. More important, Massinger has a greater interest in the inner workings of character; his faint sense of duality in the human being could lead his audience on to a tragic responsiveness inhibited by Jonson's satirical cast of mind.

Massinger, according to A. K. McIlwraith in his introduction to *Five Stuart Tragedies* (London: Oxford World's Classics, 1953), p. xvii, was interested in the problem of how a debauched man could be a good ruler. However, though Massinger may have thought of Domitian as a good administrator, the play shows him only as willful, arbitrary, obsessed with power and prerogatives, punitive, sadistic. Hence his death is only the downfall of a bad man, like that of Sejanus. The unrealized tragic potential lies in two elements that Massinger sees in Domitian—in certain conflicts within him, and in his hubris. Domitian is infatuated with his wife Domitia, and is fond of the actor Paris; hence, when Domitia makes love to Paris, Domitian's responses are more complex than those of a betrayed husband in melodrama. But this is a last-minute complication rather than an essential part of the action. On the other hand, Domitian takes his godhood quite seriously, and Massinger lays the ground for treating him as a tragic victim of his own arrogant sense of omnipotence and invulnerability. The difficulty is that Domitian never becomes a representative man experiencing a characteristic hubris; he is rather a monster of hubris in whom there is almost nothing representative. He remains a villain rather than becomes a tragic character.

half dozen years, worked from melodramatic premises in three differ-ent directions, and all but transformed the stereotype with their innovations. In *Bussy D'Ambois* (1604) George Chapman suffi-ciently complicates both a hero and his mistress to create a strong pressure toward tragedy; in *The White Devil* John Webster elects to attribute certain virtues to characters who might simply be conven-tional villains; and in *The Revenger's Tragedy* Cyril Tourneur does a fresh anatomy of the revenger, giving him new lineaments or reinter-preting old ones.

Chapman's Bussy D'Ambois

Chapman almost converts a romantic hero into a tragic hero, but his premises do not quite permit it. Bussy D'Ambois is the Renais-sance model of the modern self-made man, the possessor of "virtue" who by sheer personal quality—manliness in the sense of energy, zest, inner power that subdues others—reaches high place.[5] He is a sort of Tamburlaine whose world is the French court of Henry III; one might think of him also as having Kent's unbridled tongue, except that his unchecked candor and aggressive rhetoric are the expression, not of a king's cause, but of the speaker's own vaunting rashness. With his verbal libertinism, his swordsmanship, and his power to charm, he is a Cyrano de Bergerac who succeeds in the world and in love and whose main career, therefore, is anything but pathetic. Monsieur, the King's brother, spots Bussy as a "resolved spirit" (I.i.44)[6] who will "bear state and flourish" (line 50); takes him to court, where his "sudden bravery, and great spirit" (II.i.2) soon arouse ill feeling and lead to a triple duel of which Bussy is the only survivor; still Monsieur supports him, and the King forgives him. Bussy becomes the lover of Tamyra, wife of the Count of Montsurry (II.ii; III.i), and such a favorite of the King that he exercises a "manly freedom" to rail in all directions (IV.ii). Powerful courtiers resent him, look for weapons against him, discover his affair with Tamyra, reveal it to Montsurry, and thus set in motion the plot that leads to Bussy's death. This second half of the action, Bussy's "fall," is treated mainly in melodramatic terms: we see the net closing about Bussy, his counteractions, his being deceived at a crucial moment (though he receives supernatural advice), and his death.

Yet, for all the familiar conniving of which Bussy is a victim, the play avoids a simple, mechanical motivation, because it makes Bussy an ambivalent figure: despite his merits, he has so antagonized the court as to bring about his own downfall. In effect he has used his integrity as an offensive weapon; his exuberant energy has expressed itself in endless gestures of triumph; he has a domesticated version of Faustian hubris. In this sense Bussy is the tragic hero. But the potential tragic effect is minimized by the fact that the vaunting man finds his nemesis in such ignoble forces, and by the fact that he himself remains only the energetic competitor, unaware that he is anything more than a victim of scheming courtiers. Indeed, at the final ambuscade, far from having any tragic recognition, he is used to illustrate a pattern of noble dying: he "hath Montsurry down" (V.iii.118), but at Tamyra's plea lets him up, is fatally wounded, endeavors to find a Roman death while standing up, forgives his murderers, and urges Montsurry to forgive Tamyra and be reconciled to her (lines 118–93). While on the one hand this anticipates the death of Addison's Cato, on the other it borders on the Cyrano sentimentality. What inhibits the latter is the density of the verbal texture; Bussy's dying fidelity to the Chapman characters' practice of regularly laboring for epigram, mythic allusion, and sublimity results in a viscous rhetoric without marked effect. Dryden's disparagement was by no means all wrongheaded.[7]

Chapman complicates Bussy as an agent without really making him a divided character. It is interesting, then, that he senses a division in Tamyra and actually gives her some awareness of it. After becoming Bussy's lover, she wishes for the benefits of a "spotless conscience" and exclaims, "O the dangerous siege / Sin lays about us" (III.i.8–10); if she is troubled less by a sense of misconduct than by an awareness of a dangerous situation, still she becomes more of a character by knowing more than one motive. She keeps wrestling with the problem: "Our bodies are but thick clouds to our souls, / Through which they cannot shine when they desire" (III.i.59–60). In firmly denying her guilt to her husband, she does act simply as the one-dimensional character intent on self-preservation; she undergoes great torture before she writes the letter that will lead to Bussy's death. When Bussy enters the trap she calls a warning to him; on the other hand she asks him to save her husband, and Bussy's obedience leads to his death. After Bussy's death her one long speech registers strongly the clash between her feelings as mistress and as wife, and her last words are those of remorse for her infidelity (V.iii.210–30, 237–46). As a secondary character, she does not determine the tone of the play, but the careful treatment of her conflicting emotions gives a tragic direction not realized in the more univocal characterization of Bussy.

Webster's The White Devil

Webster's *White Devil* is like the later *Duchess of Malfi* in that the revengers are made unappetizing, even though here they have a better case. Francisco de Medicis, the Duke of Florence (whose sister was murdered), and his ally the Cardinal first subject the malefactors to a prejudiced and abusive trial and then, reinforced, track them down, with disguises and scheming, and exultingly slaughter them. Webster's reduction of the revengers to petty and ignoble plotters is a lesser originality that contributes to his greater originality: it prevents that sympathy for the revengers which would interfere with his romantic rehabilitation of the original evildoers. Webster takes a pair of adulterers and instigators of murder and invests them with personal qualities that elicit admiration; they come to seem almost sturdy and courageous victims of malice rather than willful and heartless self-seekers who let nothing stand in the way of their passion. Brachiano and Vittoria have to get rid of his wife Isabella and her husband Camillo, and this Brachiano accomplishes with executive dispatch—by poisoning and a fake accident during "vaulting." Then Webster enters on his novel treatment of the adulteress, who at least morally has had a hand in murder: tried by a court that is more personal and punitive than judicial, Vittoria becomes sharp, ironic, untruthful, of such "brave spirit" that she manages to seem the upright citizen challenging an unjust court. Brachiano attacks the court (the Duke and Cardinal) with impudent bravura (III.ii).[8] From now on, Brachiano and Vittoria are treated as great, suffering, passionate lovers: in the house of convertites (supposedly reformed prostitutes) in which Vittoria has been confined, they have a spirited quarrel based on jealousy (IV.ii) and then escape and marry. Poisoned, Brachiano dies only after a long and energetic mad scene (V.iii). Vittoria is equally brave in facing her brother, Flamineo, who wants money, and the hired assassins who finally kill her; before dying, she lavishes boldly cutting remarks on them (V.vi).

To impute an attractive resoluteness and a romantic flair to a couple whom we first see coolly getting rid of their original spouses is a great variation in pattern (and it provides another of those fascinating Jacobean anticipations of the modern: the lovers are wholly free of that "sickly conscience" that keeps coming up in Ibsen). Webster manages another great variation in the character of Flamineo, Vittoria's brother, who helps bring the lovers together and commit any murders necessary to their and his own convenience. Webster takes this subordinate machiavel, who might be only an unscrupulous and sinister agent, and makes him a rare combination of pander, Ariel, Volpone's Mosca, Edgar playing poor Tom in *Lear*, entertainer, player of games, cynical observer, energetic experimenter, and eventually tedious talker. An anticipator of Bosola, he is still harder to make into a consistent being, perhaps because there is more of the psychopath in him. The big thing, however, is his vitality, and this, behind all the facets of his unresolved personality, is a source of originality in *The White Devil*.

What is interesting about this melodrama is that Webster gets outside the usual boundaries by an imaginative sympathy with three characters who rend the ties of community. But having had a kind of fling, in which the revenge play is hardly left in recognizable form, Webster at the end retires into traditional order: Brachiano, Vittoria, and Flamineo are all murdered, and Giovanni, the Duke's nephew, announces a resumption of the order of justice. It is a nominal day of judgment after a long play's life in which ethical ambiguity is a means of aesthetic fencing with formula; this is one of the ways in which Stuart drama anticipates mid-twentieth-century drama.

Tourneur's The Revenger's Tragedy

Cyril Tourneur had already begun fencing with formula. In *The Revenger's Tragedy* (1607) his way is almost the opposite of Webster's: whereas Webster gives center stage to romanticized evildoers, and subordinates his unpalatable revengers, Tourneur leaves his offenders loathsome and secondary, and gives dramatic primacy to the searching analysis of a revenger whose good cause is less in the eye than is his dark personality. Tourneur's *Atheist's Tragedy* (1611) is best described, for the moment, as tragedy *manqué*. What each of his two surviving plays does, however, may best be seen against a background of their common elements. Both begin with melodramatic premises, that is to say, with a relationship between the very evil and their victims, and then proceed to different alterations in the generic stereotype. Up to a point, they make identical alterations. Both have, in the galleries of lustful characters, a middle-aged nymphomaniac; her sexual maneuverings, as well as those of others, provide a strong infusion of intrigue comedy. Both juxtapose intrigue comedy and bizarre sensational events; both make dramatic use of dead persons' skulls, and both so introduce these in sexual episodes as to image, in crude burlesque, the love-and-death motif of which we have since become acutely conscious. Both fill out the character of revenger with complicating elements that—as in a number of other dramas considered in this section—could, but do not, justify the word "tragedy" that Tourneur uses in his titles and sprinkles through the text more generously than most dramatists. But *The Revenger's Tragedy* treats the revenger with a consistency, force, and novel perceptiveness that justifies its traditional position as the stronger of the two dramas.

Tourneur takes the revenger, who is so often an automaton in the gestures of honor or unvarnished retaliation, and in effect exposes him; he reveals the kind of psyche that may find a haven in the role. Vendice, the title character, has been historically described as the union of the malcontent and the revenger, a placing that need not be questioned; but viewed in the light of generic analysis, Vendice is a melodramatic type in whom his creator has perceptively seen more than the usual simple motives. By the revenge conventions Vendice has grounds for getting even with the Duke and the Duke's son Lussurioso: the Duke has caused the death of Vendice's mistress, and his son tries to seduce Vendice's sister Castiza. What happens is that his technically just grounds not only free Vendice from any qualms but actually release his intense love of plotting and inflicting injury. Vendice discovers a vocation for revenge. He has secret ties with Iago. Whereas Iago revenges himself on a world that is better than he is, Vendice revenges himself on a world that is worse than he is; that is, he rails against vice, and takes a savage pleasure in torturing the vicious man. Not that Tourneur sentimentalizes the vicious man, or denies Vendice's case, but that he discovers, long before it was to become a modern truism, the sadism that may have a share in the scourge of vice. Hamlet was inhibited in his campaign against Claudius by a fear of something that Vendice does not even recognize and hence freely gives rein to—the inadmissible motive.

Tourneur has discovered in Vendice not only the zestful relisher of the physical and psychic acts to which revenge gives the coloring of necessity, but a nervous organization that requires unusual stimuli. At the outset he contemplates and addresses, at length, the skull of his late mistress, which he is holding in his hand. He derives histrionic pleasure from being disguised as pimp to the Duke's son Lussurioso, his victim-to-be, even before he is working on a revenge plot. When he is supposed to persuade his sister Castiza to accept Lussurioso as lover, he goes out of his way (still in disguise) to see if he can win his mother over to the project, and, even while praising his sister's resistance and sneering at his mother's compliance, he enjoys putting great pressure on both of them (II.i). He is in an utter ecstasy of delight when he is asked by the old Duke to arrange an assignation; he prepares a dummy female figure as a sweetheart for the Duke, uses for the head of it the skull of his mistress, and poisons the place where the lips would be (his mistress had been poisoned by the Duke). He and his brother Hippolito watch the Duke kiss the poisoned skull, and then while the Duke slowly dies, Vendice savors one punitive torment after another: taunts and sneers, the identification of the skull and of himself, and then, to "stick thy soul with ulcers" and "make / Thy spirit grievous sore," [9] the announcement to the Duke not only that he is a cuckold but also that the Duchess' lover is his own bastard son, Spurio. Furthermore, the Duke is compelled to watch ("Brother, if he but wink, . . . / Let our two other hands tear up his lids") wife and son go to their incestuous assignation (III.iv). What dominates the scene is Vendice's unflagging jubilant gusto in each detail of the physical and emotional annihilation of the Duke. Then he turns to Lussurioso, enjoying the "quainter fallacy" of now coming to serve the ducal heir in his own person (in effect a disguise, since Lussurioso had not known him), acting out his assumed character as a cynically observant rustic, taking on the assignment of killing "Piato" (his name when, actually disguised, he served Lussurioso before), and in this role having the fun of stabbing the obviously dead Duke (now dressed as "Piato") before the eyes of the Duke's son Lussurioso.

Vendice is as happy as a character in an intrigue-and-spy novel at thus shocking the son and getting the father's death blamed on the nonexistent Piato (V.i). In the meantime, entirely in the cause of woman's virtue ("Let's conjure that base devil out of our mother"), Vendice, aided by Hippolito, has been dragging his mother around by the shoulders and threatening her with a dagger for being willing to give Castiza to Lussurioso for profit; under this super-Hamletic treatment, the mother reforms (IV.iv). Finally, when Lussurioso is being installed as Duke, Vendice leads a group of maskers who, during a festive dance, stab to death Lussurioso and his friends at the high table. Unfortunately for himself, Vendice cannot help boasting about it to the succeeding Duke, Antonio (" 'Twas somewhat witty carried, though we say it"), and Antonio promptly orders Vendice and Hippolito executed (V.iii).

Tourneur's considerable achievement, then, is to analyze the stereotype revenger, who is also the voluble defender of outraged virtue, and discover an enthusiast for wily stratagems, third-degree tortures, and unsubtle vigilantism. Tourneur may have planned this novel portrait, but it seems more likely that he suddenly found that he had created, if not actually a killer, at least a person exceptionally given to a cunning kind of retributive violence. For Tourneur has Antonio, the new ruler, turn on Vendice, a fellow victim of the old ducal house and a fellow conspirator against it, after Vendice has spoken only four lines of self-congratulation about his plot against the Duke: "You, that would murder him, would murder me." Antonio's abrupt executive ruthlessness has not been prepared for; we may guess that Tourneur suddenly felt the need to do something about such a character as Vendice has turned out to be. In other words, his insight into Vendice is not equaled by his plot management. Indeed, when Tourneur starts with a revenger against the utterly corrupt ducal family and then interprets the revenger as one to whom revenge is a kind of fiendish revel, he creates a problem for himself, for he virtually eliminates a moral perspective (Antonio's dispatching of Vendice is too pat an afterthought, and Antonio may be thinking only of self-protection). The resulting cynicism resembles that of "black comedy." In fact, in this highly original melodrama, whose dramatis personae keep talking of it as a tragedy, there is constant pressure toward grotesque comedy. The sex-mad ruling family have, in their monomania, a kind of imperceptiveness that gives them a distant kinship with Molière gulls or Ben Jonson humors; there is one uproarious piece of bedroom farce when Lussurioso rushes into the Duchess' bedroom hoping to find the bastard Spurio and instead finds only the Duke; the assignations, disguises, and a misdirected death warrant are closer to comic than to tragic irony; Spurio is flippant about his sexual misconduct; and in his closing speech, Vendice speaks mostly about the ironic fact that he gave himself away unnecessarily. Another way of describing *The Revenger's Tragedy* is to say that it tends to be satire without a norm. The play is a turbulent confluence of different generic tendencies, but it is not just a hodgepodge; what comes through is a sense of melodramatic form treated with such individuality that stock responses, far from being sought, are constantly challenged.

Middleton and Rowley's The Changeling

If melodrama could go on indefinitely being written in fairly conventional ways (as in *Antonio's Revenge* and *The Cardinal*, in *Sejanus* and *The Roman Actor*), or was susceptible of change that could refresh it and make it a sharper instrument for opening up human reality (as in *Bussy D'Ambois*, *The White Devil*, and *The Revenger's Tragedy*), it could also be the source of distinction. It reached a high level in Thomas Middleton and William Rowley's *The Changeling* (1622) and in John Ford's *'Tis Pity She's a Whore* (1633). Since they are late plays, one might argue that a long history of both convention and experimentation have to precede extraordinary attainment. That may be the most generous approach to them, for if we view these plays from the Shakespearian tragic heights that we occasionally use, they fall perceptibly below greatness. Not that using the melodramatic measuring rod makes them great. But it does reveal them as strong and original, and above all, as having greater magnitude than we have so far found in Stuart drama. On the one hand, Middleton-Rowley's De Flores and Ford's Giovanni have as much vitality as Bussy, Vittoria, and Vendice, perhaps more; they have great assurance in their respective ways, and the coincidence of inner and outer life makes them essentially melodramatic in conception. They challenge others or the mores, not themselves; they are romantic entrepreneurs, off-center lovers who commit every resource to the mad affair that can end only in flaming disaster.

But what is remarkable about Middleton-Rowley and Ford is that while they can sympathetically present these specialized erotic quests, can give the outsider-antagonist his due, they can also view the passionate relationship tragically—that is, in terms of the inner tensions that give it a more meaningful status than the simple relationship of contender against convention. In each play the tensions determine the characterization of the woman—of Beatrice in *The Changeling* and of Annabella in *'Tis Pity*. We can say of both plays that they start as melodrama and become, or at least encompass, tragedy. Hence both dramas bring into play more of human reality than the others we have considered in this section. If Beatrice simply fought against her relationship with De Flores, or remained cynically content in it, and if Annabella either rejected her brother or became wholly committed to incest, we would have simpler characterizations and dramas of less magnitude; but both women have the more interwoven human organization which does not permit a clear "yes" or "no." Since the plays not only present such characters but incorporate dual points of view, both plays are worth ampler discussion than their predecessors.

The Changeling is of generic interest in several ways. With its double plot, it illustrates the companionability of melodrama and comedy, both of which, in their different keys, deal with conflicts in the world rather than in the psyche. In the major plot and in the subplot the chief business is a love intrigue; passion and marriage, actual or planned, do not always match, and both men and women are intent on schemes for getting, or getting rid of, or getting around a spouse. In the subplot, in which several gentlemen act like madmen to gain access to a madhouse (an early anticipation of Duerrenmatt's *The Physicists*) and pursue the keeper's wife, everyone comes to his senses in time; the events serve as a commentary on those of the main plot. The main plot might well function in comic terms, too: Beatrice is betrothed to Alonzo but loves Alsemero. Then it suddenly appears that she is willing to have Alonzo murdered, and the new intensity of feeling and lack of scruple take us over the boundary between comedy and melodrama: Alonzo, stabbed by De Flores at Beatrice's instigation, is another of the innumerable victims in these dramas who die to inaugurate trains of bloody consequence. But here Middleton and Rowley innovate in ways that take them beyond melodramatic stereotypes. Negatively, they all but ignore the revenge issue that for many playwrights would be the main business; Alonzo's brother Tomazo looks for satisfaction, but he is made ineffectual and kept on the sidelines. Much more important, the dramatists give a new coloring to the relationship between the instigator of the crime and the agent: the agent is not an uncharacterized person to be paid off and forgotten, but a strong personality who wants a great reward. After killing Alonzo, De Flores blackmails Beatrice into becoming his mistress. It is of course ironic that in getting rid of Alonzo in order to have Alsemero, she should fall into the hands of De Flores—an ugly man for whom she has always expressed dislike. This irony might well seem labored, but it has actually been well prepared for: from the beginning we see De Flores fascinated by and infatuated with Beatrice, from whom he can take any amount of snubbing and abuse. Since she has been aware of her power over him, it is entirely plausible that she should call upon him for an extraordinary service, and expect to secure it at no cost but money.

In a more conventional play, Beatrice might be the machiavel who, having used an agent to dispose of an unwanted person, then coolly disposes of the agent. She is not a machiavel, however, but a more complex person who is capable of crimes but not of unlimited crime. Middleton and Rowley write in terms of a moral realism that presents nemesis not as a violent end that patly comes to someone only after he has committed many acts of violence, but as a daily suffering that is the outcome of one evil deed. On the other hand, De Flores is not an agent of justice but an ugly inferior who is making a victim of Beatrice; the point is, of course, that she is not the stereotyped innocent victim but the person whose indefensible conduct has made her defenseless before another, whatever his motives. She has been active, not passive, unexpectedly finding an explicable suffering, not an irrationally punitive cosmos.

It may be that she is active in a subtler way than bluntly enlisting a trigger man to dispose of Alonzo. Much is made of her dislike of De Flores; the authors take pains to show her speaking sharply and insolently to him. It is not necessary that she dislike him; he could be infatuated with her if she were simply indifferent to him, and, being indifferent, she might the more plausibly engage him as gunman. It is possible that, without knowing it, she is perversely attracted to him;

that she goes out of her way to be disagreeable to him shows that she is aware of a man whom she would naturally ignore. When she says, aside, "This ominous ill-fac'd fellow more disturbs me / Than all my other passions" (II.i.53–54) and

> I never see this fellow, but I think
> Of some harm towards me, danger's in my mind still;
> I scarce leave trembling of an hour after,[10]
> [II.i.89–91]

she gives us evidence for suspecting ambiguity in her response to him. In choosing De Flores as tool, she may be instinctively opening the way to a relationship offering an obscure, unrecognized pleasure. At any rate, whether or not she is a diffident, confused predecessor of Strindberg's Miss Julie, she has in her the central elements more fully developed in Temple Drake in Faulkner's *Sanctuary* and *Requiem for a Nun*. For all the horror that she manifests when De Flores demands that she pay him for murdering Alonzo, not with her money but with her body, she does accommodate herself to the price. Paying it does not destroy her; she goes on; clearly, being De Flores' mistress accords with some part of her nature. Not with all of it, else she would be a simpler character than she is; her evil companion is not enough, for she goes ahead and marries Alsemero.

At this juncture the play functions as comic melodrama that even has strongly farcical details, what with ludicrous virginity tests and Beatrice's trying to conceal her own lost virginity from Alsemero by having her waiting woman Diaphanta replace her in Alsemero's bed on the bridal night. These tonal shifts are so extreme that they might wreck the play. Yet behind all the bedroom farce of the wedding night we can still see Beatrice with the divisions of the tragic character. She consents, in a not wholly defined way, to the relationship with De Flores and finds kinship with him; yet she runs from this and wants to have Alsemero's love and hand. She pushes her own guilt down out of consciousness and hopes by desperate and dishonest measures to beat the game. In this, De Flores is so cooperative that she describes him as "a man worth loving" (V.i.76), even when she is terrified that Alsemero will cease loving her. Almost to the end she is driven by counterimpulses, which establish her as tragic and the drama as spacious. When Alsemero begins to see the light, she at first makes frantic and ruthless efforts to maintain her position. Yet, when the facts are at last undeniable, she does not take refuge either in sullen silence or in blame of De Flores—the untragic postures—but confesses what she has done, does not balk at self-knowledge, and asks forgiveness. This final movement of character is in part prepared for by earlier remarks in which Beatrice, for all her nonmoral rushes toward self-gratification, reveals an ability to know what she is and does. When De Flores first tells her that she is as guilty as he, she says, "He speaks home," and a little later she adds, "Vengeance begins; / Murder I see is followed by more sins" (III.iv.87, 163–64). Hence the few last lines, in which she speaks as a guilty and self-understanding person, do not seem an afterthought, as in moralistic drama; tense, compact, figurative, they put the tragic seal on the characterization. They offer just enough contrast with those of De Flores, who kills both her and himself; he too knows that "now we are left in hell" (V.iii.163), but against her sense of shame and her plea "Forgive me" stand his proud lines of triumph that he was her sole lover:

> . . . I thank life for nothing
> But that pleasure: it was so sweet to me
> That I have drunk up all, left none behind
> For any man to pledge me.
> [V.iii.168–71]

Here is the romantic whose obsessive course is its own justification; he chooses, finally, the melodrama of conquest, devil take the cost. It is a good foil for the tragic view. Middleton and Rowley surpass most of their contemporaries in being able to understand, and make dramatic use of, both views.

Ford's 'Tis Pity She's a Whore

Ford's *'Tis Pity She's a Whore* is also of great technical interest, though in a different way. Here Ford shows the melodramatic impulse not only taking a romantic turn in a unique direction, but pursuing the new course as far as it can go. *'Tis Pity* assigns a transcendent value to the sexual love of the brother and sister, Giovanni and Annabella, or at least it permits that value to be asserted by one of the strongest, most confident voices in the play. But before looking in detail at this special development in melodrama, we should note that *'Tis Pity* also operates in terms of more familiar dramatic patterns. It contains, for instance, a heavy load of ordinary revenge melodrama— that is to say, actions in which various characters are single-mindedly trying to get even with other characters. Hippolita, the cast mistress of Soranzo, wants revenge on him; Richardetto on his wife Hippolita, for her adultery, and on Soranzo; Grimaldi on Soranzo for incivilities suffered in their rivalry for Annabella; Soranzo on Annabella, whom he has married and found to be pregnant by her brother, and on her family. To top it off, Vasques, Soranzo's Spanish servant, is bribed by Hippolita to help her gain revenge on Soranzo, but does a sudden turnabout, poisons Hippolita instead, and then—with overtones of both Iago and Bosola—gives aid and counsel to Soranzo in his machinations against Annabella and her family, and says, at the end, "I rejoice that a Spaniard outwent an Italian in revenge" (V.vi.149–50).[11] The striking heterodoxy of a key character, Giovanni, makes it easy to forget that half of the lines or more are in an old theatrical pattern; indeed, nearly all of Soranzo's revenge business could be that of any cuckold, whoever his wife's partner in infidelity, just as incest is not required to explain the troubles of Annabella's other lovers. In fact, only a little more than a third of the lines have to do directly with incest.

But the incest theme, whatever its quantitative share in the play, is the moral center, and all critics address themselves to it. Ford confounds expectations by apparently having here, as elsewhere, a strong bias in favor of the special sensibility that finds its *modus vivendi* outside the taboos; hence artist and partisan are mingled. What is interesting, then, is that he is capable of imagining Annabella largely in tragic terms, that is, of seeing sympathetically a personality not only attracted to the unique good that many lines in the play espouse but also responsive to other less idiosyncratic imperatives. He first shows Annabella as cool to suitors, devoted to her brother Giovanni but unaware of the extent of her devotion, deeply troubled by his avowal ("—'twere fitter I were dead"—I.ii.220), yet yielding to it once she recognizes her own responsiveness to it, and finally tracing her own ambiguity—"And not so much for that I lov'd, as that / I durst not say I lov'd, nor scarcely think it" (lines 250–51). We see her in one gay lovers' scene with Giovanni (II.i), but then driven

by pregnancy, and the Friar's moral accusation, to accept Soranzo as
husband. Ford has not written his scene with the Friar very clearly
(III.vi), for, in giving the Friar many lines of strong pastoral censure, and Annabella only a few monosyllables of anguished response,
Ford perhaps wanted to show her as a victim of official doctrines and
style; but at that her few words seem to indicate genuine moral
distress. When Soranzo finds she is pregnant, he abuses and mistreats
her; she is strong and independent here, refuses to tell the name of the
lover, and enthusiastically speaks his praises to Soranzo (IV.iii).
Then, however, both in a long soliloquy and in dialogue with the
Friar, we see her truly grief-stricken, thinking of "false joys" and
"weary life," of "conscience" opposing "lust," ready to "blush at
what hath pass'd" and "welcome death" (V.i.2ff.).

Ford does well in having Annabella retain for Giovanni a devotion
that makes her want to warn him against Soranzo and his hirelings,
and that keeps her from blaming him. On the contrary, she exclaims
passionately,

> Oh, would the scourge due to my black offence
> Might pass from thee, that I alone might feel
> The torment of an uncontrolled flame!
>   [V.i.21–23]

That is, she does not become the pat moralist that repentance is
always in danger of producing, but has the tragic sense of profound
involvement in which what is done is the source of both guilt and
loyalty. The doubleness persists in her final scene with Giovanni,
though her role is muted as his own desperate violence becomes
dominant. Ford conveys her attitude very subtly. He does not let us
see her actual rejection of Giovanni, as if this might give her moral
concern an undesirable harshness; we see only Giovanni's harsh replies—"What, chang'd so soon! . . . treacherous / To your past
vows and oaths? . . . Thou art a faithless sister, . . . you'll now be
honest, that's resolved?" (V.v.1–15 *passim*). She gives voice only to
a melancholy sense of ill-being ("my calamity") and of the end that
others plot ("there's but a dying time / 'Twixt us and our confusion"
—lines 17–18); even more than that, she tries to alert him to the
dangers that threaten him. Drama does not often combine so well a
firm self-judgment, a gentle acceptance of fact, and a continuing

sense of another's welfare. After Giovanni has stabbed her, Annabella speaks words a little reminiscent of Desdemona's: "Forgive him, Heaven—and me my sins! Farewell, / Brother unkind, unkind— Mercy, great Heaven!—oh—oh!" (lines 92–93). In her dividedness, her assumption of responsibility, and her unwillingness to blame her brother, Annabella takes on a tragic quality that is rare in post-Shakespearian characters. She has the spirit and the grace of the Duchess of Malfi but is much more than the victim of others.

Giovanni, on the other hand, is the melodramatic character who finds unity in a single passion from which he derives all principles of conduct and thought; nothing challenges or even affects that one intense feeling that penetrates all he does and thinks. Although at first he does not altogether shut his ear to priestly advice (Ford couches the advice in routine formulations that betray his own lack of faith in it), he is already prone to rail at "a peevish sound, / A customary form" (I.i.24–25) and to contend that incest, since its participants have an additional ground of oneness, helps bind them "by the links . . . Even of religion" (lines 31–33). He soon finds prayer and fasting "but dreams, and old men's tales, / To fright unsteady youth" (I.ii.160–61), makes a tempestuous confession to Annabella, and wins her assent ("Love me or kill me," each says to the other, in a rather mechanical repetition—lines 256, 259). Exalted by the consummation of their love, Giovanni returns to the Friar to give half-playful, half-earnest Platonic defenses of their relationship.

When Annabella becomes pregnant, he is distressed but unhelpful, and for a time he in effect disappears; next we see him jealous of Soranzo, Annabella's husband. But in soliloquy he contends that her marriage has in no way diminished their unmatched happiness, which leads him into hedonistic philosophizing—"A life of pleasure is elysium"—and a Faustian denial of hell (V.iii.16, 19–20). Annabella's news that they are discovered leads him into heroic bravura— thoughts of "glorious death," of going out with a bang ("with me they all shall perish"—V.iii.77, 80); he even tells her that, were she "more steady,"

> . . . I hold fate
> Clasp'd in my fist, and could command the course
> Of time's eternal motion. . . .
> [V.v.11–13]

Then recrimination gives way to praise of her beauty and innocence, to a prediction that their love will justify them in the future, to a final kiss, and to his killing her to forestall Soranzo's revenge.* Not content with this, Giovanni suddenly appears before all the guests in Soranzo's banquet room with Annabella's heart on his dagger, boastfully recounts their relationship, claims "the fame / Of a most glorious executioner," triumphs unmercifully over Soranzo, kills him in a duel (claiming "brave revenge is mine"), and is finally killed himself (V.vi.34–35, 76).

It is this last frenzied extravaganza that has helped call forth the adjective "decadent" from Ford's critics.[12] If decadence is the word, we should note that it is most subtly apparent in the characterization of Giovanni, that is to say in the conferring upon him of an unshaken oneness in a situation where a dividedness such as Annabella's is entirely expectable. The sense of total character has fallen before the urgency to make Giovanni a partisan, and a partisan in an eccentric cause. Giovanni's unshaken, unswerving, frantic single-track dramatic life is the source of a brilliancy and intensity of effect often associated with decadence. But Giovanni reveals the melodramatic sense of character carried to an extreme—the undividedness not of the fighter in a good cause, or of the evil man who rejoices in his evil, or of the antagonist driven by the will to survive, but of a solitary challenger, in his own interest, of long-enduring moral conviction. The ultimate untragic individualism is the perverse integrity of an angry young man with never a doubt to humanize his pedantic declaration of an overriding private law. Ford has caught quite accurately the assured doctrinaire oneness of a type wholly formed by an idea—who might be radical innovator, professional vigilante, willful martyr, or monomaniac. With great perception he carries Giovanni through into that final phase in which the aggressiveness required for the role goes wild in a gratuitous and outrageous display, a histrionic self-magnification calculated to inflict the utmost humiliation and horror on all those about him. It is sometimes felt that Ford shows his sympathy with Giovanni by giving him exceptional energy of action and poetic speech and thus letting him determine the final course of events and

---

* There is probably something, too, of the love-in-death paradox that has become familiar through Denis de Rougemont's *Love in the Western World*, trans. Montgomery Belgion (New York: Pantheon, 1956).

have his unique triumph. This is in a sense true; one wonders, too, whether Ford did not unwittingly reveal a side of himself in Giovanni.

But there is also a third possibility: that a deeper level of understanding led Ford, in the very midst of sympathy, to take this overly single-minded man on into a final phase in which, amidst all the trappings of glorious revenge, what comes through is simply the sick triumph of a sick man; and that Ford knew this. His dramaturgy suggests an artistic instinct that modified the partisanship we impute to him. If, in the final scene, the observers have little claim on our sympathy, still we are driven toward them by Giovanni's monstrous egomaniac gestures. More than that, when Florio twice calls his son mad and then dies of shock, this seems a reliable dramatic critique of the raging hero. And the rampaging of Giovanni is in contrast with the quiet resignation, just a few lines before, of Annabella, in whom Ford showed himself capable of a superior tragic sense of character. This makes it reasonable to suppose that he was not really taken in by the simpler melodramatic being of Giovanni, was not awarding him a mad triumph, but was simply tracing a disturbed being to a probable spectacular finis. If this is true, then *'Tis Pity* is one of the rare dramas in which the playwright was able, with great detachment, to carry both types of character through to ends implicit in their make-up.

VI. ALLEGORIC AND PATHETIC TRAGEDY

While now and then we see a play that starts as melodrama not only developing its generic form uniquely but also expanding and introducing a tragic perspective, we can also see plays that in structure are technically tragic and yet because of eccentric emphases become deformed tragedy. Tragedy can decline in various ways. By way of reminder, the most striking of these is that in which the sense of dividedness in character all but shrinks out of sight or reappears as an unconvincing, last-minute codicil; division within a character becomes division between characters. We can read *The Duchess of Malfi* this way—as a falling away from the Shakespeare model. In the present section, however, our concern is with what happens in plays that do retain a tragic form and yet undergo a decline or loss because of an artistic deviation. An imbalance gets into the dramaturgy, the form is distorted, and special or even bizarre effects seize our attention. We sometimes find it helpful to explain these effects as intended to gratify special kinds of audiences—general-uncultivated, middle class, puritan, jaded-genteel, courtly-sophisticated, and so on. Quite aside, however, from the impact of audiences on dramatists, there is the problem of identifying the formal abnormalities that lie behind functional specializations. A priori we might expect a commingling of atrophy and hypertrophy, of shrinking of certain elements and distension of others. This is the kind of thing that does happen.

As early as Marston's *Antonio's Revenge* (1599) we observed a "tendency to protract scenes of strong emotional impact" and "the emergence of that unstable relationship between action and feeling that is characteristic of decadence." We can now look more fully at the drift toward this kind, as well as other kinds, of formal distortion. If we could postulate an ideal process of dramatic composition, presumably it would center in the dramatist's constructing his "action" as best he knew how; the action would absorb his conscious attention, and his imaginative power would infuse it with moral significance and emotional vitality. Such a process may never take place in pure form, but as an ideal construct it provides a way of describing deviant forms. Suppose that a dramatist—for the sake of novelty, or because of biases of his own, or out of responsiveness to an audience—lets his putting together of a dramatic action be influenced by a sense of what he wants the action to mean or of the feelings that he wishes it to evoke. Then, we may conjecture, the action loses something of its pre-eminence and spontaneity, of its control over a meaning and feeling that are normally different expressions of its primary being; these latter begin to assert themselves independently, and the action partly yields to their will. Doubtless, action would never atrophy in a literal sense, but it could shrink away into a secondary position. This is a way of describing what happens in three plays that extend from the middle of Shakespeare's career almost to the end of the period— Thomas Heywood's *A Woman Killed with Kindness* (1603), Beaumont and Fletcher's *The Maid's Tragedy* (1611), and Ford's *The Broken Heart* (1633). These plays exhibit, in different ways and in different proportions, the loss of dramatic primacy by the action, and the coming into prominence of patterns of meaning or feeling, or both, that the action is designed to support. The result may be called "allegoric tragedy" or "pathetic tragedy"; that we are impelled to use such terms is a clue to the fact of decadence, and to its specific forms.

Heywood's A Woman Killed with Kindness

A Woman Killed with Kindness is most interesting generically in that Heywood, who introduces both of the principal deviations in tragic form, has the most consistent tragic sense of character outside of Shakespeare. Heywood sees dividedness everywhere. Sir Charles Mountford no sooner triumphs—in a four-against-four duel, his side kill two of Sir Francis Acton's followers—than he is overcome with remorse, and he undergoes a heavy penance. Wendoll struggles between qualms and lust before he makes overtures to Frankford's wife Anne; he has a brief period of pleasurable triumph and then, after discovery, suffers great remorse. Heywood intends that Anne undergo an inner struggle before she yields to Wendoll; he is more successful in showing her troubled state after she yields; and only too successful in presenting her self-flagellation after Frankford has discovered the affair. Sir Francis Acton plans to extend his revenge upon Sir Charles Mountford by seducing and then scorning Sir Charles's sister Susan; then he sees her and falls in love; if his haste is unseemly, at least for a moment he struggles between the impulse to triumph and the impulse to love and marriage. Released from prison by Sir Francis' payment of debts, Sir Charles is in a conflict between the joy of freedom and a painful obligation to an old enemy; Susan is caught between her loyalty to her brother and his intention to give her to Sir Francis as mistress in repayment of the loan (an anticipation of Claudio's appeal to his sister Isabella in *Measure for Measure*).

Finally, Frankford, dishonored by his wife's infidelity, embodies two remarkable variations upon the traditional revenger, both reflecting feelings more complex than the crude impulse to destroy the offender. Heywood was an innovator, as Fredson Bowers has pointed out, in substituting, for "an exterior physical revenge," the "punishment which arises from the erring characters' consciousness of their guilt. . . ."[13] Thus Frankford, lavishing a false "kindness" upon Anne, makes it possible for her to take on a tragic coloring instead of becoming just another conventional victim. Second, instead of contenting himself with the infliction of punishment, or becoming in turn the object of a counterrevenge, Frankford suffers from the sentence which he has imposed on Anne; he is miserable too, and his unhappiness serves to mitigate the impression of sadism and priggishness, which is not entirely dissipated by the other major characters' unqualified approval of Frankford's action.

These inner conflicts and the self-knowledge to which they lead evidence a remarkably thorough use of the tragic perspective. By the quantitative principle, then, *A Woman Killed with Kindness* might be saluted as a great tragedy. Yet it is not the great work that some readers have thought it (nor, for that matter, the lamentably poor one that others have judged it to be). Without entering on a catalogue of merits * and demerits, we can place *A Woman Killed with Kindness* in a secondary rank of tragedy because of a generic malformation. It exemplifies allegoric tragedy; consciously or not, Heywood has a strong homiletic intention, and this leads him to construe characters with reference to concepts that he wants illustrated.[14]

* On the credit side are the adequate sense of character, the lively realism of the lesser dramatis personae, and the thematic unification of the two plots. Although at first glance they seem separate affairs, actually they are both revenge plots, one starting with a killing, the other with an adultery. In each case the revenge, instead of leading to a series of murderous catastrophes, is liquidated, so to speak, by a kind of magnanimity. Frankford's banishment, instead of execution, of his wife is construed by all the others as a charitable form of revenge (indeed, it hardly amounts to more than a modern divorce, with custody of the children going to the father), and it is followed by forgiveness by the aggrieved party. Sir Francis Acton's vendetta against Sir Charles Mountford ends when Sir Francis, in love with Susan Mountford, acts generously to his old foe and victim. Heywood's choice of words reveals his sense of the interrelatedness of the plots. Not only does Frankford tell Anne that he has decided to "kill thee even with kindness" (IV.v), but Sir Francis Acton similarly describes his plan of action against Susan Mountford: ". . . fasten such a kindness on her / As shall o'ercome her hate" (III.iii). Though the acts of kindness are different, yet kindness may punish, as with Anne, or be hard to bear; Sir Charles Mountford says of Sir Francis' helpfulness, "His kindness like a burden hath surcharged me" (V.i). Sir Francis' kindness, meant to secure love, comes ironically close to killing; Susan threatens suicide when her brother, Sir Charles, unwilling to feel obligated to Sir Francis, would offer her to Sir Francis. The kindness that kills and the kindness that knits are strangely interwoven, and the presence of this paradox is a mild, though hardly adequate, antidote to the sentimental tendencies of the play.

This should not be overstated, for the characters are not altogether deprived of spontaneity; rather their spontaneity partly yields to different pressures as the author elects to make one point or another. The best example is of course Anne: Heywood, intent on a certain treatment of an adulterous wife, needs first to have the adultery, and so he pushes Anne into adultery without giving her any time at all to be "enchanted" as she says she is (II.iii). Intent on a certain treatment of revenger and victim, Heywood needs revenger and victim; so with extraordinary speed he enlarges a falconry dispute among old friends into a bloody fight so that Sir Charles, as leader of the more successful duelists, can be the recipient of Sir Francis' animosity. Sir Charles, penniless and jailed for debt, must be entirely at the mercy of Sir Francis; therefore, when Susan seeks help for Sir Charles, an uncle and two farm tenants turn her down with robot-like dispatch. Sir Francis is to be the enemy transformed into friend by love, so he falls in love with Susan Mountford almost as soon as he sees her, and then turns his back on revenge. To illustrate the different workings of the doctrine of honor, Heywood makes Sir Charles so sensitive to his financial rescue by Sir Francis that, quite incredibly, he will push his sister into Sir Francis' bed to make good the loan; Susan, in her honor, will then kill herself. But when she finds Sir Francis ready to marry her, she needs only two lines to overcome a long hate and to resolve to love him (V.i). In nearly all the actions that create the central dramatic situations, the characters are less naturalistic than allegorical.

Then, as situations are resolved, Heywood wants to exploit the moral quality of the action done, and he makes a legitimate tragic consciousness work overtime. Whereas at first the character had to assume a role ("I am an adulteress"), she now has to act out the author's assessment of the role ("An adulteress should be condemned"); the allegorical in definition is succeeded by the allegorical in homily. The former Heywood takes for granted, the latter he feels a passionate need to demonstrate; perhaps we can say that he hardly understands how people fall into wrongdoing, but understands only too well how indefatigably they repent. In life, different human beings may be expected to pace the reckless step and the remorseful contemplation very differently, but all Heywood's characters, with the single exception of Wendoll, marry their misdeeds in haste and then inexhaustibly repent at leisure. Before the falconry fight, Sir Charles speaks scarcely ten lines; immediately after it, he has a fifteen-line soliloquy of remorse, and in the ensuing dialogue with Susan speaks about fifteen more lines, all of the same tenor (I.iii). Anne Frankford not only does not enjoy her liaison with Wendoll—a number of her lines are self-critical—but after the discovery all the lines that she speaks, over a hundred, are full of self-blame (IV.v and following). Wendoll is given about fifty lines to mull over his errors, to feel "the sharp scourge of repentance," and to get ready to "wander like a Cain" (V.iii; however, he also expects to rehabilitate himself thus). The tragic note is diminished by excess—by the histrionic humiliation and the conspicuous contrition.

When grief and suffering are held—as in the scenes in which Anne, Wendoll, and Frankford are all wretched and unhappy (as well as in earlier scenes in which Sir Charles is in rags and in jail)—the effect is of course sentimental. Allegoric tragedy slides over into pathetic tragedy, that is to say, drama in which the structure remains tragic but in which the exploitation of feeling takes precedence over the exploration of character in action. The word *pathetic* is useful because it can apply to several kinds of feeling-dramas—those that are sentimental, i.e., that capitalize on the more relaxed and familiar emotions, and those that are sensational, i.e., that capitalize on the more tense and exotic emotions. For the sentimentalism that appears often in domestic drama and the sensationalism which begins to emerge in Beaumont and Fletcher have much in common. Here we are considering them as specializations of tragic form; they may appear in melodrama too, but there they would originate in a different structure of action. Pathetic melodrama, to give an example, would wiredraw the human suffering caused by external forces; pathetic tragedy, the suffering brought about by the individual's own conduct. *A Woman Killed with Kindness* happens to illustrate both types; though basically tragic in structure, it introduces one pure villain who victimizes another person. Shafton, a "false friend," lends destitute Sir Charles Mountford five hundred pounds to create a debt that he can use as leverage when he tries to grab Sir Charles's ancestral property. But on the whole Heywood's play does illustrate, not a movement from tragedy toward melodrama,* but a movement within the tragic structure toward two off-center forms—the allegoric, which treats motive scantily, and the pathetic, which presents the emotive copiously. We can see later dramas taking both tendencies to greater extremes.†

Beaumont and Fletcher's The Maid's Tragedy

Our two remaining examples of Stuart drama, which are separated by two decades, are advanced cases of pathetic drama. Beaumont and Fletcher's *The Maid's Tragedy* is archetypal pathetic tragedy; Ford's *Broken Heart* is generically mixed, but its primary allegiance to the exploitation of feeling is unmistakable. The pair round out the illustration of decadence.

As if revolting against their immediate contemporaries' addiction to a bewildering multiplication of characters, relationships, and lines

---

* This movement does appear in one detail. Sir Charles Mountford, after killing two men in a fight, is arrested and tried; he finally goes free, but the trial has used up all his resources. Sir Charles does not consider the trial and costs as inevitable consequences of a murder about which, as we have noted, he felt painfully remorseful. He now shifts to a melodramatic style of thought and is inclined to blame his poverty on hostile actions by others, as if their pressing the trial were an indecency. "Well, God forgive them / That are the authors of my penury. . . . O sir, they have undone me" (II.ii) betrays the familiar posture of blame, an instrument of self-exculpation.

† Tourneur's *Atheist's Tragedy* (1611) is another delinquent tragedy, and it has affiliations with *A Woman Killed with Kindness*. D'Amville starts out as little more than a melodramatic villain, but his atheism is so treated as to give some variety to the characterization. He is not secure in his atheism, and he has a more troubled consciousness than would a racy naturalist of the Edmund sort. The division between his will to believe in theories that serve his own lusts, and his increasingly painful awareness of other truths, moves D'Amville out of the realm of the insentient villain and into the realm of tragic experience. However, he is not followed through as a spontaneous character; he is rather conceived of as indicating an error of belief. Hence *The Atheist's Tragedy* takes on the lineaments of allegoric tragedy and is akin to *A Woman Killed with Kindness*. D'Amville's victims, Charlemont and Castabella, are also molded more by doctrinal intention than by sense of character. Charlemont illustrates the theory that it is better to give up revenge than to have it, and he and Castabella develop into allegorical figures of patience. In the end they are rewarded as they might be in an eighteenth-century sentimental comedy.

of action, Beaumont and Fletcher formed *The Maid's Tragedy* on a single plain plot and thus produced an unusually lucid and centered work. To provide a front for his liaison with Evadne, the King marries her to Amintor; her brother Melantius persuades Evadne to expunge the dishonor by killing the King; later, in despair, she kills herself; Amintor's original fiancée, Aspatia, manages to trick Amintor into killing her in a quasi duel; and then Amintor commits suicide.

Freed from the exhausting labors of plot manipulation (even in Act V, Webster seems always to be introducing new subplots), Beaumont and Fletcher are able to concentrate more on interior events. They develop at unusual length the scenes in which one person explores and expresses his own feelings, exerts pressure on the feelings of another or responds to such pressure, or undergoes a major emotional disturbance or alteration. These scenes are prolonged, deliberately or instinctively, to such an extent that what the character feels becomes less an accompaniment of the action in which the drama centers than the primary subject of the drama. Hence *The Maid's Tragedy* is a good representative of "pathetic tragedy," of which we first saw a hint in Heywood's *Woman Killed with Kindness*. But while Heywood, whose bent was allegoric, ordinarily hurried characters into the actions that represented chosen concepts, Beaumont and Fletcher hold characters in situations as if a full savoring of the emotional experience, by both participants and audience, were the end sought. Just as abrupt action usually means lack of self-awareness, so deliberate action implies more than usual self-consciousness. If we are correct in seeing in *The Maid's Tragedy* an especial preoccupation with feeling, both as an element in perhaps overly self-conscious individuals and as a mode of appeal to the audience, then the play represents one kind of decadence of which tragedy is capable.

In this pathetic tragedy there is a certain amount of conventional pathos, that is, of the pitiableness of the victim. Deprived of her lover when Amintor is married to Evadne, Aspatia is brokenhearted, and early in the play she is given two substantial passages of lamentation (II.i.43–111; II.ii.1–82); [15] near the end, dressed as "Aspatia's brother," she visits Amintor, labors hard to provoke a duel, then lets him wound her (V.iv.1–107), and finally enjoys a rather slow dying (lines 176–225). Here Beaumont and Fletcher are, of course, making the emotional most of a melodramatic situation, as they are likewise doing when Evadne, newly married to Amintor, slowly lets him know that he will be her husband in name only (II.i.142–368); when the King is suspicious of Evadne and Amintor (III.i.164–298); when Melantius urges (IV.i.1–180), and Evadne carries out (V.ii.1–100), revenge against the King. There is also comic-romantic melodrama in the sparring among the King, Melantius, and Calianax, Aspatia's "humorous" father (crotchety, fearful, unable to win the confidence of others), as Melantius endeavors to get the key of the fort from Calianax (III.ii.297–336; IV.ii.1–42, 63–288). Instead of following the well-worn recipe of constantly introducing new lines of action and making surprising shifts from one to another, Beaumont and Fletcher develop motifs with a fullness that invites connoisseurs of feeling to relish unhurriedly the emotive bouquet of each lingering episode.

But if there is a good deal of what we may call pathetic melodrama, still the basic conception of *The Maid's Tragedy* is tragic. The key characters do not have single emotions that easily determine their courses, but are drawn this way and that by conflicting impulses. Amintor feels guilty about leaving Aspatia but accepts marriage to Evadne; he rebels at his dishonorable situation as cuckold-in-waiting, but feels constrained by the King's divine right. Evadne takes on her dual role as nominal wife and actual mistress with cynical worldliness, but comes to feel that she has committed herself to something evil. Even Melantius, the chief proponent of honor, finds the triumph of successful revenge completely wiped out by his sorrow at Amintor's death. In the midst of his anguish at his marital role Amintor does not forget "The faithless sin I made / To fair Aspatia . . ." (III.i.234–35); nor is he simply a victim when he can find in the King's "divinity" an imperative that makes him bear his impossible situation. The disruptive strains that he feels are traced with novelistic fullness in Act III, Scene ii, in which his old friend Melantius tries to find out what is wrong; when he hears Amintor's one-sided story, Melantius feels he has to defend Evadne's honor and challenges Amintor. Amintor feels so guilty that he cannot fight. But a little later he feels so fearful of losing his honor through Melantius' revealing the story that he insists on fighting, while it is now Melantius' turn to refuse. Here the artifice of roles reversed betrays the drift toward decadence: though character is tragically conceived, the tracing of

emotion is overingenious and overrefined, and the effects are calculated rather than spontaneous.

The same tendency appears, if less markedly, in the scene between
Melantius and Evadne; we follow through every possible resistance
which Evadne can throw up against her brother's charges; then,
when she admits the facts, her resistance to his command to kill the
King. Once she accepts the duty of revenge, she sees herself in a new
perspective, and in a dialogue with Amintor goes into an abnormally
protracted self-condemnation. Here is the tragic consciousness developed as an agreeably painful end in itself; Evadne judges herself with
a thoroughness and vigor that, though it resembles the homiletic rant
of the moralistic drama, actually signifies a self-indulgence in feeling
equally pleasurable to her and the audience. We see this in another
way in the scene in which she prepares to murder the King, ties him
to the bed, lectures him, and then stabs him. On the one hand she is
the remorseful sinner being drawn into still another sin ("Oh, the
conscience / Of a lost virtue, whither wilt thou pull me?"—V.ii.2–3);
on the other she becomes a fanatic revenger enjoying all the sensa-
tions of revenge like Vendice in Tourneur's *Revenger's Tragedy*. She
tops even that by thus closing the scene: "Die all our faults together! I
forgive thee" (line 100). But at this point the authors let their quest
for sensation undermine their tragic sense of Evadne. The murder
makes no mark on her, and she dashes to Amintor to report a triumph
and cast herself into his arms. This sets up still another emotional
experience for her, since Amintor, with a dying Aspatia on his hands,
is not at all pleased; hence Evadne feels a lover's despair and kills
herself.

Evadne's actions reveal the course of *The Maid's Tragedy* from
tragic structure to pathetic tragedy and pathetic melodrama, and then
to a final eruption of emotional disaster which hardly merits a more
precise term than pathetic drama. Three broken hearts, a fourth
whose owner declares it broken, and a new good king who reprehends
rather than revenges his murdered predecessor—these are an abundant anticipation of the later sentimental mode.

Ford's The Broken Heart

Again in John Ford's *The Broken Heart* we have essentially pathetic drama, largely melodramatic, but in part tragic. The drawing

out of emotional effects is a natural accompaniment of Ford's management of plot and conception of character. The action lags in the background, and a number of episodes seem more like static conversations than dramatic dialogues with a perceptible forward movement. Hence attention is focused upon the sensibilities of the participants in the scenes, as if they were Ford's real concern; he presents an exfoliation, modulation, and sometimes simple repetition of the feelings that constitute their being. For drive of plot he substitutes drift of feeling.

Whichever may be prior—Ford's laggard plot or his sense of personality—they go naturally together; for the central dramatis personae are hypersensitive beings who live principally in affective states. One might think of them as humors except that they cling to, rather than are coerced by, their emotional centers. At least to a modern eye they hug their sufferings, and Ford passes on to us his tireless fascination with their long dwelling in unhappiness. Bassanes is so jealous of Penthea (who loves Orgilus but is given to Bassanes by her brother Ithocles) that, always animated by a check-up and lock-up spirit, he goes from one senseless scene of hyperbolic misery to another, and on one occasion accuses Penthea and her brother of incest (III.ii). Then, shocked into an alteration of conduct, Bassanes continues as unhappy over himself as he had been over his wife and settles into the grimmest forebodings of life in general (the Queen finally appoints him marshal, so that the numerous duties will "set a peace to private griefs"—V.iii.48).[16] The point is that even though he undergoes a change of direction, he still exists as little more than a capacity for feeling torment.

Ithocles returns in triumph from war, but it soon appears that he is gnawed by remorse for having made Penthea marry Bassanes; he acknowledges his error to her disappointed lover's complaining father (II.ii) and to Penthea. Indeed he appears to be made physically ill by it and speaks of his heart "now a breaking" (III.ii.46); and he goes on and on in this vein. But the scene is not clearly written, for the anguish of the remorseful brother, which is almost interminable, is merged with his undeclared feelings for the King's daughter, Calantha. Though he quells his brotherly suffering sufficiently to become engaged to Calantha, still, when he is murdered by Orgilus, his dying words, addressed to the dead body of his sister beside him, are of his "wrongs to thy forc'd faith" (IV.iv.66). Ford, having made as much as he can of Ithocles' grief by constantly bringing it into the dialogue, plays for a different feeling-effect in his treatment of the King's daughter. During a dance in the palace Calantha is informed, in three successive speeches, of the death of her father, of Penthea, and of Ithocles, who was to ascend the throne with her; having won universal admiration by showing no apparent response to this extraordinary series of disasters, she has herself crowned, arranges all the affairs of the kingdom, and then dies, in public and on schedule, of a broken heart. The scene, and especially Calantha's language, have been praised; but it is a tour de force in which all treatment of character has been subordinated to a calculated effect typical of pathetic drama.

In his addiction to extended suffering, Ford lets Calantha steal the end of the play from the two major characters, Penthea and Orgilus, the separated lovers. Orgilus is conceived entirely in melodramatic terms: he is simply the injured lover who lives in a sense of injustice, he falls into jealous spying, he blames Penthea for not acting on his philosophy that love is the only law of life (Giovanni in *'Tis Pity She's a Whore* is an ultimate development of Orgilus), and he naturally becomes an implacable revenger who, after alternately enjoying rant and dissimulation, finally murders Ithocles beside the body of the dead Penthea. In his emotional undividedness and his conceptual singleness he best embodies an allegorical bent that Ford renders explicit by giving only too meaningful names to his dramatis personae: Orgilus, indeed, foreshadows the character of avant garde mid-twentieth-century drama, which gives up fullness of personality to represent a mood or interpretive posture of the dramatist (as often in Beckett and Pinter, for instance).

Penthea, on the other hand, is more interesting. True, she is a victim; not only has Ithocles forced her, despite her love for Orgilus, to marry Bassanes, but Bassanes himself, with his fantastic jealousy, is an impossible husband. Yet despite this unpromising start, Ford wants to deal with her as a character who makes choices. Ford apparently shares Orgilus' view that, by the overriding law of love, she is really the "wife" of Orgilus and hence need not be faithful to her legal husband Bassanes. But at the same time—as with Annabella in *'Tis Pity*—Ford sees her as unable to act by so simple a rule; she is caught in a conflict between her persisting love for Orgilus and the sense of honor evoked by her marriage to Bassanes (she has the "divided mind" which Orgilus' sister Euphranea claims for herself at I.iii.67), and the conflict destroys her. That is to say, Ford is impelled, despite his philosophic premises, to treat her partly in tragic terms. But in dealing with her, Ford becomes the pathetic tragedian; he is not content to make drama of her destructive split, but he gives her a kind of Beaumont-and-Fletcher consciousness of feeling. This consciousness makes her parade that feeling and even fondle it and use it instead of just experiencing it. As she says to Orgilus,

> . . . I shall more often
> Remember from what fortune I am fallen,
> And pity mine own ruin.
> [II.iii.88–90]

When her brother reiterates his remorse for having forced her into marriage, she keeps reiterating her grief and his guilt; indeed she urges him "Pray kill me" and keeps him begging for her forgiveness (III.ii.64, 92). When she finds out that he is in love with Calantha, she asks him how he would feel if he were engaged to Calantha and her father snatched her from him to give to someone else (lines 106–9). Having reduced him to a mass of quivering guilt, she now goes to see Calantha in his behalf. Her strategy against Calantha is to talk first about her coming death and about the wretchedness of life, then to ask Calantha to be her executrix and to dispose of her youth, her fame, and her heart; she follows her plea for Ithocles with a climactic statement about his unkindness to herself, and declares herself now ready for death (III.v.7–112). Next time Penthea comes on stage, she is disheveled and mad; she not only sadly rehearses her griefs, but manages, with the sadism that often belongs to the professional sensitive woman, to put the knife into Ithocles repeatedly (IV.ii.69–169 *passim*). We learn that she has not slept for ten days; next she fasts and starves herself to death, asking her friends to play a funeral song while she is still alive, and saving her last breath to say "O cruel Ithocles and injur'd Orgilus!" (IV.iv.9). Insofar as Ford does believe in love as a transcendent law, he may be intent upon proving that she has made the wrong choice; but somehow the proof, if that is what it is, fades away into another picture of another person savoring misery and making a career of wretchedness.

Pathetic tragedy, then, is related to that kind of melodrama in which the revenger, such as Tourneur's Vendice, makes a career of retaliation and savors the details of revenge. Both tend to lose a "normal" range of character and to let a specialized personality, ill or verging on illness, take its place. It is not that such portraits are not true in their way, for the neurotic types depicted seem to us, with our own alertness to pathological and borderline cases, familiar enough. The decadence lies in the fact that they have the center of the stage and offer us experiences that purport to be those of representative personalities with a full range of human responsiveness.

VII. Genre in the Renaissance

So much, then, for this experimental playing against each other of nonhistorical concepts and a historical period, for using the work of an age to amplify and sum up the comparative exploration of concepts, and the concepts to describe, as best they might, the work of an age. To the latter end we have proposed at least quasi-chronological patterns and outlined the apparent "movements" between the tragic and melodramatic poles. This has not been, of course, a systematic accounting of the period; our concern is not the ultimate calculus of the Elizabethan-Stuart half century that might follow from the tireless reading of several hundred plays. Rather we have looked for the directions apparently taken by leading dramatists in nearly a score of dramas that have, for the most part, held the interest of later ages.

Since the period is one of adaptation and innovation, we would expect general developments from cruder to more sophisticated forms. The amazing exceptions are Marlowe's special accomplishments in melodrama and tragedy—*Tamburlaine* and *Dr. Faustus*—before foundations had really been laid. Aside from these sports we can see several kinds of movements emerging. Melodrama trifurcates: one branch continues the original form without much variation, another presses toward tragedy, a third goes deeper into its own generic possibilities. Political melodrama continues an ordinary course from Marlowe through Jonson to Massinger; at the same time it shows special developments in *King John* and *Richard III;* tentatively in *Richard III* and far less ingenuously in *Richard II*, it feels the pressure of the tragic view; in *Macbeth*—and for that matter in *Lear* as a political drama—the tragic has taken over. Revenge melodrama continues an ordinary course from Kyd through Marston and others to Shirley; in *Hamlet* and *Othello* the melodramatic is subordinate to the tragic. In *Bussy D'Ambois*, *The White Devil*, and *The Revenger's Tragedy* melodrama is at its most powerful. It remains melodrama but discovers ways of shedding the simplicity that inheres in its basic form and thus of involving the auditor in more demanding experiences. Characters move from unexamined wholeness, not into the divided motives and the troubled choice of tragedy, but into a new dividedness of appeal; this dividedness of appeal reflects not so much the contradictory impulses that determine the moral life of the individual as the ambiguity of virtues and vices themselves, the paradoxical drift of one into another, and the ambiguity of context. The free spirit develops arrogance and aggressiveness; the murderer and adulterer develops freedom of spirit; the revenger with a case becomes a casuist in cruelty and humiliation. One is not drawn into gratifying triumph or suffering, but rather is alienated, forced to take stock of an unclear, mixed responsiveness. As we have been intimating, there is something "modern" about these plays, with their inclination to alter patterns, to bring one up short, to shock, to puzzle.

Once it has developed its potentialities, tragedy seems to be under heavy pressure from ways of seeing reality that make it difficult to retain, as a dramatic center, the divided and sentient man. Plays in which the tragic sensibility has a strong foothold are fought for, as it were, by the melodramatic spirit, flourishing in its own steady stream of plays and always in humanity itself. The tragic spirit may here and there survive with a vigor that enables it to dominate major parts of plays that are strongly melodramatic, as in *The Changeling* and *'Tis Pity She's a Whore*. However, the melodramatic impulse may drive the tragic potential so far to one side that the drama becomes an unequal contest between good and bad men, as in *The Duchess of Malfi*. Or the tragic spirit may be undercut by the homiletic impulse, as in *Woman Killed with Kindness* and *The Atheist's Tragedy*, or by a craving for more emotional indulgence than a normally paced action will afford, as partly in *Woman Killed with Kindness* and eminently in *The Maid's Tragedy* and *The Broken Heart*.

In observing the interplay of the tragic and melodramatic impulses in English Renaissance drama, we have inevitably opened up another issue—that of the level of attainment on either side of the fence. In considering the criteria of generic identity, we have also turned to the criteria of generic excellence. The melodramas of half a century have revealed a double tendency—in one stream to be content with a rather conventional level of performance, in another to reach a high level of achievement. These superior melodramas are character- ized by "dividedness of appeal"; it is their way of surmounting the simplicity of approach ordinarily present in the genre. On the other hand, the tragic dramas which we have examined are characterized by kinds of falling away from the tragic heights represented in Shakespeare. Neither in this chapter nor in earlier chapters, however, have we dealt formally with the aspects of tragedy that indicate greater or lesser excellence. We have made passing mention of quali- tative problems, and we have alluded to the great touchstone works as if they automatically provided a definition of their virtues. So, while some of the criteria of melodramatic quality have now become ex- plicit, those of tragic quality have to a greater extent remained im- plicit. It is time, then, to look more directly at the problem of tragic quality—the final theme in this essay.

CHAPTER SEVEN

Problems of Quality:
The Tragic Consciousness

IT IS a considerable step from the generic nature of a work to the quality of a work. It ought to go without saying that genre and excellence are not identical, that a work may technically be tragic and yet be inferior. Lillo's *London Merchant* has a clear-cut tragic structure: George Barnwell, the hero, is a divided character; he is a "good man" who falls into evil courses—robbery, adultery, and murder—and then suffers deep remorse. We almost forget the classical pattern because of the defects of execution. Lillo lacks taste. His hyperrhythmical prose and trite figures make his language laughable. His focus slips from Barnwell's conflict to the external "causes" of his misconduct; furthermore, we are left with the impression that Barnwell's worst error is that he has betrayed the world of business. Finally, Lillo lacks the skill to make his hero plausible as a character; he cannot show motives developing so as to make us believe in what Barnwell does; and he so overplays the expression of remorse that Barnwell, in his voluble self-accusation, seems positively to take pride in himself as the king of horrible examples.

There is, then, a great difference between saying of a play, "This is structurally a tragedy" and saying, "This is a successful work of art." We should never let a structural classification become a value judgment. The distinction is so plain that insisting on it may seem to be laboring the obvious. Yet discussions of tragedy are too often confused by the assumption, generally unspoken, that calling a work a "tragedy" is like granting it an honorary degree or a status symbol, and that saying that a work is not a tragedy is snobbish or even segregationist. The literary judgment feels the pressure of socio-political emotions; the issue seems to lie between an admirable openness and an unworthy exclusiveness. We can avoid this difficulty by constantly emphasizing the qualitative range possible within tragedy (a range which we have already clearly seen in melodrama). Robert Ornstein sums up the matter nicely: "We can if we wish condemn *Richard III* as crude and immature tragedy, but it would be more accurate to describe it as one of the most successful melodramas ever written." [1] We should make the generic distinction and then, if we can, judge the distinction within the genre.

I. Aspects of Magnitude

It is not safe to attempt a close measurement of greatness, for one may quickly fall into the hazards of a rule-and-regulation calculus. But lesser and greater ranges of achievement may be discriminated. One can mark out the greater range only by boldly invoking a paradox: that here the qualitative and the quantitative are almost inseparable. By that I mean that the greatness of a tragedy is to be sought in the amount of human reality that it encompasses. In the ideal work, the maximum of human reality would afford at the same time, and not altogether distinguishably, a profound emotional experience and a sense of great call upon one's powers of knowing. If other things are equal—if, of two writers, neither is markedly defective, say, in control of language—the work that goes further in amassing human truth will seem the "larger" work. No one will claim that either Sophocles' or Euripides' *Electra* approaches *King Lear* in magnitude. It is possible, of course, to find one dimension of magnitude without sufficient immediacy or emotional substance—as in historical panoramas, Hardy's *Dynasts*, or Goethe's *Faust*, where the extensive pictorial and philosophic range is not matched by the human range or depth. Or there can be a powerful thrust of feeling without much spread in that which is to be known; if all the emotional responsiveness is drawn into a narrow channel of experience, the effect may be more than ordinarily moving. Duerrenmatt's *Visit* has shown its power, but this it has secured by cutting out nearly all of human nature but its corruptibility. Likewise in such disturbing dramas as Strindberg's *Dream Play* (1902) and *The Ghost Sonata* (1907), in which the mainstream of feeling is despair in the face of disaster. Often there is an inverse proportion between impact and range; in greatness they are reconciled.

Extent and Depth

There is no sound way of calculating "the amount of human reality encompassed." All we can do is suggest general terms for approaching the problem. In part, at least, we can identify greatness in extent and greatness in depth. *King Lear* is rich in depth of feeling and thought, and its world has hardly an equal in expanse: it spreads from the innermost scenes of mind and heart outward into the lives of two families, the human relations of love and piety, the political movements of an entire kingdom, and the metaphysical reaches of order. Only the very great plays can have such greatness in extent, and we need not make bald comparisons. But if we use *Lear* simply to define the concept of extent, we clarify the critical issue for other plays. In general, for instance, we can see that domestic plays have a more limited arena: *Othello* takes the type as far as it can go, but it takes in much less of the universe than does *Lear*. *Rosmersholm* is a more capacious play than *John Gabriel Borkman* because the domestic "triangle" opens out, at least for a time, into the universal issue of old order versus new order in the larger community. George Kelly's *Craig's Wife* (1925)—to take a minor classic of domestic drama in more recent times—is lesser in extent than Sidney Kingsley's stage version of *Darkness at Noon* (1951). Within the restrictions of the domestic plot there are choices: in *Desire Under the Elms* (1924) O'Neill admits a wider "context" of enduring and possibly understanding humanity, whereas in *A Moon for the Misbegotten* (1941–42) the circle of reality is cut down to the bare wreckage of James Tyrone. *Waiting for Lefty* (1935) opens out less than *Skin of Our Teeth* (1942), *Our Town* (1938) less than *Rhinoceros* (1960). Hofmannsthal's *Everyman* (1911), which develops a mythic theme, is a larger work than Michel de Ghelderode's *Death of Dr. Faustus* (1925), which is a sardonic elegy for a myth. The problem of "spatial" extent is paralleled by that of temporal extent: again, how much reality is compressed within the bounds of a play? If I have been right in urging that continuity is integral to the tragic view, then the play is diminished when it stops short of where it might go—when, for instance, as so often in Ibsen, everything ends in a blunt shock or a sudden death. When Solness plunges into the quarry, we are left with nothing but the crash; all the possible drama latent in his own understanding of his exploit is cut out. Webster's bent is to show a world wiped out; he cannot, like Shakespeare, imagine a future rooted in the bitterly earned wisdom of present catastrophe.

Greatness in depth: here we have to see how much of the total human endowment and potential the artist is capable of imagining—how much of strength and will and feeling and mind; how much, indeed, of dividedness and of suffering. Obviously few tragic heroes could have a maximum endowment in all ways, but by being defective in one way or another, or perhaps even excessive, a protagonist can fail of representative greatness. In one respect, we are told, Raskolnikov "differs radically from the dreamers and inhabitants of the underground: their conflicting impulses paralyze the will and leave them incapable of action; his inner seething must sooner or later precipitate an explosive deed. It is thus that Dostoevsky takes the great stride from pathos to tragedy." [2] It is true. Great tragedy is hardly possible if there is a defect of strength of will: it may be a characteristic modern difficulty, in the days of Zero as hero. Perhaps the modern archetypal example is Rosmer: he has the dividedness, the intensity of feeling, and much of the self-understanding of the tragic hero, but he is deficient in will, in human sturdiness; his manner has so much of the febrile as to border on illness. An almost parallel case is that of Treplev in Chekhov's somber comedy of frustrations, *The Sea Gull* (1896): Treplev simply gives up, almost with a whimper. The treatment of him does not go beyond pathos.

Another kind of tragic shortcoming appears in a once much-esteemed play that also ends in a suicide, Addison's *Cato* (1713). It is as different as possible from *Rosmersholm*. In Ibsen's play, there is a defect of continuity; with the double suicide, everything stops, and the final curtain note is blankness. In Addison's, there is an excess of futurity: for all the survivors—over two-thirds of the major characters

—the forecasts are as promising as if we were in the epilogue of a Victorian novel. The personal lives go so swimmingly that, despite the military defeat, there is little sense of human tempering in the fire of experience. Rosmer is emotionally overexposed; he has no protection against an excessive self-doubt and self-blame. Cato is overprotected against suffering by the chain mail of "Roman virtue" that he is ever conscious of wearing. Samuel Johnson has made the timeless judgment on the lack of emotional depth in the play. The suicide is not made dramatically comprehensible; it is simply a well-bred cessation of activity, without resonance. And yet at one point, just before Cato dies, Addison lets him have a moment of doubt:

> —And yet methinks a beam of light breaks in
> On my departing soul. Alas, I fear
> I've been too hasty. O ye pow'rs that search
> The heart of man and weigh his inmost thoughts,
> If I have done amiss, impute it not!—
> [V.iv.94–98] [3]

But it is too late to exploit this tragic possibility, and Addison slips back into the melodramatic posture of arraignment that was to plague the theater for over a century: Lucius, a senator, rebukes the "civil discord" that "robs the guilty world of Cato's life" (V.iv.108–12).

There is, I believe, a comparable failure of depth in Eliot's treatment of Becket in *Murder in the Cathedral*: the play never convinces us that Thomas is suffering deeply. He conquers temptations, subtle as they are, without much difficulty, and he has steady assurance as he combats both enemies and friends, on the way to martyrdom. At the end of *The Wild Duck* Gregers Werle seems on the edge of understanding and suffering, but we are not sure of his capabilities for this part of the tragic experience: in his rigid idealism he may be more suited for an allegorical than a tragic role. Harry Monchensey in *The Family Reunion* has a similar, if not identical, defect of feeling: in his rather complacent self-absorption he tends to regard others simply as objects, and to respond to them largely by condescension. Biedermann in Frisch's *The Firebugs* has only one motive—the desire to appease.

Goethe's Faust

The hero may be defective in the very condition which makes him tragic—namely, dividedness. We can so describe Becket, Cato, and

Werle. We have only to compare them with any of the Shakespearian heroes or with Dostoevski's Raskolnikov to see how much closer they are to singleness of being. When the character is limited because his inner split is not basic or powerful, the drama will be likely to become univocal and thus to fall away from tragic greatness. It may be impressive in parts, but not persuasive by dramatic wholeness. Goethe's *Faust* is a case in point. In Faust's character there is a steady movement from great complication to simplification, and then a thinning out into allegory. This is not a new point. But it is important to see the move as one from potential tragic greatness toward panoramic virtuosity, from character analysis toward special pleading in a cosmic arena. During the Gretchen scenes Faust becomes increasingly less at ease with himself, as his outbreaks against Mephistopheles show (Scenes xiv and xvi); on Walpurgis Night he is seriously concerned (end of Scene xxi); and when he finds that Gretchen is a prisoner, he cries out violently (Scene xxiii). But how does he cry out? He blames Mephistopheles, and he demands that Gretchen be rescued: blame and rescue—the moral and the activist phases of melodrama. Like many a tragic hero, Faust is trying to live in a melodrama (Scenes xxiii, xxiv); but he is never brought around to the final stage of tragic experience—that is, facing ineluctable tragedy. He never realizes his own guilt; there is no note of self-knowledge. There is great intensity, as often when the range is narrow, but never the human fullness that we saw in Oedipus.

The possibility of this fullness disappears entirely in Part II when Faust becomes simply an embodiment of striving or aspiration. Here we have a univocalness of thought that will account for a troubling thinness of substance. A single quality is taken out of the context of total moral possibility and made to do duty for the whole; in dealing with values, this is the exact equivalent of the method of dealing with character which defines an individual by means of a single trait. What is more, the single quality or function is morally neutral, and its relationship to virtue is begged when it is separated from the problem of ends. Striving may characterize an Oedipus, a Lucifer, a Iago, or a Hitler. In the end it turns out to be only activity or energy. When striving is proposed as the means of salvation, we feel ourselves to be in the presence of a limited partisan view, not of tragic contemplation of human wholeness. But *Faust* conceals its severely limited complexity and depth by a scarcely rivaled spread of geo-graphical, cultural, historic, mythic, and cosmic decor.

II. RANGE IN CHARACTER: INTELLIGENCE

Of the various ways in which extent of reality may be symbolized in a drama, the chief is capaciousness of character, and this requires, finally, that the tragic hero be intelligent. If he is not, the drama will evoke less of a sense of greatness. Volumnia is larger-minded than Coriolanus, and her presence contributes something to magnitude; but the play belongs primarily to Coriolanus, and it is his restricted awareness that makes the work less great than Shakespeare's chief tragedies. Not that intelligence is enough in itself; it is not a substi-tute for passion. But, except for neoclassical drama aspiring to trag-edy, and modern serious drama aspiring to clarification and correc-tion, passion comes more readily and regularly upon stage than does intelligence.

Intelligence is a general term for a wide range of perceptiveness—reflectiveness, intuition, even imaginativeness, in a word, all of the activities of consciousness by which reality may be sensed, imaged, known. A hero may, of course, have great powers of mind but never be able to employ them on the tragic substance of his divided self. John Gabriel Borkman has some justification for classing himself among "exceptional, chosen people," for he is capable of great dreams and plans. Nor is he without insight, for he can recognize in himself a "love of power" that is "uncontrollable" (Act II).[4] But in jail and subsequent isolation he retries himself and reports, "I have acquitted myself" (Act III); and at his death he is still gazing down from a mountain at an empire that might have been, still in love with "the kingdom—and the power—and the glory—" (Act IV). Borkman holds to his illusion; he does not criticize it; he does not finally have a sense of wrong action or wrong values. His mind lacks the greatness to take him in the indicated direction. This limiting of his personality leads to a reduction of the magnitude of the play as a whole; an area of potential action is unexplored.

Miller's Death of a Salesman

In one dimension, Borkman has some affiliation with Othello, whose vision of glory inhibits his final plunge into the depths of self-knowledge; in another direction, Borkman has kinship with Willy Loman in Arthur Miller's *Death of a Salesman* (1949). The relationship may be obscured, at first glimpse, by the fact that Ibsen's play of 1896 deals with an entrepreneur of the imperialistic type that one associates with the nineteenth century, whereas Miller's play of 1949 is about an expendable salesman in the lower echelons of the economic order. What Borkman and Willy Loman have in common is that at the end the once big man and the always little man go to their deaths hugging the illusion around which the wreckage of their lives is strewn. Not that both do not have moments of partial self-recognition: Borkman knows that he has been power mad; Willy can acknowledge to Charley that he is jobless and broke, that the magic of personality has failed. But neither one essentially alters his dream of looking down at a subservient world. Willy is never able to face his own guilt in the adultery that his son Biff discovered and made the cornerstone of his own continuing disaster. When Bernard asks a question that could lead to Willy's facing of his own past, Willy only replies ("angrily," the stage direction orders), "What are you trying to do, blame it on me? If a boy lays down is that my fault?" (Act II).[5] Willy has been compared to Lear, but while Lear can ask Cordelia to forgive him, Willy can only blame Biff for "spiting" him by a series of revengeful failures. It is the melodramatic blame instead of the tragic guilt. Willy not only flees from the truth of himself; he is also impervious to the truth of Biff, which Biff tries desperately to get to him. Willy is always in the first stage of the tragic rhythm—the flight from truth; but he never comes into the last stage of the tragic rhythm, in which truth breaks through to him. We are walled up within his impenetrable blindness.

It has been said that Willy's suicide is expiatory, and that he dies as a father, not as a salesman. But his death is never an atonement for an acknowledged wrong: it is a final gamble in the glory market—for Biff's profit and, vicariously, for Willy's own. Before he rushes into suicide, the very center of his dialogue is the hallucinatory exchange with Ben, who succeeded in the jungle: Ben's life is the symbol of the successful snatch, and Willy's final communion with him is the dramatic way of telling us that Willy's final vision is of the diamonds in the jungle. In death we cannot separate the salesman and the father, for the two are merged in a grandiose dream of success not really challenged by a few waking moments of factual seeing. The nature of Willy's last-minute hope and faith is betrayed in these lines:

Can you imagine that magnificence with twenty thousand dollars in his pocket?
When the mail comes he'll be ahead of Bernard again!
Oh, Ben, I always knew one way or another we were gonna make it, Biff and I!
Now when you kick off, boy, I want a seventy-yard boot, . . .
There's all kinds of important people in the stands, and the first thing you know. . . . [Act II]

This is not an act of penance, nor is it the grandeur of sacrifice; it is the last plunging investment in conspicuous triumph. To be certain that this is neither expiation nor charity, we have only to remember that in tapping the life-insurance gold mine, Willy has not once thought of an extraordinarily devoted wife. Not a penny for her. She can earn him no glory.

Willy's character is consistent, and the treatment of him has the intensity often produced by a narrow channeling of reality. My point is that he is limited, indeed so limited that he lacks tragic dimension; this appears primarily in his failure of perception; the truth never comes through to him. Charley says to him once, "When the hell are you going to grow up?" (Act II). It is his persistent failure of maturity, his sticking to the pettiness of false greatness, that makes him less tragic than pathetic. He is so constricted a character that he communicates his constrictedness to the play as a whole. It lacks tragic largeness and resonance. Hence, it is unfortunate that in the epilogue (entitled "Requiem") Charley, who speaks with considerable authority, is made to emphasize the fact that Willy is a salesman. Charley's words help seal Willy off in a special class, when he needs to take on as much of an air of human representativeness as possible.

The play is difficult to judge because it is so deeply rooted in two emotions that almost define our way of life: the pathos of obsolescence and the wracking tensions of insecurity. It is so convincing a historical document that it seems almost irreverent to look at it as art outside the stream of time. As art it has virtues: the construction is tight, the past is brought skillfully into the present, there is a hint of an escape hatch into the future, there is an effective symbolic dimension, and the naturalistic and expressionist modes are ingeniously fused. But one has to wonder whether its impact is due mainly to its contemporaneity, as was that of a comparable "common-man" drama, *The London Merchant*, over two hundred years ago; to its catching a mood that will pass. For it gives us a sense of being enclosed within an insufferable narrowness which is intensely "real" as far as it goes but which cuts off too much of reality. Miller has constructed a tight, unrelieved microcosm of bills, things, jobs, getting ahead of others. One shudders, but one is stuck there: there is no tragic transcendence. In the Everyman character, Willy, there is no saving insight into the heart of the matter. We are left with the hopeless doom that belongs to one end of the melodramatic spectrum.

To this generalization Biff, the elder son, is the exception: he comes to know, at least in part, what is wrong with both himself and his father. Biff's standards are uncertain, however; it is impossible to predict how well his definition of a better life will hold up as future history finds new symbols for values. His words, "The work and the food and the time to sit and smoke," barely avoid cliché and sentimentality, and it is questionable whether they enlarge horizons. Nevertheless the play moves out toward the tragic dimension because Biff is not locked within the prison of false dreams from which the dead Willy and the living Happy, the younger son, never escape. Biff anticipates the Tennessee Williams characters scarred by an early trauma, but while the Williams characters tend to go to pieces under such a shock, Biff owes his possible salvation to his disillusionment; though it spurs him into failures to "spite" his father, it also separates him from the paternal fantasies. At least we see him suddenly coming to the point at which he can call his theft of a pen "a terrible thing," call himself "The scum of the earth," can say, "I'm a bum," and confess, "I stole myself out of every good job since high school." Though part of his self-castigation, as well as his repeated "I know who I am," seems, in contrast with the naturalistic idiom of the rest, rhetorically inflated, still Miller does infuse into Biff something of the greater human potential that tragedy is concerned with.

In dealing with Willy, Miller hardly goes beyond a sad homily on the cul-de-sacs of commercial life; the arena is tightly closed; the doings are petty; there is little that opens out. But Miller makes Biff so define himself that he becomes more than a standard figure of triviality and muddlement; there is a real, if not resonant, echo of tragic largeness when he declares, "I could never stand taking orders from anybody! . . . I had to be boss big shot in two weeks. . . ." Behind the immediate sociology of "employment attitudes" we sense a human constant not bounded by historical limits: the short cut, the usurpation, the almost Faustian grab of the unearned or unearnable power. Miller has recognized the kind of hubris that relies on secular magic for the big takeover—the power of personality; at the end, Happy goes on in Willy's old melodrama of subduing a world by hypnotic sparkle. And although Miller makes Biff willing, even fairly close to the end, to blame Willy, he can also imagine Biff as finally surmounting the blame and assuring Willy, "There's no spite in it any more." That is to say, Biff has a share of the intelligence which can go beyond noting the causes and sources of the thing done, significant as these may be, and acknowledge the quality of the deed done. In Biff, then, Miller is not limited to popular psychological mechanics and the genealogy of disorder. Nevertheless Biff may be too easily granted a way out; he hardly contributes grandeur to a play committed to the little man and small affairs; and above all he does not have the centrality of role which finally determines the quality of the drama.

Since *Death of a Salesman* is extremely well known, it provides useful material for a discussion of the hero's power of understanding and its relevance to artistic quality. The obvious difficulty is that its thematic immediacy—the "common man" as underdog in economic competition—has made the play almost sacrosanct. Yet that fact may underscore the critical point: despite its contemporary attractiveness, the play has a hero so limited that this is a limitation of the play itself.

Opposing Tendencies

This particular argument from quantity—that, other things being equal, greatness is a function of the extent of human truth drawn upon—in our own day runs into a general cast of mind that is implicitly adverse to it. There is ground for thinking that "understanding" or "insight"—the "intelligence" which is the index of the hero's magnitude—is not valued very highly among us. What we keep praising is "reason," by which, in general usage, we mean either the denigration of traditional modes of thought and feeling, or the formulation, in general terms, of causes, effects, frequencies, correspondences. This "reason" tends to limit sense of character to an awareness of the laws by virtue of which it presumably became what it is, and self-knowledge to an identification of forces that "made me what I am today." This process is morally neutral; it implies that any view of the self is completed when the influential trauma or the decisive habits have been spotted. A criticism of an aspect of modern life is relevant here: ". . . one can be tripped by purely analytical and descriptive procedures into abandoning one's ethical values. . . ."[6] Hence a placement of self, an application of an order of values, is outside the pale of expectable activities of mind, which include only seeing in what way one is ill, not saying "I have done ill."

If the case for full range of character has to contend with a popular habit of thought in our day, it is also inconsistent with influential theatrical practice. In some ways our "serious" theater is the most allegorical and homiletic since the morality plays and the eighteenth-century didactic-sentimental drama. Great technical virtuosity, expressionistic novelties, and fanciful ingenuities are often the masks of lecture rooms; sermons are decked out as wacky or sinister conundrums. Though Brecht regularly transcends his own rules, his extensive influence has been toward making the stage a tutorial on the nature of the social organism and its contorting pressures. Sartre, on the other hand, uses the theater to define a philosophical attitude, or establish the bases of post-theistic morality. With the exception of *Waiting for Godot*, Beckett hardly makes drama out of disquisitions. Whatever the virtues of these artists, their significance, for our purposes, is the extent of their influence in diminishing fullness of character by making the dramatis personae either mouthpieces or segments of thought, semaphoric counters in an idea market. They become monosemantic, that is, analogous to the monopathic characters of good and evil in pure melodramatic structures. Shaw's characters talked their ideas; these post-Shavian beings model theirs. They may be superficially enigmatic, like Goldberg and McCann in Harold Pinter's *The Birthday Party* (1958); but the enigma is the absence of expected human dimensions, and in time they may stand out as stark images of all the pressures and customs that reduce Stanley, the artist, to a dead-alive robot. Here, as in Duerrenmatt's *Visit* and Max Frisch's *The Fire Bugs* (1958), the action is produced by sinister visitants working through weakness in those visited; the opposite structure is found in David Rudkin's *Afore Night Come* (1962) and Frisch's *Andorra* (1962), in which sinister insiders destroy a visiting outsider. Characters stand for weak or aggressive insidership, or destructive or vulnerable outsidership. The concepts represented may be philosophical, sociological, or psychological. Our rediscovery of human traits played down in post-Enlightenment hopefulness—such as death seeking, murderousness, random and eccentric lusts—leads to the subtraction of these from the complex total of human nature, and the independent representation of each as if it were a total. We have an unusual number of demonstrations of, for instance, bourgeois viciousness and human murderousness. The dramatist all but uses a pointer. The conceptual singleness from which characters are derived leads to the use of single, often monosyllabic names, for dramatis personae—Bud, Dust, Swett, Krapp; these are not names for persons, but tags for objects, as cut down from fullness as the neuters of farce. Such a limiting of personality is often breath-taking, sometimes brilliant.

This is not a complaint about the ways of the contemporary theater, which must discover what it can and frame its discoveries with what freshness it can. The habits alluded to here are one background that can help outline the problem of the magnitude of tragic drama. Actually the dramatists most in the public eye in the 1960's do not purport to be writing tragedy, though popular usage might invoke the term for their works; rather they are dominated by a sense of disaster, and their collective voice tends to be that of the prophet, with accents now of instruction and warning, now of satire and invective, now of disgust and despair. All these tones are proper to the melodramatic mode.

III. The Hero's Mind: Modes of Action

In a sense it is axiomatic that, as tragedy moves closer to the full exploitation of its potential, it will tend to include the widest ranges of feeling and consciousness, especially the activities of consciousness involved in self-confrontation. These latter are difficult and taxing; the character who lacks them is a lesser character, and his world a lesser world. Titus and Aaron, Timon and Coriolanus, and for that matter Romeo and Brutus are of smaller dimension than Othello and Lear, and their worlds are narrower. If the dramatist can encompass the larger life in which the tragic consciousness comes into play, his imagination will have a needed freedom in discovering diverse styles for the operation of that consciousness.

There is no pat formula for the functioning of the hero's intelligence. Lear comes grudgingly, by minute steps, into an acknowledgment of his error; likewise Oedipus proceeds by slow motion from the self-contented riddle solver to the unillusioned self-knower. On the other hand, Macbeth moves away from the unillusioned self-knower to the self-deceptive riddle solver ("Birnam Wood," "of woman born"). Macbeth is not stupid; rather he is, as it were, trying to be stupid, to trim down his mind for the sheer melodrama of conquest. Yet he cannot wholly prevent what he knows from returning to him in ghostly form, in the sense of what he has lost ("honour") and gained ("Curses," V.iii.25–27). We come upon Faustus at a later stage of the Macbeth cycle, enthusiasm having already got him over the hump of denying the wisdom to which he has been subject; and from there on until the end we see his mind barely holding off the driving insurgency of what he knows. Orestes knows enough about his intended deed to be unable to cherish an illusion of immunity. Hamlet differs from all the others in bringing great reflective and ratiocinative powers to bear upon a complex problem of self-knowledge: he prefers the adverse judgment upon himself as a defaulting revenger to the adverse judgment upon himself as a successful revenger with faulty motives. Sartre's Franz von Gerlach seeks in madness an escape from unbearable knowledge but cannot hold to his illness; Eliot's Celia Coplestone laboriously works toward a knowledge to escape from an unbearable life; Duerrenmatt's townspeople are brilliant in maintaining a necessary stupidity about their own doings; Ibsen's master builder develops great capacity for knowing himself, but dies before he comes to complete insight.

In none of these characters do we have only a persistent inability to turn toward the light. The hero's intelligence may work in many ways as the problem of himself and his conduct enters his consciousness; its presence, not its mode of functioning, is relevant to the problem of magnitude. The presence needs, of course, to be a true one, neither a hasty afterthought, as in the sketchy words of remorse by the Cardinal long after the death of the Duchess of Malfi, nor, at the opposite extreme, a histrionic and oppressive lingering, as in *The*

London Merchant, in which George Barnwell's protracted meditations deprive his evildoing of all plausibility. Intelligence has greatest
dramatic reality when, as in life, it is there all the time but must
always struggle, against other competitors in the personality, to maintain a precarious share in what is done, taken in, assented to.

Understanding and Dividedness

It is one thing to say that the tragic dramatist who has a feeling for
magnitude will tend to find leading characters with an actual or latent
power of understanding. We can go beyond that and say that the
power of understanding is a natural complement of tragic character.
What is to be understood is that the truth about oneself is different
from what one had believed, imagined, or indeed resolved: all the
disparities between passion and power, pride and the nature of the
world, will and the complexity of inner and outer forces set in motion,
the sense of invulnerability and the strength of moral consequences—
in a word, the nature of tragic life in its split between imperative and
impulse. The natural subject of understanding is dividedness, inconsistency, misconception, illusion, conflict—the states in which, as we
proposed in Chapter 1 and Chapter 5, tragic action has its genesis;
understanding is the natural completion or resolution of the division
in which tragedy originates. The true object of understanding is what
has been the object of misunderstanding—the motive or step that has
caused or constituted the flaw or error, be it a misdeed with unfore-
seen consequences or a monstrous crime.

The character who is undivided or whole, whatever the mode of
wholeness, provides no material for comprehension or judgment or
placement. If he is totally "good"—a Squire Allworthy (though he
can be deceived), a Daniel Deronda, a Dinah Morris, or, at another
level, the triumphant hero in "popular" melodrama of various kinds
—he has nothing to contemplate but his own virtue, so that any
inward look would shrink into moral narcissism. If he is a bona fide
victim and has the unhappy wholeness of the man treated unjustly, he
has nothing in himself to know, and can only turn upon himself the
eye of pity. If he is a wholly evil man, his very wholeness implies a
freedom from the self-understanding that might constitute a brake, if
only a tardy one, upon his corrupt course. His wholeness might
perversely include a tragic consciousness that has undergone a muta-

tion and appears only as an instrument of self-congratulation, as in Aaron's "If one good deed in all my life I did, / I do repent it from my very soul" (*Titus Andronicus* V.iii.189–90). But total evil means that there is too much to be known; so radical a knowing would be destructive, and it must be shunned by the man who could know only it. The totally evil man is saved from the tragic split between the power of knowing and the difficulty or revoltingness of what is to be known.

If a fragment of the power of knowing persists and demands indulgence, its owner may embrace revoltingness. Then he will either retreat into his own sickness, that is, into a neurosis of self-disgust; or else get more living room by generalizing the discovered revoltingness and calling for universal nausea as the only form of knowledge for the upright man. Another possibility, open only to a very subtle mind, is to use the moral intelligence to transmute evil into the practice of freedom or the achievement of sainthood; this has only the disadvantage of reducing the sinner, like the less paradoxical kind of saint, to a spectator of his own blessedness.

The more familiar evil character tends to eliminate the judicious intelligence by yielding his being to insatiable impulses that keep him always on a rigid one-way monorail toward the kind of triumphs needed. The revengers are a case in point, less perhaps the man who wants revenge on others for what they have done (Titus) than the man who wants revenge on others for what they are (Iago). The revenge of the slighted man may wear itself out, that of the spiritual defective is tireless. The deed to be revenged may fade or be canceled; the state of being that makes one a revenger is always present as a good. But in both cases there is the psychic structure of the feud, in which all value attaches to demonic energizing against what is hated, and none is left for reconsidering the loved self. Barabas, in Marlowe's *Jew of Malta* (ca. 1590), piles stratagem on stratagem in a massive accumulation of revenges, and the fatal backfiring of his own final treachery only makes him truculently rehearse his evil triumphs.[7] In *The Spanish Tragedy* (ca. 1585–88) Kyd offers us not only the unqualified machiavel in Lorenzo, whose unscrupulous practicality is never impeded by any sense of the nature of his acts, but also, in Hieronimo, both the victim who can think only of the wrongs done him, and the revenger bent upon extinguishing the evildoers and then furiously triumphant in the success of his machinations. (Hence the play "remains merely melodrama." [8]) We may conclude that to conceive of the divided personality is not only to make available the human material for self-understanding, but to imply the existence of the very power of self-understanding, whether it be denied or resisted, grudgingly accepted or fully developed. The further the dramatist's imagination takes him toward fullness of character, the less content he is with the monopathic individual and the more he tends to discover, among the permanent complexities of human make-up, the consciousness that we call tragic because, although it may neither check nor separate itself from the most strident urgencies to wrong action, it knows at some time the nature of the thing done. The gross or univalent conception of character may weaken unexpectedly: even upon that greatest of the machiavels, Richard III, Shakespeare bestows, albeit clumsily and tardily, a fragment of conscience.

The Functioning of Tragedy

It is quite possible that the proper functioning of tragedy depends upon its magnitude, that is, ultimately, upon the fullness of personality that the dramatist can establish in his leading characters. The larger these men and women are, the less easy they are to condescend to or to write off, which is what we do in effect when we find them so much of a piece that we can easily fit them into some current category of behavior. Thus we reduce the relevance of characters to ourselves, for we refrain from that circumscribing of our reality which would occur if we fitted ourselves into the same categories. We thereby attenuate the kind of experience that it is the function of tragedy to make us undergo.

Experience is a matter about which we are not consistent. In our day it is not fashionable to refuse or decry all experience, either immediate or vicarious; yet in practice we tend to be drawn in by that which is less exacting. Hence an attraction, stronger I suspect than our formal professions of faith would make likely, to melodramatic forms and to tragedies like *Death of a Salesman* at the lower end of the scale of possibility. As we said in earlier chapters, through melodrama we can participate in a triumph; we can be at one with victims, through a pleasurable pity and indignation; even the drama of despair has an inviting simplicity. We are not deeply tried; at most we are caught in some segment of our being; and whole reaches of responsiveness remain unengaged. In satire we have a free field for the mockery and chastisement which are natural to our egos; the satirist rarely has a technical way of making us see ourselves among the lashed, and he must be resigned to his fate of assisting us to an easy triumph over those whom we wish damned. Even the more recent dramatists who most perturb us with visions of cruelty, depravity, and nothingness in the heart of man, or in the cosmos, leave us a large way out: sheer flight from the narrow dogmas of secularized puritan divines, from portraits that only serve preachments, or, more subtly, from characterization not penetrating enough, from that which terrorizes without persuading. To sum up: we value all experience, but slip more readily into that which is less demanding.

But if we are tempted by ease, we are also, in the inconsistency of our nature, held aloof from one kind of ease: we have an ultimate inability to be engaged by the incomplete. The more complete the experience, the harder it is, and yet at the same time the more compelling, the more invasive, the more resistless; one's nature may shrink from, but it does not deny, wholeness (as it will the disagreeableness which seems only a part truth). In other words, the more inclusive the range of the tragic personality, the less we are able to place it or remain outside it or find ourselves unengaged by its multiple conflicting activities. We can hold aloof from or repudiate Titus or Timon or even Coriolanus more easily than we can Lear. Hence Lear is more meaningful. Through him we know more about ourselves, for we more nearly become him as he expands to full human dimension by the growth of self-awareness.

The hypothesis which I am exploring here has to do with self-knowledge, and with the communication of it from dramatis personae to audience or reader. We are always aware of self-knowledge as an ultimate possibility of character. A critic can say of a Howard Nemerov protagonist: "One wonders why the author, who has made him an intelligent man and a historian, does not allow him to understand his plight better, and thus make him a purged man at least, if not a hero." [9] Another notes that Joyce Cary "does not create much pressure toward self-recognition. He is for freedom, imagination, mother, vitality— and who is not?" [10] Another says of Robert Penn Warren's work: "The beginning of wisdom is the rational perception of the *internal* conflict between good and evil"[11] (italics added). For Ionesco, self-understanding is basic: "This understanding of self . . . rests on the answer to that most basic of existential questions: Who am I? . . . Who am I? is the central question of Ionesco's dramaturgy."[12] George Eliot attributes to her character Casaubon the habit we have noted often in dramatis personae: ". . . irritated feeling with him, as with all of us, seeking rather for justification than for self-knowledge."[13] One critic has even claimed the rarer achievement for Proust's Marcel: "The effort required, the direction voluntarily chosen, the renunciation of lesser pleasures and illusions to serve a larger end—all these aspects of self-recognition give it a moral significance which the *moments bienheureux* never achieve."[14] To sum up: "The common element of all true tragedies, Christian and non-Christian, is the knowledge or vision that suffering brings to a sensitive protagonist. Without this knowledge we have only melodrama. . . ."[15] Or in Hart Crane's view: "The imagination always spans beyond despair; beyond suffering lies illumination. . . ."[16] Henry de Montherlant puts it effectively: "The dangers to individual consciousness, to the self, are rationalization, absolutism, hypocrisy, sentimentality—in short, any impediment to an austere self-contemplation, to the discipline of self-knowledge."[17]

Dramatist and Audience: The Problem of Distance

The problem, as we have said, is the relation of the literary work, specifically of tragedy, to this self-understanding. More than one artist is aware of the problem; the less content he is to entertain, the more he contemplates measures for breaking down that resistance of the reader to seeing the artistic truth as his own rather than his neighbor's. Gogol talks directly to his audience about it: "But which of you, full of Christian meekness, not in public but in solitude, in silent communion with yourself, will peer into his own soul and ask himself this very painful question: 'Is there not something of Chichikov in me too?' Why, of course there is!"[18] In *Sweet Bird of Youth* (1959), Tennessee Williams makes his chief character speak for him; for the final speech of the play Chance comes to the forestage and, directly addressing the audience, asks "Just for your recognition of me in you. . . ." One may applaud the intent of both novelist and playwright and yet not admire the method, for the direct appeal to the audience is an acknowledgment that the drama has not been success-ful. Art does not make contact with its audience through the interven-tion of the intellect, however useful the intellect may be in clarifying the contact that has been achieved, or however much it may be present in the total personality engaged in the artistic experience. Wilde insists that art cannot even "show us the external world." He goes on: "All that it shows us is our own soul, the one world of which we have any real cognizance. . . . Consciousness, indeed, is quite inadequate to explain the contents of personality. It is Art, and Art only, that reveals us to ourselves." [19] Wilde's view that we "become" the characters in drama has recently been applied to readers of novels: "When Flaubert said, '*Madame Bovary, c'est moi,*' he affirmed not only an essential condition of the novelist's relation to his work, but one of the reader's relation to the novel as well." [20] Lawrence Durrell has put it more epigrammatically: ". . . you must think about a detective story in which the reader at the end discovers that he is the criminal!" [21]

This discovery of criminality, or more often of less sensational forms of guilt, is, as we have been saying, the problem; resistance to it is not a kind of wall which an artist can attack with a battering ram. Richard Wilbur believes that the wall is breached by the "closing speech" of Sartre's *Altona* (1959) when the author "lifts his play from the context of a limited comment on the individual in a specific national and historical situation to a universality where the spectator suddenly finds himself questioning his own conscience concerning his personal involvement in any use of force as a national policy." [22] The reader's involvement, however, has to be brought about by over-all dramatic cogency, not by an expository codicil. The closing speech in Sartre's play is a postdramatic exposition, a tape recording made by the chief character years before when his madness and sanity were not entirely distinguishable, and now played after his presumptive death. His voice says that he had taken upon himself the guilt of the self-destroying twentieth century, the victim of a "cruel enemy . . . [a] flesh-eating beast—man himself . . . his look deep in the eyes of our neighbors . . . the beast still living—myself." [23] The content of this is admirable for its shift from the melodramatic to the tragic view, and insofar as the "Voice of Franz" speaks about Franz's own role, and really bores into that role, the improvement upon the glib address to the audience in Williams' *Sweet Bird of Youth* is great. Still, it is not a continuation of the dramatic experience, but a super-imposed effort to invite thought.

Hence it falls into the Brecht pattern, as this has been summarized by Harold Clurman. Brecht's "goal is not excitement but understanding. He wants his audience, it is said, to recognize its place in society, and how it (the audience) can help change that society. He tries to induce in the spectator the attitude of an alert observer rather than that of a hypnotized person who seeks to be swept away by the show." [24] In this standard interpretation of the well-known Brecht position, the significant terms are two pairs of opposites: ". . . not excitement but understanding" and "alert observer rather than . . . hypnotized person." We are offered a pair of alternatives as if these exhausted the possibilities, and there is reason to suppose that this either-or view is widely held in our day, in which we have moved away from traditional drama in two directions. In one, there is the Brecht theater, which, as Oscar Büdel has put it, "is demonstrating situations of a mere factual nature and relationship"; [25] if things go according to plan, the audience is so separated from transactions on the stage that it might as well be attending a lecture. At the other extreme, all boundary lines disappear: in a widespread practice (for instance, in the Pirandello theater and the "happening") audience and cast, actors and the characters they represent, stage and theater, drama and life are merged. We seem to have a choice only between listening to a sermon and enjoying a drunken carouse; or, as Büdel, who is interested in the subject of aesthetic distance, puts it, "we may discern both a tendency to underdistance as well as one to the opposite, to overdistance." [26] Underdistancing includes both the state of the "hypnotized person who seeks to be swept away by the show" and the eliding of lines between art and life. Though complete surrender to the show seems naïve, and the rejection of the differentiation of art and life "sophisticated," the two really come together. For the assimilation of cast and characters, of pit and stage, in effect reduces everyone to the position of the simple-minded theatergoer who from Elizabethan times on has been laughed at for his taking stage transactions as actualities. When the whole audience is confused about boundaries, then underdistancing has paradoxically done the work of overdistancing, for the theatergoer becomes, not the possessor of an experience, but the asker of questions and the seeker of answers.

But in fact we need not be driven to these extremes, either of which vastly simplifies the experiences afforded by drama. In the theater we are neither taking in propositions nor being taken in by emotional whirlwinds, but are taking part in an experience marked by complexity, not by confusion. Büdel refers, quite accurately, to the spectator's "honest critical-emotional response." The joining of *critical* and *emotional* is one way of designating the complexity, or at least the duality, of what the spectator or reader does. He always remains in part an observer; he knows that he is reading a book or sitting in a theater seat. But the aloof student of the scientific exhibit is here also drawn into a special form of engagement and participation so natural to the dynamics of personality that it could be resisted only by effort of will. Bodily separation and imaginative union coexist; each has a share in a consciousness able to accommodate both of them simultaneously without disturbance and without simply oscillating between the two. The spectator is critical enough not to mistake art for life, but involved enough to "become" the characters as the human constants in them evoke a conscious or unconscious sense of relatedness or potential identity. One is outsider and insider, observer and agonist, spectator and secret sharer. He undergoes a two-sided but unitary experience which it is very difficult, if not indeed impossible, to replace by any one-dimensional substitute, such as being calmly lessoned, being wholly swept away, or being hung limply on an epistemological crux.

To convey something of this experience I have used the term "feeling knowledge" [27]—that is, a knowing not by intellectual analysis and mastery, but by having been "in" the actions constituting the reality known. Later one may order these by pure mind; at the time he has a "feel" or a kinesthetic awareness of them. He undergoes not ecstasy, but extension; not hypnotized subservience but empathic acceptance of other being through latent identity.

Freedom in Character

Given as Sartre is to constructing characters out of theorems or at least subjecting them to the pressure of doctrinal concepts (even when presumably driven by passions, they have about them a kind of academic chill or geometric ordonnance), he provides a good account of what goes on in our relationship with fictional characters and of the conditions of its going on. According to Philip Thody,

[Sartre] maintained that a character in a novel is brought to life only by the free decision of the reader to identify himself with him. The reader cannot do this if he suspects that each move which the character makes is predetermined, for he can only lend his powers of anticipation and sympathy to someone he believes to be free. If a novelist wishes his characters to live, he must "see to it that they are free." [28]

Leaving aside the question raised by "free decision," * we can accept the view that a sense of life in the character is a function of the ability to identify with him. More important, however, is the view that identification, in turn, is made possible by a sense of freedom in the character. We can go a step further and say that this sense of freedom in the character makes identification not only possible but necessary. The issue is the meaning of freedom, and that I take to be a freedom to make choices, which is—to come back now to the specific subject of tragedy—a *sine qua non* in tragic character. Freedom to make choices, however, is rooted in freedom of conception and of being. Freedom of conception does not exist if the character is but the representative of an idea; in Sartre's *Altona*, for instance, the father almost becomes an emblem of omniscience and omnipotence in the immediate business world. Again, freedom of conception does not exist if the character stands for one impulse or one strain of reality among the diverse and contradictory elements that constitute human actuality—say murderousness or stinginess or disillusionment: Titus or Timon or Henry VI or, less conspicuously, Richard III. (We testify to the excluding force of nonfreedom by refusing to identify with such one-trait characters as Jonsonian "humors.") Nor, finally, does the character have freedom of being if he lacks the power of understanding with which to know what the issues are, whether he rejects the knowledge, submerges it, earns it, or grudgingly comes into it. Without an adequate consciousness, actual or potential, he is too much the automaton to excite in us the imaginative participation which is the proof of his human vitality.

---

* It implies a conscious, voluntary act, whereas making or failing to make an identification would appear to be entirely spontaneous, not subject to will or preference. But the phrase may be Thody's.

Freedom, then, is a name for inclusiveness or wholeness of character, for that largeness of character which is a principal source of magnitude in tragedy. It is that largeness, we have argued, which draws in the spectator or reader, lessens his ability to ignore or reject what is difficult, exacts acknowledgment of reality—in a word, compels that assent of feeling and being for which the convenient term is *identification*. Hence occurs the kind of experiencing appropriate to tragedy. The final element in that largeness, and thus in the persuasive—the *intractive*, to coin a word—magnitude of tragedy, is the endowment of intelligence by virtue of which the protagonist knows or comes to know what he has been about.* Without it, the tragic experience is diminished or wanting. For, however much the individual may be tempted by the easier aesthetic experiences which permit him to be engaged only in part, whether in obvious or more obscure gratification (in melodramas of triumph and defeat), he will not acknowledge a oneness with the man who lacks the power to make distinctions about courses, imperatives, the quality of his own actions. He separates himself from that defect of freedom (to repeat Sartre's key word) which appears as obtuseness. What is left for him is a theatrical demonstration of how things go.

Pointed evidence of this lies in the remark of a man—this is literal reporting—whose argument in defense of *Death of a Salesman* was: "I had an uncle just like that." That is it: not, there go I, but there goes someone else. It is a reduced modern version of the familiar Elizabethan attitude: yes, there is evil in the world, just look at those Italians. The nephew goes scot free; he is not drawn in, as he is by Othello or Orestes, though their pattern of life is far less immediate. The distinction is between the tragic experience and the dramatized lesson, between the vital illumination and a perhaps perfectly valid

* Here, as elsewhere, comedy has an analogous function. At the peaks of comic achievement, the protagonist has great range and is capable of self-recognition. Molière's misanthrope has a larger, more inclusive personality than does the miser, the bourgeois gentleman, the imaginary invalid, or for that matter Tartuffe or Orgon. Hence he has more to see, and more power of seeing himself in perspective. But the comic consciousness and the tragic consciousness have different objects. In comedy the sentient character says, in effect, "I have acted foolishly"; in tragedy he says, "I have acted wrongly." One has violated the canons of good sense held by the civilized world; the other the imperatives that lie beyond worldly wisdom.

analysis presented discursively as a generalization acted out by a character (e.g., salesmanship begets and thrives on false values). Perhaps the most we need do is reiterate that, just as disaster should not be mistaken for tragedy, so the wholesome homily on the stage, however transmuted into disastrous events, should not be mistaken for tragic experience in which, from the inside, one knows the whole range of the free being. The content of "there go I" is not a proposition but a state of being with a scarcely formulated increment of awareness. The self-knowledge of the protagonist is the final means not only of involving the witnesser but of stirring his own self-knowledge. Among literary forms tragedy is the great nourisher of complete consciousness, in the individual and then in the race. Hence tragedy may be thought of as engaging the individual's wholeness, actualizing it, bringing it to life. Without tragic consciousness there would be a threat to human consciousness in its most significant ranges, and to the wholeness which it signifies.

IV. KNOWLEDGE OF SANCTIONS: MILTON AND SARTRE

In self-knowledge there is not only acknowledgment of the deed done but awareness of the sanctions by virtue of which the quality of the deed is known. Laius and Jocasta, and later Oedipus himself, thought that they had beaten the oracle, but they did not question the authority which made the prophesied actions terrible and monstrous. Milton's Samson is a figure of interest here. Milton introduces Samson in a situation rather like that of Oedipus after he has put all the evidence together and has blinded himself: Samson is blind, too; he is likewise completely clear-sighted about what he has done. "Whom have I to complain of but my self? . . . O impotence of mind, . . . of what now I suffer / She was not the prime cause, but I my self. . . . Nothing of all these evils hath befall'n me / But justly; I my self have brought them on, / Sole Author I, sole cause: . . . foul effeminacy . . . servile mind . . . that blindness worse than this, . . . let me here, / As I deserve, pay on my punishment; . . . swoll'n with pride. . . ." [29]

But Milton is aware that verbal self-punishment may be a ritual lacking sound substance, and he devises for Samson a series of tests or temptations (predecessors, if not models, of those faced by the Archbishop in Part 1 of *Murder in the Cathedral*): can he hold firm in the role of the justly punished man, or will he settle for one or another of the redemptions possible within the world—ransom by his father Manoah (who cunningly suggests that there may be a masochistic egoism in his son's sufferings), reconciliation and a comfortable home life with Dalila (who makes a fascinatingly modern explanation, and therefore justification, of her role in his downfall), or cooperation, at least trouble-avoiding if not positively advantageous, with the Philistines in the big feast to their god Dagon? Perhaps the subtlest trial is that offered by the jibes of Harapha, the rival champion; they constitute a temptation which Samson names when he says, in resistance to it, "I . . . despair not" (line 1171). The tempters are all actual persons, not symbols of forces within Samson; in resisting them Samson at times becomes strident, condemnatory (notably with Dalila), and even self-righteous. Thus in the very exercise of tragic consciousness he has also something of a melodramatic stance. The generic mixture is not only technically interesting, but is functional: the rasping or even quarrelsome tone is a symptom of the inner tensions of a man who, though he has come to a sharp vision, has not reached a false or premature peace, a bulwark from which to reject, with an easy calm, the solicitations of his visitors, hostile or well intending.

Beyond the painfully disturbing conditions of a state that, though wholly accepted, is nevertheless miserable, lie the tensions of a man who is still waiting to know the will of God. When he begins to feel the presence of that will, he moves toward an alteration of his refusal to attend the Dagon feast:

> Yet that he may dispense with me or thee
> Present in Temples at Idolatrous Rites
> For some important cause, . . .
>   [lines 1377–79]

His final act is to obey the will that once he had violated, and from the sense of obedience comes his first touch of serenity. In Samson's recognition of wrongdoing there is never merely the use of the prevailing term for what he has done, but the overriding, unpalliated awareness of the sanctions whereby the wrong became wrong: "I must not quarrel with the will / Of highest dispensation, . . . divulg'd the secret gift of God . . . what I motiond was of God; . . .

The work to which I was divinely calld; . . . I, . . . who have profan'd / The mystery of God . . . to God have brought / Dishonour, obloquie, . . . I / Gods counsel have not kept, . . ."[30] So he can make a summary acknowledgment:

> . . . these evils I deserve and more,
> Acknowledge them from God inflicted on me
> Justly.
>
> [lines 1169–71]

Though the situation is one to which the answer of more recent times would often be despair, Samson is able to reject despair because the transcendental reality always present to his mind keeps the situation infinitely open. He continues immediately: ". . . yet despair not of [God's] final pardon." True, he goes on to his death—not, however, to end the anguish of knowing the truth, but in a final redemptive effort to act in accordance with the will against which he had once transgressed. In this work, rather more rich than its bare exterior indicates, Milton exhibits the tragic consciousness in its most capacious form.

When Rosmer tells Rebecca West, near the end of Act IV of *Rosmersholm*, "There is no judge over us; and therefore we must do justice upon ourselves," he signifies the limiting of the tragic world by the removal of the standard of self-knowledge that transcends local and topical opinion, or simply personal feeling. Shortly after making this statement, Rosmer commits suicide. Whereas Samson's burden was the knowledge that he had violated the will of God, Rosmer knows only that he is weak; and whereas Samson in bringing death upon himself is recovering the power to act by God's will, Rosmer is acting by his own will and, in the main, "getting away from it all."

Sartre's rewriting of the Orestes story, *The Flies* (1943), is relevant in that he is campaigning against the "sickly conscience" that troubled a number of Ibsen characters. After killing Clytemnestra and Aegisthus, Orestes is calm and collected, "Beyond anguish, beyond remorse" (Act III). He has "the courage of his crimes"—a paradoxical way of asserting the value of resoluteness, and, on the other side, condemning what in this essay we have called the "hypertragic consciousness," that exaggeration of guilt by which one sinks into the impotent misery of self-flagellation. On the face of it, the ailment would hardly seem to need blame. But what Sartre does, with a doctrinaire simplicity that Ionesco may have been twitting in *Rhinoceros*,* is to extend "sickly conscience" to mean all conscience, to treat the ideas of guilt, remorse, repentance, atonement, expiation as devices for the maintenance of power over a nation by a king (Aegisthus) and over humanity by a god (Zeus). Orestes, having given the first blow to Aegisthus, sounds like a much more assertive Rosmer when he cries, "What do I care for Zeus? Justice is a matter between men, and I need no God to teach me it" (II.ii). He has already said, "from now on I'll take no one's orders, neither man's nor god's" (II.i). If these statements suggest the ruthlessly self-willed man criminally intent upon a coup for snatching power from its present holders (whether by revolution or by counterrevolution), it need only be pointed out that Sartre's Orestes comes to resemble a secular Christ who at the end is intent upon freeing mankind from its "sins . . . remorse, . . . night-fears" by taking them upon himself and becoming, not the sacrificial victim, but a new flute player of Scyros who by his music charmed the rats and led them away from the community they had plagued. Sartre has tried to stress sufficiently Orestes' sense of his burden, but Orestes still comes close to the race of Dorothy Sayers' Faustus, the impetuous reformer who planned to remake the world by removing unhappiness at a blow.

The specific relation of *The Flies* to our own perspective is that it shows a markedly diminishing area of tragedy. Sanctions and imperatives become subjective ("you [Zeus] have no power to make me atone for an act I don't regard as a crime"—Act III), and any self-knowledge that finds a guilt to be borne, instead of a slavery to attack, is equated with pathological self-torture, which can and will be put to their own uses by royal and divine racketeers. Whereas O'Neill undermines tragedy by declaring self-knowledge unbearable,

---

* When Berenger, who seems intended to have our sympathy, expresses regret for past conduct, his girl friend Daisy says, "You'll spoil everything if you go on having a bad conscience. . . . Guilt is a dangerous symptom. It shows a lack of purity. . . . We must try and not feel guilty any more" (Act III, quoted from Derek Prouse's translation in *Rhinoceros and Other Plays* [New York: Grove Press, 1960], p. 98). Daisy is not an ethical theorist except by implication; she has a profound sense of how the world goes, and she does not intend to be left behind. This is her mode of freedom.

Sartre attacks from a different viewpoint by declaring self-knowledge untrustworthy, the tool of oppressors.

Sartre, of course, is not trying to write a tragedy; he is using a situation from classical tragedy as the subject for a clever polemic dialogue on behalf of freedom (and he avoids banality by making freedom not an automatic privilege for trivial people but an awesome burden for a hero). Like Shaw's, his characters stand for ideas. But whereas Shaw writes intellectual farce, Sartre writes intellectual melodrama. Shaw's ideogram characters knock each other all about the place, but like Menaechmi, Dromios, and Scapins, they are never really hurt. In Sartre these ideogram characters take on feelings, like Rosson's Universal Robots in Karel Capek's play, and they are lined up either on the side of good or of evil. Sartre even inclines toward the paranoid aspect of melodrama: a conspiratorial "they" is usually causing the trouble. In *The Flies* it is Zeus, so treated that he becomes also a Christian godhead; and the play drifts into a familiar idea melodrama of our day. Whereas Aeschylus uses the Orestes story to show the coming into power of a better set of divinities, Sartre uses it to reduce divinity to the laws of nature that have no relevance to human reality. We are left with this: the sanction of the deed is the unqualified determination of the doer. This is not far from Marlowe's Tamburlaine and Webster's Vittoria Corombona.

Yet it is not clear that *The Flies* sinks into a hortatory drama of triumph, or that man's lifting himself by his bootstraps is going to exalt him permanently out of the Valley of the Shadow of Death. The satirist and the puritan preacher that are so prominent in Sartre are not permitted to cancel his sense of ineluctable fact. He does not trivialize his Flies-Furies into an illusion that can be easily banished. He drives satirical barbs deep into Orestes' rationalist-relativist tutor, the complete liberal ideologue who wishes he were back in Athens, "where reason's always right," and who regards the Furies as "More of those primitive myths!" Orestes replies tensely, "Do not try to approach me, or they will tear you in pieces" (Act III). The Furies do not evaporate. Though to Sartre's Orestes they may not be as elemental as they are to Aeschylus' Athena, who calls on every resource to convert the energy that they represent from a destructive to a beneficent disciplinary function, nevertheless Orestes is embarking on a heroically difficult exploit of attracting the Furies to himself and leading them away. We are not assured that he will not be a sacrificial victim. Sartre the artist may after all not entirely share Sartre the homilist's conviction that guilt is a put-up job, and remorse a spiritual con man's counterfeit money.

One toys with the likelihood of a faint duality in *The Flies*, because sixteen years later in *Altona* another Orestes takes upon himself, at least verbally, the burdens of an age; but he is already suffering from private Furies, which are not belittled. He has a burden of guilt and remorse which are not interpreted as the banishable instruments of someone else's tyranny, but which on the contrary are his awareness of a bestiality intrinsic to humanity ("the beast still living—myself"). If he is the carrier of a message, he is also the bearer of a conscience, and Sartre moves back toward a tragic realm which *The Flies* would have rendered extinct.

Franz von Gerlach is the son of a rich German industrialist, in this play the man without a conscience, who collaborated with the Nazis, even selling them land for a concentration camp, and either actually or in effect betraying to them a Polish rabbi who had escaped and whom Franz had brought home to conceal; the Nazis had beaten the rabbi to death before Franz's eyes. Pursued by the horror of this, Franz, now in the army, had sought death in campaigns but always won glory instead ("Twelve decorations"); finally there is a military episode in which he tortures prisoners. The war over, he comes home ill, takes to drink, secludes himself in an upper room in the family mansion, refuses ever to see his father, is attended to by a fanatically devoted sister Leni, with whom he has an incestuous relationship; he is not only "half mad" or trying to be mad, but officially dead—with records expensively secured by the all-managing father to foil blackmailers. This life goes on for thirteen years. Then the father is found to have a cancer that will kill him in six months. In trying to resolve both business and family affairs, he obliquely manipulates the others toward ends that are not disclosed until later. His daughter-in-law Johanna goes up to see Franz, and there develops between them a relationship called "love"; Johanna's influence moves Franz back toward reality, Leni's sexual jealousy leads to the disclosure of more of Franz's history, and then Johanna, shocked, draws back. The upshot is what the father had long wanted, a meeting with Franz.

In this meeting, which has resemblances to that between Brick

Pollitt and Big Daddy in Tennessee Williams' *Cat on a Hot Tin Roof*,* tragic self-recognition has a large place; it comes out of the ruinous dividedness of Franz and brings his troubles to such resolution as is possible. His anguish is valid; it is not treated as an imposition from without, as in *The Flies*. *Altona* continues from *The Flies*, it is true, in that the sanctions that hold for Milton's Samson are formally denied; Franz says to his father, repeating Ibsen's Rosmer in what is becoming a cliché of modernity,† "There isn't a God, is there?" and concludes "Then, . . . you're my natural judge." Franz has already said of them, "Two criminals. One condemns the other in the name of principles they have both violated." But "the principles" hold, it appears, and so we have at least a complexer moral world than that founded on sheer resoluteness in *The Flies*. Franz has it much harder than Orestes, who had only to declare himself free. At first Franz insists that he will not be judged. He thinks of his evil as caused: ". . . it's because you're an informer that I'm a torturer." But he gradually emerges from the melodrama of blame and wants to be judged because he sees his actions in themselves, not as the results of prior actions by his father. He admits that he shut himself up, not "so that I shouldn't witness Germany's agony," as he "pretended," but "so that I shouldn't be a witness to its resurrection," because, if Germany does not die, "I shall become a common criminal." He can say, though we see that the first part is not correct, "I'm not suffering; I made others suffer."

Amidst these recognitions and acknowledgments there is one special moment of revelation: Franz is tensely analyzing the sense of "power" that he felt at the time he tortured the prisoners, and he

* Franz and Brick both had an early shock that damaged a cherished belief; both had done things that they did not want to face; both had taken refuge in a flight from ordinary life—Brick in drink, Franz first in drink and then in ambiguous mental illness. Both fathers, dying of cancer, are powerful men; each has a special feeling for the lost son, and is less attached to the well son, who in each play is a lawyer. Each father has an empire to dispose of. Beyond this, of course, there are many dissimilarities, both in detail and in the fact that Sartre is trying to show a number of ideas in action whereas Williams sticks to personalities. But as far as the resemblances go, they reveal that singular parallel of imaginations which is always interesting.

† Arthur Miller attributes a similar thought, quite anachronistically, to John Proctor, the leading character in *The Crucible*.

finds it rooted in the feeling of "powerlessness" he had when he was forced to watch the Nazis beat the rabbi to death. Of the moment of power he says, "I am Hitler" and "I'll assume the evil; I'll display my power . . ."; of the moment as a helpless witness of evil, "The rabbi was bleeding, and I discovered at the heart of my powerlessness, some strange kind of approval." This is the moral climax of an extraordinary drama of self-discovery and self-revelation. It is this drama that draws the outsider, the witness, into active participation, for here is Sartre's "free" personality working its way into full tragic consciousness. One does not resist the personality free enough to loathe the Nazis, to be horrified by torture, to find within itself the seeds of the power to torture, and perversely to forge a link between a horrified seeing and a mad doing of the thing seen. Sartre finds a human depth into which one cannot help being drawn, and in that experience lies the genesis of whatever self-knowing one is capable of. Identification or involvement comes out of experience, not out of Franz's formal exposition, committed to a tape, of his relationship to his century.

Sartre, however, moves on from this episode of tragic achievement as though it were a lesser form of business and carries farther with that sparring between father and son which is resolved only in a joint suicide. Sartre permits Franz to find identity and then takes it away from him again by making him little more than a shadow or echo of his father. We revert from moral quality to causation. The father, the big manufacturer, takes over:

I had given you all my talents, and my bitter taste for power, but it was no use . . . the firm turned all your acts into gestures. . . . [You were] destined . . . To impotence. . . . To crime. . . . By my passions, which I implanted in you. . . . I alone am guilty—of everything . . . there never has been anything but me. . . . I built the firm which is destroying us.[31]

Here Sartre reduces Franz to a victim without really giving the father tragic status: the father's recognition is not the new light struggled to in darkness and suffering, but a coolly ironic analysis which is the final extension of the industrialist's mastery of the world. The father has not been dramatically made a sentient man; his domination of the last act is rather like that final control of the situation by the imperturbable hero of detective fiction. From being a background manipulator who provides the context for the true tragic agony of Franz, he is brought, at a late hour and in a surprise shift, forward and center (as if Zeus, in *The Flies*, were revealed as controlling, rather than as discarded by, Orestes). The reason for this is clear: he speaks less as an individual than as Sartre's voice in explicating the malign role of the giant capitalist. We have, in the end, only victims and a villain— "the firm." We have moved outside the intense engagement of the characters into a lesson about contemporary society. We have the let-down feeling of discovering, at the end of an original and often torturing plot, a cliché. But whether it is a cliché or a novel message is less important than that the idea is cutting down the freedom which Sartre declared essential to the character. Thus, in a generic conflict that apparently echoes an inconsistency in Sartre's inner world of feeling and thought,* melodrama of ideas is struggling to take the stage away from a tragedy that had possessed it, and hence us.

V. Variations in Magnitude

It is in the older tragedies, those in the long history that extends through *Samson Agonistes*, that we are most likely to find the most capacious tragic consciousness, which knows both the deed done and

* Philip Thody notes that Sartre has a strong impulse to lay general blame on the bourgeoisie (for an example, see *Jean-Paul Sartre*, p. 211); to that extent he is a "melodramatic" thinker. But in another aspect of his thought the emphasis is all "tragic." In Thody's words: "In his insistence that man must always be responsible for what he becomes, and that he can never legitimately claim to be better than his acts, Sartre is laying the foundations for an extremely healthy approach to personal morality. He does away with all alibis and excuses, and makes each person look his own failure straight in the eye" (p. 236).

In *Altona*, tragic effect also suffers from the Sartrian "nausée," that Gulliverian response which pushes the satirical mode toward total rejection. Johanna's "love" for Franz involves, and is perhaps indistinguishable from, her fascination by death and madness. "Madmen," she says, "often speak the truth," and she adds, "There's only one: the horror of living" (Act III). The death of the father and Franz is not an avenue to freedom for the others, as it might be, but a knockout blow. Leni, the sister whose incestuous love for Franz encompasses a complete knowledge of him, at the end retires, permanently we assume, into his room (in a manner reminiscent of Lavinia Mannon at the end of O'Neill's *Mourning Becomes Electra*). The point is that we draw away from a sick world as from a sick room; we are given not an experience but a shocking lesson, which we may be at pains to reject, or, if we happen to relish shock, to embrace simply for the kick it gives us.

the trans-historical claims that illuminate its character. To return now from the composition of consciousness to the presence of consciousness: that presence, we have proposed, is what establishes the proper magnitude in the tragic protagonist, and through him in the drama of which he is the center. The more defective he is in that magnitude, the less freedom he has, and hence the less compellingness as a character; that is, the less power to draw us into the tragic experience and its revelatory processes. If we do not enter into that experience—in the paradoxical participation which is less than that of the characters represented but more than that of the detached student—we are essentially listening to a lecture or watching a demonstration. If that is true, an art is aspiring to be a science and finally accomplishes the end of neither.

Granted that much will remain mysterious in the experience afforded by the work of literary art. But magnitude will impose itself, if not in every individual experience then in the mass of experience. We are spontaneously caught up by the more spacious work; we may specifically be drawn by one element or another that symbolizes the spaciousness, but it is the insight of the hero that will seal the largeness and power of the drama. As a matter of fact, this kind of perceptiveness can rescue the "villain" himself, without sentimentalizing him or paradoxically reinterpreting him, from the formal alienation natural to him in art and bring him close to home. There is, for instance, that remarkable imaginative passage in which Marlowe has Mephistophilis warn Faustus against the course he is bent upon. Quite aside from the ironic contrast with the flippant Faustus which is the overt effect, something else goes on when Mephistophilis tells Faustus:

> Why this is hell, nor am I out of it.
> Think'st thou that I who saw the face of God
> And tasted the eternal joys of heaven
> Am not tormented with ten thousand hells
> In being deprived of everlasting bliss?
> O Faustus, leave these frivolous demands,
> Which strike a terror to my fainting soul.
> [I.iii.76–82]

The anguish and the power of definition so enlarge the character that he is no longer a remote figure of evil but takes on, for the brief moment, a tragic dimension; he is "free" and we become him, knowing not only the scourge of grief for the needlessly lost, but the whole moral being that brought on the loss and must now forever maliciously try to convert the loss into gain.*

Aeschylus and Sophocles

The magnitude of Aeschylus' *Oresteia*—not the fact that it is a trilogy but the human range in each of its parts—is brought into relief by the relative constrictedness of other Aeschylean dramas. *The Persians* is the lament of the defeated which obliquely glorifies the victorious Greeks; Xerxes, the defeated general, is simply overcome by grief for the disaster at Salamis. Interestingly, the ghost of Darius censures the Persians in the conventional terms of tragedy—"pride and godless arrogance," "insolence," "overboastful / Minds" (lines 807, 821, 828–29)[32]—but this is more the recrimination of defeat than the illumination that emerges from tragic suffering. *Seven Against Thebes* is of course a ritualistic war poem in which human personality is only superficially invoked before the brief final episode. In that, Antigone resolves to bury the body of Polyneices in violation of the edict against it:

> . . . I
> am not ashamed of this anarchic act
> of disobedience to the city.
> [lines 1029–31]

A new dramatic life surges in with her awareness of the contradictory imperatives; yet this is only a preliminary to action not represented in the play.

A still better contrast is afforded by *Prometheus Bound*, in which, for all of the cosmic scene and superhuman participants, there is

---

* Cf. the problem of Iago, whom we tend to draw away from and belabor as separatist evil: "there goes, not myself, but some other." Yet in one respect Shakespeare so wrote the part as to permit the inference that he was trying to make Iago belong to the reader, that is, prevent him from disowning Iago. That is the effect of all Iago's justifications; not only are these a familiar habit, but they appear to give Iago more magnitude as a character. One more easily identifies with revenge than with autonomous malice. Or, if one does fear to find the same malice within, he may instinctively want to credit Iago's justifications and thus find a less shocking identity.

implicitly present a more ample field of human experience. Yet Prometheus, the very character who symbolizes mind or knowledge, has almost none of the self-awareness that most of the principals in the *Oresteia* either are endowed with or earn. He accepts himself as a specially gifted hero who is the victim of injustice by the oppressive tyrant, Zeus, and the view is not much challenged. So we have essentially an allegorical melodrama of torturer versus tortured, and the experience offered is that of sympathy for the suffering champion of man, and approval of his vigorous defiance of Olympian threats and revenge. There is a possibility of tragic enlargement of the role when Prometheus can acknowledge, "I knew when I transgressed nor will deny it" (line 268). But he goes on immediately to justify the transgression: "In helping man I brought my troubles on me" (line 269). At this point at least (the lost later plays might have altered the situation) his action has none of the ambiguity that so marks the principal actions in the *Oresteia* and is the genesis of the moral self-awareness in it. There are other grounds for ambiguity, too, for Prometheus reveals that he was first angered by the "savage arrogance" of the Titans (line 209) and hence decided to "join Zeus's side" (line 220); then as soon as Zeus won, he "dared" to revolt against Zeus's plan "to blot the race [of man] out and create a new" (lines 235, 236). But this rich field of possibility, in which sense of justice is at least mixed with self-righteousness, willfulness, and a quick eye for the defects of others, is not developed; Prometheus is taken straight as man's champion in the melodrama against the gods. Hence, for all of its cosmic involvement and its strong postromantic appeal, the *Prometheus* is a good example of a drama that has much narrower scope because it makes active only one segment of personality.

Among the plays using the Theban myth, *Seven Against Thebes* does far less with human possibility than the Sophocles triad. *Oedipus the King* and *Antigone* have provided us with frequent points of reference because, centering on the dividedness in human nature and human life, they are almost archetypal instances of tragic genre. *Oedipus the King* derives its essential magnitude from Oedipus' capacity for self-knowledge and from the growth in understanding toward which the whole drama moves.

Then there is a recession of magnitude in Sophocles' third treatment of the subject—the *Oedipus at Colonus* of the last year of his life. In this later treatment there is still a good deal of theatrical richness, in the mold of *Oedipus the King:* we see Oedipus in a series of confrontations in which, as he seeks to secure his own purposes and balk those of others, constant tension is generated. First he must win acceptance by the Chorus and by Theseus; then he must fight off Creon, see his daughters abducted, and plead for a recovery operation; after that there is the unwilling and furious interview with his son Polyneices; finally Oedipus gives orders for his death scene and burial. Except for the final one, the episodes are in the melodramatic vein: an Oedipus who assumes all rightness for himself and his purposes engages in all-but-military struggles against those who have different purposes (and finds an almost modern kind of *deus ex machina* in Theseus, who not only sees that things go Oedipus' way but rescues the daughters kidnaped by Creon). He easily falls into verbal violence: his abuse of his sons before Polyneices comes on the stage, and of Creon and Polyneices to their faces, constitutes a mass of invective that only the most determined partisan would be likely to find sympathetic. Aside from carrying the art of blame to heights achieved only by untragic protagonists, Oedipus devotes a good many lines to arguing his own essential innocence in his relations with Jocasta and Laius; he sounds much more like an intemperate defendant in a lawsuit than like the judge of himself that he had become in the earlier drama.

After all of this, it is difficult to see in him a man who wins the wholehearted support of Athenian ruler and citizens and whose spirit will have, after his death, a beneficent influence on the city. The key to the problem is provided in David Grene's acute analysis of the play: ". . . in no sense," he says, "is the uniqueness . . . of the character important"; "It is the theme and not the man that matters." The theme that preoccupied the aged Sophocles was, in Grene's convincing view, the "union of the blessed and the cursed" [33] in a single individual (Philoctetes as well as Oedipus). My point is that the characterological range is insufficient for the thematic paradox; there is a shift from a felt actuality of character to a conceptual problem; and the chief person of the drama has undergone shrinkage even while becoming the symbol of a doubleness of being that is of great philosophical interest. Whatever he stands for and means to others, he is, as a character, little more than a disagreeable old man.

It is clear that if magnitude of theme and magnitude of character do not have an ideal indivisibility, magnitude of theme does not compensate for limitation of character. The theme of the dual man who is obnoxious to men but also necessary to men and hence the winner of glory from men, finds, in Sophocles' *Philoctetes*, a much better embodiment in character. This gradually emerges from skillfully contrived melodrama that makes *Philoctetes* good theater in a quite modern sense: Odysseus and Neoptolemus plot to capture Philoctetes and his extraordinary bow, for without them the Greeks cannot take Troy. Their problem is that Philoctetes is not likely to be well disposed to his fellow Greeks, who had cast him out on the island of Lemnos because they could stand neither the smell of his foot, infected by a viper bite, nor his cries of pain when the disease periodically became acute. Neoptolemus dextrously executes the plot and wins Philoctetes' confidence, a disguised sailor heightens the pressure with news of Greek pursuit and the Odyssean project, Philoctetes has an extraordinary seizure of pain in the diseased foot, Neoptolemus is smitten with remorse for his trickery and reveals the plot, Odysseus shows up to forbid returning the bow to Philoctetes, there are physical and emotional struggles, Neoptolemus gives back the bow and has to keep Philoctetes from shooting Odysseus, who again theatrically appears at a crucial moment. All this is quite like our own melodrama of international intrigue.

But what lies behind the tense and varied movement, and emerges from it to claim primary attention, is the drama of character in both Neoptolemus and Philoctetes. Neoptolemus undergoes an inner contest between the political imperative to bring back Philoctetes and, on the other hand, both a revulsion against his own tricking of Philoctetes and a growing sympathy for him. He first carries out the plot, then struggles with conflicting motives, feels "repentance" (line 1270), returns the bow to Philoctetes, and even prepares to take him, as he wishes, to his own country rather than to Troy. Since his change of heart and his amends follow an action that has not irreparably damaged either him or Philoctetes, the sequence of moves is of the order of high comedy rather than of tragedy. But what is significant for us here is the range of character that Sophocles imputes to Neoptolemus: he is divided between irreconcilable motives, he acts in terms of both, and slowly and painfully he comes into self-knowledge —here of the abhorrent character of what he has done—and decides which motive he has to live with, whatever the consequences.

Even more interesting is the treatment of Philoctetes, not only because he is the central character, but because he is an early example of the human type we find so often in later drama: the man who wants to live in his grievance, to cling to his misery, and to blame those who have wronged him. To be sure, he has reason for talking, from the beginning, about being "alone and very wretched," about "all the wrongs I suffered," about "wasting with my sickness / as cruel as it is," and giving many details of his misery on Lemnos (lines 227, 252, 266–67). Still, occasional phrases such as "what they have done to me" and "poor cripple," the charge that the gods send only "the just and the good / . . . out of the world," the new idea that going to Troy would be worse than staying on Lemnos, his lengthy curse on the Greeks, his alternating between the cry, "Sorrow, sorrow is mine. Suffering has broken me, / who must live henceforth alone from all the world" and begging the Chorus to stay and to come again—all these rather subtly give the impression of one clinging to misery (lines 314, 448–50, 487, 999, 1019ff., 1101–2). They prepare not only for the forthright charge of Neoptolemus after he has given back the bow,

> But men that cling wilfully to their sufferings
> as you do, no one may forgive nor pity.
> Your anger has made a savage of you;
> [lines 1319–21]

but also for Philoctetes' holding passionately to the single picture of "wrongs to come" (line 1359) at Troy and stubbornly refusing to go there. It takes a *deus ex machina*, Heracles, to bring Philoctetes around. Though it has been criticized as an artifice, this divine intervention serves, from my point of view, as a symbol of conversion and hence as evidence of magnitude in the character. True, Philoctetes simply changes; he does not share in Neoptolemus' experience of knowing what he has been. But he has moved beyond a purely monopathic existence; Sophocles conceives of him as a larger figure than the wounded man who opts out of ordinary life. As Heracles puts it to him:

All this must be your suffering too,
the winning of a life to end in glory,
out of this suffering.
[lines 1422–24]

So a melodrama of the victim * takes on something of tragic stature.

On the other hand, although both Aeschylus and Euripides brought the Electra theme to tragic proportions through the characters' awareness of the ambiguity in their actions, Sophocles uses it for a pure melodrama of revenge oddly like the Elizabethan revenge drama in which the spirit of retaliation constitutes the whole of a personality. While Orestes, little more than a secondary character, and his tutor are cool mechanics of revenge, Electra, who is on stage for all but a few opening lines, is a tense, possessed, all-but-mad-woman who founds a life on bitterness for unavenged Agamemnon. She is a truly monopathic character; she hardly has more than a single emotion, not to mention a tragic consciousness. As David Grene remarks, Sophocles has nowhere else such "absence of nobility and magnitude in the chief character." [34] The constricted drama that results, whatever the monopathic force that may be secured by a narrowing of possibilities, scarcely penetrates the tragic scale at all. The one-dimensional characterization, that is, the tyranny of the single motive, is technically not much different from either that of the Renaissance revenge play or that of the modern "theater of cruelty" with its restrictive treatment of personality.

Euripides

Euripides does not ordinarily achieve magnitude of character; intensity through small range is rather his forte. Yet he makes of Electra a more capacious character than Sophocles does, and in *Medea* (an early portrayal of the revenger, that essentially melodra-

---

* The serpent bite that started Philoctetes' troubles seems to have come about when he accidentally wandered into sacred territory (1327–30). But the situation has tragic possibilities from the start if Philoctetes' intrusion is read, not simply as a mistake, but as a failure, through an implicit self-assurance, to guard properly against such errors. This possibility is much greater for Oedipus, who in *Oedipus at Colonus* talks a great deal about the fact that he did not err knowingly; but it can be said of him that he had a great deal more reason than Philoctetes to practice the utmost caution against falling into any acts whatever in the categories in which evil was predicted of him.

matic character who haunts the stage for two millennia), he actually achieves a temporary conflict of motives.* Medea plans to revenge herself on faithless Jason by murdering, not only Jason's new bride, but her own and Jason's children. As soon as it appears that the plot is going well, however, she is seized by anticipatory grief for the children who are to die, and one seventy-five-line scene turns on the conflict between maternal love and the scorned woman's merciless fury: "I cannot bear to do it." . . . "No, no, I will not do it. I renounce my plans. / Ah, what is wrong with me? Do I want to let go / My enemies unhurt and be laughed at for it?" . . . "Do not, O my heart, you must not do these things!" . . . "But stronger than all my afterthoughts is my fury, / Fury that brings upon mortals the greatest evils" (lines 1044–80 *passim*). For a while she has the tragic division between different impulses, and to that extent she becomes more a character and less an automaton of retaliation. But Euripides has selected, as he so often does, a victim, and the type simply does not allow much opening out, especially into the broad realm of self-understanding. After one more brief passage of resolving to carry out the child murder immediately—a passage in which she can even say "this fearful and necessary wrong" (line 1243)—Medea reverts to the more limited role of acting out the known story, with little amplification beyond the exultant words of one who has done well in destruction.

In *Hippolytus* Euripides makes remarkable approaches to tragic magnitude and then, through dramaturgic habits that are commonplaces of criticism, lets himself fall short of the heights that he is about to take. In Phaedra he presents the tragic dividedness with great intensity and fullness: Phaedra is all but literally driven mad by the conflict between an uncontrollable lust (for her husband's son

---

* He also has an unusual achievement in *Alcestis*, even though it is one of the plays that make him "the father of the romantic comedy, the problem play" (Richmond Lattimore, "General Introduction" to *Euripides* in the Chicago edition, III, vii). In this drama Admetus comes within a razor's edge of experiencing unequivocally a self-knowledge so far-reaching that it would take the play over the border line from the comic to the tragic. Though he is saved by Heracles' undoing of his crime-like selfish deed (accepting his wife's death in place of his own) and by a final minute layer of self-protectiveness, nevertheless Admetus takes on remarkable magnitude.

Hippolytus) and the knowledge that her passion is shameful and wrong. In contrast with that other basic tragic situation in which man acts passionately first and achieves knowledge later (Oedipus, Lear, Othello), Phaedra is the protagonist who from the beginning has both the passion and the knowledge of its moral status (like Macbeth and Dr. Faustus). Dividedness and knowledge, as we have been saying, go together. Not only is the division explored thoroughly in itself, but it becomes a more impressive dramatic fact through Euripides' skillful use of other characters. First, there is the contrast between Phaedra on the one hand and, on the other, the Nurse and Chorus: though when they first learn the true nature of Phaedra's illness they carry on grievously about the moral catastrophe (lines 352–73), they shift quickly to the practical problem of doing something to help her—the only step they can think of. The Nurse repudiates Phaedra's "high moralizing" and assures her, "What you want / is not fine words, but the man!" (lines 490–91). Their cynicism, later to become the keynote of Machiavelli's *Mandragola*, has a triviality that helps emphasize the largeness of Phaedra. Further, the conflict between Artemis and Aphrodite extends the tragic dimension. Though Euripides' nagging at the gods often seems less a courageous new insight than the jejune voicing of a carefully nurtured grudge, here the allocation of responsibility to Aphrodite and Artemis introduces a sense of conflicting imperatives; when the wills of gods are active, more is at stake than the divergent impulses of an individual. The drama, then, is moving toward the achievement of considerable magnitude. However, the episodicity which is almost habitual with Euripides breaks out; he kills his major character halfway through the play and has to piece out the rest with secondary characters. Further, in the last several lines spoken by Phaedra before her death (lines 727–31), Euripides imputes to her an entirely new motive: getting even with Hippolytus. Her dying words are too close to the petty; Euripides cannot resist the cynical interpretation, so that at the end he comes uncomfortably close to cutting down a tragic heroine and leaving us only with another revenger. All we know about her, after her death, is that she has grossly slandered Hippolytus. We are in a smaller and triter world.

Neither secondary character, oddly enough, is without tragic possibility. Theseus, indeed, has one of the classical forms of tragic experience: he acts passionately (his prayer to Poseidon brings about the death of Hippolytus) and learns later that he has erred. But he has hardly discovered the truth before he is forgiven by the dying Hippolytus (line 1451).

Hippolytus is much more interesting, for in him are the seeds of a real complexity. He has the virtue of keeping Phaedra's secret when he might have saved himself from her calumny by telling the truth and calling as a defense witness the Nurse, who tried to be a go-between. Yet in the worship of Artemis he is rigid and even complacent; he is self-congratulatory about his chastity, sure that he has the key to right conduct, and contemptuous of women and of Aphrodite worship. At least it is possible to read him in this way and hence to see him, not merely as victimized by Phaedra, but through a stiffness of pride contributing to his own downfall and thus becoming tragic. But that expectation, while it is aroused by the text, is not fulfilled. Threatened and sentenced by Theseus, Hippolytus seems only the upright young man who cannot make his innocence believed. In the long account of his death he is courageously resistant to the sea monster sent by Poseidon. Artemis enters to justify him completely and promise revenge against Aphrodite. If Euripides, as we suspect, has knowingly given his hero an infusion of priggishness, Hippolytus remains unaware of this trait in himself. Instead, Euripides tops off what is in effect the glorification of Hippolytus with a protracted death scene in which pure physical suffering, deathbed forgiveness, and general grief are mixed in a swell of pathos that washes away all tragic effect. One is reminded of Aeschylus' charge in Aristophanes' *Frogs*: ". . . you dress your kings in tatters / to squeeze tears out of the audience." [35] In the long-drawn-out ending the tragic being disappears in the noble victim who dies lamentably and in moral triumph.

Racine's Phèdre

In *Phèdre* (1677) Racine eliminated both the broken-backed structure and the sentimental tendencies of Euripides: Phaedra dominates the whole play, and Hippolytus' death scene is spared a lachrymose prolongation. Despite an occasional touch of intrigue and of a rather mincing courtly sensibility, Racine's drama achieves a greatness that results from consistent magnitude in characterization. Hippolytus alone remains essentially the good man as victim. Though

Racine intended, as he makes clear in his preface, to endow Hippolytus with an imperfection by having him fall in love with the daughter
of an enemy of Theseus, this does not work, "for no one," Kenneth
Muir justly comments, "takes very seriously the 'guilt' of Hippolytus.
. . ." [36] By having Hippolytus fall in love at all, Racine removes the
parthenolatrous complacency which in Euripides is a possible source
of tragic scope. Still, Hippolytus has a steady memory of that old
arrogance—"proud and scornful sentiments," "rash pride," "arrogant revolt / from love," "I have carried virtue to the point of
harshness" (lines 68, 530–32, 1110) [37]—and these recollections,
plus his own sense that his love for Aricia is reprehensible, broaden
out the personality. By shifting the false accusation against Hippolytus from Phaedra to Oenone, the nurse, Racine both expands the role
of the nurse and, what is more important, gives her character a tragic
quality: she is not only a confidante and regular adviser of Phaedra,
full of understanding and patience, but a devoted would-be savior;
after she has unscrupulously lied about Hippolytus to help Phaedra,
she has to endure Phaedra's fierce abuse. Nor can she simply join in
recrimination.

> . . . Ah, Gods,
> to serve her I have done all, forsaken all.
> And this is my reward? I have well deserved it.
>   [lines 1327–29]

For some readers her recognition and subsequent suicide may border
on the pat and automatic; yet so many lines have attested to the
centrality in her life of her relationship with Phaedra that Phaedra's
unexpected and unforgiving attack ("your impious mouth . . . ex-
ecrable monster . . . heaven pay you"—lines 1314–19) cannot fail
to create in her an immediate and crushing sense of having done evil.
A lesser character could take refuge in resentment and the quest of
revenge.

As in Euripides, Theseus appears only in the second half of the
drama, but Racine's imagining of him is subtler and more comprehensive. Returning from a dangerous expedition in which he had been
held a prisoner in "unlighted caverns," he expects the fatted calf at
home, but finds only gloomy looks and foreboding words on all sides
and begins to feel sorry for himself. Then he hears Oenone's accusa-

tion, rages against Hippolytus, threatens and banishes him, calls on Poseidon to aid his revenge; feeling clever, he misinterprets Hippolytus' denials and defenses, and belabors him with contumely. But once Hippolytus has left the stage, the heavy father, who has been largely a figure of offended justice meting out deserved punishment, confesses other feelings: "I loved you" and "I feel my vitals wrung in that foreknowledge [i.e., of the inescapable punishment]" (lines 1161–62). Aricia's hints that he is in error call up a "secret pity" (line 1457) and make him resolve to investigate, first by questioning Oenone, and then, when he learns that she is dead, by recalling Hippolytus. He even begs Poseidon to go slow in answering his prayer.

> . . . Perhaps
> I have too much believed false witnesses,
> and lifted up too soon my cruel hands.
> [lines 1484–86]

When he learns the truth, he knows that he is "doomed" to "remorse" (line 1573). He would like to blame Phaedra, and he could without injustice use her guilt and that of the dead Oenone to exculpate himself in part. But Racine sees Theseus as having that larger human range that prevents a callous forgetfulness of his own act: he must "expiate the mad curse I abhor" (line 1650). He has the tragic consciousness.

Of that consciousness the chief possessor is of course Phaedra, with her division, hardly explored so fully by any other writer of tragedy, between the uncontrollable impulse and the desire to abide by moral imperatives. That she can feel both is the source of her magnitude; if she were merely a figure of lust, she would be commonplace, and if she had the sense of sin without the inclination to sin, she would be sick rather than tragic. Commentators tend to point out, with an air of surprise, that Racine has made her a sympathetic character; but this is to be surprised that he has made her a tragic character of human fullness rather than a melodramatic villain. It is this fullness that gives her, in Sartre's term, the freedom that evokes our own sense of identity, which is not evoked by sheer perversity of passion or hypertrophy of conscience, or, if we have passed infantility, by a comfortable freedom from both. Phaedra first appears as an ailing woman who cannot confess what her malady is and yet who must endure the attendant shame to find relief in talking. After the agonizing slow first admission to Oenone there is a rush of words (lines 269ff.)—about the sudden seizure, the struggle, the rediscovery of Hippolytus even "in his father's face," the resistance by playing the "harsh step-mother," the wish to die. Then the reprieve in the report of Theseus' death, which sets the stage for the confession to Hippolytus: that remarkable exercise in indirection, deviousness, symbolic revelation, in which fear, hope, desire, and misery confect a translucent but not quite transparent fable that first leads Hippolytus into a self-accusing retreat from the correct translation before Phaedra bursts at last into full candor, intense and perceptive psychological history, self-loath-ing, the call for death, the gesture toward suicide (lines 584–711). Then shock, at herself and at his rebuff, despair, obstinate irrational birth of hope, the dream of bribing Hippolytus with empire; and suddenly a new sense of total disaster with the news of Theseus' return.

> . . . I know my perfidies,
> Oenone. I am not of those bold women
> who can live tranquilly in crime. . . .
> [lines 849–51]

Then the dread of public disgrace, the confused yielding to Oenone's initiative, the begging Theseus for mercy to Hippolytus after Oenone has accused him; on top of all other emotions, the jealousy of Aricia, the conceiving of a plot to destroy Aricia; and the sudden pull-up:

> I breathe, at the same moment, guile and incest.
> My life-destroying hands, quick for revenge,
> are burning to be plunged in innocent blood.
> [lines 1270–72]

The wish to die and the fear to die; the violent turning on Oenone, needed but not fair, but if unfair still not a device for escaping self-judgment: she tells the story implicitly to Theseus and goes to her death.

This great portrait, dominating the play in its mastery of the human range, is unobtrusively augmented by a pattern of imagery such as Racine is sometimes thought to lack. The play is full of the language of seeing—of references to what is seen and not seen, to what may and may not be seen; there is much concealing and revealing, false as well as true. There is a constant sense of light and of darkness. Hippolytus resents "so black a lie" and asserts, "my heart is candid as the light of day" (lines 1087, 1112). When Aricia defends Hippolytus, Theseus thinks she is trying to "obscure his deed" (line 1439). But shortly he must say, "I would have more light," and, after Hippolytus' death, acknowledge, "My eyes would still be blindfolded"; after Phaedra's death he refers to "the blackness of her deed" and describes himself as "too well enlightened of my error" (lines 1459, 1599, 1645, 1647). After Hippolytus' death his tutor Theramenes takes pains to mention his own "hating the light" (line 1589). Phaedra is especially conscious of her image in the eyes of others. Her very touch had made Hippolytus' sword "horrible in his inhuman eyes"; she had always suffered from his "proud" eye, his "cruel eyes"; to Theseus she confesses "incestuous eyes," grieves that Oenone made Hippolytus "guilty in your eyes," and is at pains to show "remorse in your sight" (lines 751, 1206, 1210, 1624, 1630, 1635). This careful rectification of sight ironically justifies Oenone's way of describing to Theseus the supposed suicide attempt by Phaedra (in Oenone's lying account, the result of a sexual assault by Hippolytus): ". . . would have put out the clear light of her eyes" (line 1018); and it reverses Phaedra's earlier longing to cover things up. Now, in dying, she sets the record straight, whereas once she hoped "by dying to . . . hide from view a longing so infamous" (lines 309–10). In mid-drama the methods are less extreme: "Hide me," she pleads to Oenone, and since Hippolytus, she is sure, will not "conceal . . . my burning love," she has "no thought . . . but to hide myself" (lines 740, 846, 922). It had always been her role, she realizes when she hears about Hippolytus and Aricia; while their days "rose calm and clear," "[I] hid myself from the morning, fled the light" (lines 1240–42).

So there is a constant poetic extension and intensification of physical and psychological action, primarily that of Phaedra. Her imaging of her moral awareness in terms of the seeable is not altogether simple. When Phaedra speaks her final words,

> . . . death,
> stealing the brightness from my eyes, gives back
> to the light, which they defiled, its purity,
> [lines 1642–44]

the light that she believes she has soiled is the ordinary world in its moral aspect. When she blames Oenone in these terms—"When I fled the light, it was you that turned me back" (line 1310)—the light is at once the seeing world and the world of possibility in which life would always include the Hippolytus danger. These late speeches continue and reflect earlier and more important passages in which the interrelated concepts symbolized by light are active and in which their activity adds, however imperceptibly, to the dramatic magnitude. At her first appearance Phaedra says, "My eyes are dazzled to see the light again" (line 155), and a few lines later she addresses the Sun: "Noble and brilliant author of a sad race, . . . you, red with shame, perhaps, for my wretchedness, / Sun, I have come to see you for the last time" (lines 169–72). Helios was the divine father of Pasiphae, Phaedra's mother: hence the light that Phaedra cannot endure is implicitly a judgment both by ancestral and by divine authority.

Phaedra's knowledge extends to the sanctions that establish the quality of deeds. This is made more emphatic in a climactic passage near the end in which she refers both to Helios and to Zeus, the father of her father Minos:

> And I live, and can bear the eye
> of that holy Sun from whom I am descended?
> My grandfather is master of the Gods;
> my ancestors crowd heaven, the universe.
>   [lines 1273–76]

Like Samson's, her ultimate consciousness is of a misdeed against heaven. Then Racine gives a brilliant new turn to the concept. Phaedra goes on immediately with a Faustian question:

> Where hide? Let's fly into the night of hell.
> But no. There my father holds the fatal urn
> in his strict hands: they say it is his lot.
> There Minos judges each pale human traveler.
> Ah, how my shade will tremble when he sees
> his daughter led before his eyes. . . .
>   [lines 1277–82]

The final dark into which she would flee from the light of the seeing world and seeing gods has its own light of justice; the ultimate irony is that both the ancestral and the divine eye are as active in the underworld as in the upper. Thus Racine dramatizes the knowledge of a justice that is allied to the order of the universe. He approaches a magnitude of the *Lear* kind.

VI. MAGNITUDE IN THREE MODERN PLAYS

An effort to judge magnitude is at best a touchy business. One tries, not to achieve finality, but to apply the chosen perspective to enough different plays to show how it works. The quantitative hypothesis—that greatness is related to the extent of human reality encompassed in main characters, and that extent implies division and tragic consciousness—appears to be applicable to a considerable range of dramas and to permit at least some tentative judgments and distinctions. It permits us to separate out what one might call classes of largeness. There are the characters of extraordinary range whose self-knowledge is related, albeit diversely, to a sense of transcendent authority—Oedipus, Lear, Samson, Phèdre. Almost opposite them, in terms of human dimension, are the revengers whose being is taken up with a single passion: Sophocles' Electra, Kyd's relentless Spaniards, Webster's Duke and Cardinal, Shakespeare's Titus and Aaron. Then there are the revengers who begin to open out in small or great degree —Medea with her occasionally rebellious scruples; the Electra and Orestes of both Aeschylus and Euripides, in their different ways never untroubled by scruple; Hamlet, driven into regular ambiguities of conduct by scruples that, emerging from inconsistent motives, almost overwhelm him. There are the principal characters who agonize without any awareness of their own complicity in their fates, from Prometheus to Willy Loman; and those whose agonizing centers in what they know, or come to know, about themselves, from Dr. Faustus to Phèdre to Sartre's Franz von Gerlach. Related to the lesser of these categories is a type of character who is symbolically interesting but whose being is much less than his meaning—Sophocles' later Oedipus and his Philoctetes, who represent the paradox of beneficence inseparable from a grave handicap. I suggest that Coriolanus belongs in their camp: he has a kind of charisma that makes him valuable to either side, and it is related to an ungoverned, unthinking energy that also causes him to be cast out.

If we take his defect of self-awareness along with that of Romeo, Brutus, and Cassius, we have, in characters who are by no means contemptible, a contrast for the four major Shakespearian tragedies.

They are major precisely because the protagonists have a fullness of being, both in their complex responsiveness to others and to situations, and in their large share of tragic consciousness. It is this range of character which erodes away in Jacobean tragedy, as we saw in Chapter 6, and then, except for sporadic reappearances, awaits reconstruction by Ibsen and his successors. These latter, too, have had to reconstruct, if their beliefs so directed them, an older order of imperatives that had also eroded away; or to do without, and accept an accompanying constriction of range; or to participate in the agonizing search for replacements—whether by logic, by metaphysical intuition, or by the exploitation of psychological doctrines that for some have been heuristic and for others, who apprehended them mechanically, confining. But whatever the beliefs that have modified the sense of personality in post-Ibsen drama, the personalities created show great fluctuations in range, from one extreme at which they stand for single impulses or ideas, to the other at which they approach a traditional fullness. We had earlier glimpses of the practices of O'Neill, Eliot, and Duerrenmatt; in the present chapter we have sampled the problem in Miller and Sartre. Three plays that have something in common will suffice for the present consideration of magnitude.

The plays are not far apart in time—Maxwell Anderson's *Winterset* (1935), Brecht's *The Private Life of the Master Race* (1934ff.), and Sidney Kingsley's dramatization (1951) of Arthur Koestler's *Darkness at Noon* (1941). Based on historical events in America, Germany, and Russia, respectively, they examine different aspects of one large theme: the separation of power and justice in the actions of public authority, and the impact of this on the victims of power.

Anderson's Winterset

While Brecht and Kingsley portray authoritarian regimes, Anderson, working from the Sacco-Vanzetti case, develops the irony of a legitimate court's acting on the theory that

> justice, in the main,
> is governed by opinion. Communities
> will have what they will have. . . .[38]
> [Act II]

Here is the material that can produce a satirical or even cynical tone, and indeed that tone is almost always present in *Winterset*. Mio

Romagna, the avenging son of Bartolomeo Romagna, the man unjustly executed for murder in connection with a mail robbery, repeatedly slips into the contemptuous manner of premature disillusionment. Anderson always presents police as heavy-handed, stupid, or
corrupt. By the final scene Trock Estrella, the man who really committed the murder for which the elder Romagna was executed, has
killed three other people to protect himself for the remaining six
months of life that fatal illness allows him. Such actions point toward
the despair that marks some extreme melodrama of disaster.

Yet Anderson, as his prefatory essay makes clear, aspires to the
tragic mode, and in four characters he finds a dividedness that could
reach tragic proportions. The first of these is Judge Gaunt, who
sentenced Romagna to death, and whose sense of guilt, or at least
doubt, has driven him, at the start of the play, into mental disorder.
But the judge, who could become a tragic hero, disappears for good
before the end of Act II, and is never carried through to an ultimate
confrontation of himself; he wavers between anxiety and self-justification, falls into pettiness and even whining, and finally is incapable of
sustaining our interest. Two other characters that could be treated
tragically are Garth Esdras and his father Rabbi Esdras; Garth
knows that Trock Estrella was the murderer, but, with the entire
approval of his father, keeps quiet to protect himself (Trock and his
gunmen are always rather incredibly standing around ready to shoot
anyone who displeases Trock). Thus they not only prevent justice but
contribute to the death of Garth's sister Miriamne and of Mio Romagna, whom Miriamne loves. But Garth seems only annoyed by this
outcome, and Esdras, after a brief request for forgiveness, drifts off
into a vague philosophical essay. Neither has much strength of motive
beyond the son's self-protectiveness and the father's there's-nothing-
much-that-can-be-done-about-anything line; hence the tragic possibility is completely unrealized. Finally, Miriamne Esdras is caught
between her love for Mio, whose mission in life is to clear his father's
name, and her devotion to her brother, who could clear that name at
some risk to himself; at a crucial moment she opts for her brother and
then in penance lets herself be shot by the gunmen. But her struggle
is given neither centrality nor tension, and at most she seems a sweet,
mild, and pathetic girl rather than a desperately tried Antigone.

Closest to the dramatic center of the play is Mio Romagna; his role is melodramatic, and at one point, like a detective and district attorney in one, he seems on the edge of a triumph. But love for Miriamne makes him irresolute; the situation gets away from him; the tables are turned, and instead of bringing out the truth he is hemmed in by gunmen. At this moment he declares "I've lost / my taste for revenge" and begs Miriamne,

> . . . teach me a treason to what I am, . . .
> . . . teach me how to live
> and forget to hate!
> [Act III]

Here is the widening out of the revenger's monopathic character, and theoretically this should lead us to sense magnitude in the play. But Mio's sentiments, however admirable, seem misplaced; he has not committed an evil that has suddenly overwhelmed his consciousness and made all action in the world irrelevant; rather he is in undeserved danger in which all energy ought to go into self-preservation. An actual melodrama makes a legitimate demand on him, and he falls inappropriately into the gestures of a tragic hero coming into insight. The renunciation of revenge is meaningful only if one has power and opportunity to commit revenge; an ambush by thugs calls for a different focus of energies. When Mio achieves, presumably, a nobler code of life, and then simply walks out and gets shot by a gunman, and thus inspires his girl to expose herself and get shot too, Anderson loses a grip on both melodramatic and tragic character and falls into the operatic.

Brecht's Private Life *and* Kingsley's Darkness at Noon

Anderson's difficulty, one may suggest, is that he tried to write tragedy with his eye not on character itself, but on ethical problems, on the idea of poetry as the tragic medium (the speech is often self-conscious rather than convincing), and on the idea of tragedy (there are echoes of the *Romeo and Juliet* plot, the mad trial scene in *Lear*, and of reflective and antic Hamlet). Brecht and Kingsley both write with eye firmly on the object—the ways in which people act under the stress of power evilly used. Our interest is in the contrast in method between *The Private Life of the Master Race* and *Darkness at Noon*, but the contrast stands out because of the resemblances between these two treatments of socio-political disaster. One portrays Germany under Hitler, the other Russia under Stalin; one shows how the dictatorial party affects the lives of the citizens generally, the other how it affects party members. Brecht traces the ways in which constant fear of irrational power corrupts both individuals and the relationships between individuals; his sense of what happens to men and women is neither doctrinaire nor hackneyed, but penetrates into a multitude of distortions that occur when a disaster damages the moral as well as the physical being. The pressure of survival cuts off the inner life implicit in scenes where individuals are coming to decisions about their next moves; or rather, the playwright's desire to introduce numerous episodes documenting the types of response to political ruthlessness prevents a full dramatization of a conflict between the passion to survive and the pressure of imperatives (integrity, loyalty, decency) that, if heeded, might weaken the chances of survival. The tragic dimension, though it is always pressing for entry, is held out. On the other hand, the fidelity and concreteness of scene, and the absence of banality in the treatment of political victims, make this "Documentary Play" (the subtitle) a work of high quality in the melodramatic mode.

The eleventh episode, "The Old Nazi," gives us one look at a disillusioned party member: a butcher who was an enthusiastic Nazi long before 1933 (when Hitler came into power), who therefore feels a certain freedom to complain and to run his business in his own way (to get meat for his customers where he can), and who comes under official displeasure. When he learns that "they came for" his son while he was away, he hangs himself in his shop window, wearing on his chest a legend, "I Voted For Hitler!" [39] Here is a move toward the perspective adopted in *Darkness at Noon*—that of the political insider who becomes a victim, rather than of the outsider who is a victim by definition.

In Brecht one sees the party member only at a distance and must guess what goes on in his mind; in the Koestler-Kingsley work we see the entire action from the point of view of Rubashov, the old Communist. A leader who has shown great fidelity to the party (in flashbacks we see him carrying out missions that require the utmost discipline and the utmost in ruthless indifference to the convictions, hopes, and ideals of party members in different countries) and has suffered heroically for it (the Nazis captured him and relentlessly tortured him, smashing his jaw and breaking both his legs), he is now arrested by the party under a new race of younger and still tougher leaders, tortured, driven to a confession to be made in a public trial, and taken off to execution.

This story could be merely a topical exposé of the 1937 purge trials in Moscow, and since the actual torture of Rubashov is a prominent part of the action, the play might stop at being a high-grade melodramatic rendering of revolutionary terror (the fierce conflict within the torture scenes would establish its excellence in this mode). It is that, as is Brecht's *Private Life*, but *Darkness at Noon* at the same time uses the tragic perspective. For we come to see that Rubashov is a divided man—a divided revolutionary who could always act in terms of the harshest party rules but had to keep quoting them in order to gloss over an awareness of the cruelty and cynicism to which the application of the rules led. Within the party he could make ironic jests about the imperfections of the revolution; some such careless remark led to his arrest, since, to the pure psychological robots of the new leadership, it evidently signified an obscure, unarticulated political disloyalty. His own consciousness of the disparity between revolutionary ideals and the actual state of Russian life is in sharp contrast with the parochial, doctrinaire, unwavering, undivided mind of Gletkin, the scarcely human, machine-like inquisitor who by untiring, savage torture breaks Rubashov, gets his confession, and marches him off to death. According to Ivanoff, another old revolutionary, Gletkin is "something new in the world—the Neanderthal Man! He came after the flood. He had no umbilical cord to the past" (Act II).[40] The Gletkins, he adds, are "brutes. They don't count." Rubashov immediately retorts, "Who made them brutes? We did." This carries much further his earlier words of disillusionment: "Our golden dreams—! What a stinking mess we've made of it"; just as this exclamation had advanced beyond an earlier questioning, worried uncertainty: "We wanted to build a new and better world. . . . I don't understand why [it has gone wrong] myself. Our principles were right" (Act III—a flashback).

Out of Rubashov's dividedness, which had been so long under taut control, there is developing the knowledge of his own complicity in a monstrous catastrophe. This presents two dangers to tragic effect, and Koestler and Kingsley seem to have recognized both. One is the too easy coming around, the speedy recognition that makes a glib, unearned peripeteia; the gradualness of Rubashov's understanding, and his resistance to it, guard against this kind of falseness. The other danger is the sheer self-congratulation of Western audiences: here, heaven be praised, is a Communist who sees what a fraud Communism is—a response which would irretrievably identify *Darkness at Noon* as second-rate melodrama. The play protects itself against this kind of response by keeping Rubashov, despite his painful awareness of the facts, a convinced revolutionary. Ivanoff works on Rubashov by accusing him of having a "bourgeois conscience" and asks him if he wants "To become a Christian martyr? For the Western democracies?" This elicits from Rubashov a strong attack on "Western democracies—. . . those decadent humanists—those phantoms of religion and superstition?" Throughout the inquisition in Act III he never becomes non- or anti-revolutionary; he vehemently defends the old revolutionaries to Gletkin, and he says, "My whole life has but a single purpose: to serve the Cause." In resisting the confession that will be a lie, he does not challenge the argument—a regular part of the pressure put upon him—that the confession will be a service to the party. Nor, in the closing scene, do the slightly rhetorical words repudiating revolutionary methods constitute an apostasy from revolutionary faith.

In other words, the dramatist has not violated Rubashov's personality in order to make him a mouthpiece of sentiments agreeable to a given audience. But he has given Rubashov a legitimate conscience, one struggling to a sense of evil done without really reaching clear answers to the ultimately difficult problems inherent in the courses he has followed. The actions of that conscience are not sentimentally protracted; it is only in the dozen or so speeches between sentence and execution that Rubashov's statements of wrongs committed take on the forthrightness of conviction. His growing insight into "where . . . we failed" works at several levels. At one, there is the acknowledgment of victims generally. If "My hundred eighty million fellow prisoners, what have I done to you?" is not quite one with Lear's "Poor naked wretches" lines, nevertheless the question reveals an independent working of the same kind of consciousness. But still more important is his final exchange with Gletkin, the new-era, utterly inhuman revolutionary, the undivided man, who has destroyed Rubashov and is now taking him out to be shot. As Rubashov, formulating a "last wish," tries to reach Gletkin with a fragment of his new knowledge, Gletkin tells him not to "waste" his "last words." Rubashov goes on: "You don't build a Paradise out of concrete. My son—" Gletkin interrupts, "I am not your son." Rubashov insists, "Yes, you are. That's the horror. (*Pause*) The means have become the end; and darkness has come over the land." Rubashov's "Yes, you are. That's the horror," which has great dramatic power, certifies the tragic dimension into which the play has moved.

Rubashov might make a good case for the old revolutionary against the new streamlined brand; he might accuse Gletkin of betraying the ideals which up to the present the revolution had served. This would be the perennial line of keeping oneself safe by falling into indignation and putting blame elsewhere—the initial phase of the tragic hero, who must go beyond it if he is to develop fully as tragic hero. Rubashov does go beyond it to find his own ultimate guilt in the moral siring of the most loathsome and sinister figure of the new political race. It is possible that his "You don't build a Paradise out of concrete," as well as his earlier "If History is all calculations" speech, is too bluntly expository; but it is also possible that they may serve to help lift the topical theme into universal relevance. However, the essential means to universalization is the tragic structuring of the materials; the playwright has looked at evil from the point of view, not simply of the victim, but of the evildoer, and then imagined an evildoer with the power to know what he has done. The drama presents, finally, not only the corruption which ensures disaster, but along with it the new insight which, as the completion of the tragic action, permits the sense of recovery beyond present disasters. This is the continuity implicit in tragedy. That continuity is one of the sources of magnitude.

VII. Oedipus as Exemplar

The ancient and the modern, both glanced at in this chapter, come together revealingly in a modern interpretation of an ancient myth. The myth is that of Oedipus, and the modern interpretation—in a novel by Mary Renault—exactly seizes on the tragic essence of the events. In the novel, Oedipus is like Macbeth in knowing the nature of his acts; he is anything but the innocuous pilgrim trapped by incredible coincidences, or the victim, as in Cocteau, of a melodramatic infernal machine contrived by divine plotters. He is a representative human aggressor who will not be balked by even the most explicit forewarnings of his moral destination. To frustrate the oracle, he would have to accept frustrations. But if he is like Macbeth in somehow hoping to get away with the illicit that he will not forego, he goes beyond Macbeth in looking directly at the heart of his tragic action. Not only did he know what he was doing, but he knows that he knew. He tells Theseus, the king of Attica:

Did I not know that every man or woman past forty must be my father or mother now, before the god? I knew. When the redbeard cursed me from his chariot's road and poked me with his spear, and the woman laughed beside him, did I not remember? Oh, yes. But my wrath was sweet to me. All my life, I could never forego my anger. "Only this once," I thought. "The gods will wait for one day." So I killed him and his foot-runners, for my battle-fury made me as strong as three.⁴¹

It is entirely right. However, Oedipus appears only in a subordinate episode in the novel, and the question of magnitude does not arise. But the Oedipus of this brief autobiographic report is remarkably close to the Oedipus fully characterized in Sophocles' play—the intemperate man who must have his will and is furious when others do not accede wholly to it. The magnitude that we feel in Sophocles' version would not come from the pathos of an innocent, unchoosing man driven to murder by a mysterious compulsion not in himself but in the nature of things.

Like Sophocles, the novelist shows Oedipus not easily accepting truth. In the novel, however, he faces not only the knowledge of what he did, but the knowledge that he knew at the time what he did. We learn that for a long time he fought off the knowledge that he acted knowingly. He was self-protective. As he reports this, his words cast a bright beam of light on tragic experience and quality. Theseus, as both considerate host and ruler of the state which will benefit from Oedipus' promised blessing, proffers Oedipus a way out of his history —the way out that charms everyone in love with innocence. He says, soothingly, "Fate was your master. You did these things unknowing. Men have done worse at less cost." Oedipus receives this well-meant aid with gentleness and wisdom: "He smiled." Then he speaks words

that brilliantly summarize both the human passion for self-exoneration, and the transcending of that passion: "So I said always till I
became a man."

"So I said always"—the eternal pre-tragic longing to be free of
guilt. "Till I became a man"—a true definition of the growth of
tragic character. Only by remaining forever young can one blame
external forces, or the ultimate symbolization of them—fate. When
one becomes a man, he knows what he has done, and in some way that
he always knew. Or better, when he knows this, he becomes a man.
The knowing and the growing are the hardest of human tasks, and
perhaps the hardest for the dramatist to envisage and transmit. So
they are a measure of the greatness in his imaging of experience.
Tragedy not only overcomes our reluctance and initiates us into
self-knowledge; the imaginative entry into that knowledge opens the
route to maturity. The final mark of quality in tragedy is that it
nourishes consciousness and ripeness.

CHAPTER EIGHT

Retrospect and Prospect

ORE THAN one contemporary writer has thought of great
writing as the discovery of permanencies underlying the
shifting surfaces that reality presents to the changing eye.
Hence Nikos Kazantzakis attacks "realistic representation"—that is,
presumably, representation of the present scene by current visual
habits—as "a disfigurement and caricature of the eternal." [1] "The
great artist," he says, "looks beneath the flux of everyday reality and
sees eternal, unchanging symbols. Behind the spasmodic, frequently
inconsistent activities of living men, he plainly distinguishes the great
currents which sweep away the human soul." Joyce Cary, employing
a flatter rhetoric, starts with the same noun phrase but pluralizes it:
"all great artists." They, he says, "assume, from the beginning, that
it is their task to reveal a truth about some permanent and fundamental real." [2] These are not altogether fashionable views in a day that is
wary of constants and that suspects constants to be an illusion or a
calculated entrapment. Since these views are not clichés of our time,
they encourage the assumption that, in the continuing quest for the
permanent, artists reveal certain basic kinds of perception which
emerge in recurrent formal structures. That is to say, whatever the
alterations by accident, by conscious experiment, or by the influence

of personalities that spontaneously deviate from received practice, genres are quietly persistent, reflecting modes of intuiting or imagining a "permanent and fundamental real" that abides underneath cultural changes or personal idiosyncrasies. If we are convinced that generic formulations of human truth endure behind the multiplicity of phenomenal variations that we first see in literature, we can then do what we have done here: look at literary works of different ages as if what they have in common is no less notable than the special marks of time that separate them.

I. Generic Distinctions: Necessity and Risk

In this process, based on the assumption of generic durability, there are a number of issues. One wants to avoid "mere classification"; if he categorizes, as he can hardly avoid doing, he hopes rather to bring the play into better view than to drop it like a parcel into some concealing receptacle. "Better view" implies change: if one can take a group of works conventionally called tragedies—say those of Sophocles or Marlowe or O'Neill, or the commoner Jacobean works —and discover significant generic variations within a supposed identity, he may make possible a better idea both of the given body of plays and of what goes on in any one play. He may relieve the obscurity caused by loose and inconsistent use of generic nomenclature. This is an ample project, for the stability of forms is almost matched by the instability of terms.

Terminological indiscriminateness may threaten adequacy of experience, either in knowing the past or assessing the present. A few years ago Theodore Greene wrote about "crucial and irreplaceable" words that get into difficulties because of vulgar usage—words such as *beauty, freedom, democracy, nature,* and *God.*[3] He might well have included *tragedy* and, for that matter, *melodrama;* if the former has been cheapened by being applied where the latter is fitting, both have been debased by being used for much less exacting experiences than those which they properly denote and for which we lack other terms. After remarking, "The word *tragedy* is often used loosely," Robert Penn Warren goes on to define its "deepest significance: the image in action of the deepest questions of man's fate and man's attitude toward his fate."[4] If this judgment is right, as I think it is, then clearly a not very exacting standard is being used when Gabriel Fallon tells us that O'Casey's *Juno and the Paycock* is "one of the great tragic masterpieces of our time" [5] and John Raleigh awards a prize for tragedy to O'Neill's *Long Day's Journey*. Debasement of the term goes on dizzyingly when one journalist terms a pet's death in a domestic fire "a tragedy" and another describes a tennis defeat at Wimbledon as "stark tragedy" (Associated Press, June, 1966). Here, as in much popular discourse, the "tragic" is no more than the unfortunate, the painful, the disappointing. Virtually all users of *melodrama*, for whom the word means conventional villainy meeting conventional defeat, are by their habits incapacitated for facing or placing the true protagonists of melodrama—the Tamburlaines, Richard III's, Iagos in whom melodrama carries out its essential function of portraying the world's evil in characters of single-mindedness rather than tragic dividedness.

Greene proposes: "The effort must be made again and again to strip such key words of their false and sentimental associations and to put them back, if possible, into responsible currency." In the present "effort" in the direction of "responsible currency" I have felt that the "false associations" of *tragedy* needing most serious attention are those of popular usage because they constitute, not a *faux pas* worthy only of laughter from academe, but a threat to the necessary understanding of a central human experience. In another context one might want to inquire into the theory that tragedy is an autumnal rite or a sacrificial rite or an enactment of membership, or that in tragedy man is undone by what is admirable in him, or that the adversity that comes to him is undone by his endurance and courage, or that tragic suffering is essentially unmerited and inexplicable.[6] Such views, some of which might lend support to this essay or seem seriously open to question, ordinarily circulate in the library study rather than in the street. From the present point of view, the library study is least helpful when its ideas separate tragedy entirely from the street, or, at the other extreme, justify the habits of the street. The library study does the latter when it advances theories that treat accidents, misfortunes, injuries inflicted by others, and unjust actions—all coming upon him from without—as constituting man's tragedy. For the self-exonerating and the self-indulgent are at the heart of the commonest and the least reliable conceptions of the tragic. Hence, if we are to put *tragedy* into responsible currency, we must try to strip away the sentimental association in which suffering man is never responsible for what happens to him.

In denying that accidents, misfortunes, injuries inflicted by others, and injustices are tragic, we naturally do not deny that they frequently occur and stimulate the healthy literary imagination. The problem is to distinguish kinds of catastrophe—the kind that comes from other persons and other forces, and the kind that comes from one's own actions. A man may be a victim of others, or a victim of himself; he may do injury to others or to himself. Richmond Lattimore speaks of "the murder committed not against an external enemy but against a part of the self." [7] His words imply two typical situations—the one in which man's relations, whether he is aggressor or victim, are essentially with others, and the one in which all the important relations, though they may impinge ruinously on others, are inner, a conflict between unreconciled urgencies of man's own being. In the former, man is undivided, whether good or bad, strong or weak; if he is an aggressor, he has got rid of all motives but one; and if he is a victim, what happens to him naturally blots out questions about his moral being. In the latter, man is divided axiomatically, in Lattimore's terms, into the part that murders and the part that is murdered. We can let the murderer and the murderee stand for all the conflicting elements that constitute the tragic being.

Undivided man creates the world of melodrama. When we make *tragedy* stand for that world, we fail to distinguish the humanly central drama of the wrongdoing that comes from the man who is not essentially evil and whose deeds finally recoil upon himself, from the simpler realm of disaster, whether inflicted, suffered, or surmounted. For thus we encourage the blurred, muddy life in which self-pity, the most persistent of moral ailments, is most able to take over and to increase the difficulty of knowing what is disaster and what is tragedy. The critic must try to pry these worlds apart. Up to a point he may do it by disparaging the melodramatic, by showing that, as a sole way of looking at life or as a dominant literary form, it spoils man by demanding of him less than he is capable of, while tragedy puts him in a much more difficult role. But the denigration of melodrama is a permissible strategy in a given context rather than a permanent mode of action to be justified on grounds of incurable generic unregeneracy. Melodrama is not indissolubly bound to the meretriciousness which, in our unconscious but habitual debasing of forms, we take to be its normal state. It is not meretricious when it portrays recognizable evil —as in Renaissance revengers or Count Cenci or Brecht's Nazis or Koestler's Gletkin—or plausible courage and fidelity, as in the Talbots in *Henry VI*.

So, though I have more than once alluded to melodrama in minimizing terms, I have wanted also to rehabilitate it, to recover for it a stature of which it had been deprived by our clichés.[8] It reaches its own heights when it evokes, even with unmixed themes and essentially undivided characters, a certain duality of response. A recent critic says of Virgil, alluding to his interpretation of Aeneas: "The narrative of spectacular successes is never an end in itself for him: he is always aware of the cost, and presents, in one phase after another, the sufferings which purchase the triumphs." [9] Hence the *Aeneid* may be thought of as mature melodrama—the account of victory which also records the price of victory; we enjoy the triumph, but we feel the anguish and suffering that pay for it. Sartre's *Flies* is similar: if a single-natured Orestes wins a victory for freedom, at least freedom, instead of shrinking into a subject for simple hurrahs or a façade for whatever we want to do, is treated as a burden, and the bearing of it as not without peril. The quality of melodrama depends principally on how perceptively the dramatist deals with the hero. In *The Revenger's Tragedy* Tourneur takes a revenger with a just cause and reveals him as a master of machination and a virtuoso in sadism. If the unmasking of the "good man" is one route to melodramatic excellence, another is the reinterpretation of the bad man by endowing him with virtues that claim admiration: Webster does it with Brachiano and Vittoria in *The White Devil*, employing a pattern that has had considerable attractiveness in the twentieth century. It is the pattern, incidentally, that takes over in the latter part of *Macbeth*, which can most adequately be described as moving from a tragic to a melodramatic posture. These are some of the complexities of which melodrama is capable; we need to keep them in mind to encourage our use of the category in placing individual dramas. If we do not use it, we simply fail to recognize a nontragic dramatic structure, one that corresponds to a pattern in human behavior itself and in our ways of understanding human behavior.

Patterns intermingle, of course; there is no need to fall into a rigid dualism of types, an either-or judgment of postures. Not that we need rule out either-or as always unusable: the tragic dominates *Lear* and *Dr. Faustus* as clearly as the melodramatic dominates *Richard III* and *Edward II*. On the other hand we can see *Richard II* as seesawing back and forth between modes. Beaumont and Fletcher's Evadne, driven to an awareness of her moral status as king's mistress and as false wife, flees into the melodrama of revenge and falls into that of despair; in its treatment of her *The Maid's Tragedy* does not again resume the tragic view. In *Oedipus the King* Oedipus is a self-seeing and self-judging tragic hero; in *Oedipus at Colonus*, though he embodies a paradox of human experience, he becomes a self-righteous and accusing man of melodramatic cast. Euripides' Phaedra has a real tragic split, but Euripides' rather Mephistophelian skepticism makes him picture her, at her death, as mastered by the melodramatic revengefulness of the woman scorned. Ibsen's Rosmer and Rebecca experience tragic conflict and self-knowledge but finally pull the play toward the melodrama of neurotic troubledness; on the other hand, Ibsen's Gregers Werle first enjoys a melodrama of power by enforcing on others the claims of the "ideal," and then approaches the tragic experience of knowing himself injuriously wrong. He is a special version of the archetypal melodramatic character whom the narrator of Camus's *The Fall* describes with a bluntness that may seem less veridical than provocative: "The truth is that every intelligent man, as you know, dreams of being a gangster and of ruling society by force alone." [10] The melodrama of power that literally or figuratively originates thus—from Tamburlaine to Emperor Jones, from the revengers to the reformers such as Dorothy Sayers' Faustus —may eventuate in melodramas of triumph, defeat, or decay, or as tragedies in which the user of power judges himself. While Clytemnestra kills the king in the ironic belief that justice is being established, Orestes takes two lives only with misgiving; the melodrama of the feud is giving way to the tragedy of guilt and expiation.

Often the drama that is centrally melodramatic has what we might call tragic accents. This is not the easiest accomplishment for a dramatist who is dealing with a victim, yet Sophocles manages it in *Philoctetes:* he permits other motives to disturb Neoptolemus, the Greek plotter against Philoctetes, and to interfere with Philoctetes' persistence in the woefulness of the mistreated man. The tragic ingredient is more easily introduced if the victimized character has the strength and the opportunity for retaliation: Euripides' victimized Medea has become a revenger, but she is troubled by countermotives that enrich the characterization. If some characters find a unity in suffering, punishing, injuring, or self-serving, others have a distinguishing awareness that thrusts them into painful conflict. In *The Duchess of Malfi*, while the main villains drive on maniacally in the destruction of others, Bosola feels revulsion at what he has done. While others in Duerrenmatt's *Visit* are driven by revenge and material desires, Alfred Ill can feel guilt for a gross, if not unusual, self-protective deed.

II. THE CONCEPTION OF TRAGEDY

All such distinctions in form—all endeavors to separate from each other the misfortunes and misdeeds of life, the active and passive roles in the realm of suffering, the kinds of personalities that disrupt moral order—depend on one central idea, the conception of tragedy. My basic working theory, that the heart of the tragic is the divided personality, reformulates, with changes in emphasis, an idea often expressed elsewhere. George Moore was being more than antiromantic when he made a character assert, "We cannot invent ideas; we can only gather some of those in circulation since the beginning of the world." [11] Ideas may circulate because they are easy enough to become clichés, or sound enough to remain in mind when fashions change. An idea of tragedy, if it is sound rather than trite, will have to be rooted in a fundamental sense of the human make-up out of which catastrophes arise. Only thus can it "image," in R. P. Warren's words, "the deepest questions of man's fate and man's attitude toward his fate." The concept of tragic dividedness appears to go deeply enough into the human situation to make possible a profound imaging of man vis-à-vis his fate. It implies a human being fundamentally drawn toward irreconcilable opposites. One of these characteristically acts as an imperative (reason, courage, duty), and the other then becomes the impulse that cannot be reconciled with it; the same conflict will exist if the radical reversals that come from perversity, love of novelty, or obsessive heterodoxy should make imperatives out of unreason, cowardice, or animality. Always there will be the need to contravene an imperative, and thus to express a will and escape limitations.

Though division may be a very subtle affair, not amenable to precise formulation, general models do appear. A man may seek two different ends which are incompatible. Most frequently, his conflict is between a passion (for gain, power, revenge, enhancement of the ego in whatever way) and a limiting obligation (as expressed in law, faith, tradition, or solitary conscience) — in our words, between impulse and imperative. It simplifies actuality too much to say "between a right and a wrong," but the introduction of these two words opens the way to a description of the most disruptive conflicts: perhaps between two wrongs, more probably between two rights, and ultimately between two courses, each compelling in its own way, and in some measure combining right and wrong. Here we face what we usually describe by the phrases "choice of evils" and "no perfect choices," except that, while those terms imply meditation upon alternatives, the tragic situation is one of passionate involvement in which clarity of mind may be no more than anguished doubt, or may occur only in brief flashes, or may be earned only after one has made crucial choices.

However, we differentiate structures less to classify than to render the idea of inner conflict tangible and meaningful. We have to concretize that idea both for its own sake and to set it off as sharply as possible from the other type of conflict in which an individual is in effect freed from an inner disturbance because he is engaged in, or in order that he may engage in, a struggle with other persons or with forces outside himself. For the moral engagement in which the antagonist is a part of the protagonist's self is the fundamental mark of the tragic form. We can hardly go beyond that, or propose a deeper human ground of tragedy. Not that a conflict in the soul and a conflict in the world may not go on simultaneously. Hamlet has to do combat with Claudius and Claudius' agents as well as with his own motives; Lear has to confront hostile daughters as well as his own folly; Oedipus faces a plague as well as his own past. The greater the dramatist, the more he will include of both conflicts. But he does not simply report all, using now this point of view, now that, like a succession of camera angles; he finally chooses a prime field, and he makes us attend to it.

The intensest reality in *Hamlet* is Hamlet's debate with himself. Or, to change the terms, Macbeth murders not only Duncan but a part of himself. It is the self-murder that the play is "about." The rape and purification of Scotland are socio-political echoes of the prime event.

The dramatist who can imagine the elemental human reality of dividedness might be thought by this feat itself to have entered the high region of greatness. Certainly he has taken on a larger task than the artist who produces figures of undivided goodness, a nineteenth-century staple now turned out largely by popular confectioners, or the artist who produces undivided figures of evil or illness, such as have had quite a run among the customers of the present century. (Imagine, for instance, a play built around Iago but without Othello; it would lack all the magnitude conferred by the truly spacious character who contains both a potential Iago and many other potentialities —a loss not to be compensated for by any number of duped Roderigos and even Emilias and Desdemonas.) It may be an impulse to reward the more ambitious choice that leads some people, when they call a play a "tragedy," to intend the term honorifically rather than descriptively. But the word should make a technical distinction rather than confer distinction. For a dramatist may have a valid perception of human dividedness and yet not make impressive use of it. Why does Webster's Bosola, though a memorable character because of his sharp fluctuations of feeling and loyalty, not seem to us a great tragic character? In part, surely, because he is one thing at one moment and another thing at another moment; rarely do we see him as a human totality in which rival urgencies are operative at the same time.

The dramatist's avenue to greatness is, in my view, the magnitude that he can imagine in his chosen characters—the strength, the range, the inclusiveness, the kind of wholeness created by the simultaneous activity of divergent parts. The final evidence of magnitude is the hero's intelligence as it becomes the capacity for self-understanding. Self-awareness is the seed of greatness simply because it is the ultimate achievement of human struggle and growth. Yet it is also necessary to the functioning of drama, to its coming home fully to the reader and spectator. In stressing "totality of perception" as a major source of the "value" of a writer, Cleanth Brooks declares that the writer's "role is to give us an awareness of our world . . . as it involves ourselves—in part a projection of ourselves, in part an impingement upon ourselves. In making us see our world for what it is, the artist also makes us see ourselves for what we are." [12] It is not difficult to accept the view that the summary accomplishment of the literary work is the reader's self-recognition: the external evidence is the longevity of the view, and the indwelling logic is the sheer difficulty of self-recognition—the response to which we come last of all, when the easier satisfactions are exhausted but do not exhaust what the work demands of us. We come to it because of the writer's "totality of perception," which by definition embraces the self-awareness of the protagonist: it is the self-recognition of the character that not only earns, but indeed compels, that of the reader. Through an uncomprehending character the dramatist may make an interpretation which we rationally comprehend; but only in the identification with a character who has come to knowledge has the spectator had a complete dramatic experience. Nobody has said this better than Henry James in the preface to *The Princess Casamassima:* we do not care, he says, for "what happens to the stupid, the coarse, and the blind," but only for "what happens to . . . the really sentient." [13]

Granted, a dramatist may not have the art to manage successfully the hero's experience of finding the meaning in what he has done and has been. Webster's Cardinal is made to undergo a moment of self-recognition in which, because of the weight of the evidence afforded by his moral history, we do not believe. Again, the hero can become painfully self-conscious in his self-placement. The repentant sinners in *A Woman Killed with Kindness* and *The London Merchant* almost betray a pride in themselves as above-average horrible examples. There is an interesting parallel in public life: what appear to be the voices of conscience may take on a stridency and condemnatory insistence that make it hard to accept them as evidence of tragic awareness in the community soul.

In drama, as elsewhere, what is at stake is the quality of the imagination at work. A dramatist, I have proposed, can write tragedy only if he is imaginatively able to adopt the point of view of a man who can commit a wrong but can also know himself, that is, can accuse himself and accept the accusation. The dramatist may imagine other kinds of characters acutely; his excellence will then be in a nontragic genre. O'Neill can imagine self-recognition only as an unbearable experience; so he veers away from the last phase of the tragic rhythm. Or, without knowing it, a dramatist may be able to imagine self-recognition only as an egotistic or a histrionic act, and so he will inevitably render it in that tone. (Shakespeare's Iachimo in *Cymbeline* has a theatrical personality; so his rather flamboyant acknowledgments at the end are in character.) Or he may be unable really to imagine self-recognition but may endeavor to use it dramatically, perhaps because it is in the air or is expected or seems scenically effective; hence it will lack plausibility. Or he may simply consider it a moral desideratum, as Heywood and Lillo obviously do. In the latter cases he will introduce it by act of will, rather than come to it naturally by act of imagination. The structure of tragic experience has to be fulfilled by an imagination that is adequate to it; that imagination will reveal itself in the painfulness, the intensity, and the inevitability of the character's illumination.

True illumination rests on a certain aesthetic and moral decency; one sign of this is a mediation between the perfunctory and the prolonged, between the mechanical leap and the clinging embrace, or, in other words, between the too easy forgiveness of oneself and the refusal of forgiveness. The mediation appears in what I have called the "Oresteian conversion": Orestes never disguises the enormity of matricide, yet through his penance he struggles for his own and for divine forgiveness. On the one side Wendoll, in *A Woman Killed with Kindness*, sentences himself to exile abroad but quickly begins to think of the advantages of travel. Richard III speedily recovers from his brief attack of conscience. At the opposite extreme are those who cannot forgive at all: Ibsen's Rosmer, Hardy's Sue Bridehead, and to an extent Sartre's Franz von Gerlach. Those impotent to forgive, be it themselves or existence, must despair and embrace death or suffering; this is a frequent O'Neill pattern. They represent James's "really sentient" man in a morbid state; though penalties are inalienable, an undying zeal for penalties—an incapacity for self-forgiveness—becomes a subtle self-gratification. If facile forgiveness falls short of tragedy, nonforgiveness is an excess on the other side of tragedy.

Forgiveness can be a slippery, ambiguous matter. It can pitch one, in no time, toward sentimentality. Self-forgiveness can be the moral façade of self-indulgence. Yet the value of forgiveness is that it implies knowing what there is to forgive. Forgiveness implies that man neither shrinks from what he must forgive nor is crushed by it. Hence forgiveness can be a metaphor for the most penetrating self-recognition and for survival in it—in a word, for those last actions by which divided man brings the tragic rhythm to its representative, health-bearing fullness.

III. Past and Present

With such criteria in mind, the selective observer of the drama of three ages—ancient, Renaissance, modern—finds, within the large area that usually remains undifferentiated under the banner of "tragedy," two basic structural types that continue to show up time after time: the melodrama of the man, be he strong or weak, in conflict with other men or with the world, and the tragedy of the man whose essential conflict is with himself. A dramatist may utilize both structures, may shift from one to another, may execute a structure with conventionality, with grandeur, with sometimes piquant innovations. Sophocles' sense of character varies drastically from Antigone to Electra; Euripides moves in opposite directions as he develops Medea, in whom there are traces of tragic conflict, and Phaedra, who gravitates toward the ordering single motive. Marlowe excels once in each genre, is so-so in other dramas; we lack the sure chronology which would permit us to see a pattern of development. Not so with Shakespeare, in whom, though we have used him mainly as a touchstone rather than as ore for formal assay, we can discern an alteration in sense of character that might almost be plotted on a curve: beginning, in the "tragedies," with the more nearly monochromatic characterization in *Romeo and Juliet* and *Julius Caesar* (not to mention *Richard III*), advancing into the extraordinarily complex polychromatic portraits in the major dramas, and then again cutting back to the less ample range of Antony and the near simplicity of Coriolanus—in other words, framing the pure work in tragedy with high achievement of a more melodramatic cast.

If we use the tight integration of these elements in Shakespearian drama as a standard, we can see one or another of these breaking out of disciplined equilibrium into an exaggerated prominence in the work of other dramatists: the moral implication is heavily explicated, as in Heywood and later domestic drama (allegorical tragedy); feeling is intensified and extended, and action diminished, as in Beaumont and Fletcher; violent and bizarre actions swell out and hence restrict the range of feeling and thought, as in Webster and Tourneur (modes of pathetic tragedy). Revenge melodrama, somehow making frenzy monotonous, shrieks away in continual surges from Kyd to Shirley. But some writers of melodrama develop the form brilliantly: Chapman in the portrayal of Bussy D'Ambois, a bold combatant who takes incorruptibility as a warrant for bursting aggressiveness; Ford in the portrayal of Giovanni, who claims moral authority for deviant emotions and whirls off into erratic spectacle. And most of all Middleton and Rowley, who in Beatrice portray another reckless, insurgent soul and present her as an unscrupulous overreacher countered by hard fact, which does not crush her but coerces her into a knowledge of it and of herself. Hence Beatrice takes not only the unusual step from victimizer to victim, but the rare step up from the victim of disaster to the tragic heroine, from the monopathic to the polypathic experience.

In the past the transformations of disaster and of tragedy are numerous, continually striking, often brilliant. We are not likely to slip into disparagement of these past accomplishments, that perennial gesture by which an age shores up its self-esteem. We are more likely to fall into the opposite gesture—also a melodramatic one, incidentally —of finding in the past the standards by which to disparage the present. Yet such disparagements of ages are hard to make either just or convincing. In art we establish greatness by a continuing act of memory; the memory that must judge our own artistic deeds is not in being. We may guess but can never know what is memorable among the things that have not entered into memory. We have, in the end, no more than comparative impressions.

From the reading of these plays, ancient and modern, it is difficult to escape the impression that the strong, active, energetic, driving character (whether commanding, seeking, competitive, revengeful, or destructive; with or without moral consciousness) found rather frequently in the past is more rare today. Our minds turn easily and naturally to the themes of disability, illness, and weakness that are frequent with us—in O'Neill's *Iceman*, in Williams' Blanche DuBois and Brick Pollitt, in Miller's Willy Loman. The theatrical history of victims from Gorki's *Lower Depths* on is a large one. When we are especially attentive to victims, the atmosphere can easily make us feel like victims: hence Osborne's Jimmy Porter, whose self-pity, metamorphosed into verbal aggressiveness, has been internationally fascinating rather than tedious. The other side of awareness of the victim is awareness of iniquities: we have a long history of problem plays [14] and crusading drama. Gabriel Fallon is the voice of a popular attitude when he lauds O'Casey's *Juno and the Paycock* (1924) as a "blistering indictment of the stupidity of men." [15] In criticism, *indictment* is as popular an honorific as is *compassion;* the frequency of the two words shows our profound attraction to the two monopathic, unity-giving extremes of melodramatic life (accusation of villains and pity for victims). When the two are rather simply conjoined, as in Hochhuth's *The Deputy*, the effect, for most audiences, can hardly be less than irresistible (though, for a minority, very tedious).

Very obviously, however, generalizations about the modern and the contemporary state of affairs are not possible at this point because we have not looked directly at enough plays. A more thorough survey of the taste and practice of the twentieth century, in its degree of attraction to the tragic and melodramatic poles in the artistic interpretation of experience, is still to be done. The world around us is naturally the final testing ground of a theory which endeavors to be tied to no particular world. That kind of theory makes it possible to juxtapose widely separated ages as a way of setting them off. Suppose, for instance, that we were to look at modern drama and Jacobean drama in the light that each might shed on the other. It is imaginable that the "decadence" often imputed to the Jacobean theater might lead us to discover a comparable phenomenon in our own. It is also imaginable that the sense of reality conveyed by our own theater might lead us to see in the Jacobeans a richer, less specialized, more deeply grounded drama of character than appears in the more conventional estimates. Whatever the conclusions, the juxtapositions should reveal indicative common grounds between the Jacobeans and us: the sense of the runaway motive, of the centrifugal personality, of the freed destructiveness, the wide-ranging malice, the despair, the vision of nada. There would still be the problem of how the dramatist treats such material—settling for the immediate and most accessible intensity, seeking the melodramatic excellence of divided appeal, or searching out the tragic implications; in a word, of how much centrality he finds in the centrifugal.

Suppose we widen the early comparative materials from the Jaco-

beans to English Renaissance drama generally. It would be too easy
to say that we appear not yet to have produced a Shakespeare or a
Marlowe of the great plays, or perhaps even the great melodramatist
whose work at times feels the pressure of the tragic—a Webster, a
Tourneur, or a Ford. Hence we might take a different tack and
suggest that, whatever the heights of the great first period of English
drama, still the tragic sense did not have, over five decades, a consistently sure position. We might then ask: if that is true, what a priori
expectations would be justified by the habits and postures of our own
age? We can envision different forecasts. One maker of comparisons
might urge that the self-consciousness of the Renaissance has increased vastly in our own day. He might argue that we should
therefore expect a flowering of the lyrical and the confessional and a
decline of the drama, which has its origin in the unselfconscious leap
into action. But he might also argue that an age of self-consciousness,
with its commitment to unearthing true motives and to seeing behind
the more eligible façades, should strengthen the phase of tragic experience in which a sure insight follows the confused plunges and
dashes, or the unquestioned driving pursuits, that come out of unruly
emotions. He might point to the tragic elements in *Altona*, *The Visit*,
and *Darkness at Noon*. Another maker of hypotheses might reply
that, on the contrary, an age mastering a new view of motives would
use them mechanically rather than with moral insight, and would
indeed be so fearful of eligible façades that it might regard any
modifying or judging of motives as a façade. Hence uncriticized
urgencies would be the order of the day, and we could expect a
thriving melodrama of instinctual life.

Another maker of comparisons might insist that we are more
self-consciously antitraditional and assertively individualistic than the
age of Tudors and Stuarts. With us, he might contend, to be antitraditional (or, since it is within easier reach, anticonventional) means
ordinarily the stance of the opponent and the crusader. To be individualistic seems to imply less a quiet self-reliance guarded against
idiosyncrasy by faithful self-questioning than a vigorous thrusting
forward of one's own will, and a posture of attack in private projects
or public causes. Whether we oppose and crusade out of the most
unassailable goodness, whether causes are impeccable or are public
fronts for private needs, and whether attack is an expression of

principle, an automatic way of life, or a projection of disorder within, the phenomena all reveal a strongly melodramatic temper. In the theater, then, we might expect this temper to release a sense of wrongdoing, topical criticism, polemics, and suspicion of the immediate world and of the cosmos, to discover, in sadness or anger, the hell that is other people. In this theater, it is likely, there would be limited room for the sense of reality that would discover the vice within and present it, not as removable nor as controllable, but as able to be known by the man in whom it moves, and to be judged rather than held always to be the self's just cause.

To bandy hypotheses, however, is only a way of pointing up the problem encountered in a move from the older to the more recent theater. A priori expectations are starting points that may serve their purposes by being defeated. They are really questions—the only possible counterparts to the assertions that it now appears possible to make about the past.

Both assertions and questions are always likely to imply a predisposition in favor of tragedy, an impulse to enlarge its realm. The impulse is understandable, but it may need to be reined in. Tragedy is not always called for; there are occasions when the melodramatic response is right and necessary. We are in trouble, as I said earlier, only if we respond in one way all the time, or in one way when the other way is called for. But if for most of us the problem is to distinguish situations which invite pity or indignation from those which invite self-knowledge, the writer's problem is a different one. He does not determine what the situation is and then report on it. Rather he chooses the perspective from which follows one kind of interpretation or the other. We do not dictate perspectives to writers; we only hope that their perspectives will be varied enough. We do not prescribe for the artist's vision, but we may legitimately point to the consequences of the optical habits of an age.

Notes

Chapter One

1. This is in "A Tory Philosophy," reprinted in *The Life and Opinions of T. E. Hulme*, by Alun R. Jones (Boston: Beacon Press, 1960), p. 190.

2. Honor M. V. Matthews, *Character and Symbol in Shakespeare's Plays* (Cambridge: Cambridge University Press, 1962), pp. 63, 202, 203.

3. Robert Graves, Foreword to *Collected Poems* (New York: Random House, 1938), p. xiii.

4. George Eliot, *Middlemarch* (Riverside Edition; Boston: Houghton Mifflin, 1956), p. 113 (Bk. II, chap. xv).

5. George Eliot, *Silas Marner* (Riverside Literature Series; Boston: Houghton Mifflin, 1962), p. 106 (chap. xiii).

6. All Shakespeare quotations are from *The Complete Plays and Poems of William Shakespeare*, ed. William A. Neilson and Charles J. Hill (Boston: Houghton Mifflin, 1942).

7. Christopher Fry, *A Sleep of Prisoners* (New York and London: Oxford University Press, 1951), p. 10.

8. Theodosius Dobzhansky, "Evolutionism and Man's Hope," *Sewanee Review*, LXVIII (1960), 282, 284.

9. Arnold Stein, "The Image of Antony: Lyric and Tragic Imagination," *Kenyon Review*, XXI (1959), 603.

10. Eliseo Vivas, *D. H. Lawrence: The Failure and Triumph of Art* (Evanston, Ill.: Northwestern University Press, 1960), p. 167.

11. Patricia Marx, "An Interview with Rolf Hochhuth," *Partisan Review*, XXXI (1964), 368.

12. Quoted by Fred C. Thomson, "The Genesis of Felix Holt," *PMLA*, LXXIV (1959), 577.

13. Quoted from *Life* magazine by Ralph E. Hone (ed.), in *The Voice Out of the Whirlwind: The Book of Job* (San Francisco: Chandler, 1960), p. 298.

14. Vivian Mercier, *The Irish Comic Tradition* (Oxford: Clarendon Press, 1962), p. 240.

15. See Sections V, VI, and VII of this chapter, and Chapter 2.

16. Albert Guerard, *Thomas Hardy* (Cambridge, Mass.: Harvard University Press, 1949), p. 152.

17. Christopher Fry, *Venus Observed* (London: Oxford University Press, 1950), p. 95.

Chapter Two

1. C. G. Jung, "On the Psychology of the Trickster Figure," in *The Trickster*, by Paul Radin (New York: Philosophical Library, 1956), p. 207.

2. John A. Meixner, "The Saddest Story," *Kenyon Review*, XXII (1960), 264. The reference is to the characters in F. M. Ford's *The Good Soldier*.

3. Quoted by Monk Gibbon, *The Masterpiece and the Man: Yeats As I Knew Him* (New York: Macmillan, 1959), pp. 108, 184–85.

4. In 1965 the play was available in *New English Dramatists*, No. 7, ed. Elliott M. Browne (Penguin Plays, No. 47; Harmondsworth, Eng.: Penguin, 1963).

5. This is in Duerrenmatt's Postscript, in the translation of *The Visit* by Patrick Bowles (New York: Grove Press, 1962), p. 107. Citations are from this edition.

6. Alvin B. Kernan, "A Theory of Satire," in *Modern Satire*, ed. Alvin B. Kernan (New York: Harcourt, Brace and World, 1962), p. 173.

7. Preface to *The Battle of the Books*. Cf. Robert C. Elliott, *The Power of Satire* (Princeton, N.J.: Princeton University Press, 1960), pp. 231ff., for Wyndham Lewis' elaboration of Swift; pp. 269ff., for Cowper's doubt of the efficacy of satire and for the efforts of the sociologist Frederick E. Lumley to determine "whether satire accomplishes its purported end." Cf. the footnote on p. 131 of the present study.

8. Quotations are from Maxim Gorki, *The Lower Depths*, trans. by Jenny Covan, in *A Treasury of the Theatre*, ed. John Gassner (New York: Simon and Schuster, 1960).

9. Quotations are from Eugene O'Neill, *The Iceman Cometh* (1st ed.; New York: Random House, 1946).

10. Albert Camus, *The Fall*, trans. by Justin O'Brien (Harmondsworth, Eng.: Penguin, 1963), p. 16.

11. *The Iceman Cometh* was copyrighted as an unpublished work in

1940; Sherwood's *There Shall Be No Night* was first produced in March, 1940.

12. Roland M. Frye, *God, Man, and Satan* (Princeton, N.J.: Princeton University Press, 1960), p. 30.

13. Trans. by Allan H. Gilbert, in *Literary Criticism: Plato to Dryden* (New York: American Book Company, 1940), p. 85. Bywater translates "odious."

14. Peter Alexander, *Shakespeare's Life and Art* (New York: New York University Press, 1961), p. 84.

15. Cf. F. L. Lucas (ed.), *The Complete Works of John Webster* (London: Chatto and Windus, 1927), II, 23–24. Line numbers are from this edition. Spelling and punctuation are modernized.

16. The figure originates in Sidney's *Arcadia*, noted by Lucas in the *Complete Works of Webster*, II, 162.

17. They may be compared with the source in *Arcadia; ibid.*, II, 199.

Chapter Three

1. The article "Melodrama" in *The Oxford Companion to the Theatre*, ed. Phyllis Hartnoll (2nd ed.; London: Oxford University Press, 1957), contains a good brief summary of history, motifs, types, and so forth. Naturally I find congenial the more recent revaluations of melodrama by Eric Bentley in *The Life of the Drama* (New York: Atheneum, 1964), pp. 195–218, and by James L. Rosenberg in *The Context and Craft of Drama*, ed. Robert W. Corrigan and James L. Rosenberg (San Francisco: Chandler, 1964), pp. 168–85.

2. Cf. Alan S. Downer, *The British Drama* (New York: Appleton-Century-Crofts, 1950), p. 276. Downer defines melodrama more narrowly than I do, but remarks that "it was never wholly gone from the stage, and was not wholly a creation of the late eighteenth and early nineteenth century."

3. In most of these, of course, there are complications of character that draw the works in part beyond the basic structure represented in them.

4. Disasters by natural forces are so little accommodated to staging that the theme is not frequent in drama. It is more suited to the novel, e.g., *The Last Days of Pompeii* and Aldous Huxley's *Ape and Essence*.

5. Cf. Walter H. Sokel, *The Writer in Extremis: Expressionism in Twentieth-Century German Literature* (Stanford, Calif.: Stanford University Press, 1959), chaps. i and ii. In tracing the eighteenth- and nineteenth-century origins of modern expressionism, Sokel defines, as philosophical and social sources, romantic subjectivism and sympathy with the outsider.

Chapter Four

1. Eric Bentley uses the same metaphor independently in *The Life of the Drama* (New York: Atheneum, 1964), p. 202.

2. Tennessee Williams, "The Timeless World of a Play," Introduction to *The Rose Tattoo* (New York: New Directions, 1951), pp. vi, ix.

3. There is also a notable return to biblical myths in serious modern drama: André Obey's *Noah*, Christopher Fry's *Sleep of Prisoners*, which utilizes a number of Old Testament stories, Nikos Kazantzakis' cinema of the Christ story (*He Who Must Die*) and his play *Sodom and Gomorrah*, Archibald MacLeish's version of the Job story, and Jean Giraudoux's *Sodom and Gomorrah*.

4. See Leo Weinstein, *The Metamorphoses of Don Juan* (Stanford, Calif.: Stanford University Press, 1959).

5. This does not exclude the possibility of contemporary allusions by the dramatist, or the sensing of immediate relevance by the audience of the day.

6. Dwight Macdonald, "Masscult and Midcult: II," *Partisan Review*, XXVII (1960), 628.

7. John H. Raleigh, "O'Neill's *Long Day's Journey into Night*," *Partisan Review*, XXVI (1959), 573ff.

8. Nicola Chiaromonte, "Eugene O'Neill" (1958), trans. by Barbara Melchiori Arnett, *Sewanee Review*, LXVIII (1960), 497.

9. Philip Rahv, "Dostoevsky in *Crime and Punishment*," *Partisan Review*, XXVII (1960), 398.

10. Cf. Kenneth Burke, *The Philosophy of Literary Form* (Baton Rouge: Louisiana State University Press, 1941), pp. 48ff. The Stevenson quotation is from *Virginibus Puerisque*, chap. ii, first paragraph; John Steinbeck makes use of it in "Junius Maltby."

11. Several of my examples involve citations of historians. Perhaps this is not altogether a coincidence. Melodrama, I have said, is topical, and a historian is more concerned with topics than with constants.

12. Avrahm Yarmolinsky, *Dostoevsky: His Life and Art* (2nd ed.; New York: Criterion Books, 1957), p. 410.

13. David T. Bazelon, "A New Kind of War," *Partisan Review*, XXIX (1962), 555.

14. Steven Marcus, "The Novel Again," *Partisan Review*, XXIX (1962), 193.

15. Quoted in the *New York Times Magazine*, Dec. 20, 1959, p. 22.

16. James W. Hall, *The Tragic Comedians* (Bloomington: Indiana University Press, 1963), p. 47.

17. Henry Treece, *Electra* (Consul ed.; London: Bodley Head, 1965), p. 91.

18. Simone de Beauvoir, *The Mandarins*, trans. Leonard M. Friedman (Cleveland and New York: World Publishing Company, 1956), pp. 165, 191.

19. Bertolt Brecht, *Mother Courage and Her Children*, English version by Eric Bentley (New York: Grove Press, 1963), p. 14.

20. Thornton Wilder, *Three Plays* (New York: Harper, 1957), pp. 221, 227, 236.

21. The episode is recounted in Jeremiah Melford's letter dated "London, June 11," and written to Sir Watkin Phillips.

22. The interview is described in chap. xvii, "Sir Abraham Haphazard." But the relevant materials appear in many other chapters.

23. Albert Camus, *The Fall*, trans. Justin O'Brien (Harmondsworth, Eng.: Penguin, 1963), p. 60. Earlier the narrator has said, with incisive wit, "If pimps and thieves were invariably sentenced, all decent people would get to thinking they themselves were constantly innocent, . . .— that's what must be avoided at all costs. Otherwise everything would be just a joke" (p. 32).

24. Beauvoir, *The Mandarins*, p. 235.

25. Attributed to the psychoanalyst Wilhelm Stekel (1868–1940) by J. D. Salinger in *The Catcher in the Rye* (1951), chap. xxiv. In the Modern Library edition (New York: Random House, 1958), this is on p. 244.

26. The quotations are from William C. Havard, "The Burden of the Literary Mind: Some Meditations on Robert Penn Warren as Historian," *South Atlantic Quarterly*, LXII (1963), 522.

27. The quotations from Ibsen's *Rosmersholm* are from Charles Archer's translation in *Ibsen's Prose Dramas*, ed. William Archer (New York: Scribner and Welford, 1890), Vol. V.

28. In the Wessex edition of 1912 the quoted passages occur on pp. 416, 423, 425, 427, 435.

29. *Ibid.*, pp. 416, 417, 476, 478.

30. Patricia Marx, "An Interview with Rolf Hochhuth," *Partisan Review*, XXXI (1964), 374.

31. *The Correspondence of André Gide and Edmund Gosse, 1904–1928*, ed. Linette F. Brugmans (London: Peter Owen, 1960), p. 158. For some ancillary remarks on man's impulse to lose self-hood, see V. L. O. Chittick, "Yeats the Dancer," *Dalhousie Review*, XXXIX (1959–60), 338; Eliseo Vivas, *D. H. Lawrence: The Failure and Triumph of Art* (Evanston, Ill.: Northwestern University Press, 1960), p. 56; Lionel Trilling, "On the Modern Element in Modern Literature," *Partisan Review*, XXVIII (1961), 35.

32. Quoted by Samuel H. Monk, *The Sublime* (New York: Modern Language Association of America, General Series, 1935), p. 9.

33. Eliseo Vivas makes a useful distinction between the "healthy conscience" and the "pathological conscience" in "Freedom: The Philosophical Problem," *Modern Age*, VI (1961–62), 14–15.

34. Nikolai Gogol, *Dead Souls*, trans. David Magarshack (Harmondsworth, Eng.: Penguin, 1961), p. 293. Gogol does it the other way round in an episode in which the rascally Chichikov sees that he was to

blame for some social annoyance. Gogol goes on, ironically: "He was not, however, angry with himself, and there, of course, he was quite right. We all have a little weakness for sparing ourselves and we try to find someone we know on whom to vent our spleen . . ." (p. 185).

35. Fyodor Dostoevski, *The Devils*, trans. David Magarshack (Harmondsworth, Eng.: Penguin, 1953), p. 458.

36. Jerome Thale, *The Novels of George Eliot* (New York: Columbia University Press, 1959), p. 17. Thale uses the phrase in a special context. I lift it here because it contributes something to the present analysis: the person whose anger makes him blind about the world will obviously enjoy, a fortiori, a blindness about himself.

37. Cf. Robert C. Elliott, *The Power of Satire* (Princeton, N.J.: Princeton University Press, 1960), p. 209, note 19, on "our pleasure in vituperation."

38. David Daiches, *A Critical History of English Literature* (New York: Ronald Press, 1960), I, 280.

39. James Cox, "Walt Whitman, Mark Twain, and the Civil War," *Sewanee Review*, LXIX (1961), 185.

40. Philip Thody, *Jean-Paul Sartre: A Literary and Political Study* (New York: Macmillan, 1960), p. 177.

41. Gogol, *Dead Souls*, pp. 270–71.

42. Camus, *The Fall*, p. 15. Cf. p. 22.

43. Beauvoir, *The Mandarins*, pp. 569, 582.

44. Saul Bellow, *Herzog* (New York: Fawcett, 1965), p. 67.

45. Walter Allen, *All in a Lifetime* (London: Michael Joseph, 1959), p. 209. Earlier, the narrator describes a woman who "lived in an excessively simple universe and was strident and domineering, quivering always . . . with indignation" (p. 145).

46. Edward H. Rosenberry, "The Problem of *Billy Budd*," *PMLA*, LXXX (1965), 490.

Chapter Five

1. Thomas Mann, *The Story of a Novel: The Genesis of "Doctor Faustus,"* trans. Richard and Clara Winston (New York: Alfred A. Knopf, 1961), p. 163.

2. Robert Penn Warren, *World Enough and Time* (New York: Random House, 1950), p. 506.

3. Robert Penn Warren, *The Legacy of the Civil War* (New York: Random House, 1961), p. 23. On the next page Warren quotes James Russell Lowell's retrospective remark that northern reformers "stood ready at a moment's notice to reform everything but themselves." A decade after *World Enough and Time* Warren is still interested in the human capacity for the "flight from innocence." See note 2, above.

4. The Hesse quotation is from Basil Creighton's translation of *Steppenwolf* (New York: Henry Holt, 1929), pp. 163–64. The comment on

Hesse is based on Ernst Rose's *Faith from the Abyss: Hermann Hesse's Way from Romanticism to Modernity* (New York: New York University Press, 1965), pp. 58, 80. Rose's analysis of the divisions within the hero of *Steppenwolf* reveals an essentially tragic cast in that work.

5. Jean Anouilh, *Becket*, trans. Lucienne Hill (New York: Coward-McCann, 1960), p. 46 (Act I, near the end).

6. The phrase is used by Robert Jordan in "Poetry and Philosophy: Two Modes of Revelation," *Sewanee Review*, LXVII (1959), 13, in referring to the antimetaphysicalism of current American philosophy. He is arguing that poetry must bring about "a conversion, a 'turning toward' objective being" (p. 23). I am proceeding analogously, I believe, in proposing that the tragic view is the whole view of the "objective being" of humanity.

7. For this formulation I am indebted to Leonard Dean.

8. John Osborne, *Look Back in Anger* (London: Faber and Faber, 1957).

9. Quoted by Janet Dunbar in *Mrs. G.B.S.: A Portrait* (New York: Harper and Row, 1963), p. 276.

10. The quotations are from Philip Vellacott's translation, *Medea and Other Plays* (Harmondsworth, Engl.: Penguin, 1963), pp. 138, 141, 142. I have also made use of Vellacott's Introduction, pp. 11–14. The passages quoted here are translated differently by Emily T. Vermeule in *The Complete Greek Tragedies*, ed. David Grene and Richmond Lattimore (Chicago: University of Chicago Press, 1959), Vol. IV, but even with the verbal differences, the effects seem to me to be the same.

11. Smith Palmer Bovie, "The Truth Realized in Time," *Sewanee Review*, LXVIII (1960), 331.

12. John A. Meixner, "The Saddest Story," *Kenyon Review*, XXII (1960), 264. The omitted words are "which in its heroism." Whether Meixner's view and my own entirely coincide depends partly on what meaning is given to "heroism." I should regard the highest heroism as being able both to know the self and to live with the knowledge.

13. J. A. Bryant, Jr., *Hippolyta's View* (Lexington: University of Kentucky Press, 1961), pp. 148–49.

14. L. S. Dembo, *Hart Crane's Sanskrit Charge: A Study of "The Bridge"* (Ithaca, N.Y.: Cornell University Press, 1960), p. 16. Dembo elaborates on this idea for the next several pages. Cf.: "Society will be redeemed when it understands its tragic nature and through its imagination, which speaks through the poet, moves beyond tragedy to a knowledge of divinity" (p. 18). Also: ". . . a blind but redeemable society—a society in which tragedy was possible—" (p. 19).

15. This is in Sidney Kingsley's stage version of *Darkness at Noon* (New York: Random House, 1951), p. 117 (end of Act III). The play sharpens up the more diffused recognition that gradually emerges in the latter part of the novel.

16. I am indebted to the analysis of the *Eumenides* by Maud Bodkin in *The Quest for Salvation in an Ancient and a Modern Play* (London and New York: Oxford University Press, 1941), which seems more perceptive than the critiques that call Aeschylus to task for finding a solution outside the original dramatic situation. Actually, the *Eumenides* is highly unified, though its unconventional unity depends somewhat on the parabolic. The role of Orestes is continued by the city of Athens; the hiatus is well bridged. The freeing of Orestes is a repudiation of the Furies principle, which anticipates the Furies' own renunciation of their primitive role. For an illuminating account of comparable conversions in the lives of artists, see Walter H. Sokel, *The Writer in Extremis* . . . (Stanford, Calif.: Stanford University Press, 1959), pp. 155ff.

17. Roland M. Frye, *God, Man, and Satan* (Princeton, N.J.: Princeton University Press, 1960), p. 163.

18. Norbert Fuerst, *The Victorian Age of German Literature: Eight Essays* (University Park and London: Pennsylvania State University Press, 1966), p. 25.

Chapter Six

1. All Marlowe references are to *The Complete Plays of Christopher Marlowe*, ed. Irving Ribner (New York: Odyssey Press, 1963).

2. Up to this point in Act V, Scene iii, a scene on Richard's side of the field (lines 1–18, 47–78) is balanced by one on Richmond's side (lines 19–46, 79–117), and the contents are roughly similar. First we have the Richard scene, then the Richmond scene. True, Richard's soliloquy scene (lines 177–222) is followed by a Richmond scene, so that the sequence of sides is not disturbed. But after Richard's soliloquy there is an abrupt shift in the subjects of the scenes: Richmond now addresses his troops and prepares for battle (lines 223–70), and afterward Richard closes the act by going through the same procedure (lines 271–351). These two scenes, which close the act, restore the initial symmetry, even though the earlier order is reversed.

3. See George Lyman Kittredge, Introduction to *Richard II* (Boston: Ginn and Company, 1941), p. vii; Mark Van Doren, *Shakespeare* (New York: Henry Holt, 1939), pp. 84, 95; Theodore Spencer, Introduction to *Richard II* (New York: Crofts Classics, 1949), p. viii.

4. Quotations are from Ben Jonson's *Selected Works*, ed. Harry Levin (New York: Random House, 1938).

5. Cf. Eugene M. Waith's *The Herculean Hero in Marlowe, Chapman, Shakespeare and Dryden* (New York: Columbia University Press, 1962).

6. Quotations are from *Bussy D'Ambois*, ed. Nicholas Brooke (The Revels Plays; London: Methuen, 1958). Brooke's urbane and knowledgeable introduction is noteworthy.

7. *Bussy D'Ambois*, ed. Brooke, Introduction, p. lv.

8. The act and scene divisions are from *The Complete Works of John Webster*, ed. F. L. Lucas (London: Chatto and Windus, 1927), Vol. I.

9. Quotations are from *John Webster and Cyril Tourneur: Four Plays*, ed. J. A. Symonds (Mermaid Dramabook; New York: Hill and Wang, 1956).

10. Quotations are from N. W. Bawcutt's edition in The Revels Plays series (London: Methuen, 1958). Bawcutt's introduction is interesting both for his own discussion of Beatrice, with which mine is in general agreement, and for his comments on prior discussions of her by Una Ellis-Fermor, T. S. Eliot, Helen Gardner, and Fredson Bowers (pp. lii and following).

11. Quotations are from the text in McIlwraith's *Five Stuart Tragedies*.

12. Cf. Stuart P. Sherman's introduction to the Belles Lettres edition, G. B. Harrison's introduction to the Everyman edition, and the comment in Alan S. Downer's *The British Drama* (New York: Appleton-Century-Crofts, 1950), pp. 175–76. More recent stress is on Ford's determinism and individualism, as in G. F. Sensabaugh's study, *The Tragic Muse of John Ford* (Stanford, Calif.: Stanford University Press, 1944), and McIlwraith's introduction to *Five Stuart Tragedies*.

13. Fredson T. Bowers, *Elizabethan Revenge Tragedy, 1587–1642* (Princeton, N.J.: Princeton University Press, 1940), p. 225.

14. On the historical relationship between domestic tragedy and morality plays, see R. W. Van Fossen's edition of *A Woman Killed with Kindness* (The Revels Plays; London: Methuen, 1961), pp. xxiv–xxvi. Van Fossen gives various secondary sources. My own concern is not with sources and parallel cases but with the aesthetic impact of a homiletic consciousness in the dramatist. Quotations are from Van Fossen's text, but line numbers are omitted because there is no standard act-and-scene division and lineation.

15. Quotations are from the text in McIlwraith's *Five Stuart Tragedies*.

16. Quotations and line numbers from John Ford's *The Broken Heart* are from the Belles Lettres edition, edited by Stuart P. Sherman (Boston: D. C. Heath, 1916). The prescription of therapeutic activity is an almost jolting intrusion of common sense into a world dominated by uncommon sensibilities.

Chapter Seven

1. Robert Ornstein, *The Moral Vision of Jacobean Tragedy* (Madison: University of Wisconsin Press, 1960), p. 226.

2. Avrahm Yarmolinsky, *Dostoevsky: His Life and Art* (New York: Criterion Books, 1957), pp. 208–9.

3. *Plays of the Restoration and Eighteenth Century*, ed. Dougald MacMillan and Howard Mumford Jones (New York: Holt, 1931), p. 546.

4. Quotations are from the translation by William Archer in *The Works of Henrik Ibsen*, with introductions by William Archer (New York: Wiley Books, n.d.). This edition was by arrangement with Charles Scribner's Sons, who held the copyrights in 1911 and 1912.

5. Quotations from Miller's *Death of a Salesman* are from the original edition (New York: Viking, 1949), as reprinted in *Masters of Modern Drama*, ed. Haskell Block and Robert G. Shedd (New York: Random House, 1962). There are sharper comments on the dreariness of *Death of a Salesman* in John Simon, *Acid Test* (New York: Stein and Day, 1963), pp. 95–97.

6. Robert Brustein, "The Madison Avenue Villain," *Partisan Review*, XXVIII (1961), 591. Brustein adds, "when you begin to ask 'What is it?' instead of 'Is it good?' you are already on the way to joining it."

7. *The Complete Plays of Christopher Marlowe*, ed. Irving Ribner (New York: Odyssey Press, 1963), V.v.77ff. True, a little earlier Barabas could say to himself "by wrong thou got'st authority" (V.ii.35); but this is a technical rather than a moral statement, a part of a cool assessment of the strength of his present situation and of the strategy called for.

8. J. A. Bryant, *Hippolyta's View* (Lexington: University of Kentucky Press, 1961), p. 121.

9. Andrew Lytle, "The Displaced Family," review of Howard Nemerov's *The Homecoming Game*, in *Sewanee Review*, LXVI (1958), 126. There may be an echo here of words spoken to Harry Monchensey by Agatha, an authoritative voice in Eliot's *Family Reunion:*

> . . . sin may strain and struggle
> . . . to come to consciousness
> And so find expurgation.
> [II.ii]

She adds that Harry may be "the consciousness of your unhappy family."

10. James W. Hall, *The Tragic Comedians* (Bloomington: Indiana University Press, 1963), p. 82.

11. William C. Havard, "The Burden of the Literary Mind: Some Meditations on Robert Penn Warren as Historian," *South Atlantic Quarterly*, LXII (1963), 520.

12. Richard Schechner, "The Inner and Outer Reality," *Tulane Drama Review*, VII (1963), 202.

13. George Eliot, *Middlemarch* (Riverside Edition; Boston: Houghton Mifflin, 1956), p. 241 (Bk. IV, chap. xxxiv).

14. Quoted from Roger Shattuck's *Proust's Binoculars* by Joseph Frank in a review, "Proust: Remembrance and Recognition," in *Partisan Review*, XXXI (1964), 141. Frank disagrees with the analysis. For my purposes, the point is not whether Shattuck is correct, but rather his choice of this mode of defining Proust's achievement.

15. Bryant, *Hippolyta's View*, p. 111.

16. L. S. Dembo, *Hart Crane's Sanskrit Charge* (Ithaca, N.Y.: Cornell University Press, 1960), p. 17.

17. Gene Baro, "Montherlant and the Morals of Adjustment," *Sewanee Review*, LXIX (1961), 705. In this section, of course, we are speaking of self-knowledge simply as an end in itself, as achievable by humanity. It is beyond our scope to speak of self-knowledge as a starting point for further developments. Other writers often do. Robert Penn Warren speaks of the story in which the participants find "a reconciliation by human recognition" (*The Legacy of the Civil War* [New York: Random House, 1961], p. 103). A Lawrence Durrell character specifies, very perceptively, "you have to find yourself before you can really give yourself" (*The World of Lawrence Durrell*, ed. Harry T. Moore [Carbondale: Southern Illinois University Press, 1962], p. 167). Ionesco hangs the "meaning of the universe" and of "the world of experience" on the "understanding of self." "Who am I? Once the individual can satisfactorily answer that question, finding in the answer an integral sense of selfhood, the chaotic universe will again take a meaningful shape" (Schechner, "Inner and Outer Reality," p. 202).

18. Nikolai Gogol, *Dead Souls*, trans. David Magarshack (Harmondsworth, Eng.: Penguin, 1961), p. 257.

19. Oscar Wilde, "The Portrait of Mr. W. H.," in *The Riddle of Shakespeare's Sonnets* (New York: Basic Books, 1962), p. 242.

20. Steven Marcus, "The Novel Again," *Partisan Review*, XXIX (1962), 189.

21. "The Kneller Tape (Hamburg): Lawrence Durrell Speaking," in *World of Lawrence Durrell*, p. 167. Or he may get the word at the beginning, as in Baudelaire's famous words "Au Lecteur," "Hypocrite lecteur! mon semblable, mon frère!"

22. Richard Wilbur, "The Existential Hero," *Partisan Review*, XXIX (1962), 606.

23. Jean-Paul Sartre, *Altona*, trans. Sylvia and George Leeson (Harmondsworth, Eng.: Penguin, 1962), p. 165. This volume also contains *Men Without Shadows* and *The Flies* (trans. Stuart Gilbert), cited below.

24. Harold Clurman, "The Achievement of Bertolt Brecht," *Partisan Review*, XXVI (1959), 625.

25. Oscar Büdel, "Contemporary Theater and Aesthetic Distance," *PMLA*, LXXVI (1961), 286.

26. *Ibid.*, p. 281. Büdel not only gives numerous examples in the theaters of different countries but identifies the theoretical origins and notes anticipations in earlier theatrical practice.

27. In "Literature and Growing Up," *English Journal*, XLV (1956), 303–13. Maynard Mack, using different basic terms, discusses interestingly the dual relationship of reader to imaginative work in "Engagement and Detachment in Shakespeare's Plays," *Essays on Shakespeare and*

Elizabethan Drama in Honor of Hardin Craig, ed. Richard Hosley (Columbia: University of Missouri Press, 1962), pp. 275–96.

28. Philip Thody, *Jean-Paul Sartre* (New York: Macmillan, 1960), pp. 42–43.

29. The passages cited are at lines 46, 52, 233–34, 374–76, 410, 412, 418, 488–89, 532, as edited by Helen Darbishire in *The Poetical Works of John Milton* (Oxford: Clarendon Press, 1955), II, 65ff.

30. Cf. lines 60–61, 201, 222, 226, 377–78, 451–52, 496–97. The long passage, lines 633–51, is important in this connection.

31. The quotations in this section are all from Act V in the Leeson translation cited in note 23 (pp. 149–66).

32. The quotations are from the translation by S. G. Benardete in *The Complete Greek Tragedies*, ed. David Grene and Richmond Lattimore (Chicago: University of Chicago Press, 1956), Vol. I. In the subsequent pages the citations of Greek dramas are all in the Chicago translations—of Aeschylus' *Seven Against Thebes* and *Prometheus Bound* by David Grene (Vol. I), of Sophocles' *Oedipus at Colonus* by Robert Fitzgerald, of his *Electra* and *Philoctetes* by David Grene (Vol. II), and of Euripides' *Medea* by Rex Warner, and his *Hippolytus* by David Grene (Vol. III).

33. The quotations are from David Grene's "Introduction: 'The Theban Plays' by Sophocles" in the Chicago edition, II, 6, 7.

34. In his "Introduction to the *Electra*" in the Chicago edition, II, 330.

35. Scene vii of the translation by Dudley Fitts (New York, 1955), p. 108.

36. In the Introduction to *Jean Racine: Five Plays Translated into English Verse* (New York: Hill and Wang, 1960), p. xxiv.

37. Quotations are from *Three Plays of Racine*, trans. George Dillon (Chicago: University of Chicago Press, 1961), pp. 127ff.

38. Quotations are from the American edition of Maxwell Anderson's *Winterset* (Washington, D.C.: Anderson House, 1935).

39. Quotations are from Eric Bentley's translation (London: Victor Gollancz, 1948).

40. Quotations from *Darkness at Noon* are from the acting edition (New York: Random House, 1951).

41. Mary Renault, *The Bull from the Sea* (New York: Pantheon Books, 1962), p. 93. The subsequent quotation is from p. 92.

Chapter Eight

1. Nikos Kazantzakis, *Report to Greco*, trans. P. A. Bien (New York: Simon and Schuster, 1965), p. 173.

2. Joyce Cary, *Art and Reality* (New York: Harper, 1958), p. 85.

3. Theodore M. Greene, "Beauty in Art and Nature," *Sewanee Review*, LXIX (1961), 236. The later quotation is from the same passage.

4. Robert Penn Warren, *The Legacy of the Civil War* (New York: Random House, 1961), p. 103.

5. Gabriel Fallon, *Sean O'Casey: The Man I Knew* (Boston and Toronto: Little, Brown, 1965), p. 26.

6. These and numerous other views of tragedy may be approached most conveniently in the collection edited by Robert W. Corrigan, *Tragedy: Vision and Form* (San Francisco: Chandler, 1965).

7. Richmond Lattimore, in the Introduction to his translation of Aeschylus' *Oresteia* (Chicago: University of Chicago Press, 1953), p. 27.

8. Eric Bentley's method of rehabilitation is different. In a strategic maneuver he endeavors to say as much as can be said for what I have considered low-grade melodrama. Cf. *The Life of the Drama* (New York: Atheneum, 1964), pp. 196ff.

9. L. Proudfoot, *Dryden's Aeneid and Its Seventeenth Century Predecessors* (Manchester: Manchester University Press, 1960), p. 216.

10. Albert Camus, *The Fall*, trans. Justin O'Brien (Harmondsworth, Eng.: Penguin, 1963), p. 42.

11. George Moore, *Evelyn Innes* (New York: D. Appleton, 1920), p. 157.

12. Cleanth Brooks, *The Hidden God* (New Haven and London: Yale University Press, 1963), p. 132.

13. Henry James, *The Art of the Novel: Critical Prefaces*, with an Introduction by Richard P. Blackmur (New York: Scribner's, 1934), p. 62.

14. The best account of the development of problem plays since the eighteenth century is the chapter, "Tragedy in Modern Dress," in Eric Bentley's *The Playwright as Thinker* (New York: Reynal and Hitchcock, 1946), pp. 45ff.

15. Fallon, *Sean O'Casey*, p. 26.

Index

Addison, Joseph: *Cato*, 196, 230–31
Aeneas, 289
Aeschylus, ix, 92, 93, 120; use of Orestes story, 255
—*Works*
  Eumenides, 308; Orestes, 14, 15, 17, 93, 120, 156, 157–58, 160, 240, 250, 275, 290, 295; as divided character, 9, 10, 12*n;* Electra, 266, 275; Clytemnestra, 290
  Oresteia, 261, 262; the "Oresteian conversion," 295
  The Persians, 261
  Prometheus Bound, 261–62; Prometheus, 17, 275
  Seven Against Thebes, 261, 262
Albee, Edward: *The Zoo Story*, 138*n*
Alexander, Peter, 63, 303
Allen, Walter, 306; *All in a Lifetime*, 131
Anderson, Maxwell: *Winterset*, 276–78
Andrea Doria (ship), 134 and *n*

Annapurna, 79
Anouilh, Jean, 307; use of myth, 92; *The Fighting Cock*, 106; *Becket*, 142
Antiheroic, the, 85*n*
Ariosto, Ludovico, 170
Aristophanes, 97; *The Frogs*, 269
Aristotle, 26, 62, 67; definition of the tragic hero, 7, 91; the "good man," 16; on catharsis, 84*n*, 131*n;* on politics, 91*n;* on nontragic characters, 193
Arnett, Barbara M., 304
Arnold, Matthew, 4
Austen, Jane: *Pride and Prejudice*, 111

Baras, Edith, xi
Baro, Gene, 311
Battenhouse, Roy, xi
Bawcutt, N. W., 309
Bazelon, David, 105, 304
Beaumont, Francis, and Fletcher, John, 296; *The Maid's Tragedy*,

Para-tragic, the, 20
Pathetic: mistaken for tragic, 21*n*
Pearl Harbor attack: as disaster and as tragedy, 23–24
Pinero, A. W., 83
Pinter, Harold, 138*n*, 222; *The Birthday Party*, 238
Pirandello, Luigi: theater of, 247
Plato: on effect of art, 84*n*, 131*n*
Poe, Edgar Allan: Roderick Usher, 155
Point of view: as key to genre, 136ff.
Polemics: impact on generic form, 144ff.
Polypathic, the, 89, 297
Popular words: loss of meaning, 5
Price, Martin: *To the Palace of Wisdom*, 132*n*
Problem plays: historical task, 96
Prohibitionism: as melodrama, 99
Proudfoot, L., 289, 313
Proust, Marcel: *Remembrance of Things Past*, 245
Psalms, 26

Quasi-tragic, the, 20

Racine, Jean: *Phèdre*, 269–75
Radin, Paul, 302
Rahv, Philip, 304
Raleigh, John H., 96, 287, 304
Raphael, D. D., vii, 20*n*
Renaissance drama: tragic and melodramatic elements in, 163ff.; and modern, compared, 299
Renault, Mary: *The Bull from the Sea*, 282–84, 312
Response to theater: nature of, 247–51; freedom and identification, 249–51
Responsibility: flight from, 24–25
Restoration heroic drama, 170
Revelations, 57
Revenge drama, 60–61, 198, 199–202, 207, 213, 220, 224–25, 297; *Hamlet*, 165; developments after 1600, 188ff.; in Renaissance, 266; in Euripides' *Medea*, 266–67; in Euripides' *Hippolytus*, 268

Revengers, 242, 275, 278, 289, 290
Ribner, Irving, 308, 310
Richardson, Samuel, 94
Robbe-Grillet, Alain: *The Voyeur*, 137
Rose, Ernst, 307
Rosenberg, James L., 303
Rosenberry, Edward, 131, 306
Rosenheim, Edward W., Jr.: *Swift and the Satirist's Art*, 132*n*
Rostand, Edmond: *Cyrano de Bergerac*, 195, 196
Rougement, Denis de: *Love in the Western World*, 210*n*
Rudkin, David: *Afore Night Come*, 40–41, 42, 239

St. Paul, 57
Salinger, J. D., 305
Sartre, Jean-Paul, 238, 276, 311; use of myth, 92; on anti-Semitism, 102, 130; on identification with characters, 248–49, 250, 271; as melodramatic thinker, 259*n;* as tragic thinker, 259*n*
—*Works*
Altona, 143, 246–47, 249, 256–59, 299; Franz von Gerlach, 240, 275, 295
The Flies, 253–56, 259, 289
Satan, 60
Satire, 46–47, 97, 131*n*, 202, 244; in Jonson's *Sejanus*, 193, 194; in Sartre, 255, 259*n;* in Anderson's *Winterset*, 276–77
Satire: as literary word only, 4, 5
Saunders, James: *Next Time I'll Sing to You*, 122*n; A Scent of Flowers*, 124*n*
Sayers, Dorothy: *The Devil to Pay*, 115 and *n*, 116, 118, 130, 144, 254, 290
Scapins, 255
Schechner, Richard, 310, 311
Schiller, J. C. F. von, 83
Schmitt, Carl, 91*n*
Sensabaugh, George F., 309
Sentimental comedy, 217*n*